The Ritual Animal

The Ritual Animal

Imitation and Cohesion in the Evolution of Social Complexity

HARVEY WHITEHOUSE

OXFORD
UNIVERSITY PRESS

Great Clarendon Street, Oxford, OX2 6DP,
United Kingdom

Oxford University Press is a department of the University of Oxford.
It furthers the University's objective of excellence in research, scholarship,
and education by publishing worldwide. Oxford is a registered trade mark of
Oxford University Press in the UK and in certain other countries

© Harvey Whitehouse 2021

The moral rights of the author have been asserted

First Edition published in 2021

All rights reserved. No part of this publication may be reproduced, stored in
a retrieval system, or transmitted, in any form or by any means, without the
prior permission in writing of Oxford University Press, or as expressly permitted
by law, by licence or under terms agreed with the appropriate reprographics
rights organization. Enquiries concerning reproduction outside the scope of the
above should be sent to the Rights Department, Oxford University Press, at the
address above

You must not circulate this work in any other form
and you must impose this same condition on any acquirer

Published in the United States of America by Oxford University Press
198 Madison Avenue, New York, NY 10016, United States of America

British Library Cataloguing in Publication Data
Data available

Library of Congress Control Number: 2021910144

ISBN 978–0–19–964636–4

Links to third party websites are provided by Oxford in good faith and
for information only. Oxford disclaims any responsibility for the materials
contained in any third party website referenced in this work.

Dedicated to Merridee

Acknowledgements

This book is a result of several decades of research, much of it undertaken collaboratively with my present and former graduate students and postdocs, many of whom have taught me new skills and introduced me to new literature and ideas, and all of whom have provided constructive criticism that has humbled and inspired me, often at the same time. I should like to thank all of them here (in alphabetical order by surname): Quentin Atkinson, Adam Baimel, Kiran Basava, Nicolas Baumard, Emily Burdett, Enrico Cioni, Emma Cohen, Christina Collins, Oliver Curry, Julia Ebner, Pieter François, Michael Gantley, Steph Grohmann, Patricia Herrmann, Dan Hoyer, Steven Hrotic, Oratios Ierodiakonou, Gordon Ingram, Robert Jagiello, Ben Johannes, Jonathan Jong, Jean-Luc Jucker, Rohan Kapitány, Christopher Kavanagh, Florian Keissling, Nicola Knight, Justin Lane, Jonathan Lanman, Pierre Liénard, Lee McCorkle, Ryan McKay, Brian McQuinn, Gudmundur Ingi Markusson, Miriam Matthews, Camilla Mazzucato, Michal Misiak, Joel Mort, Daniel Mullins, Adrian Murzac, Barbara Muzzulini, Yo Nakawake, Martha Newson, Selin Nugent, Jenny Reddish, Paul Reddish, Rebekah Richert, Robert Ross, Peter Rudiak-Gould, Kaisa Ruokanen, Yvan Russell, Veronika Rybanska, Patrick Savage, Jesper Sorensen, Mark Stanford, Tara Tasuji, Valerie van Mulukom, Rachel Watson-Jones, Claire White, Aiyana Willard, and Dimitris Xygalatas. I am particularly grateful to Chris Kavanagh and Jonathan Lanman for commenting on full drafts of the manuscript. Although the list of colleagues I have co-authored articles with over the years is too long to mention, I should like to single out for special acknowledgement collaborators and friends who have had a sustained impact on my thinking: Justin Barrett, Brock Bastian, Amy Bogaard, Pascal Boyer, Joanna Bryson, Tom Currie, Richard English, Robin Fitzgerald, Kevin Foster, Sergey Gavrilets, Michele Gelfand, Angel Gomez, Jamin Halberstadt, Paul Harris, Mike Hochberg, Ian Hodder, Dominic Johnson, Ken Kahn, Cristine Legare, Luther H. Martin, Robert N. McCauley, David Macdonald, Jennifer Larson, James Laidlaw, Tom Lawson, David Parkin, Idhamsyah Eka Putra, Elaine Reese, Martin Stokes, William B. Swann, Eddie Tong, Peter Turchin, David Sloan Wilson, and Masaki Yuki. During the busiest part of Hilary Term 2021, as I was rushing to submit, my Oxford Anthropology colleagues, David Gellner, Ramon Sarró, and David Zeitlyn, and my student Robert Jagiello, all generously provided last minute feedback and advice on various aspects of the final draft. Finally, I should like to thank my erstwhile mentors, Alfred Gell, Ernest Gellner, and Gilbert Lewis, for encouraging my early interest in the nature of ritual.

In the writing of this book, I was supported as Principal Investigator by a Large Grant from the UK's Economic and Social Research Council (REF RES-060-25-467 0085), an award from the Templeton World Charity Foundation entitled 'Cognitive and Cultural Foundations of Religion and Morality' (TWCF0164), and an Advanced Grant from the European Research Council (ERC) under the European Union's Horizon 2020 Research and Innovation Programme (grant agreement No. 694986). The book incorporates excerpts of edited text from several previously published journal articles and book chapters by kind permission of the original publishers. Where there was more than one author on the original piece, only portions authored by me are included. The introduction and Chapter 1 both include material from Whitehouse (2011, 2013b); Chapter 2 from Whitehouse et al. (2012) and Whitehouse & François (2017); Chapter 3 from Whitehouse (2012a); Chapter 4 from Whitehouse (2012a, 2016b), Whitehouse et al. (2019), and Whitehouse & Kavanagh (2020); and Chapter 5 from Whitehouse (2013c, 2016a).

My deepest thanks go to my wife, Merridee, and my son Danny, for their boundless encouragement and intellectual stimulation. Almost from infancy, Danny has presented me with challenging questions about the nature of ritual, only some of which science can (partially) answer. And Merridee's eye for detail and her rigorous empiricism as an historian when commenting on final drafts of chapters were potent reminders of all that I admire most in the humanities disciplines. This book is dedicated to her.

Contents

Introduction	1
The Varieties of Ritual Experience	4
Ritual and the Symbolist School	10
Overview of the Book	16
1. Overimitation and the Ritual Stance	24
Ritual and Instrumental Stances in Overimitation	26
Irremediably Opaque Behaviour and the Ritual Stance	28
Ritual and Instrumental Stances in Magical Thinking	36
Causal Opacity, Meaning, and Communication	40
The Evolutionary Origins of the Ritual Stance	46
Conclusions	51
2. Ritual Frequency, Emotionality, and Modes of Religiosity	53
The Modes Theory	55
The Kivung as Case Study	58
Modelling Doctrinal-Imagistic Oscillations	64
Case Studies from History, Anthropology, and Archaeology	68
Quantifying Ritual Features Cross-Culturally	74
Modes and the Transition from Foraging to Farming	76
Conclusions	80
3. Imagistic Ritual, Fusion, and Self-Sacrifice	82
Rites of Terror and Group Bonding	84
Dysphoric Ritual and the Search for Meaning	85
When Personal and Group Identities Fuse	89
The Imagistic Pathway to Fusion	91
Social Consequences of the Imagistic Pathway to Fusion	99
Fusion and Self-Sacrifice from an Evolutionary Perspective	101
Conclusions	105
4. Doctrinal Ritual, Identification, and Social Complexity	106
The Doctrinal Pathway to Identification and Extended Fusion	107
Sociocultural Evolution and the Doctrinal Mode of Religiosity	112
Doctrinal Religions, Credibility Enhancing or Undermining Displays, and Normative Tightness	120
Relational Mobility and the Doctrinal Mode	123
Conclusions	124

5. Ritual's Evolutionary Landscapes	127
Are Rituals Evoked or Transmitted?	128
Proximate Causation and Development in the Evolution of Ritual	130
Epigenetic Landscapes	133
Cognitive-Developmental Landscapes	135
Social-Historical Landscapes	138
Multilevel Landscapes	139
Conclusions	143
6. Challenges for Society	145
Multilevel Landscapes and Public Policy	147
Imagistic Pathways to Intergroup Violence	152
Doctrinal Pathways to Populism, Polarization, and Global Action	161
Conclusions	168
7. Challenges for Science	170
The Unnaturalness of Social Theory	172
The Two Cultures Problem and the Silo Effect	182
Diversifying Cross-Cultural Comparison and Collaboration	187
Conclusions	194
Epilogue	196
References	205
Author Index	233
Subject Index	238

Introduction

Throughout world history, people have joined together to perform customary behaviours, in obedience to seemingly arbitrary rules and conventions, that make their cultural tradition distinct from any other. Despite the globalization of many cultural practices, locally distinct ritual traditions continue to flourish and evolve. Even the most secular political systems ever devised, for instance under the sway of historical materialism and its vision of a communist utopia, were as devoted to ritual as any in human history. Each time a child is born, a new bearer of rituals from the past is created. And much of the psychology responsible for this is uniquely human. We are truly the ritual animal.

The word 'ritual' is commonly used to denote a diversity of behaviours, ranging from highly elaborated collective religious rites and ceremonies of state through to quite simple individual actions, like crossing oneself or observing locally prevailing rules of dining etiquette. The term is used also to refer to rites of passage such as birthing rituals, weddings, funerals, and initiatory ordeals, as well as calendrical ceremonies to celebrate the winter solstice or the first fruits of the harvest. Such collective behaviours can range in emotional intensity from being tedious and soporific to excruciating and terrifying. Participants often invest precious effort, money, and time in the performance of rituals, whether by frequent collective chanting and praying or the performance of sporadic but flamboyant outbursts of conspicuous consumption and sensory pageantry.

Despite their costliness, however, many rituals have no obvious instrumental value, and even those that do are assumed to achieve any outcomes by magic rather than by knowable causal mechanisms. This is because, unlike technically useful behaviours, rituals *lack a fully specifiable causal structure*. If your computer crashes, you might call up a technician for advice and be talked through various steps to repair and reboot the device. Even though you may not understand why each of these steps is necessary, or why they must be done in that order, you can reasonably assume that they contribute to the desired outcome in a way that conforms to specifiable processes of physical causation. As soon as you cease to make that assumption, and imagine that the technician is simply asking you to observe some formulaic sequence of actions that nobody could fully justify in mechanistic-instrumental terms, the activity becomes something altogether different: a ritual.

But if rituals have no knowable causal structure—and therefore no objective technical value—and if they are also a drain on time and resources, why do them at all? This book sets out to answer that question, using scientific methods grounded in an evolutionary framework that incorporates evidence from child development research, group psychology experiments and surveys, brain scans, ethnographic observations, historical archives, archaeological discoveries, agent-based models, and economic games. The research discussed in the chapters that follow is the culmination of decades of collaborative work across many disciplines. The goal is to uncover the psychological causes, lifespan trajectories, environmental triggers, historical predictors, and adaptive functions of ritual in a comparative framework, spanning evolving patterns of culture globally and over many millennia.

To explain why people everywhere perform rituals, four key questions need to be addressed, commonly known as 'Tinbergen's four whys' (Tinbergen, 1963). These 'four whys' seek to explain the existence of particular characteristics of an organism (from physical traits like feathers or hands to behavioural traits like head-bobbing or cultural rituals) by asking: (1) how the characteristic is assembled during the creature's development; (2) what immediate triggers or 'proximate mechanisms' cause the characteristic to be deployed or expressed; (3) whether or how the characteristic contributes to the animal's survival or reproduction; (4) how the evolution of the characteristic was constrained or shaped by preceding forms. Much research in the social and behavioural sciences can be seen as relevant to answering one or more of these four types of questions. In some cases, entire disciplines may be devoted mainly to just one of the four questions—for example, child psychology and paediatrics on development; cognitive sciences and behavioural economics on proximate causation; evolutionary psychology on adaptive functions; and archaeology and comparative linguistics on history and phylogeny. The beauty of Tinbergen's four whys is that they encompass very nearly everything one might wish to know about in order to explain the existence of a characteristic, while emphasizing the complementarity of different approaches and the need to combine them to obtain a fuller picture. Although Tinbergen's four whys were formulated around the middle of the last century, their importance for biologists has not diminished over the ensuing decades (Bateson & Laland, 2013), even if their value for the unification of the social and behavioural sciences is only beginning to be more fully appreciated (Wilson, 2020).

Applying Tinbergen's framework to the study of ritual, a key developmental question becomes why and how do children acquire the causally opaque conventions of the communities around them? In this book, I will present evidence that children have an evolved predisposition to imitate causally opaque behaviour, one of the key building blocks of rituals everywhere, and that this is motivated by the desire to affiliate with groups. Turning to the problem of proximate causation, what are the immediate environmental triggers of ritual behaviour? A range of factors may come into play, ranging from the hope for magical assistance when outcomes are particularly uncertain or the means to accomplish them are risky, to the desire to band together in the face of outgroup threats and natural disasters.

Tinbergen's questions also pertain to a given trait's evolved functions. What are the adaptive benefits of ritual participation, if any? One potential function of rituals is the role they play in generating social glue and driving cooperation. This glue appears to come in two main varieties: a very strong adhesive that motivates extreme self-sacrifice in small bands when facing challenging collective action problems such as outgroup threat, and a less powerful but highly spreadable adhesive that motivates conformism in much larger 'imagined' communities (such as nations or world religions), where group survival depends on being able to amass and centralize resources gathered from widely distributed populations. The strongest kinds of social glue are generated by rare but emotionally intense rituals as an adaptation to harsh environments, whereas the more diffuse but expandable form of cohesion would seem to be a cultural adaptation to cooperative challenges and intergroup competition in much larger coalitions. The fourth question is historical: for example, how have rituals contributed to different scales and intensities of social cohesion over the course of sociocultural evolution? I will describe efforts to answer that question by quantifying various dimensions of ritual and social complexity over thousands of years of world history and prehistory.

This fourfold approach to the puzzle of why humans perform rituals is increasingly recognized (Legare & Nielsen, 2020), but we are still a long way from being able to provide a comprehensive account of ritual's evolutionary origins, functions, causes, and consequences. The main goal of this book is to present a theory that *could* be wrong and thus is falsifiable in the face of new evidence. While many books have been written about the nature of ritual, very few advance a set of precise hypotheses that are then systematically tested scientifically, for instance using carefully controlled experiments or quantitative analysis of observations that take account of problems of selection bias, nonindependence of data points, and other potential confounds.

Testing the theoretical framework presented in this book has so far involved empirical investigation of topics as diverse as neural activity during interactions with rival groups, physiological responses during stressful rituals, prosocial behaviour following participation in collective ceremonies, and memory for participation in life-changing ritual ordeals. It has led researchers to carry out psychological experiments in a great diversity of populations around the world, from remote islands in the Pacific to war zones in the Middle East, and from football fans in Brazil to Islamist fundamentalists in Indonesia. It has also entailed quantitative analysis of patterns in the ethnographic record, regional archaeology, and world history via intensive collaboration with hundreds of scholars and scientists. As this process continues, the theoretical framework advanced in this book will no doubt have to be modified and improved. But whether or not the weight of scientific evidence eventually confirms the core hypotheses advanced here, the preeminent goal is to contribute to the establishment of a new paradigm for research in the social sciences, one that bridges across disciplinary silos, samples the full diversity of the world's populations, and plumbs our richest sources of information about cultural systems, past and present.

In view of this goal, what follows is aimed at a broad readership, but especially at students and professional practitioners of social science. If a paradigm shift is indeed to be accomplished, it will require encouragement from social scientists, particularly those starting out on their careers. Nevertheless, our intellectual milieus are also shaped by the general public, including those creating or implementing public policy in areas of social life where ritual and group bonding feature prominently. Thus, I hope this book will be read widely among all those who are intellectually curious about the origins and consequences of human nature and culture and who are personally invested in applying that knowledge in their lives and in the various ways they influence others.

The Varieties of Ritual Experience

Many efforts have been made to build typologies of ritual or theories that carve up the diversity of ritual forms at the joints. For example, Van Gennep (1960[1909]) identified an apparently distinct class of rituals that he called 'rites of passage' (*rites de passage* in the original French). Rites of passage mark transitions, for example, between changing seasons (calendrical rituals) or between social statuses such as the transformation from child to adult (initiation or puberty rite), or from prince to king (coronation). Van Gennep argued that these transition rituals had a universal tripartite structure, involving rites of separation (detachment and sacralization), liminality (segregation), and incorporation (reaggregation), all of which were symbolically marked.

Since the publication of Van Gennep's seminal work, the study of ritual has stimulated a kaleidoscopic variety of debates, each focusing on a different aspect of the phenomenon (for overviews, see Platvoet, 1995; Kreinath, Snoek, & Stausberg, 2007; Stewart & Strathern, 2014). For example, scholars have at turns attempted to define ritual in terms of such features as formalized rigidity (Nadel, 1954; Goffman, 1967), sacredness or transcendence (Durkheim, 1912); expectations of supernatural reward (Wilson, 1957; Gluckman, 1962a; van Baal, 1981); meaningfulness (Leach, 1954; Bocock, 1974; Tambiah, 1979; La Fontaine, 1985; Bell); meaninglessness (Staal, 1989; Humphrey & Laidlaw, 1994); framing (Michaels, 2016)' routinization (Weber, 1947; Werbner, 1977; Turner, 1969); performativity (Geertz, 1966; Bull & Mitchell, 2015); normativity or obligatoriness (Stark & Glock, 1971; Staal, 1989; Parkin, 1991); theatricality (Schechner, 1977); mimesis (Gunter & Wulf, 1996; Wulf, 2013); deference to tradition (Bloch, 1974; Bell, 1992, 1997); conventionality (van Baaren, 1983); habituation (Connerton, 1989; Bourdieu, 1977); separateness from everyday life (Kapferer, 1991); environmental context (Smith, 1987); relational aspects (Houseman & Severi, 1998); metaphorical qualities (Fernandez, 1971); multivocality (Turner, 1974; Kertzer, 1988); ritual syntax (Payne, 2004); action representation (McCauley & Lawson, 2002); hazard precaution (Boyer & Liénard, 2006; Dulaney & Fiske, 1994); goal demotion (Kapitány & Nielsen, 2016); and social synchrony (Hove & Risen, 2009). This is by no means an exhaustive list of the various aspects of ritual that have been the focus of scholarly attention, but it illustrates the multifaceted nature of the phenomenon.

One way of accounting for this multifaceted-ness is to regard all definitions of 'ritual' as the product of a unique history of power contestation, negotiation, and domination (Asad, 1988). But while that perspective may yield instructive insights, it also overlooks the historically and cross-culturally recurrent nature of many of the features mentioned above Indeed, many efforts to define 'ritual' more or less explicitly aim to exclude historically contingent or locally distinctive aspects in favour of more generic and globally recurrent ones. A more balanced approach might be to try to capture both features that are universal, or extremely widespread, as well as more variable ones, and to regard both recurrence and variation as equally worthy of explanation.

Some of the researchers on ritual whose work is cited above advance explanatory frameworks that are, at least in principle, both generalizable and testable. For example, McCauley and Lawson's 'ritual form hypothesis' (2002) starts from the proposal that in religious rituals, the agents, actions, patients, and instruments are attributed supernatural properties in a finite and predictable combination of ways. Thus, in the case of *rites of passage*, the agent of the ritual (e.g. the priest or master of ceremonies) is most closely associated with supernatural powers, whereas in *sacrificial rites* the patient of the ritual (e.g. the burnt offering) is imbued with sacredness, and in *blessings*, it is the instrument (e.g. the holy water). Generalizable theories like the ritual form hypothesis commonly focus on the role played by reliably recurrent mechanisms operating somewhat independently of historically and culturally unique particularities, such as evolved cognitive architecture (Boyer, 2001), recurrent sociological dynamics (Douglas, 1966), or biological stressors such as parasite load (e.g. Fincher & Thornhill, 2012).

A related strategy for carving up ritual behaviour at the joints, however, is to focus not so much on a single cluster of underlying causes (whether cognitive, social, biological, or some other) but on the clustering of observable characteristics across the ethnographic record as a whole. Based on statistical analysis of characteristics associated with hundreds of rituals from scores of language groups from around the world, my colleagues and I have shown that ritual features tend to cluster according to the kinds of emotions they evince (in particular whether the rituals are predominantly euphoric or dysphoric) and how frequently they are performed (Kapitány, Kavanagh, & Whitehouse, 2020). In the course of this book, I will delve deeper into the question of *why* emotionality and frequency should play such an important role in our ritual lives, and the ways in which these variables influence the scale and structure of human groups and the nature and intensity of our group alignments.

Another potentially instructive way to organize and classify the varieties of ritual experience, however, is to focus on a set of distinctive behavioural *outcomes*, rather than causes or attributes of the rituals themselves. Are there, for example, recurrent forms of cooperation associated with rituals performed collectively? Although it seems clear that some of the psychological processes underlying the appearance and spread of rituals are associated with purely solitary procedural habits and conventions, many rituals are performed in groups, and this would seem to have important implications for cooperation in social systems at all levels of organization. Moreover, group rituals, which may range in scale from dyads and families to large crowds and even globally coordinated communities, have been documented in all human societies, thus making it possible to develop general theories of the impacts of such rituals on cooperative behaviours of various kinds. Based on game theoretic assumptions, at least seven distinct types of cooperation may be distinguished in the natural world (Curry, 2016), and these are universally judged to be morally good in all societies (Curry, Mullins, & Whitehouse, 2019; although see also Gellner et al., 2020 for a debate). The seven cooperative rules are: help your group, support your family, return favours, be brave, defer to superiors, divide resources fairly, and respect other people's property. All the collective rituals of the world can be classified according to which of the seven cooperative moral concerns they are intended to serve most directly. An advantage of this framework is that it focuses on a small set of cooperative functions of ritual, in a way that does not commit us in advance to any particular explanatory strategy or theory. This is a useful device for introducing the great variety of ritual behaviours in human societies, but, as I shall explain, there are also many other dimensions that we need to consider if we are to explain why and how rituals do what they do and how they have contributed to the evolution of social complexity and cultural diversity.

Rituals Promoting Loyalty to Group

Most collective rituals bond participants to each other and inspire loyalty to the group. Examples are legion, particularly from the ethnographic record but also from historical accounts (Bell, 1992; Kertzer, 1988; Whitehouse & Lanman, 2014). People participate in collective rituals in part because they wish to affiliate with a group, and, as I will argue in the next chapter, even very young children join in with ritualistic behaviours more fervently when they are fearful of social exclusion or ostracism. But there are also certain elements of collective ritual that can further bolster a sense of belonging. One is social synchrony—moving or chanting in time with others creates an illusion of being part of something much larger and stronger (Wiltermuth & Heath, 2009). Another is emotional arousal which, as will become clearer in several chapters that follow, can help to create personally transformative shared experiences and produce some of the strongest forms of social cohesion known to humankind. Rituals that emphasize common ancestry, such as the mortuary rituals of descent groups, can also create a powerful sense of shared essence. And, finally, highly repetitive rituals may help to establish standardized identity markers and unify large populations. This book will explore the psychological processes underlying these forms of group bonding and consider how they have evolved over time.

Rituals That Bond Families

Rituals that strengthen familial ties and promote caring for kin include rites of passage that focus on the life cycle: birthing rituals and baptisms, puberty rites, weddings, and funerals. But kin groups also engage in more regular rituals that foster cohesion such as religious ceremonies, birthday parties, calendrical celebrations, and family hobbies, sports, and pastimes. While some of these activities are obviously rituals, many of the elements involved (e.g. observing culinary etiquette at family gatherings, chanting and clapping in football stadia) may be so familiar that we scarcely notice we are doing them or that they entail causally opaque behaviours. Moreover, although the family is an important locus for ritual life in most settled societies that rely on farming, it has not always been that way. Prior to the Neolithic revolution, most humans lived in foraging bands and it was commonly the band rather than the household that constituted the primary group around which social life, including ritual, was conducted (Leacock, 1978). At least some family rituals, such as daily mealtimes, probably only rose to prominence with the establishment of the household as the core unit of production and consumption in agrarian societies (Sahlins, 1974). It follows that we cannot take family rituals for granted, for example, as an evolved behaviour programme that is naturally expressed in all human societies. Indeed, in the contemporary world, the ritual life of families may have been eroded by the advent of television, computer games, social media, and changing work patterns, leading to a decline in even the most basic of family rituals such as eating together, observing customary table manners, and socializing around the domestic hearth.

Rituals Promoting Reciprocity

Many rituals emphasize the idea of a reciprocal relationship between performers and invisible agents. This idea is central to the logic of animal sacrifice, for example, in which an offering to the gods, ancestors, or spirits is made in the hope of receiving some kind of benefit in return. In some of the most popular religions today, such as Christianity, Judaism, and Islam, the idea of reciprocity is strongly associated with forgiveness for sins. That is, if the adherent dutifully performs a confession or carries out an act of piety or atonement, God will repay this with the gift of absolution. In many traditional societies, rituals not only established reciprocal relations with the gods but among the living too. One of the most striking examples of this from anthropology is Bronislaw Malinowski's (1922) description of the Kula ring—a highly ritualized exchange of arm shells and necklaces, allowing these valuables to circulate in opposing directions around participating islands in the Western Pacific, tying them together into a vast trading network and political system on the basis of the ritual obligation to give and receive. Another anthropologically famous example of ritualized reciprocity would be the ceremonial exchange systems of the New Guinea highlands, through which local big men and their factions challenged rivals to repay ostentatious gifts of locally valued goods (Young, 1972).

Rituals That Foster Bravery

Rituals celebrating or memorializing acts of heroism are ubiquitous in military groups but also in civilian populations that have lived through wars (Kertzer, 1988). Many commemorative rituals express admiration for the courage of those who died in battle but often also of those who supported them, for instance the medics who risked their lives to save others or the workers who kept the war machine fuelled and women who were seen to 'keep the home fires burning'. Rituals fostering bravery also celebrate the lives of cherished ancestors or past culture heroes, exemplifying forms of courage valorized in the societies commemorating them. Contemporary examples include ritual events in honour of those who have shown exceptional tenacity advancing causes that were unpopular or highly controversial at the time, such as campaigners for the abolition of slavery or the emancipation of women (Ward-Jackson, 2011).

Rituals Encouraging Deference to Hierarchy

A common theme in political rituals is the value of deference to authority and the status quo. The pomp and ceremony of royal rituals and state ceremonies emphasizes the wealth, power, and status of the figurehead or leader, often linking this idea to illustrious histories of power holders who precede them (Kertzer, 1988). In the most hierarchical societies of all, a curious phenomenon of 'ritual inversion' is also common—rituals in which the poor and lowly exchange roles with the rich and powerful. In Southern Europe, for example, during the Catholic tradition of the Carnival held every year before the arrival of Lent, the aristocracy waits hand and foot upon the commoner; processions are held reversing the usual order of precedence; figures of state authority are ridiculed and mocked; and sexual mores blatantly flouted (Mauldin, 2004). On certain Pacific islands, such as Samoa, where chiefs are usually treated very respectfully, there are moments in the ritual calendar when the lowliest of people impersonate chiefs, making fun of their styles of speech and portraying them as unintelligent and ignorant (Shore, 1996). These forms of 'ritual inversion' often appear to have a cathartic effect on the population, diffusing frustration and envy and ultimately legitimating tightly observed social hierarchies (Gluckman, 1962b).

Rituals Promoting Fairness

Rituals supporting equitable distribution of resources are common in hunting and gathering societies, including so-called levelling mechanisms designed to prevent status inequalities arising as a result of variable hunting success (Woodburn, 1982) and ritual rules governing the butchering and distribution of meat in the community (Lee & DeVore, 1969; Bodenhorn, 1990). Or to take a very different set of examples, in situations of rapid social change or upheaval, rituals commonly appear that highlight and challenge social injustices and celebrate a millenarian vision in which wrongs will be righted and inequalities levelled (Worsley, 1957). An extended example of such a ritual tradition is considered in Chapter 2.

Rituals Promoting Respect for Property

Most societies have at least some rituals that emphasize the importance of respect for other people's property. In many cases, such rituals are embedded in the ceremonial of the criminal justice system, but they are also often found in rural communities and indigenous groups where rights over land or other resources are ritually enacted. Examples range from beating the bounds in medieval English villages (Berwick, 2007) to ritually tabooing the exploitation of marine resources during certain periods of the year in Melanesian lagoons (Hviding, 1996). A particularly instructive example of such rituals is found among the Manambu, a group living in the Sepik region of Papua New Guinea (Harrison, 1991). The Manambu say that all the vital resources of nature that humans require to survive are magically controlled through the male cult, which assigns responsibility for different resources (e.g. land, sun, water, crops, fish, and game) to different subclans. The rights of each subclan are embodied in the names it possesses. The Manambu have in total somewhere in the region of 32,000 names, and each subclan lays claim on average to about one or two thousand names. Each person is only allowed five or so names, however, and if the population of a given subclan declines, it is unable use up all its names, risking the loss of ritual powers over natural resources and corresponding loss of status and ritual precedence at major ceremonies.

Although far from being a comprehensive survey of the world's rituals, the above should at least convey a sense of the diversity of ritual traditions and their cooperative functions. Of all seven types of cooperation considered here, one has exercised the anthropological imagination far more than any of the others—namely *loyalty to group*. Variously described as solidarity, *esprit de corps*, collective effervescence, social cohesion, deference to tradition, and *communitas* (among other things), this apprehension of being bonded and loyal to one's group has been the object of voluminous writings and extended empirical observations in social and cultural anthropology. Arguably the most influential scholarly framework for understanding the cohesive power of ritual is that provided by the so-called symbolist school, pioneered by the French sociologist Emile Durkheim.

Ritual and the Symbolist School

According to Durkheim (1912), people everywhere are aware, if only obscurely, of a complex and dramatic internal battle raging within them, rather like the struggle between Robert Louis Stephenson's celebrated fictional characters, Dr Jekyll and Mr Hyde. Durkheim famously characterized our species as *homo duplex*, forever torn between egoistic psycho-organic drives and impulses and the obligations and duties incumbent upon us by virtue of station and office. As the bearers of social roles, we defer to a social order that requires sublimation of our antisocial tendencies for the betterment of all. But there was also another, rather less Hobbesian aspect to Durkheim's conception of *homo duplex*, further elaborated by his students, such as Hertz (1960) and Mauss (1979), and their intellectual heirs such as Douglas (1966) and Bloch (1992). In terms of their bodies, human beings go through irreversible phases of life: birth, growth, reproduction, ageing, and death. This irreversible progression constitutes, for Durkheimians, the core of that which people everywhere recognize as profane, transient, and 'worldly'. By contrast, social institutions, such as the monarchy, have a notional permanence: individual monarchs die and have to be replaced, but the kingship itself persists. According to Durkheim, religion and ritual provide a way of conceptualizing and cultivating attachment to the permanent, transcendental quality of society. Rituals transcend us in three senses: they outlive us; we are socialized into them rather than creating them ourselves; they regulate our behaviour.

Durkheim referred to these three forms of transcendence conjointly as 'the sacred', a dimension construed as more powerful than the individual, the ultimate source of creativity in the cosmos, and unchanging—liberated from the transience of worldly activity, growth, and decay. Indeed, religious rituals commonly portray a mirror image of biological reality, postulating an otherworldly dimension in which there are no bodies and no sense of processual change. But such imagery merely *symbolizes* the unchanging and transcendent order of society itself. For this reason, Durkheim is often described as the founder of the 'symbolist' perspective on religion and ritual.

As noted above, Durkheim's ideas on ritual deeply influenced subsequent generations of anthropologists. An early example would be the work of French sociologist Robert Hertz, whose essay entitled 'A Contribution to the Study of the Collective Representation of Death' (1960) focused on the widespread Malayo-Polynesian practice of double burial, whereby corpses are not immediately taken to a final resting place but instead placed in a temporary location such as the family house for a period of time. It was said that the corpse should not be permanently buried until it had thoroughly decomposed so that only the skeleton remained. Bodies allowed to rot in this way were sometimes sealed in coffins, and the putrefying liquids drained from time to time. In certain parts of Borneo relatives of the deceased mixed this decomposing material with rice, eaten during the period of mourning. Hertz observed that the condition of the corpse corresponded to the imagined condition of the dead person's soul. While the corpse was rotting, the soul was considered to remain in a kind of limbo, and could not find rest until the decomposing material had drained away, leaving only the dried skeletal remains. By eating the fleshy part of the corpse, mourners hoped to expedite the process of drying out necessary for the release of the soul, but these acts of endo-cannibalism also provided a means of consuming the vitality of the corpse, the flesh that made the person strong and active during life, but which must now be left behind. This vitality is of value to the living insofar as society requires strong and healthy members if it is to survive.

Hertz's understanding of the cultural logic of double burials drew heavily on Durkheim's notion of *homo duplex*: a distinction between the person as a physically and psychologically distinct being and the person as the bearer of social roles. When a person dies, his or her body is destroyed and along with it the particular hopes, fears, loves, and hates of the individual. But what of the social roles and obligations that person had acquired over the course of a lifetime? These must somehow be redistributed and preserved. The transition may be awkward, however. If the deceased was a pillar of the community, upon whom many depended, death would be a source of major social disruption. Hertz believed that in the small-scale societies of Borneo, where social cohesion was strong, the disruption caused by death was experienced as a kind of outrage against the group itself. Death destroyed not only the profane, biological part of the person but also the social or sacred side, and the purpose of the double funeral was to correct this outrage, to respond to the sacrilege of death. This logic was plain to see, Hertz argued, in the symbolism of double burials. Recall that the corpse was separated into two parts: the flesh (symbolizing the profane, psycho-organic aspect of the individual) which must be pared away, its destruction being of no consequence to society; the dried skeleton (symbolizing the sacred aspect of the individual, his social roles) that must be preserved after death. Thus, according to Hertz, the bones represented the everlasting soul, but the root of this symbolism was the social organization itself. The 'other world', to which the souls of the dead ultimately repaired, was in reality the social order itself—a way of conceptualizing the everlasting nature of society.

More than half a century later, Hertz's ideas were taken up by anthropologists Maurice Bloch and Jonathan Parry (1982) in an attempt to develop a comparative theory of funerary rituals and, more ambitiously still, a general theory of ritual symbolism. While rejecting Hertz's seemingly anthropomorphic conception of society as being in some sense outraged by the death of its members, they agreed that funerals provide an occasion for dramatizing and re-establishing the transcendence of society.

Consider the notion of transcendence as super-permanence, in other words, the idea that both social institutions and the sacred realm are conceptualized as timeless and unchanging. According to Bloch and Parry, this is expressed in mortuary symbolism in three particularly common ways. First, it is expressed as a denial of our subjective experiences of time as linear and irreversible: funerary rituals portray the other world as frozen or as participating in a cyclical process of death and rebirth. Second, the permanence of society is symbolized through the imagery of durable objects: gravestones, tombs, pyramids, dried skeletons, and other durable artefacts featuring in mortuary rituals to convey a sense of the permanent, unchanging nature of the sacred realm. Third, in many patrilineal societies, mortuary rituals use images of masculinity to emphasize the permanence of the sacred order. In such societies, it is argued, male substance is seen as the stuff of everlasting descent groups, in contrast with the worlds of women dominated by biological reproduction and child-rearing. Whereas households are merely transient groupings, the descent group is conceptualized as a permanent entity, a masculine realm that epitomizes the permanence of the ancestral world.

Another aspect of the transcendence of society and the sacred realm concerns the location of creativity. In many traditional social systems, we do not on the whole see ourselves as creating society but rather as being born into it. Correspondingly, we envisage the sacred realm as something already there, rather than being our own creation. In fact, religious dogma widely proclaims that we are the creations of gods, or other supernatural forces, and not the other way around. According to Bloch and Parry, this idea is most commonly expressed in mortuary rituals through the use of fertility symbolism emphasizing the idea that death is really a kind of rebirth and that the soul of the dead person is now embarking upon a new phase of existence. Thus, mortuary rituals often focus on images of birth and fertility, asserting that although a body has been destroyed, an ancestor has been created. This, of course, involves seeing death as a highly creative event. And the creation of ancestors is upheld as superior to the act of biological reproduction.

A further point about the transcendence of society and of the sacred order concerns their moral control over our lives. Durkheim understood this as a process by which our biological drives are felt to be regulated by social forces acting on us from above. According to Bloch and Parry, mortuary symbolism is fundamentally concerned with underlining the authority of the sacred order and the superiority of the sacred over the profane. At funerals, cyclical time is portrayed as superior to linear time; durable objects, like bones and tombs, are superior to perishable objects, such as flesh and skin; masculinity and male solidarity are superior to femininity and family life. Thus, mortuary symbolism is not only concerned with constructing images of permanence—it also emphasizes the transcendence of these permanent objects over transient ones.

A recurrent thread in these Durkheimian studies of rites of passage is the changing balance between physical and spiritual aspects of the person over the course of the life cycle. In the case of funerary rituals, this transformation is especially dramatic: the physical aspect of the person is destroyed and discarded, leaving only the everlasting spirit. In many other rites of passage, such as initiations, a less radical kind of change is supposed to take place. The spiritual side of the person is enhanced, without destroying the body. According to Durkheimian logic, spirit substance and sacredness are really just symbols of the abiding authority of society. Society has to be seen as more powerful than the individual in order to regulate people's antisocial tendencies. A convenient way of conceptualizing this is through religious symbols, and so people are seen as becoming increasingly spiritual as they get older. When they end up in the ancestral world, they are completely sacred and represent the authority of the social order in the purest and most irrevocable sense. So, one might imagine the life cycle as a process of accumulating spirit-substance: as an infant, one has only a little of this substance, but it grows over the course of the lifespan, so that, at death, one ends up being an entirely spiritual entity. Each rite of passage delivers another 'dose' of spirit substance.

Following the logic of Hertz's Durkheimian interpretation of double burials, Bloch (1992) has argued that the accumulation of spirit substance over the course of life symbolizes the acquisition of rights, obligations, social roles, and responsibilities. When we start out in life, as babes in arms, our psycho-organic demands are incessant, but our contributions to society negligible. As we mature, assuming roles and obligations, we wield greater authority in society (conceptualized as an increase in sacredness or spirituality). But as this authority grows, our vitality diminishes. The older we get, the more powerful we may be in social life, but the weaker we become physically. In very old age, there is hardly any of our physical vitality left. Our bodies crumple and diminish, and the process of decay is drastically accelerated after death, as we become completely spiritual. We enter the world of the ancestors—a world without bodies, without processual change, and without reproduction.

This logic would help to explain why spiritual authority is invested in older people in many traditional societies and why ancestors are venerated. Authority is measured in terms of spiritual purity. The most powerful authority is that of pure spirits—the ancestors—who confer misfortune on the badly behaved and who are seen, more positively, as the mystical source of continuity in the world. Elders are closer to the ancestors in the way they are constituted, so they are naturally the holders of authority in 'this world'. Growing old is only one way of being close to the ancestors—another possible way is to become a chief or a king. Such figures are usually seen as vehicles for the will of the ancestors, and they have to undergo special rituals to assume this high status. It is thus the imagined balance between bodily and spiritual attributes that warrants how much authority the individual can assume in society. The more spiritual you are, and therefore the less physical vitality you possess, the more powerful your position in the world.

Building on this general line of reasoning, Bloch has advanced a general theory of 'rebounding violence' in ritual symbolism, suggesting that funerary rituals are essentially truncated versions of initiation rites. Initiations typically begin by caricaturing the bodily aspects of people and then contrasting this caricature with images of the spiritual world, portrayed as much more powerful and desirable. A particularly common way of expressing this idea is that novices undergoing initiation are symbolically killed, their flesh beaten, lacerated, or mutilated, before being sent to a place of seclusion (often explicitly analogous to the place of the dead). The same kind of process is enacted at funerals. In Borneo, as Hertz observed, the corpse is dried out by draining off rotting material, and only when the bones are completely dry can the deceased enter the realm of the ancestors. The difference between funerals and initiations is that mortuary rituals end at the point when the human object has been totally transferred to the spirit world. But novices in an initiation have to be brought back from the dead. Bloch refers to this as 'rebounding violence'. Novices cannot leave 'this world' behind forever, unlike a corpse that can and must. The re-entry of the novices is not simply a matter of returning, but of coming back as conquerors, more powerful than before, and asserting dominance over the people they once were. Much the same may be said of other rituals that confer authority and sacredness by symbolically destroying the body and then establishing the dominance of the social/spiritual order over it, such as royal rituals and installations, whereby the office holder must be sent (at least symbolically) into the realm of the sacred, later returning violently to regain control over the earthly body but with a new balance of sacred and profane (the former now enhanced and the latter conquered and controlled). *Homo duplex*, it would seem, is a dynamic conception of the person, a progressive victory of

Dr Jekyll over Mr Hyde, performed through a series of ritual dramas from cradle to grave.

The Durkheimian view of religion and ritual has prompted anthropologists to document a wide variety of contrasts drawn in ritual symbolism between sacred and profane characteristics, juxtaposing body and spirit, birth and death, vitality and stillness, hot and cold, wet and dry, left and right, femininity and masculinity, pollution and purity, nature and culture, consumption and abstinence, moon and sun, and flesh and bones, among other recurrent dichotomies (Bloch & Parry, 1982). It has been suggested that the way these characteristics are portrayed in rituals conforms to widely replicated patterns, an argument formulated perhaps most sharply in Bloch's (1992) theory of rebounding violence. According to this theory, rituals endow us with sacredness, justifying the exercise of authority in this world by demonstrating that it originates in a transcendent source.

The legacy of Durkheim's theory of ritual and religion is not restricted to the symbolist school but has also deeply influenced other theoretical traditions in anthropology, including Bronislaw Malinowski's (1944) and A.R. Radcliffe-Brown's (1952) brands of functionalism, Victor Turner's juxtaposition of structure and *communitas* (1969), and Mary Douglas's ideas about pollution and taboo (1966). In these and many other scholarly works, especially in the twentieth century, anthropologists have contributed innumerable insights into the nature, causes, and consequences of rituals (see Bell, 1992). Many have concurred with Durkheim's fundamental insight that rituals elevate us above the world of everyday profane concerns by establishing traditions that transcend us: preceding us, outliving us, and directing our behaviour. Along with these three forms of transcendence comes an uneasy balance between symbolic communication and political control and legitimation. But in addition to the rich meanings and social consequences of rituals, they are also commonly ascribed efficacy as magical procedures capable of improving our fortunes and healing our ills. Rituals, in other words, seem to have many salient properties and affordances. Partly for this reason, it has proven hard to establish what, if anything, rituals all have in common or to provide a simple answer to the question why humans perform rituals at all.

As compelling as the symbolist perspective may seem, at least as a narrative framework, if it is to have explanatory power, it needs to be scientific. Ideally, it should generate hypotheses with sufficient precision that they can be tested empirically. This is not a minor detail. After all, ideas are cheap, whereas evidence capable of supporting or refuting those ideas is typically much more costly to generate. If rituals do indeed bind us to groups, making us defer to the interests of the collective even when these conflict with more selfish ones, then we need to develop and apply ecologically sound measures of self-sacrifice and prosocial action. Likewise, if we are to disambiguate the potentially complex psychological processes, and their developmental origins, that give rise to pro-group action, then we need to create theoretical constructs and psychometric measures to investigate the causal pathways from ritual to cohesion to cooperation. This book attempts to show how such an enterprise might unfold, in ways that are both theoretically parsimonious and empirically tractable. The aim is less to provide an authoritative alternative to existing approaches to explaining ritual, than to help map some of the many pathways through which those approaches can be made more scientific, as part of a cumulative process. The scientific study of ritual is still in its infancy, and so the programme of research described here comprises little more than baby steps. But such steps are essential if we are to make more substantial progress in the future.

Overview of the Book

Seven chapters and an epilogue follow this introduction. Chapter 1 delves into the psychology underlying ritualistic behaviour and its emergence in development. Here, I focus in particular on the role of imitation of causally opaque behaviour (also known as 'overimitation') in social learning and especially the transmission of cultural conventions. It has been appreciated for some time that overimitation can support efficient transmission of instrumental skills by enabling learners to acquire useful technical procedures without needing to understand fully how they work. Our collaborative research suggests, however, that overimitation also plays a central role in the transmission of group-defining rituals, enabling learners to acquire behaviours that are stipulated by convention rather than because they have any technical use. Social learning of causally opaque behaviour can involve either ritual or instrumental stances, depending on available cues, giving rise to contrasting patterns of overimitation associated with distinct motivational systems. The ritual stance appears to be primarily affiliative, functioning also as a means of reinclusion when primed with the threat of ostracism. In addition, the ritual stance plays an important role in learning to tamp down egoistic impulses in order to implement group-oriented or future-minded strategies.

The ritual stance in human development explains not only why humans voraciously imitate behaviour that has no causally transparent instrumental value, but also why rituals become such a magnet for meaning making and exegetical interpretation. It helps to explain, for example, why the symbolist perspective on ritual is such a seemingly compelling narrative. Since ritual actions are not constrained by causal structure, they could incorporate almost any conceivable procedural rules and consequently may be invested with a vast array of meanings or symbolic motivations. But causal opacity also makes it quite possible to imagine rituals as having no meaning whatsoever. The paradox that rituals are capable of being both deeply meaningful and utterly meaningless is explained by their causally opaque character.

Causal opacity and the ritual stance also help to explain why rituals become such powerful identity markers and therefore capable of lifting us out of our profane everyday lives by providing us with a feeling of attachment to something far greater, the realm of the collective and the sacred (as Durkheim envisaged it). Rituals demarcate group identities precisely because they prescribe behaviours that are both arbitrary and instrumentally useless. They have little value except as ways of marking membership of a collective. But because they can also be invested with meanings, the exegesis attributed to rituals—just like the procedures themselves—can be socially learned and distributed, thereby also serving as identity markers. Indeed, it is typically the combination of belief and practice, myth and ritual, that lies at the core of every cultural tradition. Rituals and their meanings tend to come as a package—the one complementing and embellishing the other, as folklore warrants ceremony and as doctrines demand rites. Insofar as rituals define groups and motivate affiliation, loyalty, and a sense of higher purpose, they are also powerful instruments of political control. But just as rituals can be used to bolster the powers of elites, they can also mobilize support for revolutions and rebellions. This also means that in highly stable social systems, where revolutions are unheard of, rituals can provide catharsis for the exploited and oppressed, without risk of posing a serious threat to power holders.

Causal opacity also explains why rituals are so often attributed magical efficacy. Ritual and instrumental stances on causally opaque behaviour are always finely balanced, and while some actions strongly gravitate to one or other pole, others tend to cluster in the middle. Such actions may prompt a *quasi-instrumental* stance—oriented to influencing real-world outcomes but in ways that are only partially knowable. Opacity thus transforms into a magical mystery, the invisible essence that is left after the homeopath has diluted the remedy so many times that not a molecule of the original medicine remains. Magic resides in the grace uttered before a meal, the bottle cast against the hull of a ship as it is launched, the self-crossing of a footballer before taking a penalty kick. Embedded in many such instrumental actions are the vestiges of rituals, and this is where most everyday magic also lurks.

Rituals come in many varieties. One of the most striking ways in which they vary is in their frequency, emotionality, and sensory pageantry. Chapter 2 introduces the theory of divergent modes of religiosity (hereafter the modes theory), which makes a series of testable predictions about the effects of ritual frequency and arousal on group size, structure, and patterns of transformation in a religion over time (Whitehouse, 1995, 2000, 2004). The modes theory seeks to explain the differences observed between two broadly distinct patterns of religious organization and transmission: the doctrinal mode exemplified by the many forms and offshoots of the world religions, embracing vast followings and promulgating a body of standardized teachings, and the imagistic mode, typically uniting much smaller communities cultivating somewhat personal and esoteric revelations. The doctrinal mode appears to be relatively recent, originating in the rise of agriculture and complex social organization. The imagistic mode is much older, originating in small-scale traditional societies and persisting today largely in the form of local traditions on the fringes of much larger doctrinal systems. Three main types of evidence are offered in support of these claims: detailed cases studies of rituals cross-culturally and historically, quantitative analysis of rituals across a global sample of contemporary cultural groups, and longitudinal research on the evolution of social complexity using archaeological and historical datasets.

Chapter 3 focuses attention on the imagistic mode and in particular its capacity to produce highly cohesive military units willing to fight and die to protect the ingroup. In this chapter, I consider how and why rituals bond participants in ways that give rise to extreme forms of loyalty and self-sacrifice. Participation in collective rituals is a potent cause of ingroup cohesion and outgroup hostility in many societies. But the modes theory suggests that doctrinal and imagistic practices contribute to bonding and conflict in different ways, and to different degrees. One of the hallmark features of the imagistic mode is that its rituals trigger transformative experiences through the enactment of traumatic ordeals, searing themselves into the memories of participants and driving a process of exegetical reflection that can last for years, even for a whole lifetime (Whitehouse, 1995, 2000, 2004; Martin & Pachis, 2009). Traumatic experiences, especially ones that are surprising and consequential for participants, are remembered, even vividly relived, in visceral moments of recall or 'flashbacks', over longer time periods than less arousing events. In the case of traumatic 'rites of terror' (Whitehouse, 1996a) that are recalled for many months and years after the actual event, questions of symbolism and purpose are also typically a major focus of attention, further contributing to their transformative effects on personal identity.

An important development in understanding the link between emotionally intense ritual and extreme group bonding is the discovery of 'identity fusion'—a visceral sense of oneness with the group in which personal and group identities are activated synergistically (Swann et al., 2012). When people's personal and group identities are fused in this way, any attack on the group feels personal. Consequently, highly fused individuals will stop at nothing to defend other groups members, expressing willingness to fight and die for the group (Swann et al., 2009) and in some cases actually laying down their lives in armed conflicts (Whitehouse et al., 2014). A growing body of research suggests that there are at least two pathways to fusion, both of which involve feelings of shared essence with other members of the group. One pathway involves strong perceptions of shared biology, based on common ancestry, phenotypic characteristics, and other cues indicating genealogical relatedness (Vázquez et al., 2017a). Another pathway involves strong perceptions of shared experience, based on undergoing similar life-changing events, such as imagistic rituals, with other group members (Whitehouse, 2018a).

Several possible models for the evolution of imagistic practices have been proposed. One idea is that fusion, with its strong focus on familial ties, came about as a result of kin selection but has been hijacked by cultural institutions, such as painful initiation rites, so as to create bonds of psychological kinship among warriors (Whitehouse & Lanman, 2014). But other possible evolutionary explanations have also been advanced, ranging from extreme reciprocity to behaviours that condition cooperation on past experience (Whitehouse et al., 2017). Given that evolution often engages multiple mechanisms in tandem, these explanations for fusion and the rise of imagistic rituals are not mutually exclusive. Nevertheless, while the imagistic mode may have featured in human societies far back into the Neolithic and beyond (Whitehouse, 2000), the doctrinal mode—with its emphasis on highly repetitive collective rituals, centralization, and hierarchy—would appear to be a more recent cultural innovation, emerging with the advent of farming (Whitehouse & Hodder, 2010).

Chapter 4 explores the role of doctrinal ritual in the evolution of social complexity. The doctrinal mode heralds not only the first large-scale societies but also the first complex political systems in which roles and offices are understood to be detachable from the persons who occupy them. High-frequency ritual (or *routinization*) is a hallmark of world religions and their offshoots, but is also characteristic of a great many regional religions and ideological movements. Routinized rituals would seem to have played an important role in the cultural evolution of large-scale group identities, enabling strangers to recognize each other as members of a common ingroup, and facilitating trust and cooperation on a scale that would otherwise have been impossible.

The idea that frequent repetition of a body of teachings allows them to be shared in a stable fashion within a classroom, congregation, or wider community is widely recognized. For example, it lies at the root of the rote-learning system of education first fully elaborated early in the twentieth century (Ebbinghaus, 1913), and still widely practised in schools and doctrinal religions. While rote learning is often criticized by advocates of critical thinking (Schunk, 2008), in part because it seems to suppress independent reflection and critical engagement, such qualities are precisely what is required to preserve intact a large body of religious beliefs and practices. If adherents to a doctrinal tradition simply carry out the rituals and regurgitate the doctrines and narratives in a highly formulaic and predicable fashion, this can have the positive effect of enabling the tradition to spread and stabilize. Deviations from the norm are easy to detect and, especially with the advent of priestly hierarchies, relatively easy to sanction.

Participation in routinized rituals not only facilitates the emergence of much larger groups with stable orthodoxies but may also foster identification, motivating ingroup favouritism and norm enforcement as well as outgroup derogation and rivalry (Tajfel & Turner, 1979). Identification can help motivate group members to contribute to collective goals, for example, by paying tax or tribute and punishing free-riders, and it can also encourage coalitional behaviour and protectionism, but it is not a sufficiently strong form of social glue to motivate extreme self-sacrifice for the group, as in the case of imagistic groups discussed in Chapter 3. At the same time, however, large groups formed on the basis of shared beliefs and practices can also become the target of extended fusion, which can motivate quite strong forms of cooperation, even if not to the same extent as local fusion. I provide numerous contemporary examples of this, including studies conducted with religious fundamentalists.

I then turn to the origins of the doctrinal mode in world history, beginning with evidence of the rise of more routinized ritual practices at the richly documented Neolithic site of Çatalhöyük in central Anatolia, and then broadening it out to consider evidence from a much larger number of archaeological sites across the Neolithic Middle East, spanning over time from the end of the Epipaleolithic and to the beginnings of the Chalcolithic. Building on this, I consider efforts to uncover the earliest traces of the doctrinal mode in world history using a new databank known as *Seshat* which codes information on ritual practices and social complexity over thousands of years, using a stratified sample of thirty natural geographic areas chosen to maximize diversity. Taken together, this evidence points to the appearance of doctrinal practices around the time that farming emerges, potentially helping to explain how groups become larger from that point onwards. I also consider how new challenges for group cohesion may have emerged as societies grew beyond a certain threshold (around a million individuals). In particular, archaic states that relied on top-down coercion as a way of maintaining centralized, hierarchical systems may have become less stable as they grew larger, and more religiously and ethnically diverse, for example, as a result of conquest or the expansion of trading networks. In order to compete with other rapidly expanding empires, new forms of cooperation may have been necessary, based on the spread of beliefs in moralizing gods and other features associated with the so-called Axial Age.

Chapter 5 seeks to expand the theoretical framework with which we might understand the role of ritual in the evolution of social complexity. I consider in particular, various ways in which the developmental trajectories of biological organisms, minds, and social systems intersect. This is not always obvious when conducting research at discrete explanatory levels, in light of discipline-specific questions, theories, and methods. For instance, research highlighting cross-cultural differences in ritual behaviour might pay little attention to evidence for genetically canalized aspects of the behaviour. More generally, social scientists are often sceptical of psychological and biological reductionism and wary of efforts to examine the shaping and constraining effects of cognitive and physiological processes. The resulting silo effect would not be a problem if processes unfolded at these different levels independently. But they do not. Efforts to show how they are related tend to approach the subject in a rather arbitrary and piecemeal fashion.

This chapter proposes a more integrated conceptual scheme, one that generates systematic hypotheses and provides a more comprehensive and flexible understanding of proximate causation and development in the evolution of ritual systems. The conceptual approach advanced in this chapter distinguishes in particular three interacting levels, or 'landscapes': epigenetic, cognitive-developmental, and social-historical. My aim is to present a more encompassing framework for understanding how sociocultural systems evolve, not only over millennia (e.g. studied by quantifying patterns in global history) but in the lives of individuals (e.g. studied using psychometric measures in multicountry surveys). In this way, very different temporal scales, explanatory levels, and patterns of global variation can all be studied within a single overarching scheme.

Chapter 6 discusses a wide range of ways in which the theoretical framework and findings described in this book could be applied to real-world problems, beginning with the overarching multilevel landscape model advocated in Chapter 5. To the extent that public policy is informed by empirical evidence, it tends to look to only one level at best, with a strong preference for findings from the 'harder sciences', but seldom at all three levels at once, or the way they impact each other. An example of a rare exception would be research on the so-called urban poverty trap, and, drawing on this, I consider how the UK's response to the global Covid-19 pandemic of 2020–2021 might have proceeded differently if epigenetic, cognitive-developmental, and social-historical landscapes and their interactions had been considered together in designing and implementing lockdowns and other measures to lower infection rates. A major impediment to such an approach is the relative newness and lack of integration of research at higher (and more complex) levels in the multilevel landscape model. Thus, the rest of Chapter 6 focuses more closely on how the modes theory can help to fill gaps especially at the middle (cognitive-developmental) level, drawing on what has been learned about the causes and consequences of imagistic and doctrinal patterns of group alignment and cooperation.

A substantial part of this chapter focuses on relatively localized forms of group cohesion in which *imagistic* experiences feature prominently. For example, I explore the possibility that many forms of intergroup conflict might be the predictable outcome of just a small number of variables, such as identity fusion combined with outgroup threat (Whitehouse, 2018a). If so, it should be possible to build a volatility index—a way of predicting the likelihood that violence will break out and escalate in any given population—that can be used as a conflict management tool in a wide variety of settings around the world. Likewise, a version of such an index could be used as a diagnostic tool to detect potential terrorists in larger populations of hard-line extremists. I also consider interventions that could help to *defuse* volatile populations and individuals before they turn to violence. Finally, I consider how fusion resulting from imagistic experiences could be positively harnessed to achieve positive prosocial outcomes, such as reducing recidivism among ex-prisoners (Whitehouse & Fitzgerald, 2020). As an extended example, I describe a project that seeks to channel the cohesive power of football fandom to help ex-offenders stay out of prison and to motivate the receiving community to contribute to reintegration programmes and employment opportunities (Newson & Whitehouse, 2020).

The rest of the chapter looks at more global issues in which the *doctrinal* mode could play an increasingly important role. Starting with research on the divisive effects of the UK's Brexit campaign, our research suggests that a key motivation for Remainers was not a lack of patriotic commitment to Britain but comparatively high levels of fusion with Europe (Curry, Buhrmester, & Whitehouse, 2019). Moreover, I consider evidence that shared suffering in the wake of the 2016 referendum result helped to increase fusion among Remainers. Extended fusion and identification, crossing national boundaries, is also a striking feature of the world religions and their offshoots. I propose various practical ways in which this kind of cohesion could be harnessed to address global problems, such as the climate crisis. I also consider evidence that panhuman moral intuitions (Curry, Mullins, & Whitehouse, 2019) could be more systematically exploited in tackling global challenges. Currently these intuitions are underexploited by environmental activists (Curry et al., 2019). What is needed is a set of global moral norms capable of applying our evolved cooperative instincts to address not only the climate crisis but also a much wider range of collective action problems. We stand, perhaps, on the brink of a new era in human history. The challenge is to use what we are rapidly learning about the causes and consequences of human rituals to build a more globally cohesive and cooperative world.

Chapter 7 turns to the wider scientific implications of the research discussed in preceding chapters. If social science is to be a science of anything then it must be capable of building cumulatively on the theories, methods, and findings of each preceding generation. Anthropology, for example, has for decades been embroiled in continual turf wars between competing factions with widely differing foundational assumptions about the nature and purpose of social scientific enquiry. Lacking any dedicated cognitive machinery for reasoning about social complexity, scholars have been prone to borrowing intuitions adapted for processing information about quite unrelated ontological domains (artifacts, natural kinds, agents, and minds). Consequently, we are all tempted at turns to reify institutions, biologize social categories, anthropomorphize offices, or mentalize corporate groups. This chapter attempts to show how these strategies come to grief, and it suggests a more productive way forward that grounds social theory in the cognitive and evolutionary sciences.

If basic epistemological disagreements about the nature of the subject matter of social science can be set aside, if only provisionally, cumulative scientific progress will become possible, at least in theory. In practice, however, it is far from inevitable that this potential will be realized. Among the many impediments to progress, one of the most daunting is arguably the so-called silo problem—the fact that different academic disciplines are often relatively isolated and inward looking, making it difficult to see how their methods, specialized concepts, and datasets could be relevant to researchers working in other fields. A particularly promising solution to this is to identify problems that are recognizable and interesting to researchers across a range of disciplines. Problem-centred research projects can rapidly become engrossed in the search for solutions, adapting methodological tools and creating new theoretical constructs that allow researchers from different silos to work together effectively. Thus, in the process of building novel collaborations, cohesive teams of scientists can take shape, and this can have both positive and negative consequences. On the positive side, interdisciplinary teams can break free of the familiar patterns of intra-silo research in ways that open up unexpected discoveries or new directions for fruitful research. On the negative side, teams can come into fierce competition as they stumble upon similar ideas at the same time or develop contrasting views on how to proceed methodologically or how to analyse and interpret the data. When contests of this sort involve groups, rather than merely individual scholars, the results can divide entire teams and cause collaborative efforts to run aground.

Even if all these problems can be successfully navigated, problem-centred collaborative research in the social sciences tends to be much more challenging and costly than conventional intra-disciplinary work. This is partly because of the amount of retooling that needs to happen for research networks to form and collaborate successfully and partly because implementation typically requires the recruitment and training of full-time postdoctoral posts, research assistants, and numerous research staff. Comparative projects can operate economically by sourcing expertise locally to some extent but ensuring diversity of samples in cross-cultural research will also necessitate expensive forms of data collection requiring long-term team-based fieldwork or the construction and maintenance of labour-intensive databanks and data curation platforms. Despite all these daunting challenges, a strong case can be made that problem-centred collaborative approaches together with the creation of publicly available resources, such as open-access databases, are key to developing the study of the social as a scientific enterprise.

Although this is a book about the role of ritual in the evolution of social complexity, it is more broadly intended as a model for social theory that is inspired by real world observation while also remaining grounded in the cognitive and evolutionary sciences. More ambitiously still, it is to be hoped that cumulative theory building will have practical benefits for society at large, perhaps even to address problems on a global scale by harnessing the formidable cohesive and cooperative capacities of the ritual animal.

1
Overimitation and the Ritual Stance

Until around ten thousand years ago, all humans lived in relatively small-scale foraging groups. Since then, human cultural systems proliferated and diversified, giving rise to ever more elaborate technologies, art forms, architecture, systems of governance, economic organization, and religious traditions. The cumulative nature of this process of cultural evolution (Hodder, 2012) depends on the ability not only to invent novel cultural artefacts and ideas but also to store those innovations (Henrich, 2016). This combination of abilities—to innovate and to conserve—has been described as a 'ratchet effect' (Tomasello et al., 1993). When used as intended, a ratchet not only produces a forward-moving process of driving a bolt into its thread, but it also prevents backsliding by holding the advancing bolt in place while preparing to exert further pressure. In an analogous way, inventors of novel artefacts and institutions continually expand the stock of cultural innovations by adapting and improving upon existing designs (a process of driving culture forward), while imitators help to preserve the stock of past discoveries by reproducing them in the cultural repertoire (a process of holding onto the cultural achievements of forebears). This ratchet effect features much more prominently in human populations than in other primate groups. Efforts to explain why have focused on the uniquely human propensity to *teach* (especially one's offspring), to *imitate* the observed behaviours of trusted experts, and to *follow and observe norms* (Tennie, Call, & Tomasello, 2009). But this still leaves many unanswered questions about the nature of the mechanisms driving innovation and copying in human learning.

Recent research suggests that the key to understanding the ratchet effect may lie in the seemingly odd phenomenon of *overimitation*—the tendency to copy behaviour that has no obvious instrumental function. In what follows, I will refer to such behaviour as 'causally opaque', by which I mean that at least some components of the observed procedural sequence do not contribute in any obvious way to the outcome. For example, the posh English way of drinking tea involves peculiar behavioural rules (grasp teacup between thumb and forefinger, with little finger pointing outwards) that have no obvious causal rationale, since it would be just as easy to drink from the cup by grasping it in whatever fashion happens to be most convenient at the time. Children are very sensitive to the presence of such rules and, having acquired them, respond strongly to perceived deviations. Often, the rules of proper behaviour in our community are so ingrained that it is only in the breach that their existence becomes consciously apparent to us. Nevertheless, all cultural groups have a vast array of causally opaque rules of this kind that each new generation must learn—pertaining not only to dining etiquette but also to many other aspects of human affairs, from production, consumption, and exchange to the discharging of obligations towards kin, in-laws, ancestors, and gods.

Learning when and how to imitate causally opaque behaviour, as demonstrated by others, is not a simple matter. One particularly vexing aspect of the challenge is deciding whether the behaviour in question is causally opaque simply because we lack a fuller understanding of its technical contribution to the end goal or, as may also commonly be the case, because it is an arbitrary norm that must be followed for the sake of politeness or in order to fit in. When we assume that a behaviour is only causally opaque because we have not yet fully understood its underlying causal structure, then we may be emboldened to try out different versions—to innovate so as to establish which elements of the action are genuinely useful and which can be jettisoned. I call this the 'instrumental stance' on behaviour. It involves hunting for ever more efficient ways of achieving a recognizable end goal. By contrast, when we assume that a modelled behaviour is causally opaque because it is simply a random normative convention, then (assuming we wish to be accepted into the group) we copy it in every detail, without deviating or making up variants of our own. I call this the 'ritual stance'.

In this chapter, it is argued that the ritual stance is largely responsible for the diversity of human cultures globally and historically. Whereas instrumental imitation leads to unconstrained flows of cultural information, ritualistic imitation allows groups to differentiate and establish boundaries. Contiguous communities continually borrow useful skills, techniques, tools, and materials (e.g. visible archaeologically in methods of building construction) as they seek ever more effective or efficient ways of extracting raw materials, processing them, or producing useful tools and artefacts. Such cultural information is not only shared among immediate neighbours but also passed on through long-distance trade and exploration. As such, instrumentally useful cultural knowledge and its products are highly spreadable and cannot be easily restricted to any particular local or regional group identity or tradition. By contrast, most rituals have no material value, and this makes them socially valuable in a rather special way. While being of little or no use to outsiders, unless they are seeking entry or acceptance, shared rituals serve as very effective identity markers for members of an ingroup. The main exceptions to this principle are magical rituals which, just like technical skills and tools, can be passed on (e.g. borrowed, bartered, and sold) across group boundaries, if thought to be efficacious. Magic, as we shall see, is a special case insofar as it combines elements of both ritual and instrumental reasoning.

The ritual stance is motivated primarily by the desire to affiliate with a group, but it also plays an important role in learning to tamp down egoistic impulses in order to achieve higher or longer-range goals. Since rituals are not, even in principle, intelligible in purely instrumental terms, they commonly trigger expectations of magical efficacy, as well as elaborated systems of meaning. In this chapter, I explore all these affordances of the ritual stance.

Ritual and Instrumental Stances in Overimitation

When we adopt an instrumental stance on behaviour we seek out the most technically efficient ways of achieving an end goal. By contrast, when we adopt a ritual stance we are concerned primarily with observing normative conventions as a way of affiliating with a group (Whitehouse, 2011; Watson-Jones, Whitehouse, & Legare, 2015; Kapitány & Nielsen, 2015; Legare & Nielsen, 2015, 2020; Legare, 2019; Jagiello, Heyes, & Whitehouse, Under Review). Acquiring instrumental skills from a more competent model, such as a parent or teacher, entails an expectation that all the actions demonstrated, and the artefacts used, are designed to contribute in a maximally efficient way to an intended outcome. For example, if we are being taught how to use a fishing rod, we would expect the angler instructing us to demonstrate the procedures of baiting a line, casting out, and reeling in so as to contribute most effectively to the end goal of extracting fish from the water. Similarly, we would assume that the instruments deployed (such as the rod, reel, line, hook, and bait) are intentionally designed to contribute in a causally efficacious way to the same intended result. Even aspects of the process that are not immediately visible, such as the inner mechanisms of the reel, are assumed to have been fashioned in such a way as to help us in our efforts to catch a fish. As such, any causally opaque elements of the angler's kit or her methods of using it are assumed to be resolvable, with sufficient relevant knowledge. By contrast, when we adopt a *ritual stance* on the behaviour of models, such as other members of our peer group or religious congregation, we assume that all apparently deliberate aspects of the actions performed are important to reproduce faithfully without regard to causal structure as a means to accomplishing end goals. For example, if we are learning from others how to pray in church, we attend closely to not only obvious aspects such as kneeling down or clasping of hands but also more subtle behavioural modulations such as the timing, volume, and tonal regulation of utterances or the aversion of gaze. In copying these very minor adjustments in behaviour, the ritual participant assumes that the causal opacity of the actions being imitated could never be resolved into a causally transparent structure. Ritual actions such as kneeling and hand clasping are not intended to contribute to an end goal via potentially knowable processes of physical causation. Indeed, if it turned out that people were kneeling in church because that was the most efficient way to observe what the priest was doing at the altar and desisted from doing so whenever they could observe just as easily by sitting or standing, then the whole business of kneeling down would cease to be a ritual. It is precisely the irresolvable nature of the causal opacity that makes such gestures, bodily postures, and stereotyped behaviours recognizable as rituals.

Psychologists refer to the copying of causally opaque behaviour as 'overimitation' (Lyons, Young, & Keil, 2007). Typically, it is studied using puzzle boxes containing a reward that can only be accessed by carrying out a series of causally necessary steps (e.g. removing a successsion of barriers to the reward in a causally constrained sequence) but with various unnecessary procedures mixed in during the demonstration (e.g. superfluous twirling or tapping of the objects used in the extraction of the reward) (e.g. Horner & Whiten, 2005). Overimitation, also sometimes referred to as 'indiscriminate imitation' (Gardiner, 2014) or 'blanket copying' (Whiten, 2017), is the copying of the causally unnecessary elements as if they were just as important as the causally necessary ones. In some of these experiments, the target behaviours for overimitation contribute precisely nothing to the recognized end goal (Lyons, Young, & Keil, 2007), while in others they do contribute to the end goal but only inefficiently (e.g. Buttlemann et al., 2007; Nagell, Olguin, & Tomasello, 1993). The phenomenon of overimitation has been most extensively studied in children, showing that it is an early developing aspect of human learning, but it has also been shown to occur readily in adult samples (McGuigan, Makinson, & Whiten, 2011; McGuigan, Gladstone, & Cook, 2012; Flynn & Smith, 2012; Whiten et al., 2016). Moreover, it appears to be a panhuman propensity, observed in a broad range of societies, from foraging bands to slash-and-burn horticulturalists, as well as in urban populations and educated elites (Nielsen & Tomasello, 2010; Nielsen et al., 2014, Taniguchi & Sanefuji, 2017; Clegg & Legare, 2016; Corriveau et al., 2017). This propensity is not found to a comparable degree in other primates (Horner & Whiten, 2005). All the above suggests that overimitation is an evolved feature of human behaviour but the question is why? What motivates it and what function (if any) does it have? I would argue that there are two fundamentally distinct motivations for overimitation, cued by very different expectations of social learning, producing behavioural outcomes that have contrasting functions. One, the instrumental stance, is oriented to learning technically useful skills from accomplished experts, while the other, the ritual stance, is oriented to normative conformism that will help to secure one's place in the group.

These two contrasting perspectives giving rise to overimitation constitute 'stances' in much the same way that philosopher Daniel Dennett (1987) talks about an 'intentional stance'—a strategy of assuming that beliefs and desires govern the decision to act in a certain way. But by differentiating between instrumental and ritual stances, I am drawing attention to two very different kinds of strategic assumptions about these beliefs and desires. In the case of the former, we assume that the actor is attempting to change the physical state of the world in a mechanistic fashion, whereas, in the case of the latter, we assume that the actor is attempting to change the social state of the world by appeal to our psychology, particularly our desire to belong. Whereas the instrumental stance is a way of learning and improving useful technical skills via goal-directed imitation of both causally transparent and (theoretically resolvable) causally opaque behaviour, the ritual stance is a way of preserving cultural traditions via imitation of irremediably causally opaque behaviour. If this is correct, we should predict that adopting the instrumental stance would lead us to parse action sequences into components most likely to help accomplish a desired end goal via chains of cause and effect, whereas adopting the ritual stance would lead us to parse action sequences so that they can be faithfully copied as a means of similarity cuing, so as to trigger feelings of belonging and loyalty to a common tradition. While most research on overimitation has focused heavily on the *instrumental stance*, using puzzle box paradigms in which the achievement of end goals is made highly salient, in the next section, I describe a growing body of evidence from my own research collaborations, focusing on the role of the *ritual stance* in cultural evolution.

Irremediably Opaque Behaviour and the Ritual Stance

When learners adopt a ritual stance on modelled behaviour, they assume that irrespective of whether it is causally necessary or efficient to do things a certain way, it is nevertheless the culturally prescribed ('done' or 'proper') way to do it (Whitehouse, 2011, 2012b; Kapitány & Nielsen, 2015). When we first began to investigate properties of the 'ritual stance' experimentally, little was known about the processes by which children come to recognize the difference between rituals and instrumental actions. Developmental psychologists had for a long time tended to regard children first and foremost as little scientists, exploring their environments by testing more or less explicit hypotheses (Piaget, 1928; Gopnik, 2000). Nevertheless, children not only need to learn about the physical-causal affordances of the world around them but also the social-conventional ones. The latter is fundamental to basic functions such as learning how to speak, for example. Language acquisition depends on the willingness of young children to copy arbitrary phonemes in labelling features of the environment, with no expectation that there is a physical-causal rationale behind the link between sound and object. The mechanisms driving such learning are primarily social (e.g. joint attention) rather than instrumental (e.g. causal reasoning). The same may be said more broadly about the acquisition of group norms, conventions, and identity markers (Whitehouse, 2004, 2011). Building on this insight, recent experimental research suggests that the ritual stance activates distinctive motivations for social learning, as well as increasing imitative fidelity for observed body movements and object manipulations (Gellén & Buttelmann, 2018; Legare et al., 2015; Herrmann et al., 2013; Watson-Jones et al., 2014; Watson-Jones, Whitehouse, & Legare, 2015).

In one series of experiments (Legare et al., 2015: 353–6), we presented four to six year olds with a series of novel objects, allowing them to play with them. Afterwards, an adult model in a video used these same objects to demonstrate a series of arbitrary actions. There were two versions of this video and each child participating in the study was shown only one of these (in a between-subjects design). In one treatment, children viewed an action sequence that ended just as it began and, as a result, it made little sense to regard the action sequence as goal directed. We called this the 'ritual condition' because the observed action sequence that was not only causally opaque but in the absence of any end goal, there was little motivation to search for an underlying causal structure. In the second treatment, children observed a set of actions identical to those in the first condition *except* at the conclusion of the sequence, a new object, unrelated to the opaque sequence, was placed inside a box, thus creating an end-state that was distinct from the start-state. In this second condition, children could reasonably infer that the behaviour modelled in the video had a goal: to place an object in a box, albeit after carrying out some rather puzzling actions. We called this the 'instrumental condition' because although the action sequence was causally opaque, there was still some motivation to anticipate the presence of an underlying causal structure and thus to regard the causal opacity as potentially resolvable.

When we handed the objects over to the children (even without any instruction to copy what they had seen) we found that children in the ritual condition copied the modelled actions more rigidly and were less likely to invent novel actions as compared with the instrumental condition. Thus, when causal reasoning is less relevant to understanding a modelled action sequence, children are significantly more predisposed to copy what they have seen and less likely to depart from the observed script. By contrast, when children recognize that an action sequence has some kind of end goal they may still copy irrelevant elements but not to the same extent. As such, the presence of an end goal would actually seem to reduce rather than increase imitative fidelity. This suggests that, under certain conditions, imitation is motivated not by the expectation of learning something technically useful but by the desire to adopt quite arbitrary, causally opaque group conventions.

To explore this interpretation further we introduced a new experimental intervention using four conditions (again, based on a between-subjects design). As before, children were shown a video of an adult model demonstrating a novel action sequence. But instead of using the end-versus-start-state manipulation to prime expectations of conventionality versus instrumentality, we used verbal framings. Our new ritual conditions used two kinds of verbal framings: conventional-consistent ('this is how she always does it') in one condition and conventional-collective ('this is how we do it') in a second condition. We had two further conditions in which we presented instrumental framings:

instrumental-goal ('she puts it in the box') in the third condition and instrumental-process ('she moves blocks') in the fourth condition. Thus, we had four conditions in total, two of which were designed to trigger the ritual stance and two the instrumental stance. Afterwards, in all four conditions, children were not only tested for imitative fidelity and innovation after being given the stimuli to play with but were also presented with a new task in which they observed a model repeating the original action sequence but with some variations. We were interested to see whether children in the ritual conditions (conventional framings) would be more sensitive to deviations from the original script. After all, if the ritual stance motivates imitation of arbitrary behaviour without any expectation of underlying causal structure, then none of the observed elements of the modelled action sequence could be disregarded as superfluous and instead it would be necessary to encode *all* observed behaviour as equally salient. Our results showed that, as in the previous studies using end/start-state manipulations, our verbal framings produced significantly higher levels of imitative fidelity in the ritual than in the instrumental conditions. Moreover, we also found that overall, children assigned to the ritual conditions were significantly better at spotting deviations from the original script, and thus showed greater alacrity than children in the instrumental condition at detecting differences between the action sequence in the original video and the subsequently modelled version.

One possible explanation for this is that children adopting the ritual stance needed to pay attention to all aspects of the modelled behaviour, on the assumption that every detail could be a necessary part of the ritual procedure. This implies, of course, that when learning ritual procedures, the novice must encode more details of the modelled actions than would be the case in more goal-oriented instrumental learning, where ends matter more than means. This aspect of ritual learning has been described as 'goal demotion', the tendency to focus on the way ritual actions are performed (e.g. gesture, style) rather than on intended outcomes or goals (e.g. Boyer & Liénard, 2006). There is evidence that when the goals of an action sequence are removed or obscured, the action sequence itself is parsed into more minute component segments, suggesting increased processing of procedural detail. For example, in one between-subjects study (Kristoffer & Sørensen, 2011), participants were either shown an efficacious coffee-making procedure or one in which the end goal of drinking coffee was removed. Participants were invited to press a button each time they considered that a distinct segment of the action sequence had been completed. As predicted, they pressed the button significantly more frequently in the 'goal-demotion' condition. While it is clear that goal demotion has psychological effects, it is less clear how these relate to the social functions of ritual. For example, there is little evidence that goal demotion in itself produces affiliative motivations or that it enhances cooperation (Mitkidis et al., 2014). Following a series of studies aimed at disambiguating the effects of ritualistic actions, Kapitány and Nielsen (2016) concluded that causal opacity but not goal demotion increased liking for the objects used in the ritual.

If ritualistic overimitation is more demanding cognitively than instrumental overimitation, it raises the question whether ritual participation provides a form of mental training, strengthening capacities for encoding, memory, and executive control, in turn fostering future mindedness. To explore that idea, we designed a series of studies to explore the effects of ritual participation on children's capacity to control bodily appetites for the sake of more rewarding but less immediately accessible outcomes. In these studies, we had schoolchildren regularly participate in games designed to improve their 'executive control' (i.e. their attention, inhibitory control, and working memory—and specifically their ability to recall and apply instructions) (Rybanska, McKay, Jong, & Whitehouse, 2018). These so-called circle time games (see Tominey & McClelland, 2011; Schmitt et al., 2015) were conducted over three months, serving in effect as a training period. Some of the children were assigned to an instrumental condition, in which they were given a verbal framing each time they participated, emphasizing the causally efficacious nature of the game (e.g. 'this way of playing will teach us about different animals'). Others were assigned to a ritual condition, in which they were provided with a verbal framing or rationale for the activity emphasizing its causally opaque and conventional character (e.g. 'this is always how the game has been played'). In a third (control) condition children remained in the classroom following the usual school curriculum. After the three-month intervention, we ran various measures of executive function for all the children as well as a test of their ability to delay gratification (i.e. resist immediate temptation to gain a greater reward later). The latter task involved presenting each child with a sweet (or 'candy') and giving them the option to eat it right away or wait for fifteen minutes and be rewarded with three more treats of the same type. Touching, smelling, or tasting the sweet counted as eating it and thereby forfeited the reward.

What we found was that children in the ritual condition showed improved executive function and were better able than those who were provided with an instrumental rationale for the games to delay gratification. It is possible that regularly participating in collective rituals helps children to wait for a reward by improving their ability to tamp down impulses. Adopting a ritual stance entails the assumption that the action sequence is irremediably causally opaque and so there is no motivation to seek out a physical-causal rationale for the observed behaviour. But this also means that the various components of the action sequence are harder to parse than in the case of instrumental actions (Nielbo & Sørensen, 2015). This in turn increases the cognitive load on the ritual learner, potentially taxing executive control capacities to the limit (Schjoedt et al., 2013). While this might be expected to impair recall for very complex ritual sequences, there is also some evidence of improved recall for simpler ritual gestures (Kapitány et al., 2018). Thus, merely believing that you are following tradition and adopting the 'ritual stance' could cause children to pay closer attention and improve both inhibitory control and working memory. Whatever the explanation, however, the 'take home' finding from this is that children in the ritual condition were better able to forego the appeal of an immediate gain in order to secure a bigger reward later on.

The participants in our study were recruited in two very different settings: one a Western country (Slovakia) whose schooling system emphasizes individualism, analytic reasoning, and instrumental problem solving, the other a Melanesian country (Vanuatu) whose approach to schooling is more traditional, emphasizing collectivism along with deference to authority and tradition. Sampling younger age groups would have been impracticable in Vanuatu, as would the use of video presentations and other techniques suitable to lab-based experiments. Cross-cultural comparison was important, however, because it made it possible to explore whether children raised in a relatively traditional society would be more sensitive to the effects of our intervention games than Western children. What we found was that children in both countries were equally affected by the experimental manipulation. This suggests that ritual participation trains children's ability to inhibit desire and delay gratification irrespective of differences in their cultural environments, a point to which I return in Chapter 7.

To the extent that learning via the ritual stance places especially heavy demands on attention, encoding, and self-regulation, this would seem to imply strong motivational states, encouraging us to imitate faithfully despite the cognitive costs of doing so. There is growing evidence that these motivations are essentially affiliative and are routinely activated in the most commonplace of social interactions. But before this line of research began, it was not an obvious direction to pursue. Part of the reason for this is that the ritual stance is embedded implicitly in many of our daily activities, so much a part of the furniture of everyday social life that it easily escapes conscious inspection. Consider how, for example, British conversations at the bus stop about the weather tend to follow a well-worn, platitudinous pattern of discourse, as might tasting the wine in a restaurant or nodding approvingly when the barber shows us the back of our heads in a little mirror. These commonplace rituals are so familiar that we might not even notice we are deferring to a set of normative expectations rather than actually making judgements about the weather, the state of the wine, or the quality of a haircut. Nevertheless, on rare occasions the ritual stance may suddenly seem especially salient, jolting us into a more or less explicit concern with normativity. Consider how it might feel, for example, to join an organization for the first time: a new school or workplace, sports club, or religious congregation. In these circumstances, we are exceptionally alert to what others are doing, saying, and wearing. We are eager to follow suit and not to stand out. This tendency appears to be early emerging.

In a series of studies, with a sample of 259 three to six year olds, we again used verbal framings to trigger ritual and instrumental stances, respectively (Herrmann et al., 2013). But in this new line of research, our aim was to explore the effects of various cues likely to influence conformism, such as whether the novel actions are demonstrated by one or by multiple models or whether the demonstration is performed only once or successively. To investigate these effects, we developed a design involving eight conditions, in which ritual versus instrumental framings were crossed with four modelling scenarios: a single model performing the actions twice; two models performing the actions successively; two models performing the actions in synchrony twice; two models performing the actions in synchrony once only. Children were found to copy the modelled behaviour more precisely in the synchronous conditions, suggesting that the most powerful cue for conformism was the presence of a group rather than merely an individual model. But these effects were also stronger when ritual as opposed to instrumental framings were used, suggesting high-fidelity imitation in group settings is motivated more by the ritual rather than the instrumental stance. These findings provided an important corrective to the dominant view, mostly using puzzle box experimental paradigms, that overimitation is primarily a way of acquiring instrumental skills more efficiently (without needing to understand fully in order to acquire useful techniques). Our research suggests that there is much more to overimitation than that: when the ritual stance is engaged, participants are more interested in affiliation through conformism rather than skill acquisition via technical learning.

To explore further the affiliative dimension of the ritual stance, we designed a series of studies to see whether rituals might be used by children as a re-inclusion behaviour, for example, when security of tenure in the group was in doubt. In ancestral conditions, and even nowadays where social networks provide the most effective form of insurance against penury, violence, or other kinds of existential threat, exclusion from the group would carry heavy costs and might even be fatal. Therefore, our evolved psychology should be sensitive to the risk of ostracism threat, prompting effective re-inclusion behaviours. Inasmuch as ritual conformism is a way of signaling commitment to the group and bonding with its members, the presence of ostracism threat should trigger the ritual rather than the instrumental stance. To test that hypothesis, we designed a series of further studies with young children.

In an initial study (Watson-Jones et al., 2014), we adopted our original procedural paradigm for three to six year olds, described above, using the end/start-state manipulation to trigger ritual and instrumental stances and we crossed these with ostracism-threat and ostracism-neutral conditions, respectively. To prime ostracism threat we showed the children dots on a screen that appeared to move away in a group whenever a single dot approached (whereas in the ostracism-neutral condition the dots moved around on the screen randomly). Our dependent variables, as in previous studies, included imitative fidelity, as well as children's explanations for their behaviour. We found that participants copied the modelled action sequence significantly more faithfully as compared with all other conditions when both ritual cues (end/start-state equivalence) and ostracism threat were present. A plausible interpretation is that children were conforming to group conventions as a re-inclusion behaviour.

Nevertheless, in our initial study, children were not actually experiencing ostracism directly, they were merely primed with scenarios in which the theme of ostracism was present (and then only in a rather abstract form, involving the movement of dots on a screen rather than social interactions among human beings). We therefore designed a further study, involving a more direct, visceral experience of ostracism (Watson-Jones, Whitehouse, & Legare, 2015). In this new design, five to six year olds were told individually that they had been assigned to a group known as the 'yellows' and were given yellow hats and yellow armbands. To strengthen their sense of identification with the yellows, the children were then asked questions about their favourite foods, animals, and toys—and given to believe that members of the yellow team shared these preferences. Each child was then invited to play a computer game called 'cyberball', involving three other participants, said to be in another room (so not physically present). The child was assigned an onscreen avatar with a yellow shirt. The three imaginary participants' avatars also had coloured shirts, and here came the first experimental manipulation. In the ingroup condition, all of the other three avatars wore yellow shirts, whereas in the outgroup condition, all three wore green shirts. Half the participants were assigned to the ingroup and half to the outgroup treatment. But there was also another manipulation. The cyberball game involved the avatars passing a ball between them. Half the children in both ingroup and outgroup conditions were assigned to either an ostracism treatment in which the other avatars refused initially passed the ball fairly, but then stopped doing so, or an *inclusion treatment* where they received their fair share of passes throughout. Then all participants observed a video demonstration of a causally opaque action sequence associated with verbal framings suggesting that the actions performed were ingroup conventions for the yellow team. As predicted, children ostracized by the yellows displayed increased levels of anxiety and engaged in significantly higher fidelity imitation of the causally opaque behaviour modelled in the video, as compared with children in all the other conditions. These findings further support the view that ritualistic behaviour and conformism more generally is motivated by the desire to affiliate with groups. The implications of this for the study of overimitation are profound—the copying of causally opaque behaviour is not simply a speedy way of transmitting technical skills, it lies at the root of human custom, tradition, and group identity.

It may be tempting to regard ritual and instrumental stances as mutually exclusive alternatives. That is, the copying of causally opaque behaviour is *either* motivated by expectations of hidden causal structure based on the imputation of pedagogic motivations (hereafter the 'instrumental stance') *or* by expectations of convention-learning based on imputation of normative motivations (the 'ritual stance'). But it is also possible that humans oscillate between both stances when engaged in social learning, depending on the kinds of cues available to them when they observe the behaviour of potential models (Whitehouse, 2011). When the model is thought to have expertise in the performance of a task (signalled by cues like confidence, experience, success, and authority) one may infer an opportunity to learn something of practical use about the affordances of objects and so adopt an *instrumental stance* on the behaviour. But when the model is thought to be exemplifying a 'proper' or normative way of behaving (signalled by cues relevant to affiliation, conformism, or deference to tradition) it may be more appropriate to adopt a *ritual stance* on the behaviour and assume that it is simply the correct or 'done' way rather than the most causally efficacious way of acting.

Acquiring the conventional beliefs and practices of a community requires both normative and technical learning, and so it would make sense that humans are predisposed to deploy both instrumental and ritual stances flexibly, as changing social situations require. In practice this can be a messy business. Consider a very simple cultural convention that might apply in a kindergarten or junior school: shoes and clothes should be placed into lockers in a certain way, coats on pegs, shoes down below. Some children might adopt an instrumental stance when learning this procedure: coats are hung on pegs to prevent them from getting crumpled; shoes go down below so that they don't make other things dirty. Other children may adopt a purely ritual stance, never considering why coats go this way and shoes go that: they just do. Probably for most children both stances have some salience but for different aspects of locker-related etiquette. For instance, one might readily appreciate the instrumental rationale for placing shoes at the bottom but not why the teacher gets cross if the shoes are tossed in rather than placed carefully. Throwing things may achieve just the same result as placing them (from a young child's perspective), but placing them is more respectful than throwing (because more faithful to modelled behaviour) when seen through the lens of the ritual stance.

The lens metaphor is instructive: to some extent, ritual and instrumental stances are like the alternate views of the world afforded by bifocal spectacles. The upper half of the lens is used naturally when gazing at more distant objects (one might think of this as analogous to an instrumental perspective focusing on the bigger picture, oriented to end goals), whereas the lower part of the lens is better for examining things in close up (analogous to the ritual perspective focusing on detailed action parsing, oriented to the gestural level). We naturally flit between the two as we judge the occasion to warrant. But it is also possible to arrive at some peculiar admixtures of ritual and instrumental thinking, most notably when we assume that a causally opaque action sequence is instrumental in intent (it has a clearly defined end goal, such as healing a patient), but the causal pathway adopted is assumed to be unknowable (i.e. involves supernatural causation that cannot in principle be brought into conformity with intuitive or theoretical physics). This kind of 'hybridization' of ritual and instrumental stances is typically described as 'magic'. It resembles the instrumental practices of medicine but is conducted in the spirit of observing normative rules, thus taking the form of a ritual. In the next section, we explore the implications of the distinction between ritual and instrumental stances for a fuller understanding of magical thinking.

Ritual and Instrumental Stances in Magical Thinking

When we learn technically useful skills from a more experienced model, we do so via an understanding of cause and effect (e.g. she did this in order to make that happen, which in turn allowed her to do such-and-such, and so on until the end goal was accomplished). Reflecting on behaviour in this way leads to explicit representations of causal chains, thereby shedding light on why that particular sequencing of the actions was necessary (e.g. she had to do a before b otherwise she couldn't have done c). As such, the learner develops a theory of how technical procedures work, eventually filling in gaps or grey areas as the contributions of previously opaque elements in the action sequence become clearer. As I have argued, however, in the case of rituals nobody expects or seeks out a physical-causal rationale for the procedures adopted. But even though rituals lack a transparent causal structure, participants may interpret the action sequence in *quasi-instrumental* terms, such that any gaps in the causal chain between actions and intended outcomes can be attributed to the invisible hand of 'magic'. Examples include pushing needles into a doll's abdomen in order to harm an enemy or sacrificing to the gods in order to obtain good harvests. However far-fetched, the logic underlying voodoo dolls and burnt offerings resembles the way we reason about quite ordinary technical actions. What is special about the doll and the sacrificial lamb, however, is that the assumed connection between actions and outcomes is of a *supernatural* kind.

Psychologists have shown that supernatural thinking is widespread and early developing (Hood, 2009; Subbotsky, 2004), and there is growing evidence that supernatural explanations often have intuitive foundations that cannot be entirely 'educated out' of us and, in some environments are, on the contrary, heavily reinforced by salient cultural content (Barrett, 2012; McCauley, 2011). Anthropologists have long maintained, however, that natural and supernatural explanations are not necessarily stark alternatives but are often seen as complementing and augmenting each other. For instance, E. E. Evans-Pritchard argued that supernatural explanations commonly address questions that more rational or scientific frameworks do not and so are not competing for the same explanatory turf. To illustrate his point, Evans-Pritchard famously described a tragic but all too common event among the Azande of Southern Sudan, whereby the supports of a granary gave way killing the people sitting in its shade (Evans-

Pritchard, 1937). The Azande typically attributed all misfortunes to witchcraft and the deaths on this occasion were no exception. When Evans-Pritchard pointed out that the supports of the granary had been eaten away by termites, severely weakening the structure, the Azande heartily agreed. But this, they argued, was only the physical cause of the tragedy. The granary could have collapsed at any time but to explain why this happened at the precise moment those particular people were sitting there required a further explanation: witchcraft. For the Azande, Evans-Pritchard maintained, natural and supernatural accounts coexisted without contradiction. Could this be a consequence of the coexistence of instrumental and ritual stances?

When we adopt a ritual stance on behaviour, we assume that the link between actions and declared end goals cannot be rendered in physical-causal terms. For example, if we are told that the ritual is necessary to ensure crop fertility, to heal sickness, to reverse the effects of witchcraft, or to achieve some other desired outcome, any effort to explain *how* must inevitably be *post hoc*—at best being credible only on the basis of associational or thematic principles rather than causal ones. The question as to how exactly rituals might have palpable effects on the world is unanswerable in terms of physical causation and so perhaps quite naturally prompts a search for supernatural explanations. If our stock of ideas about supernatural causation is already populated with notions of ghosts, ancestors, and deities then the causal opacity of ritual might more readily trigger ideas about the intervention of transcendent forces in preference to other kinds of interpretations. Often, however, we find that magical explanations are invoked alongside purely technical-instrumental ones, as in the case of the Azande. The coexistence of natural and supernatural explanations may be puzzling because it seems irrational in a post-Enlightenment world—a problem that needs to be resolved for instance by positing different levels of processing or reasoning. But what if supernatural reasoning were not so much a failure of natural explanation as an altogether different *kind* of discourse? What if it were a kind of discourse that dispensed with the very notion of ordinary causation, one that is not just causally opaque, but irremediably so? This is really the hallmark of the ritual stance.

Consider the way some anthropologists have tried to understand the relationship between culturally variable approaches to the treatment of illness. According to Robin Horton (1993), African divination, like biomedical science, sets out to explain the causes of various diseases. But whereas scientists might seek to discover the physical-causal effects of microscopic entities, such as viruses, parasites, and proteins, diviners seek to understand the causes of illness in terms of a few types of human failing, such as jealousy, adultery, or the breach of taboos. On this view, the theories of scientists and diviners are cast in qualitatively different explanatory frameworks: the framework of the scientist is mechanistic, concerned with theoretical entities (like viruses) that cannot think or feel; the framework of the diviner is social, concerned with theoretical entities (like gods, ancestors, and other spirits) that act more like people.

Natural and supernatural explanations may therefore result from quite distinct strategies for understanding causally opaque behaviour. Insofar as we are ready to learn technically efficacious procedures even when their causal structure is unclear, we may adopt a strategy of overimitation that is rapidly supplanted by goal emulation as trial and error reveals what is really essential (and what is not) to accomplish desired outcomes (Whiten et al., 2009). And yet we must *also* be ready to acquire technically unnecessary but socially salient information, such as the random signifiers of a language, the arbitrary identity markers of a group, and the norms of politeness towards social superiors. Arbitrary conventions of this kind, once learned, tend to stick but not because their causal rationale has been discovered. Indeed, for the learner to interpret this kind of behaviour in terms of physical-causal reasoning would be quite the wrong way to think about it, even ridiculous or subversive.

Thus, the notion of supernatural causation is arguably little more than a *post hoc* rationalization of irremediably opaque processes *as if* they were somehow equivalent to events with an intelligible causal structure. On this view, we treat magic as 'like' medicine but know that it is not really the same thing. What crucially distinguishes the two is that magic is premised on an unknowable causal rationale and medicine on a potentially knowable one. When we invoke supernatural causation, we are making claims primarily about the social rather than the mechanical structure of the world, claims that can really only be 'right' in a normative rather than an epistemological sense.

In light of these observations, we might say that ritual and instrumental stances are largely complementary rather than contradictory. Only where ritual procedures are accorded a quasi-instrumental, and thus a magical, purpose do they come into contradiction with a scientific world view. After all, magical explanation is by definition irremediably incomplete. For those less concerned about that incompleteness, however, the coexistence of magical and scientific thinking presents little dissonance. Across the world's cultures, stretching back over the millennia, the general tendency has been to deploy technical and magical cures flexibly, often in tandem, depending on their perceived costs and potential benefits. Indeed, it may only be in modern educated circles, influenced by the philosophical traditions of the Enlightenment, that this flexible approach to medicine and magic seems contradictory.

Magical rituals abound primarily whenever there is a felt lack of control over day-to-day problems (e.g. illness, infidelity, poverty) and more efficacious forms of intervention are unavailable, distrusted, or too expensive to procure. Nearly a century ago, the pioneering anthropologist Bronislaw Malinowski observed that seafaring activities among Trobriand Islanders were more elaborately ritualized than horticultural pursuits. He attributed this to varying levels of risk and uncertainty (1935, 1945; see also Homans, 1941). On the whole, Trobrianders could be fairly confident that if they planted a sufficient volume of root vegetables and other crops in their fertile soils they would generally be assured of adequate harvests. But efforts to exploit marine resources and to engage in trade with more distant islands were fraught with dangers and presented highly unpredictable outcomes. Lives were often lost at sea in unforeseen tempests; the locations of shoals of fish were hard to predict; the cooperativeness of exchange partners in foreign lands was difficult to ensure. In the absence of more pragmatic methods of reducing risk, Trobrianders turned to magic. Much subsequent experimental research has lent credence to the view that magical thinking may be triggered by perceived risk (Felson & Gmelch, 1979; Case et al., 2004; Rudski & Edwards, 2007; Womack, 1992; Wright & Erdal, 2008) and lack of control (Whitson & Galinsky, 2008), whether this takes the form of lucky charms and mascots used by athletes and their fans (Bleak & Frederick, 1998; Burger & Lynn, 2005; Gmelch, 1971, 1992), the superstitions of gamblers (Bersabe & Arias, 2000), or prayers and incantations in the shadow of warfare and terrorism (Sosis, Kress, & Boster, 2007).

The finding that people more readily seek assistance from rituals when outcomes are uncertain might help to explain why only certain kinds of problems are presented to healers and therefore why they need a particular repertoire of treatments. That is, if antibiotics or pain killers are sufficient to address our particular maladies, we may be less likely to solicit the costly and perhaps uncertain interventions of the witch doctor. The pragmatist astutely seeks out supernatural solutions only for the trickier problems: symptoms that refuse to go away, relationship problems that seem insoluble or hopeless, and diseases of the mind that natural therapies and drugs seem unable to cure. But when confronted with a variety of healers and treatments, how are we to decide which ones to invest in? A common solution is to favour procedural elaborateness and complexity. Since the link between the subgoals and end goals in rituals is intrinsically opaque, anything that reinforces the idea that such a link really exists seems to lend credence to claims of efficacy. So, for instance, the more complex and numerous the procedures and/or the more insistent the healer's injunctions to observe them, the stronger will be our impression that they must have a purpose (Legare & Souza, 2012). And perhaps the more closely a set of ritual procedures resembles a set of technical procedures, the more likely we think it will be to succeed. For instance, rain magic among the Orokaiva of Papua New Guinea involves squeezing the juice from a succulent palm to simulate rain (sunny weather is produced by a variant of this ritual in which the juice is made to dry out)—although the causal mechanism is obscure, such rituals hint at the presence of mechanistic principles rather than offering merely abstract or thematically unrelated procedural rules (Whitehouse, 2004).

Magical actions help bring into focus the fluid relationship between ritual and instrumental stances. Not only are both stances capable of being activated flexibly in rapid succession as we oscillate between technical and affiliative goals, but also magical thinking presents us with a peculiar midway point between the two. Describing this liminal position as 'quasi-instrumental' captures its technical character—the fact that magical acts are techniques in much the same way as medical treatments or horticultural skills. But at the same time, they are not fully instrumental insofar as they incorporate elements that are not only causally opaque but irremediably so. As such, the magical healer is also a ritualist, a master of ceremonies, and potentially a cult leader with whom his or her clientele long to affiliate. Many such figures—from the mai- and pai-de-santos of Candomblé and Quimbanda religions of Brazil to the faith healers of evangelical churches in Eurasia—gather around them devoted followings in a way that a mere technician could not hope to do. This is because such leaders tap deeply into both ritual and instrumental stances and their associated intuitions, motivations, and imitative behavioural repertoires.

Causal Opacity, Meaning, and Communication

Another striking consequence of causal opacity is that rituals can be invested with indefinitely many exegetical interpretations. Even if exegesis is unforthcoming or unknown, participants recognize that this is a possible affordance of their rituals. Social anthropologists have often observed that their informants may struggle to articulate the rationale for locally prevailing ceremonies, appealing in the end simply to tradition or the ancestors. But it is also noteworthy that nobody has any difficulty understanding the anthropologist's question, when she asks what the rituals mean. People know that ritualized actions can be invested with symbolic properties even though they may struggle on occasion to identify what those may be, often pointing the hapless researcher in the direction of somebody older or wiser. On other occasions, people may have very strong intuitions about the meaning of a ritual, even if they are powerless to explain why that particular action sequence rather than any other is the privileged vehicle for symbolic expression. Thus, there are many ways of responding to the puzzle of why ritual actions must be conducted in conformity with normative conventions.

A longstanding debate in anthropology focuses on whether rituals are more about saying or doing something (Seligman et al., 2008). There are those who have emphasized the communicative aspects of rituals (e.g. Leach, 1954), while others have documented the variability of meaning making (Humphrey & Laidlaw, 1994) or have pointed out that rituals may mean nothing at all (Staal, 1989). According to one anthropologist (Bloch, 1974), all actions entail a mixture of propositional force (making statements of various kinds) and illocutionary force (deference to procedural scripts), and the stronger the illocutionary force evoked by an action, the weaker its propositional content will become and thus the more readily we will interpret the action as a ritual. This framework, though perhaps intuitively appealing, raises but fails to answer a number of tantalizing questions. What exactly is illocutionary force and how can it be observed or measured empirically? Why and how do some actions and not others require deference to the script? Moreover, if propositional and illocutionary force are inversely correlated on a scale then what drives behaviours in one direction rather than the other? Besides, the debate about whether rituals 'say' or 'do' is not simply about whether or not they entail deference to rules (a point few would dispute). It is also about whether rituals are understood as acts of communication or as quasi-technical operations. In this regard, much may depend on whether the rituals are intended to influence the mental states of an imagined agent (e.g. god, spirit, ancestor) or whether they are simply formulaic procedures that, if only they are performed correctly and according to a specified sequence, should automatically lead to a set of intended outcomes.

Where the efficacy of rituals is attributed mainly to quasi-instrumental principles (i.e. if you perform it in a certain way then a given outcome is expected magically to ensue), one might say that the emphasis is more on 'doing' rather than 'saying' something. Such rituals are the stock-in-trade of healers and witch doctors and hence predominate in the magical therapies described in the preceding section. If supernatural agents come into the frame at all, they do so mostly in positions of servitude, by magical compulsion rather than by petition and sacrifice. Much the same may be said of various forms of ritual celebration. Participants dress up, dance, and sing along according to custom, without necessarily wondering why they should do so. The euphoria, camaraderie, entertainment, and sense of occasion may all be reason enough. Many perhaps suspect that there exists also some kind of rationale for the event: to commemorate an ancestor, to ward off evil spirits, or to celebrate a celestial event. One might call this the 'fiesta' syndrome. Those participating in fiestas might vaguely assert that various ritual actions or objects represent sins or demons, or that certain dances promote fertility. But for most, detailed knowledge of that kind belongs in the temples and monasteries (if they exist), and the main concern is simply to join in.

Nevertheless, there are undoubtedly also rituals that attract a great deal of meaning making and some ritual traditions actively encourage prolonged reflection on the symbolism of the acts and artefacts involved. For example, mystics commonly use ritual as a pathway to revelation, a vehicle for exploring insights and understanding that lies beyond our familiar experience and immediate environment. The emphasis is on unusual or especially salient experiences, epiphanic illuminations, and the discovery of esoteric knowledge through acts of heroism and endurance. Interpretive quests of this kind entail a passionate concern with exegesis (Barth, 1975, 1987), often requiring trials and ordeals to be surmounted in order to peel away layers of meaning (Tuzin, 1980). These characteristics contribute to the formation of enduring episodic memories, fostering subsequent reflection on matters of ritual meaning and exegesis (Whitehouse, 1992, 2004).

Although revelatory rituals may be accorded magical potency (as in the petitionary or placatory rituals discussed above), the focus of attention is more on meaning than efficacy. What primarily exercises the imaginations of participants is the idea that ritual actions establish relationships between performers and the complex, powerful agentic forces that lie in some sense 'above' or 'beyond' them. Cosmological adventure matters more than technical control. The rituals of mystical quests are typically performed rarely and in secret, entailing agonizing or frightening trials and ordeals. This combination of rarity and dysphoric arousal contributes to the formation of enduring episodic memories, and provides a fertile psychological basis for subsequent reflection on matters of ritual meaning and exegesis. Perhaps the reason this process privileges meaning over efficacy is that the discovery of quasi-mechanistic interpretations offers closure, whereas the quest for meaning is never-ending. Final answers may actually be the enemy of mysticism, even if they are the ostensible purpose of the quest.

Yet another way in which rituals are invested with meanings is typically found in large-scale organized religions rather than in local esoteric cults. Adherents of such rituals are like pupils, endlessly lectured and tested. In performing rituals, what matters above all is what, by the lights of the orthodox canon, they mean, express, and accomplish. Scriptural religions typically demand belief via the argument of authority. Rather than inspiring a personal quest for revelation, the aim is to quell further enquiry by simply saying that it is an obligation or duty to accept things 'on faith'. For example, Roman Catholic theologians may insist on the dogma of transubstantiation whereby the wafer received in Holy Communion becomes flesh and wine becomes the blood of Christ. This is presumed to occur not through the manipulation of divine intentions but as a mystical outcome of following a series of steps, beginning with blessings conducted by an ordained priest. In this way, Catholicism provides a more or less systematic and comprehensive account of the meanings and purposes of its officially sanctioned rituals.

Thus, according to the above account, rituals spawn at least four distinct modalities of meaning making: one based on magical efficacy (therapies), another emphasizing celebration (the fiesta syndrome), yet another motivating revelatory quests (cultic ordeals), and finally one that invokes authoritative dogma (theological schools). Although religions may foster all four ritual modalities, particular traditions tend to place special emphasis on only one or two of them. In the case of scriptural religions, the magical and theological modalities of ritual interpretation are often exploited in equal measure. For instance, the Roman Catholic Church, like other doctrinal religions, provides a more or less comprehensive account of what all its officially sanctioned rituals say and do. These accounts are seldom generated spontaneously by individual adherents but are mostly acquired through the testimony of others. To the extent that practising Catholics are knowledgeable about matters of ritual exegesis, they acquire this expertise from higher authorities: teachers, nuns, priests, and catechists. And the authorities in turn owe their doctrinal mastery to others and are closely monitored and policed by an ecclesiastical hierarchy centrally regulated from the Vatican.

But scriptural religions also commonly harbour popular forms of worship that more closely resemble the 'fiesta complex'. For example, for several centuries the Roman Catholic church managed to achieve a balance between maintaining a disciplined professional priesthood and literati while also tolerating locally distinctive cults of saints, Easter parades, Lent carnivals, varieties of pilgrimage, and so on. This tolerance on the part of professionalized priesthoods towards popular expressions of religiosity is often somewhat pragmatic. Excessive discipline saps morale and induces tedium, but with so many calendrical celebrations to look forward to, demoralization can be counteracted, and motivational levels maintained. This has long been recognized in societies where 'little traditions' composed of local or regional forms of ritual expression more or less comfortably rub shoulders with the 'great traditions' of learned specialists and religious authorities (Redfield, 1955). But not all doctrinal religions exhibit such tolerance. For instance, the Greek Orthodox Church has for centuries publicly forbidden sacred parties, such as the practice of walking on red-hot coals carrying icons annually 'stolen' from the Church (Xygalatas, 2012). Protestant churches, and similarly iconoclastic varieties of other world religions, have likewise taken a stern line on popular festivals. But some of those very same iconoclasts have adopted a more cunning approach: rather than allowing the coexistence of great and little traditions, they have integrated more entertaining rituals into the very fabric of worship, ushering tambourines and electric guitars into their churches or whirling dervishes into their mosques (Shankland, 2004).

The fiesta syndrome can of course also flourish in isolation from a doctrinal school. In many traditional kingdoms, including those of the Swazi and Zulu of Southern Africa for instance, religion does not inculcate an orthodoxy, distinguishing traditions one from another but accomplishes rather specific political ends such as the resolution of conflicts among equals (Norbeck, 1963), the legitimation of aristocratic and royal privileges and powers (Gluckman, 1962b), or the mobilization of resistance in the face of colonial imperialism (Lincoln, 1987). With these kinds of sociopolitical concerns taking centre stage, issues of meaning and efficacy are commonly left vague or underspecified (Kertzer, 1988).

Ritual therapies abound both inside and outside doctrinal religions. Like popular festivals, unauthorized therapies may be censured by missionaries and iconoclastic evangelists, but many leaders of doctrinal traditions simply live and let live. And why not? Therapists offer little in the way of serious competition to imams, prophets, priests, and gurus. Healers typically preside over small operations, and their rituals are seldom used as markers of identity. They compete as individuals, each requiring a modest but steady stream of patients. A healthy list of clients has a low ceiling, because only so many sick people can be treated in a given day. True, therapies do occasionally spread to service larger populations, eliminating and absorbing the clientele of rival clinics but they are typically market-driven. What clients want is what the therapist must provide. Treatments must look plausible, and in practice this means that rituals and potions must have some intuitive appeal. This is much less true of esoteric cults and theological schools.

Efforts to disentangle these diverse aspects of ritual systems have led to the postulation of a variety of classificatory schemes. For example, Alan Strathern (2019) makes a richly elaborated distinction between 'immanentism' and 'transcendentalism' which captures many of the key features of the distinction I make above between therapies and theological schools. Among the key defining features of immanentism are an emphasis on harnessing supernatural power to prevent or ameliorate misfortune in the here and now, the adoption of a pragmatic stance on the value of ritual, and the tolerance of local variation and lack of concern with systemizing. In such traditions, figures of authority are typically seen as healers rather than as gurus, pursued by clients seeking assistance rather than followers seeking revelation or enlightenment. By contrast, transcendentalism emphasizes the notion of doctrinal orthodoxy as a coherent and transportable system of beliefs and practices—a universalist, hegemonic creed. It encourages the rise of expertise, authority, oratory, and hierarchy and, with it, a focus on higher values such as otherworldliness, truth seeking, and the pursuit of a more ethical way of life. Strathern's framework partly originates in ideal types proposed by Max Weber (1958[1916]), which have inspired other dichotomous formulations along comparable lines. These include, for example, David Gellner's (1988, 1992) contrast between soteriological (as transcendentalist) and this-worldly (as social or instrumental and in this sense immanentist) forms of religion and Louis Dumont's (1980) distinction between salvific religions and 'religions of the group' in his musings on world renunciation.

It is noteworthy that most dichotomous models of this kind, as with Weber's ideal types that inspired them, include a strong emphasis on belief content (e.g. thematic emphases on soteriology, transcendence, and salvation), in addition to features of social organization, ideological integration, and the way beliefs and practices are rehearsed and transmitted. An advantage of this is that such models capture much of the richness of the clusters of covarying features observed across the world's religions historically and ethnographically. A limitation of these approaches, however, is that they tend to skirt around the question of underlying causation—what exactly makes a particular religion gravitate towards immanentist, transcendentalist, or soteriological poles? This is arguably where attention to the underlying psychology becomes important.

A more psychologically grounded way of characterizing the contrasts between therapeutic immanentism and theologically elaborated transcendentalism is to focus on the relative ease with which human minds are able to generate, process, and transmit their content. Some forms of religious thinking and behaviour are highly intuitive, spreading like wildfire, whereas others are more demanding cognitively, for example, requiring elaborate mnemonic supports and disciplined practice to maintain. Pascal Boyer describes the former as 'wild' and the latter as 'doctrinal' (Boyer, 2019). Wild religion comprises beliefs and practices that are poorly regulated, heterogenous, fluid, intuitive, and disjointed, whereas doctrinal religion comprises beliefs and practices that are relatively regulated, shared, stable, elaborated, and systemized. It has been suggested that small-scale societies vary in the extent to which their religious traditions exhibit systemic, doctrinal characteristics. For example, anthropologists have long debated the extent to which the indigenous religions of Melanesia may be characterized as coherent, integrated, shared, and stable systems (Brunton, 1980). In the sample of cultural groups considered in this debate, Kunimaipa religion appeared to score low on all four dimensions (McArthur, 1971), while, at the other extreme, it was argued that Yafar religion scored higher on all of them (Juillerat, 1980), and still others appeared to fall somewhere in between on various combinations of dimensions (Barth, 1987). But what these early debates lacked, and Boyer's distinction might help to provide, is a way of explaining why some religions are more ordered than others.

The factors that push religions towards wilder or more doctrinal ends of the spectrum may be hard to disentangle, but Boyer's central idea is that they are shaped and constrained by our evolved psychology, as regulated by particular institutional arrangements. Doctrinal traditions require top-down enforcement by professionalized priesthoods and ecclesiastical hierarchies, whereas wild religions spread when religious policing is weak, for example, because in remote rural areas or urban slums, educational institutions and sanctions for deviation are hard to establish or maintain. A related idea might be that wild traditions are loose, whereas organized doctrinal religions are a result of much tighter norms (Gelfand, 2018). The tightness-looseness framework focuses more on peer-to-peer enforcement of the orthodoxy than on top-down policing. A core hypothesis here might be that existential threats (e.g. natural disaster or warfare) lead to normative tightness and therefore closer adherence to doctrinal religion and lower tolerance for wild variants. I return to these kinds of questions in great depth later in this book (especially in Chapter 4).

Viewed within the framework advanced here, one of the main factors driving variation in coherence, integration, consensus, and stability of religious traditions is the frequency with which religious beliefs and practices are repeated. While small-scale societies may perform some collective rituals on a regular basis, full-scale routinization is more typical of larger-scale cultural groups (Whitehouse, 2004). Frequent (e.g. daily or weekly) repetition of religious beliefs and practices facilitates rote learning and other forms of high-fidelity doctrinal transmission, making it easier to detect unauthorized deviation from the orthodoxy and allowing increasingly elaborate and counterintuitive doctrinal systems to stabilize, systemize, and spread. Religious representations that are not curated and regulated frequently may become garbled in a way that favours more easily transmitted (e.g. more intuitive and easily learned) variants of the belief system. These 'catchier' variants may take the form of either immanentisms and magical therapies or colourful fiestas and ritual celebrations. Both kinds of ritual activity are 'wild' in the sense of comprising beliefs and practices that spread naturally, without any need for institutionalized inducement or enforcement.

The wild-doctrinal framework, however, is not sufficiently encompassing in scope to capture all varieties of ritual experience. Revelatory quests, for example, based on esoteric cult rituals and other epiphanic experiences, do not fit so easily into the wild versus doctrinal scheme. To the extent that they trigger elaborated processes of exegetical reflection on personally transformative and group-defining experiences, they are psychologically very costly and challenging and therefore restricted to somewhat specialized communities. As such they could hardly be described as 'wild' in the sense of fast-spreading and available to all. On the other hand, the idiosyncratic beliefs and locally variable practices promulgated in traditions of this kind are not cultivated into systemized orthodoxies of a kind that may be observed in a doctrinal tradition. A large portion of this book (especially Chapter 3) is given over to trying to penetrate the complex psychological underpinnings of these kinds of revelatory or 'imagistic' practices.

At any rate, the point to emphasize in the present context is that the tendency of doctrinal systems to morph into forms that are more easily spread may be conceptualized as a 'cognitive optimum effect' (Whitehouse, 2004), denoting a recurrently observed pattern in which 'wild' religious traits 'reappear despite the political dominance of doctrinal organizations' (Boyer, 2019: 1). The establishment of doctrinal religions is thus analogous to the cultivation of ever more elaborately manicured gardens (highly elaborated and often counterintuitive orthodoxies), which require regular tending to maintain their regimented structure and which, if neglected, rapidly become overgrown with weeds (rapidly propagating variants of the religious tradition that flourish in almost any local ecology).

The Evolutionary Origins of the Ritual Stance

If rituals have evolved functions, one of them is surely to generate group cohesion and loyalty and to promote cooperation. Social scientists have long appreciated that rituals bind groups together (Khaldūn, 1958 [1377]; Smith, 1889). Since at least the 1950s, psychologists have shown that liking for the group is linked to the costs involved in ritual participation: the higher the investment in group rituals, the more dissonant feelings of ill-will towards fellow participants will become, a state of affairs that is resolved by stronger expression of pro-group feeling and tolerance towards fellow members (Aronson & Mills, 1959). There is a growing body of evidence that ritual participation increases trust and cooperation among participants (e.g. Hobson et al., 2017), for example, by acting as a costly and therefore hard-to-fake signal of commitment to the group (Sosis & Alcorta, 2003; Sosis & Bressler, 2003). For all these reasons, rituals promote social cohesion, demarcating groups and binding members to each other and to their collective goals.

As well as bonding groups together, rituals create meaning and identity. The fact that the ritual actions are not transparently linked to any particular causal structure and function means that they can be invested with a great variety of potential meanings, emotions, moods, and associations (Geertz, 1966). Insofar as people reflect on exegetical matters (and as noted above this is not always the case) the resulting meanings may be quite idiosyncratic. But if interpreters do not know very much about what others are privately thinking, they can easily form the impression, however illusory, that what is personally meaningful and motivating about the ritual experience is shared by all other participants—a long-established phenomenon in psychology known as the false consensus effect (Ross, Greene, & House, 1977). This point is also widely recognized by political scientists and anthropologists, who have observed that the common experience of publicly observable aspects of ritual (e.g. the actions and props) can foster the illusion of collective emotion and interpretation (Kertzer, 1988).

If rituals evolved to create group bonds and identities, then this was plausibly a process of both cultural and natural selection. So, while humans may have an evolved predisposition to learn and participate in group rituals, the rituals themselves have been honed by cultural evolution allowing those performing them to adapt to novel environments, in much the same way as humans have invented new forms of clothing adapted to different climates and subsistence strategies (McKay & Whitehouse, 2015). Like clothing styles, rituals differ from one cultural group to the next. Indeed, special robes and other bodily adornments are often an integral part of ritual and may themselves be seen as products of the ritual stance, in addition to any instrumental benefits they confer. But the variability of rituals and clothes is not unconstrained or limitless. Ultimately clothes must be wearable, just as rituals of all kinds must be learnable. And rituals, like clothes, must also adjust to varied circumstances. When people move into cold climates, their clothes become thicker and warmer. And as technologies have advanced and diversified, the functions of body armour have become ever more specialized, allowing us to explore increasingly inhospitable environments such as the ocean floor or the vacuum of space. But even the most high-tech forms of clothing must still be constrained by the unique structure and functions of the human body. Broadly speaking, the same may be said of our cultural rituals. For example, as ancient foragers became more reliant on domesticated animals and cultivated crops, the cooperative challenges facing our ancestors changed quite drastically, and the changing role of ritual in group alignment and social bonding formed an integral part of this transformation. Although these developments would have been cognitively constrained, our capacities for memory, reputation management, interpersonal trust, group bonding, and other building blocks of cooperation were also extended and augmented by technologies of codification, transmission, and storage of cultural knowledge, including rituals. In short, rituals (like clothes) are quite plausibly the products of both biological and cultural evolution.

It is tempting to speculate that clues to the biologically evolved functions of human rituals are to be found in the mating displays of birds, ranging from the exquisite choreography of red-crowned cranes to the ornate temple-like structures of the tropical bowerbird. Complex forms of courtship in birds have adaptive functions, for instance by cementing the bond between mates or displaying signals of fitness. Stereotyped behaviours in animals may also contribute to the building of long-term cooperative relationships, for example via blood sharing in vampire bats, or the adoption of supine postures in canids. Human rituals, albeit uniquely based on overimitation of causally opaque behaviour, serve similar functions. For example, the grandiosity, pomp, and sensory pageantry of many human rituals, just like the riotous colours of the peacock's tail, may plausibly serve as signals of fitness (Ridley, 1993). In many traditional societies, men perform public rituals before audiences of women in a manner reminiscent of the behaviour of the bowerbird, designed to attract critical and discerning females (Loncke, 2008). Avian displays may also involve dance-like movements similar to those observed in human rituals, and in both cases, these contribute to interpersonal bonding. Penguins and albatrosses (among many other families of birds) pair bond through synchronous head-bobbing, not unlike the Simbu courtship dances performed in the New Guinea highlands (Brown, 1972) or the famous tango dancing of Argentina (Chasteen, 2004). Social synchrony is indeed a widely recurrent feature of human rituals and recent research suggests that this increases social attachment and cooperation (Wiltermuth & Heath, 2009).

With the move from jungle to savannah, our hominin ancestors became increasingly omnivorous in their food procurement strategies. Among the advantages of being a generalist would have been reduced vulnerability to food shortages resulting from climate change, disease, or competition with other species. Openness to trying out new potential foodstuffs, however, would have carried a greatly increased risk of imbibing toxins (Rozin, 1999). It has recently been argued that humans evolved a unique method of reducing such risks: the 'hazard-precaution system' (Boyer & Liénard, 2006). According to the theory, dubious objects and substances trigger a programme of stereotyped actions involving cleaning and separating, and a concern with symmetry, exactness, or boundary marking. This mechanism, it is suggested, evolved to protect us from contaminants by impelling us to take precautionary action when a risk is suspected. The neural systems responsible for producing hazard precaution routines would seem to malfunction in patients suffering from obsessive-compulsive disorder but are quite useful when operating normally. According to Boyer and Liénard, a by-product of the hazard precaution system is that humans readily pick up behaviours, however random and unnecessary, which resemble the system's stereotyped outputs, primarily cultural rituals.

By-product theories of why humans have rituals have some appealing features. Indeed, it is quite possible that even the peacock's tail or the synchrony-and-cohesion arguments best explain cultural rituals as by-products of mechanisms whose original adaptive functions have been lost or diminished. Another potential by-product explanation, worthy of further consideration, is that overimitation and the ritual stance are side effects of language acquisition. In order to build vocabulary, infants and toddlers must be prepared to imagine that novel phonemes relate to features of the world in a quite arbitrary fashion. The link between lexical items and their referents is established purely by convention, just like the many traditions, norms, and customs (collectively, the rituals) of a cultural group. Perhaps the initial desire to imitate the utterances and other behaviours of caregivers during early development sets the stage for *all* forms of overimitation, whether verbal or procedural, and motivated by both the instrumental stance (copy all, correct later) and the ritual stance (copying to affiliate). Although little is known about how these stances form or diverge during early development, the evidence summarized earlier in this chapter suggests that by at least four years of age, children differentiate quite sharply between opportunities to learn causally opaque (but potentially resolvable) technical knowledge versus irremediably opaque normative conventions (rituals).

If overimitation is indeed a biologically evolved by-product of language acquisition, this capacity has proven to be highly adaptive in cultural evolution. Culture spreads mainly by copying. Imitation conserves and passes down the creations and discoveries of previous generations. Creation and discovery are, by contrast, relatively rare events. Not only in traditional conservative cultures but also in societies undergoing seemingly rapid change, a vast wealth of cultural knowledge is preserved from one generation to the next by means of imitation. Thus, the imitation of causally opaque behaviour is a conservative force, a means of preserving the hard-won discoveries and innovations of generations past. Of course, it is not the only such mechanism of intergenerational transmission. Writing and other external mnemonic devices have also played an important role in knowledge preservation, as well as many ancillary developments such as the creation of archives, libraries, and most recently computers (Mullins, Whitehouse, & Atkinson, 2013). But imitation is by far the most basic and ancient of all such mechanisms and it remains as relevant today as it has ever been.

While overimitation has undoubtedly played a crucial role in transmitting and conserving hard won technological knowledge, it has also played a crucial role in the establishment of ritual traditions, serving as a functional adaptation in competition between cultural groups. At one time, it was seen as the primary task of anthropologists to document the social functions of rituals (Malinowski, 1944). Unfortunately, however, many social anthropologists nowadays have abandoned the functionalist paradigm on the dubious grounds that some social institutions appear to be dysfunctional, and that functionalism may be taken to assume that traditional societies are incapable of changing unless disrupted by some external force, such as colonization or invasion (Goldschmidt, 1996). These objections throw the baby out with the bathwater, however. The evidence gathered in support of functionalism was very substantial, and the fact that it does not explain all rituals all the time is hardly a good reason for abandoning it, a point to which I return in Chapter 7. A more serious criticism of functionalism, however, is that it did not provide an adequate theory of how and why certain institutions acquired their functional properties. But the problem rapidly evaporates when one reconsiders the above arguments in an evolutionary framework.

Cultural evolution is governed by many of the same fundamental principles as biological evolution, except that inheritance is by learning (rather than by genes), selection by consequences for cultural traits tends to be rapid, adaptive cultural mutations arise frequently (often as a result of deliberate innovation), and prior cultural forms are only loosely constraining (cultural revolutions do sometimes happen). Nevertheless, the study of how ritual variability affects the survival of cultural groups can be understood in the same basic terms that any evolutionary biologist would recognize. Specifically, we need to understand how changing features of a given group's ecology and resourcing needs might make the adoption of particular ritual forms *adaptive* (by contributing to group survival and reproduction over time), allowing also for the possibility of drift (random factors contributing to the ritual's persistence), and phylogeny (the constraints imposed by pre-existing ritual traditions).

There is now growing interest in evolutionary approaches to the study of sociocultural and political variation and change (Boyd & Richerson, 2005; Mesoudi, Whiten, & Laland, 2006; Henrich, 2009). Like genetic evolution, sociocultural evolution is an extremely complex process, but relatively simple transmission models can often capture essential properties of population dynamics (e.g. Pagel, Atkinson, & Meade, 2007). Such a framework holds the promise of linking individual psychology, cultural transmission biases, and social dynamics operating daily on a micro scale, with macroscale patterns of global cultural diversity and evolution operating over hundreds or even thousands of years. Ritual traditions typically flourish as adaptations to particular ecological problems, including resource-extraction challenges and the strategies of group formation and competition they require.

In subsequent chapters, we will see that the successful spread of doctrinal orthodoxies produces trust and cooperation in communities too large for their members to know each other personally. This in turn facilitates the extraction of small but cumulatively large resources across larger populations through the expansion of trading networks and the extraction of taxes or tribute from widely dispersed populations. Such processes in world history allowed large, unified populations with hierarchical and centralized systems of governance to outcompete their rivals in the global evolution of social complexity, a topic that may be investigated using statistical analyses of comparative historical data, as discussed at greater length in Chapter 4.

By contrast, cultic ordeals tend to flourish where group survival depends on very high levels of social cohesion as a means of countering strong temptations to defect. Such rituals proliferate in groups that are hard to get into: military academies, masonic sects, priesthoods, and political elites and are often linked to extremely costly forms of self-sacrifice. Severe physical and psychological tortures seem to be standard features of the rituals of such groups, not only in traditional rites of initiation (e.g. in regions of sub-Saharan Africa, first nations groups in the Americas, and indigenous populations in Highland Philippines, Melanesia, Amazonia, etc.) but also in the hazing rituals and boot camps of modern armies, terrorist organizations, criminal gangs, and insurgent groups (Whitehouse, 2016c). Such practices may be the cultural by-products of multiple evolutionary pathways, including kin selection (Whitehouse & Lanman, 2014), conditioning cooperation on past experience (Whitehouse et al., 2017), and extreme reciprocity (Whitehouse, 2018a), all of which are considered in more detail later in the book.

Conclusions

The uniquely human capacity to adopt a ritual stance—that is to engage in behaviour that is assumed to lack a knowable causal structure—lies at the root of cultural diversity and persistence around the world and over the course of history. Whereas our formidable abilities for instrumental learning have allowed humans to develop and spread technological innovations in ever more inventive ways, our more ritualistic propensities have helped us to conserve cultural traditions and cooperate in ever larger communities. These propensities are universal and early emerging in development, suggesting that the ritual stance may be an evolved adaptation. But because it facilitates the emergence and spread of group identities, ritual systems have also evolved culturally, allowing groups to adapt swiftly to a great diversity of ecological niches. In the remaining chapters of this book, we will explore these processes of cultural evolution in much greater detail. Of the four ritual modalities discussed in this chapter, two have especially important consequences for the scale and structure of human groups. That is, whereas magical therapies and ritual celebrations or 'fiestas' respond to human psychological needs and desires at an individual or familial level, revelatory quests and theological schools mobilize social cohesion in ways that allow larger groups to solve collective action problems. As we shall see, these constitute powerful modes of religiosity in world history that have contributed not only to the creation of ever more complex systems of governance and economic organization but also more deadly forms of intergroup competition. Thus, ritual lies at the root of our most prosocial ambitions and also our most dangerous instincts.

2
Ritual Frequency, Emotionality, and Modes of Religiosity

The theory of divergent modes of religiosity makes a series of testable predictions about the effects of ritual frequency, arousal, memory, and exegetical thinking on the evolution of social complexity (Whitehouse, 1995, 2000, 2004). As the term 'modes of religiosity' implies, the original focus of the theory was primarily on the role of religious rituals in group formation, but over the decades, the range of groups considered has been greatly expanded to include also cultural rituals that are not usually classified as 'religious', ranging from the chanting of football fans to the memorial ceremonies of armed revolutionaries.

Anthropologists have long recognized that there are two quite starkly contrasting kinds of ritual systems, and have debated how best to characterize and differentiate them. For example, in the 1930s, Ruth Benedict attempted to ground the difference in the Nietzschean categories of Dionysian versus Apollonian, arguing that some ritual traditions resembled the ancient Greek cult of Dionysus in their emphasis on emotionally intense experience and 'abandon', whereas others more closely resembled the cult of Apollo, valuing order and temperance (Benedict, 1934). Her extended example of the Dionysian pattern was the Kwakiutl first nations group of the Northwest Pacific coast, famous for their intense forms of dancing and feasting associated with the potlatch. She contrasted this with the more sober and disciplined ritual lives of the pueblo peoples of the Zuni River valley in Western New Mexico. But Benedict's pioneering efforts to capture the difference of ritual modes was criticized for being imprecise and overgeneralizing (Aberle, 1960).

Subsequently, numerous other scholars have attempted to capture the distinction in more fine-grained detail, leading to a profusion of dichotomous theories of ritual. For example, Victor Turner (1969) attempted to clarify the differences between ritually induced experiences of spontaneous *communitas* (intense cohesion within a community) and more highly structured, rule-governed forms of ritual experience. Others focused on the differences between rural and urban forms of religion, the one emotional and expressive and the other literate, disciplined, and intellectual (Gellner, 1969). These and many other such theories have sought to capture dimensions of ritual that the modes theory (elaborated in this book) has tried to bring together, and to explain in a way that is both more encompassing theoretically but also testable empirically. Unlike most dichotomous models advanced in the past, the modes theory is concerned not only with describing how two clusters of features coalesce and diverge but also with explaining how they come into being and how they evolve. As one notable anthropologist succinctly put it, the framework of the modes theory 'is Darwinian, since it is about what religions have to do/be in order to survive and perpetuate themselves' (Peel, 2004).

At the core of the modes theory is the idea that contrasting forms of group bonding arise from divergent ways of understanding the meanings of rituals. As discussed in the previous chapter, there are several possible ways of responding to the puzzle of what rituals mean. One is simply to avoid the interpretive challenge and to explain the form and content of the ritual by appeal to tradition or the ancestors. Another is to adopt some quasi-instrumental or magical rationale. Some rituals, however, can prompt a process of extended internal reflection, resulting in the elaboration of idiosyncratic exegesis. And yet another way of responding is to accept on authority from others a set of conventional meanings or symbolic motivations. To the extent that rituals engender socially salient meanings, they can give rise to cohesive groups, united by common identities, shared experiences, or both. In this chapter, I argue that the relationship between ritual, meaning, and cohesion is greatly influenced by the frequency and emotionality of collective performances. Highly repetitive rituals may take the form of largely implicit automated procedures, triggering comparatively little exegetical reflection but at the same time leading to passive acceptance of culturally conventional interpretive frameworks. Rare, climactic rituals, by contrast, produce explicit procedural schemas, potentially fostering a rich process of exegetical reflection over time.

Investigating the factors that promote or inhibit reflexivity in the domain of ritual may sound like a somewhat scholastic exercise, of little value for the scientific study of culture more broadly. But nothing could be further from the truth. The stabilizing effects of ritual repetition on cultural transmission may help to explain the emergence and persistence of regionally and even globally distributed cultural systems and identities. Meanwhile, in promoting a more intensely reflexive stance, rarely enacted rituals constitute a major source of localized cohesion and potentially also intense intergroup competition and violence. Understanding these processes can help us to explain how cultural traditions form, spread, and change over time.

The modes theory aims to solve a number of long-standing puzzles in the study of religion. For instance, those seeking to understand recurrent patterns in the history of religions have used this theory to explain why routinized traditions sometimes break up into splinter groups or sects (Gragg, 2004; Hinde, 2005; Pyysiäinen, 2004). Archaeologists have used the theory to account for the great transition from small-scale foraging societies to the vast and complex civilizations of the Near East, Mediterranean, and North Africa (Mithen, 2004; Johnson, 2004;

Whitehouse & Hodder, 2010; Whitehouse et al., 2014). The modes theory has now been critically evaluated in light of scores of case studies based on ethnography (Whitehouse & Laidlaw, 2004, 2007), history, classics, and archaeology (Whitehouse & Martin, 2004; Martin & Whitehouse, 2005; Martin & Pachis, 2009), and the cognitive sciences (Whitehouse & McCauley, 2005; McCauley & Whitehouse, 2005). Some of the evidence needed to test the modes theory was not available from established scholarship (Barrett, 2004), and so new field research projects have been undertaken, targeting topics on which the evidential needs of the theory were considered to be especially pressing (e.g. Ketola, 2005; Xygalatas, 2007; Lane, 2019). To obviate potential problems of researcher and selection bias, additional strategies have been adopted, including experimental research (e.g. Buhrmester et al., 2018; Jong et al., 2015; Kavanagh et al., 2018; Newson et al., 2020), mathematical modelling (e.g. Whitehouse et al., 2012; Whitehouse et al., 2017), and the construction of large-scale comparative datasets coding selected features of ethnographic descriptions of hundreds of rituals from a diverse sample of cultural traditions (Atkinson & Whitehouse, 2011; Kapitány et al., 2018). This chapter summarizes a range of examples from this diverse body of research, focusing in particular on two main types of evidence in support of the modes theory: detailed cases studies of rituals cross-culturally and quantitative analysis of rituals across global samples of cultural groups, past and present.

The Modes Theory

The modes theory seeks to explain a series of observed differences between two broadly contrasting patterns of social organization and cultural transmission: the doctrinal mode exemplified by the many varieties of world religions embracing vast followings and promulgating a body of standardized beliefs and practices, and the imagistic mode, uniting much smaller and more cohesive communities cultivating somewhat idiosyncratic revelations (see Figure 2.1). The doctrinal mode is relatively recent, associated with the advent of agriculture and the rise of social complexity. The imagistic mode is older, dating back at least as far as the Upper Palaeolithic (Whitehouse, 2004). In contemporary societies, imagistic groups are often embedded within larger doctrinal organizations, for example in the form of esoteric cults, paramilitary cells, or fraternities and sororities. Some imagistic groups also continue to persist independently of larger organizations, for example in small-scale traditional societies, criminal gangs, or civil war armed groups (Whitehouse & McQuinn, 2012; Whitehouse, 2018a).

The doctrinal mode is characterized by frequently repeated teachings and rituals. The group's defining beliefs are codified in language and transmitted primarily via recognized leaders and authoritative texts. High-frequency ritual performances may allow complex networks of ideas to be repeated, and rote

VARIABLE	DOCTRINAL	IMAGISTIC
	Psychological features	
1. Transmissive frequency	High	Low
2. Level of arousal	Low	High
3. Principal memory system	Semantic schemas and implicit scripts	Episodic/ flashbulb memory
4. Ritual meaning	Learned/acquired	Internally generated
5. Techniques of revelation	Rhetoric, logical integration, narrative	Iconicity, multivocality and multivalence
	Sociopolitical features	
6. Social cohesion	Diffuse	Intense
7. Leadership	Dynamic	Passive/absent
8. Inclusivity/exclusivity	Inclusive	Exclusive
9. Spread	Rapid, efficient	Slow, inefficient
10. Scale	Large-scale	Small-scale
11. Degree of uniformity	High	Low
12. Structure	Centralized	Non-centralized

Figure 2.1 *Modes of religiosity contrasted*
(Source: Whitehouse, 2004)

learned, suppressing innovation, thus helping to establish stable beliefs and practices. The emphasis on verbal transmission in doctrinal traditions facilitates highly efficient and rapid spread, for example through processes of evangelism and missionization. The emphasis on oratory and learning also facilitates the emergence of venerable leaders and teachers: gurus, prophets, and priests. These features taken together may favour the emergence of centralized ecclesiastic hierarchies, helping to police and conserve the content and organization of authoritative religious knowledge.

By contrast, the imagistic mode of religiosity is based on infrequent, dysphoric rituals—for instance, the traumatic ordeals of initiation cults, millenarian sects, or vision quests—typically involving extreme forms of deprivation, bodily mutilation and flagellation, or participation in shocking acts. Such practices trigger enduring and vivid episodic memories for ritual ordeals, encouraging long-term reflection on the mystical significance of the acts and artefacts involved. Imagistic practices are much harder to spread than doctrinal traditions. A major reason for this is that the religious knowledge is created through collective participation in costly rituals rather than being summed up in speech or text. Traumatic rituals create strong bonds among those who experience them together, such that people remember exactly who else was present when a particular cycle of rituals took place. This tends to generate localized cults based on direct transmission in face-to-face communities, making them hard to spread efficiently or to achieve the same degree of uniformity, centralization, or hierarchical structure that typifies the doctrinal mode. As I shall explain, these differences between doctrinal and imagistic modes appear to have had major ramifications for the way human societies have evolved.

An early effort to explore the psychology involved in imagistic rituals is to be seen in the pioneering fieldwork of anthropologist Fredrik Barth in the 1960s focusing on the agonizing initiation rites of the Baktaman people of inner New Guinea (1975). A prescient insight of Barth's research on the meanings of Baktaman rituals was that the symbolism was not codified into a standardized framework but comprised continually evolving networks of conceptual and emotional associations among participants' memories for the acts and artefacts involved. Barth (1987) described this process of kaleidoscopic meaning making as 'analogic' rather than 'digital'—involving the production of 'fans of connotations' rather than stable or rigid parables, narratives, or allegories (see also Whitehouse, 1992). Sharing especially salient, symbolically charged ritual experiences, as well as the process of revelatory meaning making that follows from them, lies at the core of imagistic bonding. In part, this is because the very same experiences that shape each individual ritual participant are also recognized to be hallmark features of the entire group. In part, it is also that the memories for such experiences are quite unique and unrepeatable, specifying who else was present. The groups formed in this way have somewhat rigid boundaries—those who were not present during the formative ritual performances could not be inserted into one's memories after the fact, nor could anybody who had been through the ordeals be excluded subsequently. Part of the reason why painful initiations are especially thought-provoking, is that dysphoric rituals, like all rituals, are by definition 'causally opaque'—comprising strings of procedures for which nobody would expect there to be a sufficient physical-casual explanation (see Chapter 1). Since dysphoric rituals are remembered so well and for so long, they can prompt a protracted search for meaning common to many mystery cults and other esoteric religious traditions (Whitehouse, 1992, 2000, 2004; Martin & Pachis, 2009).

Doctrinal and imagistic modes often occur together as part of a single religious tradition, thereby achieving the best of both worlds: a mainstream tradition, constructed around regular worship under the surveillance of an ecclesiastical hierarchy, may tolerate much more colourful local practices, involving rare, dysphoric rituals (such as self-flagellation at Easter parades in the Philippines or walking on red hot coals among the Anastenaria of Northern Greece). While these localized practices undoubtedly produce highly solidary groups distinct from a mainstream tradition, the resulting cohesion can be projected onto the larger community, rejuvenating commitment to its unremitting regime of repetitive rituals (Whitehouse, 1995). In some cases, religious traditions swing back and forth between doctrinal and imagistic modes as part of a process of periodic splintering and reformation (I discuss the case of the European Reformation in greater detail below).

To the extent that religious traditions dominated by doctrinal practices are vulnerable to boredom and lowered motivation, because of their unrelenting repetitiveness, efforts to prevent unauthorized innovation may become less effective over time, resulting in the emergence and spread of simpler, more intuitive, or truncated versions of the orthodoxy. This so-called 'Tedium Effect' (McCauley & Lawson, 2002), is thought to be a significant factor driving reformations in doctrinal religions of all kinds (Pyysiäinen, 2004). Typically, movements of reform entail high levels of religious excitement, triggering imagistic-type revelations and a rejuvenation of doctrinal authority. Once the religious police are back in power, we often see a return to routinization. Other patterns are also possible, however. One grand theorist in the Weberian tradition, Ernest Gellner, argued that rural tribes bound together by high-arousal rituals formed the most formidable military units in the Muslim world, capable of periodically toppling urban dynasties, whose more routinized rituals and doctrinal beliefs failed to generate the kind of cohesion needed to mount an effective defence. Once in power, however, the invading rural tribe in turn came to adopt the less cohesive forms of ritual associated with doctrinal, urban lifestyles and were in turn vulnerable to being usurped in their turn by another rural tribe whose imagistic characteristics had meanwhile remained intact (Gellner, 1969). All these ideas can seem very abstract, however, and a more concrete way of introducing the modes theory is, perhaps, to consider an extended example.

The Kivung as Case Study

The modes theory was initially developed to make sense of the internal dynamics of a religious tradition in East New Britain Province, Papua New Guinea (PNG), known as the Kivung, which I studied via immersive field research for nearly two years in the late 1980s (Whitehouse, 1995). In *Tok Pisin* (the lingua franca of PNG), the word 'Kivung' means 'a meeting' or 'to meet', but for several ethnic groups in New Britain, it also designates a large religious movement, partly inspired by the teachings of Christian missionaries, exemplifying all the main features of the doctrinal mode of religiosity. Established in the early 1960s and spreading to encompass scores of villages in some of the more remote regions of the island, the movement has a centralized leadership, based at the coastal settlement of Malmal, from which regular patrols to outlying villages are sent: bringing news, collecting taxes, and policing the orthodoxy. Each Kivung village has its designated orators, trained at Malmal, charged with the responsibility of preaching a standard body of doctrines and overseeing a wide range of authorized rituals. At the heart of Kivung teachings is the idea that the ancestors of followers will one day return from the dead, bringing with them all the wonders of Western technology. It is said that the returning ancestors will take the physical appearance of white men and women, describing themselves as British or American financial investors and scientists. They will establish factories and shops where all the goods on display will be freely available to members of the Kivung. After this era of plenty, known as *Taim Bilong Kampani* (the period of the companies), there will be a great Day of Judgment, presided over by God and the ancestors. Those who use their riches wisely will be saved, but those who are greedy and debauched will be cast into Hell. The saved will then enjoy eternal Paradise on earth, known as *Taim Bilong Gavman* (period of the government), during which there will be no aging, no illness, no hunger, no childbirth, and no pain.

In order to persuade the ancestors to return from the dead and fulfil this eschatology, Kivung followers are required to perform a great variety of rituals and to obey various religious laws. Kivung rituals fall into four main categories: temple offerings, spiritual cleansing, sermonizing, and garden/cemetery rites. There are three categories of temple in each Kivung village: a cemetery temple, a temple dedicated to one of the movement's spiritual leaders (now deceased), and family temples. All have basically the same function, which is to provide a suitable setting to lay out offerings to the ancestors of food, water, and (if available) money. Each village has only one cemetery temple where offerings are presented twice a week. After the tables are laden, one man described as a 'witness' remains behind in the temple sitting on a rough bench in the corner listening for signs that the ancestors are present (such as a creaking door or sounds of chewing or drinking). Sometimes the food is found to have been disturbed (for instance a morsel mysteriously removed), also taken as evidence of ancestral presence. At an appointed time, the witness emerges into the daylight to find the whole village assembled, eager to learn what has been seen or heard within the temple. The witness whispers into the ear of an orator who solemnly conveys the news. If evidence of ancestral presence is lacking, this is a cause for concern, suggesting that somebody in the community has offended the dead.

Kivung ancestors are quite easily offended. The most common affront is to break one of the ten sacred laws, based loosely on the Decalogue of the Old Testament (as taught originally by Catholic missionaries in the region). Although invisible, the ancestors are thought to be present at any given time and take a keen interest in people's comings and goings. They are pleased when people obey the ten laws and offended by sinful behaviour. Only when the living have eliminated sin will the ancestors return from the dead. The observations of the witness in the cemetery temple provide a way of gauging levels of sinfulness and the offerings when received are thought to strengthen the resolve of the ancestors to return. The sins of individuals, families, and whole communities are regularly absolved through special rituals designed to restore harmonious relations with the ancestors.

Other regular communal activities that take place in the Kivung are special tasks and rituals associated with the village cemetery (where the dead are said to be 'planted' rather than 'buried') and communal gardens. An important site in any Kivung village is the 'Paradise Garden', representing the environment of Adam and Eve prior to the original sin. In Kivung accounts of the fall, offence was caused not by the eating of forbidden fruit but by Eve climbing a betel palm in which Adam had implanted a sharpened stone. As Eve slithered down, she cut herself between her legs producing a strong flow of blood, the origin of her childbearing capacities (and those of her female descendants). For this reason Kivung followers distinguish themselves from most other New Guinea peoples by abstaining from the chewing of betel nut. They say that the red substance spat out by chewers is like menstrual blood, regarded as a hazardous, supernaturally charged substance in many indigenous cultures of PNG. One of the laws of the Kivung is that menstruating women cannot help to prepare offerings for the ancestors.

Such beliefs and practices are common to all Kivung villages, expressed regularly in public acts and pronouncements. Routinized transmission of Kivung beliefs and practices produces a high level of standardization of the mainstream orthodoxy, with even minor innovations and infractions being easy to identify and collectively policed. As noted above, in terms of modes theory, the mainstream Kivung has all the features of the 'doctrinal mode' (Whitehouse, 1992, 1995, 2000). The resulting shared tradition comprises a shared meaning system roughly depicted in Figure 1 as a 'semantic network' (Carley & Kaufer, 1993) of related ideas. Semantic networks are an analytic tool useful for evaluating theories like the modes. The nodes in Figure 1 represent publicly transmitted concepts, framed in everyday discourse, in ritual, and in the speeches of Kivung leaders and orators. The links between nodes represent especially close thematic or implicational associations, such that discourse pertaining to any given node has a high probability of referring also to those nodes to which it is directly linked.

However exotic the Kivung may seem to Western observers, the mainstream semantic network is grounded in a number of implicit beliefs grounded in panhuman intuitions. One such intuition is that mind and body are divisible, the body serving as a temporary vehicle or envelope for mental operations. From an early age (Bering, 2006), humans everywhere seem to assume, if only implicitly, that invisible bundles of psychological traits (e.g. the 'spirit') persist after death (as ghosts or ancestral beings) and can even move between bodies via spirit possession and mediumship (Cohen, 2007). Several psychologists have argued that mind-body dualism is a human universal (Bloom, 2004; Hood, 2009).

Similarly, humans everywhere seem to share the intuition that many features of the natural world and of the cosmos were designed that way by intelligent agents (Kelemen, 2004). That is, we seem to find teleological explanations for the world around us more intuitively credible than purely mechanistic explanations, such as weathering and erosion or evolutionary ones, such as natural selection. This promiscuous application of teleological reasoning (Kelemen, 1999) constitutes another putatively universal component of religion, explaining the prevalence of creation stories and myths cross-culturally.

Another panhuman intuition is that hazardous or sacred substances and places should be encountered only via a set of precautionary procedures, typified by concerns with cleaning, separating, threshold/entrance, symmetry, and exactness (Boyer & Liénard, 2006). These 'hazard precaution routines' resemble the stereotyped behaviours of sufferers from obsessive-compulsive disorder, suggesting that the latter is a pathological expression of an underlying mechanism that evolved to protect humans from harmful contaminants. According to the hazard precaution theory, many features of cultural rituals are a by-product of this panhuman mechanism, meeting its standard input conditions and so helping to explain why we sponge up and pass on routines of that kind.

Yet another example is the tendency to attribute a causal link between moral actions and outcomes, as if misdeeds somehow cause misfortune to the perpetrator whereas virtuous acts are mysteriously rewarded. Ideas of this kind are thought to be driven by so-called immanent justice intuitions, documented extensively in children but also shown to play an important role in adult reasoning (Callan et al., 2014). Just as mind-body dualism and promiscuous teleology help to foster the spread of cultural concepts of spirit/soul and creator beings, so immanent justice intuitions would seem to support a range of culturally transmitted constructs involving notions of supernatural punishment (Johnson, 2015).

These implicit beliefs or 'intuitive anchor points' are depicted as black rectangles in the four corners of Figure 2.2. Such anchor points are widely recurrent across religious traditions: (1) mind-body dualism delivers the ubiquitous intuition that higher level cognitive capacities such as beliefs, memories, and desires can occur outside bodies (e.g. in incorporeal beings such as ghosts, ancestors, and gods) (Bloom, 2004); (2) promiscuous teleology supports the recurrent belief that features of the natural world were designed with a purpose (e.g. as proposed by creation myths) (Kelemen & DiYanni, 2005); (3) hazard precaution helps to explain the obligatory character of ritual, accounting also for the exaggerated concern in many rituals with, for example, symmetry and exactness, threshold and entrance, and redundant repetition (Boyer & Liénard, 2006); (4) immanent justice is the ubiquitous intuition that bad deeds lead to punishment and prosocial behaviour leads to rewards (Callan, Ellard, & Nicol 2006). As is typical of religions generally, most Kivung teachings and practices are directly rooted in one or more of these anchoring implicit beliefs. The more distantly a belief is connected to an anchor point, the more mnemonic support and cultural scaffolding it requires to be preserved intact, for instance, in the form of regular repetition in sermons or sacred texts. In the absence of such pedagogic aids, religious beliefs over time tend to be converted into more intuitive expressions (Whitehouse, 2004). Although

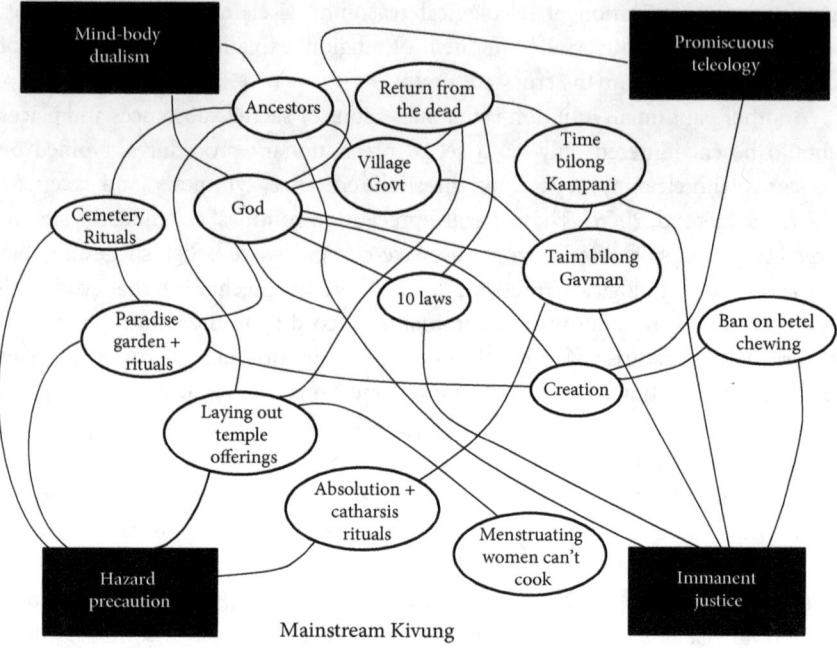

Figure 2.2 *Mapping the mainstream meaning system*
(Source: Whitehouse et al., 2012)

Figure 2.2 features just four anchor points, a more complete model might incorporate many more (Whitehouse, 2008).

Life histories collected in the field indicated that the mainstream orthodoxy of the Kivung depicted in Figure 2.2 is occasionally eclipsed by small splinter groups comprising no more than a few villages at most, who break away temporarily from the larger religious movement, claiming that they have a new plan for bringing the ancestors back from the dead (Whitehouse, 1995). Outbursts of this kind occur in most Kivung villages roughly every five years. Each time a splinter group occurs, its prophesies fail, and followers typically return to the fold, resuming their daily rounds of mainstream Kivung rituals more or less as if nothing had happened. Splinter groups are usually inspired by some extraordinary event, interpreted as a sign that the ancestors are ready to return. It is quite common for individuals to claim to have witnessed such a sign, but generally the consensus is sceptical. When motivation levels are high among mainstream followers, scepticism is strong. But after years of unremitting commitment to routinized practices, people grow weary and impatient, becoming more credulous of claims that *now* at last the longed-for miracle is finally due. Splinter-group activities invariably whip up high levels of excitement, in stark contrast to the dullness of everyday ritual life. Once hopes are dashed, some followers defect. But a more common pattern is for followers to

RITUAL FREQUENCY, EMOTIONALITY, AND MODES OF RELIGIOSITY 63

return to the mainstream movement with renewed vigour and conviction, listing any number of rationalizations for the failure of prophesy. Overall, splinter groups would seem to rejuvenate commitment to Kivung orthodoxy. Similar patterns have been observed in millenarian movements and 'activist' religions more generally (Whitehouse, 2000). Groups predicting impossible events such as the return of a messiah or of the ancestors tend not to endure, whereas those with less falsifiable prophesies may turn into more lasting mainstream traditions in their own right (Stark & Bainbridge, 1979). But either way, group morale following splintering events in the Kivung tends to be elevated rather than diminished.

Figure 2.3 shows a semantic network generated by one instance of a splinter group documented during my field research in the region (Whitehouse, 1995). The trigger for this particular splintering event was the alleged possession of a young man, Tanotka, by a local ancestor. During his spirit possession, Tanotka uttered various cryptic statements such as 'I am a post'. This was interpreted as a reference to the construction of traditional round houses, where the rafters of the roof converge upon a central post. For many, this meant that the possessing ancestor (post) would support the community (multiple rafters) in its efforts to be reunited with the village government. As this idea gained currency, a series of new rituals were invented, involving the symbolism of circles and posts (e.g.

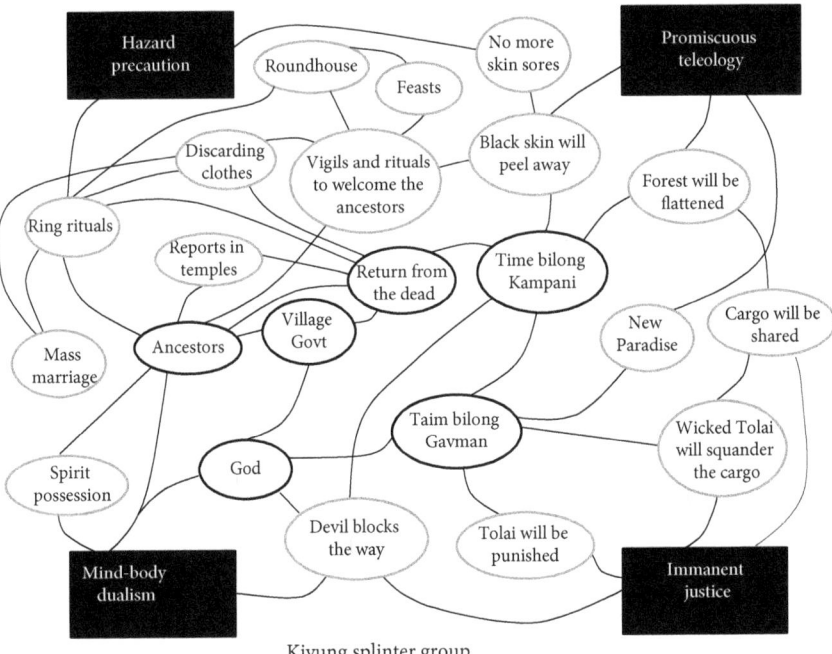

Kivung splinter group

Figure 2.3 *The meaning system of a Kivung splinter group*
(Source: Whitehouse et al., 2012)

dancing in a circle or creating rings of human bodies with Tanotka in the centre). Other novel ideas rapidly caught on. For instance, it was suggested that people should discard all Western-style clothes such as shorts and T-shirts and go virtually naked as their ancestors had once done. Since the sudden appearance of naked bodies prompted widespread erotic excitement, the leaders of the splinter group decided to organize a mass marriage to pair off those at greatest risk of temptation to fornicate (especially youths). Witnesses in the temples who had previously only heard noises attributable to the visiting spirits now claimed to be hearing fully articulated statements from the ancestors, which became known as 'reports' (reminiscent of the authority of government reports). Great feasts were held to celebrate the imminent return of the ancestors. New teachings became widely accepted, for instance that when the ancestors returned, the living would peel away their black skins to reveal a fresh white skin underneath, free of blemishes and sores. The forest would be flattened, and a concrete 'paradise' of high-rise buildings would replace it. The dominant ethnic group in the region, the Tolai (who had long ridiculed the Kivung), would receive a share of the riches brought by the ancestors. But this would be their undoing because they would squander their wealth and be cast into Hell. In preparation for these much-desired events, splinter group members constructed a traditional round house where they held nightly vigils to await the returning ancestors. Feasting continued until all local food stocks had been depleted, but there was no sign of the returning ancestors. A government patrol ordered everyone back to their homes and gardens. Most people claimed that the Devil had blocked them but next time they would succeed.

The splinter group lasted only a matter of months. During this period, it produced a novel belief system consisting primarily of new nodes, depicted in Figure 2.3 as oval shapes drawn in red font. This system overlaps with core elements of the mainstream movement, depicted with oval shapes drawn in black font. At its height, the short-lived semantic network shown in Figure 2.3 gained general acceptance in a few neighbouring villages but never spread more widely. In terms of modes theory, this splinter group exemplifies the 'imagistic mode', summarized above. A diagnostic feature of this shift from the doctrinal to the imagistic is the appearance of low-frequency, highly arousing rituals.

Modelling Doctrinal-Imagistic Oscillations

One way of investigating the precision and coherence of the modes theory, and of its predictions, is to build an agent-based model, incorporating major features and allowing us to run simulations to see if the systemic features behave in the manner anticipated. Some of our first attempts to do this began with sketching out a number of modular components associated with the doctrinal and imagistic characteristics as observed in the oscillation between mainstream and splinter-group meaning systems and intuitive anchor points in the Kivung (Whitehouse et al., 2012). Individuals interacting in these models were designed to update their belief networks in light of those interactions.

Our model contained two kinds of individuals: leaders (Kivung orators) and followers (rank-and-file Kivung adherents). Orators were initially assumed to subscribe to the meaning system depicted in Figure 2.2 and to transmit its content to audiences at twice-weekly meetings, while lay followers were assumed to update their individual meaning systems based on what they heard in the orations. Whenever new beliefs emerged, they became linked (directly or indirectly) to anchor points in the network. The ability of each node to be maintained in the system was modulated by its proximity to anchor points and its motivational intensity. The more distant a given node from an intuitive anchor point, the more likely it was to be forgotten or garbled, potentially leading to the decay of entire networks, but frequent repetition of more distant nodes allowed them to be preserved intact. On the other hand, the more times a node was activated, the lower its motivational intensity became, corresponding to the tedium effect brought on by excessive repetition. When motivation levels were high, Kivung followers rejected innovations as heretical, but when enough nodes in the system had dropped below a certain threshold of motivational intensity, innovation became more likely, and splinter groups could emerge. The visualization tools used in this model assigned different colours to the nodes: those towards the red end of the spectrum exhibited high levels of motivation, and those towards the blue end, lower levels. Figure 2.4 shows the distribution of colours in the meaning system of a typical lay adherent to the Kivung roughly halfway through a simulation, during which some of the nodes in this person's meaning system had begun to turn blue as a consequence of repetition in the public speeches heard, taken in conjunction with the effects of relative distance from intuitive anchor points.

This effort to model Kivung meaning systems and the way they can change over time allowed us to explore the consequences of changing the weightings of different variables specified by the modes theory. Figure 2.5 shows examples of buttons that could be used to increase or decrease the effects of a range of variables so that we could see how each of them effected the outcomes of simulations. This is a valuable method not only of disambiguating potentially relevant variables in a precise fashion but also of exploring whether such variables could, even in theory, affect each other in the ways hypothesized (Whitehouse et al., 2012).

Specifying in this way the causal pathways hypothesized by the modes theory also generated new predictions. For example, early formulations of the modes theory proposed that high-frequency ('routinized') rituals and associated doctrinal transmission would serve to rigidify both orthodoxy and orthopraxy by making unintended innovation more readily detectable (and therefore more readily sanctioned) than in lower-frequency traditions. As frequency drops, so the potential for modifications to the belief system to occur undetected would increase.

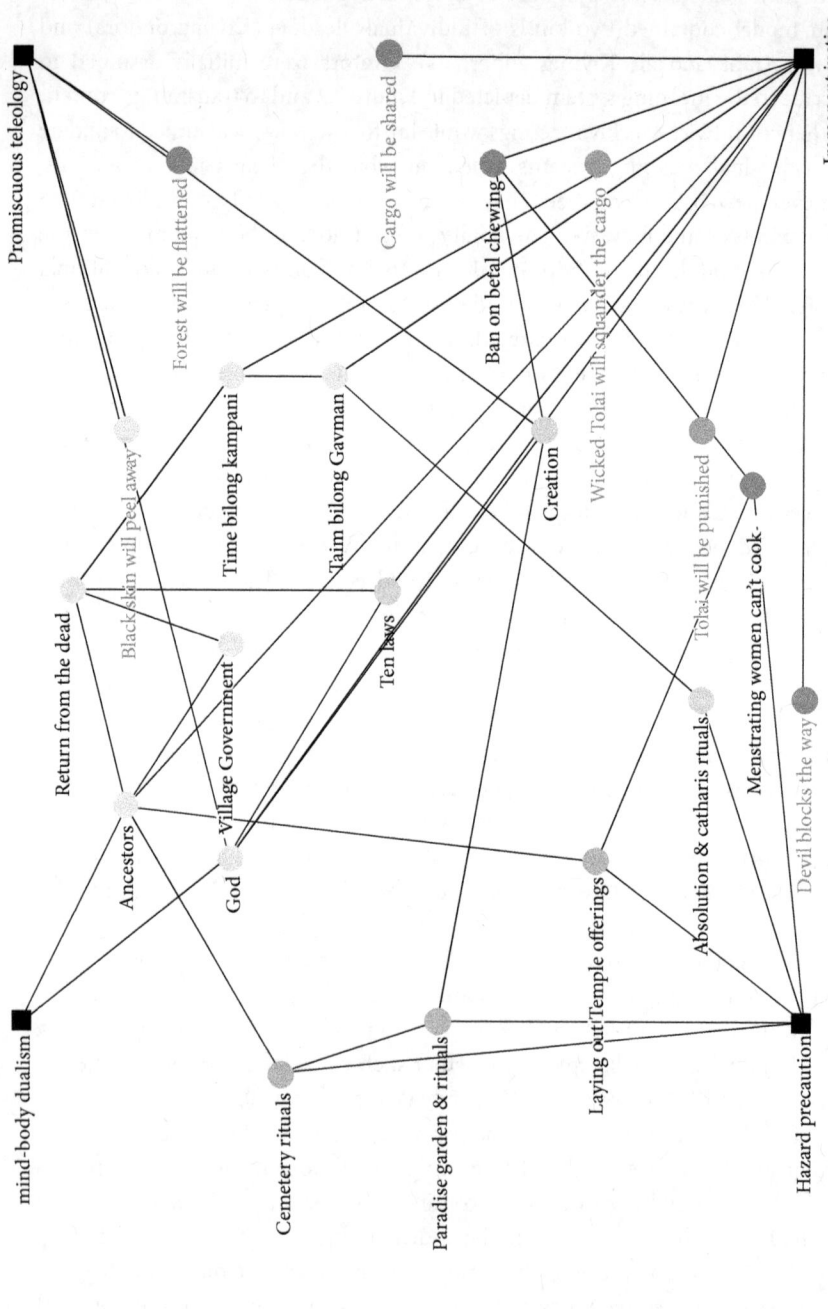

Figure 2.4 Snapshot of the meaning system of a Kivung adherent
(Source: Whitehouse et al, 2012)

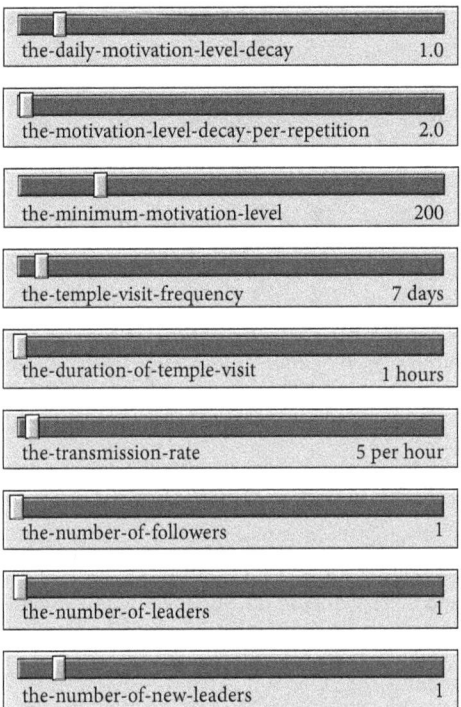

Figure 2.5 *Adjusting the effects of variables in the model*
(Source: Whitehouse et al., 2012)

Building an agent-based model, however, forced us to recognize that some sectors of the meaning system will be subject to decay (e.g. due to forgetting or garbling) more rapidly than other sectors, thereby helping to explain patterns of change in religious systems at a more detailed level. For the purposes of modelling changes we needed to specify those rates of change and their consequences explicitly.

Another example concerns the relationship between transmission frequency and intuitiveness in the meaning system. Processes of decay (garbling and forgetting) in doctrinal systems are nonrandom, being skewed towards more intuitive versions of the orthodoxy (Whitehouse, 2004), producing many instances of 'theologically incorrect' variants of the tradition (Slone, 2004). Building an agent-based model, however, made us consider how the *relative proximity* of beliefs to intuitive nodes might affect *rates of decay* as frequency drops. Simulations showed how beliefs that were distantly related to intuitive anchor points would decay as compared with those located closer to them, leading to refined predictions with regard to patterns of transformation in religious systems over time.

Modelling the variables thought to influence changes in Kivung beliefs also helped clarify the relationship between ritual frequency, arousal, and motivation.

According to the modes theory, the more frequently a belief is repeated in public oratory, the lower its emotional impact and motivating force are likely to be, all else being equal. But having to specify the effects of frequency on levels of commitment and emotional arousal associated with specific nodes in our agent-based model made us realize that the rate of decay in the affective and motivational qualities of beliefs and practices will also be moderated by their intrinsic content, leading to a more nuanced and explicit set of predictions regarding the processes by which demoralization and the tedium effect come about.

Field research on the Kivung showed that splintering events were recurrent across many villages where the mainstream movement had spread (Whitehouse, 1995). But prior to building an agent-based model, little thought had been given to the effects of sequencing in the appearance of novel splinter-group beliefs on people's emotional and motivational states, either during the lifetime of a splinter group or following its collapse. In order to simulate the process of splintering, our model required explicit formulation of the effects of sequencing, assuming that early-established beliefs lost emotional salience and motivational force through repetition whereas late-appearing beliefs would remain relatively fresh. Exploring these previously neglected aspects of doctrinal-imagistic oscillations also forced us to consider more explicitly how the collapse of splinter groups impacts emotion and motivation within the mainstream tradition in which they occur.

Case Studies from History, Anthropology, and Archaeology

If the theory of doctrinal and imagistic modes were merely intended to capture a set of dynamics unique to the Kivung, a religion found only on a relatively remote part of one island in Melanesia, it would be a parochial theory indeed. But, in fact, the modes theory has developed in a way that should be generalizable to other parts of the world, perhaps even to all ritually constituted groups. Initial efforts to generalize the modes theory were quite modest, however. The process began by examining case studies drawn from same ethnographic region as the Kivung, focusing mainly on indigenous and nativistic religions, such as the initiation cults of inner New Guinea and some of the more famous millenarian movements of coastal and island Melanesia. Yet this initial effort at generalization also made one tentative leap beyond Melanesia, to the transformations in Christianity that occurred in late medieval and Early Modern Europe—the Protestant Reformation (Whitehouse, 2000). My argument ran like this. Late medieval Christianity was predominantly doctrinal in the monasteries and convents but mostly imagistic among the laity. Nevertheless, the emotionality of Christian rituals changed during the Reformation, and with it, forms of group bonding. Medieval imagistic tendencies were suppressed, and a more thoroughly doctrinal mode of religiosity enthusiastically embraced. In their effort to tamp down or even eliminate imagistic practices, Reformers sought instead to establish more repetitive, logocentric forms of worship.

Among the first historians of medieval Christianity to engage with these ideas was Anne Clark (2004), an expert on monastic life communities and their rituals. Clark broadly agreed with my characterisation of monastic rituals in the Middle Ages as routinized, observing that, in theory at least, monks and nuns performed as many as eight rituals in the daily diurnal-nocturnal cycle, as well as frequent recitations of psalms, antiphons, and hymns. Such rites were low in emotional intensity, required deference to an ecclesiastical hierarchy, and entailed strong identification with a large 'imagined community' of fellow adherents. Yet there were also aspects of the doctrinal mode that were lacking or muted in the monasteries. For example, there was not a great emphasis on the oratory as a vehicle for the transmission of doctrinal orthodoxy, and not all monks and nuns were equally learned in religious matters. The emphasis instead was on the repetition of textual materials.

While acknowledging that monastic ritual life lacked high emotional intensity, however, Clark is at pains to emphasize that it was far from *emotionless*. Moreover, although the doctrinal mode is thought to rely on the social transmission of beliefs and practices, rather than the construction of shared personal experience as in the imagistic mode, Clark observes that monastic rituals involved meditative reflection and emotional engagement in ways that were probably experienced as transformative and self-shaping. Of particular note are the well-documented visionary experiences and revelations of both monks and nuns. In an extended account of the lives of Elisabeth of Schönau (a twelfth-century Benedictine nun) and Gertrude of Helfta (who lived a century later), Clark presents evidence of a richly personal engagement with God bearing many of the hallmarks of imagistic ritual experience. She concludes (2004: 130-1):

> So, were medieval monasteries islands of doctrinal religion? Semantic schemas abounded, authoritative interpretations were available, hierarchy was enforced, policing of orthodoxy was more possible than in the world outside the monastery walls. Yet the highly routinized ritual of the divine office offered its congregants the opportunities for intense emotional, visionary experience that became the foundation for personal spontaneous (and later deliberative) exegesis that may or may not have accorded with the prevailing orthodoxy.

Clark's meticulous case study material suggests that although medieval monastic life might be accurately characterized as conforming to the doctrinal mode, it did not exclude the kinds of intense religious experience associated with imagistic practices. A crucial question to ask from our theoretical perspective, however, is whether the ecstasies of individuals like Elisabeth and Gertrude were perceived as shared with other members of the monastic community and, as such, capable of motivating strong forms of cohesion within such groups. Clark tells us they were not, for while revelatory episodes may have formed an important part of individual religious experience in the monasteries, they did not become a group-defining experience, as would be the case in a truly imagistic mode of religiosity. In other words, although nuancing the characterization of late medieval monasticism as doctrinal, Clark's account does not contradict it.

Clark goes on to consider whether the religiosity of the medieval *laity*, at least, could be justly portrayed as 'imagistic'. Specifically, she addresses my claim that 'it is precisely within those populations that lack access to the authoritative corpus of religious teachings, and so cannot be adequately motivated by these teachings, that we find the greatest profusion of imagistic practices' (Whitehouse, 2000: 15). Clark acknowledges that lay Christians in the Middle Ages were unsophisticated in matters of theology and religious scholarship, and agrees that their religiosity was experienced in a much less doctrinal fashion than in the monasteries and universities. By way of illustration, she focuses on the cult of the Virgin Mary that, although part of the Christian tradition from much earlier times, took on a special importance among the laity in the eleventh to fifteenth centuries (Clark, 2004: 131–2):

> Effusions of love, dedication, and praise overtake the more staid, theologically centred hymns and prayers of the early Middle Ages. Devotion to the Virgin Mary was expressed in major feasts celebrated publicly (there were four annual feasts dedicated to the Virgin) and in private domestic practices. The public festivals were celebrated with Mass in a language that lay people did not generally comprehend.

Clark is reluctant, however, to describe these practices as 'imagistic' since they did not typically evince strong emotions and self-shaping episodic memories. Yet she goes on to discuss evidence of the often very intense relationships lay Christians developed with Mary. Moreover, as Clark also acknowledges, the violent nature of visionary experience, iconography, and Marian devotion complicates the picture.

According to Theodore Vial, the European Reformation did indeed create a more thoroughly doctrinal mode of Christian worship, largely to the exclusion of imagistic elements. Early Protestantism, he argues, was defined by a highly routinized programme of doctrinal transmission and supervision, often expressed in a highly codified form. Focusing on one such programme, instigated by Martin Luther in Saxony, Vial describes efforts to abolish or eliminate folk ritual practices while strengthening doctrinal ones. He illustrates this argument by describing how rituals surrounding baptism and the Eucharist were systematically modified, reducing or de-emphasizing elements of exorcism and 'magic', respectively, so prominent in their medieval forms. With regard to Luther's reforms of the rites of baptism, Vial concludes (2004: 148):

The result is a service that was just as long as the Catholic one, but one in which explanations and exhortations took the place of repeated exorcisms... Surely this is an example of a doctrinal mode seeking to displace an imagistic one... Civil authorities, with the encouragement of religious leaders, began cracking down on the festivities surrounding baptism, especially the lavish parties, the practice of delaying baptism to allow friends and relatives time to travel to the party, and expensive gifts.

Following a careful description of Luther's many reforms to the practices associated with the Eucharist, Vial goes on to argue that the process was one of strengthening its doctrinal character. Communion, and other major rituals, became occasions for doctrinal transmission and instruction, emphasizing that the efficacy of ceremonial depended on the understanding and faith of participants as much as on the acts themselves. According to Vial (2004: 151) these same patterns of transformation were evident in the Catholic Reformation as well:

> Protestants and Catholics were both purveyors of logically coherent persuasive bodies of teachings; both had clearly marked leaders and systems for checking on the orthodoxy of their adherents; both stressed frequent repetition of rituals during which doctrine was rehearsed and authorized exegeses of the rituals provided; both made efforts to transmit these bodies of beliefs far and wide.

The idea that similar patterns of ritual and group dynamics might help us to understand religious systems in such disparate contexts as sixteenth-century Europe and twentieth- century Melanesia, encouraged others to go further still, both temporally and ethnographically. To a great extent, the doctrinal mode of religiosity in PNG has undoubtedly been deeply influenced by missionary Christianity, and thus the changes in religious life forged by the European Reformation. Consequently, there is an obvious problem of nonindependence of the two cases under comparison. This is somewhat less true of the classical world, however, and scholars contemplating the rituals of ancient Greece and Rome have found some striking resonances with the idea of divergent modes of religiosity.

Some particularly lurid examples of imagistic practices come from Graeco-Roman case studies. Roger Beck's account of the Roman cult of Mithras, for instance, presents evidence of emotionally intense collective rituals triggering reflection on cosmological (especially astronomical) imagery as part of a highly cohesive mystery cult (Beck, 2004). In these rituals, everyday assumptions about the nature of the cosmos were systematically undermined and progressively replaced by 'deeper' esoteric knowledge. But as well as confirming many already established features of the imagistic mode, case studies of this kind revealed hitherto unanticipated patterns. In the case of Mithraism, for example, the process of cultural transmission was quite remarkable. Recall that a hallmark feature of the imagistic mode is that it produces localized groups whose traditions are hard to spread across the landscape because they inhere in collective performances, requiring the presence of all participants at a particular time and place.

By contrast, the doctrinal mode is far more efficient to transmit to wider populations because such traditions are codified in an eminently transportable medium—namely the teachings of proselytizing leaders (gurus, prophets, and missionaries). But Mithraism, despite its imagistic character, spread widely across the Roman Empire. How was that possible? The answer, it turns out, is that Mithraism became embedded in a much larger institutional framework—the Roman army. And where soldiers travelled in ritual groups, they carried their imagistic practices with them.

The problem of nonindependence of data points remains a concern, however, even when we consider ancient examples. After all, much of the modern world—from its systems of governance and law through to its culinary traditions, languages, and architecture—have been deeply influenced by classical civilizations. Perhaps divergent modes are products of this uniquely Western history, exported to regions like Melanesia via colonization and the spread of world religions. Thus, in efforts to extend the geographical and cross-cultural reach of the model, anthropologists have interrogated evidence for doctrinal and imagistic dynamics in ethnographic case studies in regions as far apart as West Africa (Peel, 2004; Højbjerg, 2004; Berner, 2004), the Middle East (Shankland, 2004), and Asia (Laidlaw, 2004; Bayly, 2004; Howe, 2004).

One of the more striking implications of this work has been to show that the scope of the modes theory needed to be more clearly circumscribed. Recall that the theory pertains to rituals that demarcate groups and foster cohesion within them. Ethnographic accounts revealed seemingly countless examples of rituals that did not contribute directly to the formation of collective identities, whether via imagistic revelations of doctrinal teachings. Many such rituals are of the quasi-instrumental or 'magical' types discussed in the last chapter. Like useful medicines and tools, such rituals are commonly bartered and exchanged in the marketplace rather than being ways of affiliating to a club, sect, or other group. But a more generally recurrent feature is that their significance and *raison d'être* is rooted in intuitions described in our agent-based models as 'anchor points'. Far from being linked to cognitively challenging traditions of exegesis, whether generated by internal reflection in the imagistic mode or by authoritative canon in the doctrinal mode, such rituals provided a more instantly understandable value or meaning. As noted above, these rituals and their exegeses may be described as 'cognitively optimal', which is to say that they have strong intuitive appeal and are culturally contagious, requiring little in the way of individual effort or institutional support to thrive and spread. Engagement with the modes theory from a wider range of ethnographic regions suggests that modes of religiosity do not simply swing between doctrinal and imagistic poles, as observed in the Kivung or in the European Reformation, but also can also be replaced by popular cultural practices that are neither maintained as an official orthodoxy nor as mysteries guarded by elders and ritual experts (Whitehouse, 2004). It is tempting to describe these cognitively optimal traditions as the cultural equivalent of weeds that can invade and take over gardens that are not studiously cultivated and maintained. When gardens are engulfed in this way, they lose their distinctive features; their borders become blurred with the surrounding terrain; and they eventually disappear altogether. The same can happen to ritual groups and their identities when either doctrinal or imagistic dynamics give way to cognitively optimal practices (see Chapter 1). Indeed, this is often what is happening when globalized cultural traits, with their cognitively optimal features and broad appeal, invade and supplant local traditions that historically required considerable ritual work and mnemonic support to maintain and transmit.

Another equally striking implication of efforts to compare doctrinal and imagistic dynamics cross-culturally was the finding that they were in no way unique to Western European religious history and its imperialistic missionary legacies. A compelling example of this is provided by the parallels drawn by anthropologist Leo Howe (2004) between late medieval Christianity in Europe and *agama*, a form of *adat* Hinduism, in Bali. Moreover, just as many of Europe's monasteries were besieged by reformers in the early modern period, so forms of devotional Hinduism reacted against the erosion of fundamental doctrinal principles in *agama* orthodoxy in late twentieth-century Bali. The modes theory would explain why these patterns repeat themselves even in very different ethnographic and historical settings.

Considering how modes theory might apply to a broader range of ethnographic and historical contexts has also raised questions about the relationship between local and extended forms of group cohesion that (as I shall explain in subsequent chapters) set the stage for debates that subsequently came to involve social psychologists and cultural evolution theorists. At the core of this is the question of whether forms of group bonding based on shared memories for episodic ritual events can help to unify people who were not present at the events in question. Initial forays into ethnographic case studies suggested otherwise. For example, like the Kivung splinter groups and initial cults of PNG mentioned above, Christian Højbjerg (2004) observed that the secret male Poro cults of West Africa bound together localized and fiercely exclusivist communities based on the sharing of memorable ritual ordeals with small groups of age-mates. Højbjerg documented how attempts to expand these forms of group bonding to larger communities continually failed, apparently requiring more doctrinal forms of codification and transmission in order to accomplish this.

As valuable as these historical and ethnographic case studies have been in developing and refining the modes theory, they could not reasonably be seen as testing the theory scientifically. Apart from anything else, there was an obvious risk that any observed relationships between variables of interest might be a consequence of 'cherry picking' examples that fit the model. Were case studies more likely to be selected because they confirmed the predictions of the modes theory? Note that bias of this kind does not even need to be conscious. Perhaps some scholars were interested in the theory because it resonated with their data, maybe prompting questions and criticisms, as well as confirmatory evidence, but in a way that nevertheless skewed the sample of available case studies in such a way as to favour the theory. Perhaps other ethnographers and historians would regard the doctrinal/imagistic distinction to be simply irrelevant to the groups they know about, or just plain wrong? To avoid the charge of confirmation bias, a more objective way of testing the modes theory was required.

Quantifying Ritual Features Cross-Culturally

In order address the risk of cherry picking when testing the main predictions of the modes theory, it was necessary to organize cross-cultural data in a way that was less vulnerable to selection bias and capable of being analyzed statistically. To make a start on this process, we constructed a database, recording performance frequencies, arousal levels, and other contextual information for 645 rituals from seventy-four cultures around the globe (Atkinson & Whitehouse, 2011), based on data extracted from the electronic Human Relations Area Files (eHRAF), a vast storehouse of ethnographic writings (Ember & Ember, 1998). A primary aim was to establish whether rituals from this large and diverse sample of the world's cultural traditions tended to occupy either low-frequency, high-arousal or high-frequency, low-arousal positions in the 'morphospace' of all possible ritual forms, as predicted by the modes theory. Although the modes theory does not predict that all rituals will conform to one or other of these types, it does predict that rituals will *tend to cluster* around these so-called 'attractor positions' (Sperber, 1996; Whitehouse, 2004), a claim that cannot be adequately tested using hand-picked case study material but which instead requires large representative samples of the world's cultures capable of being analyzed statistically.

For the purposes of this study, we coded data on a range of ritual features for each of the cultures in our database. Some relevant variables had already been coded as part of an earlier project known as the Ethnographic Atlas (Murdock, 1967) and so we incorporated those pertaining to group size, hierarchy, agricultural intensity, and beliefs in moralizing gods. But most of the variables used in our study had to be coded for the first time and included general features of the ritual (such as its overt purpose and duration), categories of participant, performance frequencies, movement and sound (e.g. dancing, singing, social synchrony), dysphoria, euphoria, form, and meaning. Statistical analysis of the data revealed a striking series of patterns cross-culturally. As shown in Figure 2.6, we found, as

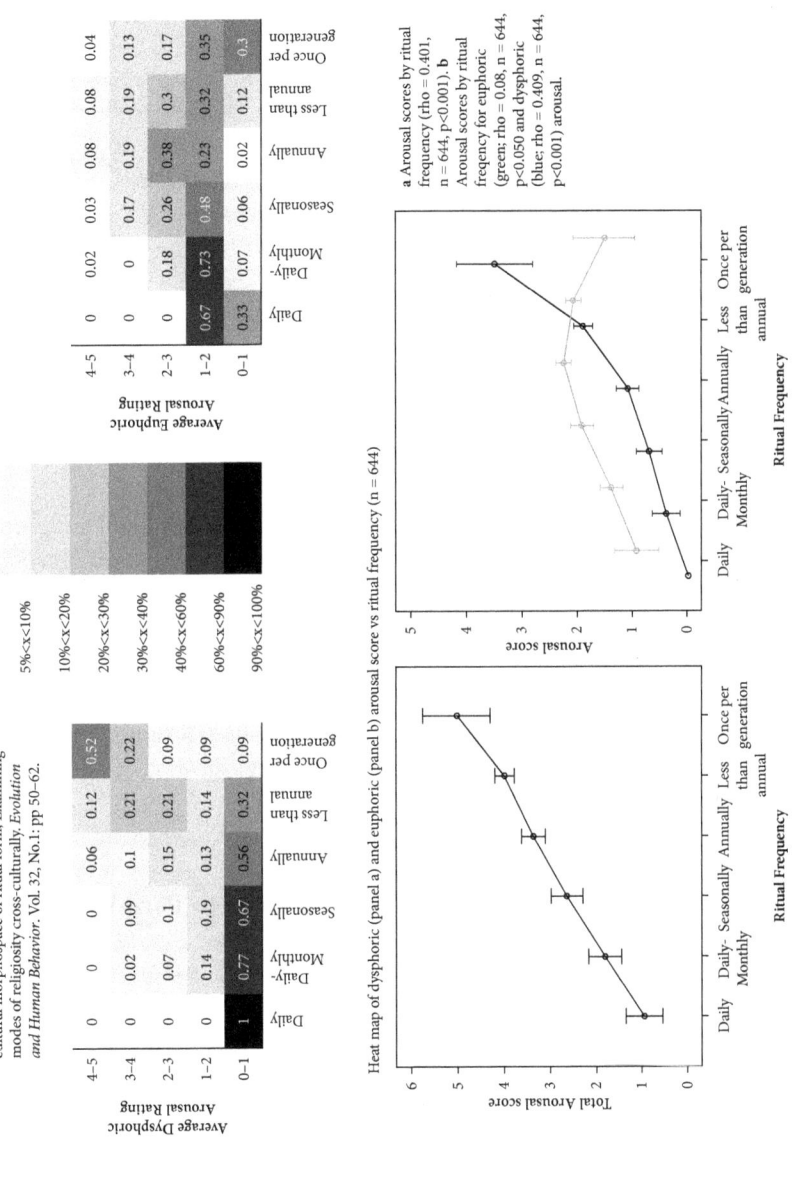

Figure 2.6 *The cultural morphospace of ritual form*
(*Source: Atkinson & Whitehouse, 2011*)

predicted, that the most rarely performed rituals tended to involve intensely dysphoric arousal (pain, fear, or other aversive emotions and sensations), whereas high-frequency rituals tended to score low in emotional arousal. Importantly, there was a noticeable bunching of rituals around the low-frequency/dysphoric end of the spectrum and the high-frequency/low-arousal end (shown as red cells in the 'heat map' top left of Figure 2.6). Nevertheless, the relationship between frequency and euphoria (the green line in the graph, bottom right—see also heat map top right) took the form of a U-shaped curve, with the most euphoric rituals peaking around annual frequency. As we shall see in Chapter 3, this finding helped to stimulate much subsequent research on whether dysphoria is more important than euphoria in generating imagistic effects in ritual communities. Some theories suggest that initiation into a group will commonly entail dangerous and painful ordeals (e.g. Sosis, Kress, & Boster, 2007), and since one can only be the patient of such a ritual once in a lifetime this might seem to explain their low frequency. But the analysis of our data suggested that the relationship between low-frequency performance and dysphoric arousal was a general pattern across a great variety of rituals and did not seem to be readily explainable purely in terms any particular function, such as initiation rites conducted to facilitate entry into a group.

We also discovered something else that turned out to be very important for subsequent directions in our work on the modes theory. This key finding was that as rituals become more frequent and less dysphoric, *agricultural intensity increases*. This pointed to the possibility that the kinds of rituals prevailing in a given cultural tradition are related to the kinds of collective action problems its members need to address. For example, whereas highly dysphoric but rarely performed rituals might be especially useful in small-scale foraging societies, as agricultural intensity increases there may be a growing need for more routinized rituals. If so, this could shed new light on what was arguably one of the greatest revolutions in world history: the transition from foraging to farming.

Modes and the Transition from Foraging to Farming

From an archaeological perspective one of the most intriguing implications of the link we had discovered between ritual frequency, arousal, and agriculture was that the transition from foraging to farming in world history may have entailed a basic shift from imagistic to doctrinal dynamics. Our first efforts to investigate this question centred on archaeological evidence from Çatalhöyük in Turkey. At this site, an ancient civilization flourished during the period of transition from hunting and gathering to settled farming, but still long before the first agrarian states emerged.

Çatalhöyük was a large, densely populated settlement established around nine-and-a-half thousand years ago and lasting for nearly two millennia. At Çatalhöyük we have found evidence of a gradual shift from the imagistic practices of small group living to much larger-scale group bonding based on higher-frequency doctrinal rituals (Whitehouse & Hodder, 2010). Some of our evidence for this shift comes from pictorial representations of imagistic practices in the early phases of settlement—for example, paintings that show the teasing and baiting of bulls, deer, bear, and boar by crowds of participants and depicting what look like rattles and drums, as well as dancing figures. The animals in these paintings would have presented a grave threat to human life and limb. Wild cattle at Çatalhöyük were much larger than their domesticated descendants—adult bulls standing two metres in height at the haunches. Faunal remains at the site show that these animals were slaughtered at large feasting events. We know from the nature of these deposits that feasting rituals occurred sporadically, perhaps once or twice in a generation, consistent with imagistic dynamics. Moreover, the rituals associated with the closure and rebuilding of houses occurred every seventy to one hundred years on average and seemed to elicit strong emotions associated with the handling of human remains.

One of the many clues to the imagistic character of early ritual life at Çatalhöyük is the pervasive emphasis on hiding and revealing, or what Hodder and I have called 'revelatory' practices. Obsidian hoards were placed beneath floors and periodically retrieved. Paintings were repeatedly remade and then covered over. Claws of bears, teeth of foxes and weasels, tusks of wild boars, and beaks of vultures were being placed in walls, repeatedly extracted, replaced, and then covered over. Bucrania were installed in walls and on upright posts. Human skulls and body parts were continually being removed from the floors of domestic dwellings and then reburied, and the hiding and revealing of body parts showed remarkably detailed and durable memory for burial locations.

Roughly halfway through the period of settlement at Çatalhöyük the ritual life seemed to change, however. Evidence of the hunting-feasting complex fades, and it seems as if imagistic practices were progressively replaced by a more doctrinally codified belief system, stewarded by orators and expert cosmologists. Hodder and I found many indicators of a more 'discursive' style of religiosity, for example, manifested in the designs of stamp seals, paintings, and narrative transmission in what we came to describe as 'history houses'. We saw evidence of increasing standardization of group ideology in the recurring themes of acts and artefacts and especially the way pottery and obsidian production become more homogeneous and centralized. We think the emergence of the doctrinal mode at Çatalhöyük constituted a milestone in the evolution of human civilizations, paving the way for more centralized, large-scale, and hierarchical patterns of political association.

Much previous theory had proposed that this step forward in political evolution was rooted in changing technology and modes of production. But Hodder and I have argued, by contrast, that larger-scale, centralized patterns of social organization were triggered by a shift in people's ritual lives, beginning somewhat earlier than is generally supposed. One of the ways we have been able to test this hypothesis is by building longitudinal databases. The excavations at Çatalhöyük have so far produced more than 50,000 units of archaeological material, each carefully catalogued in a massive electronic store. We began by recoding selected portions of this material in our own database to include proxies for social complexity, agricultural intensity, and the frequency, scale, and emotionality of ritual performances. This in itself was a major operation and of course raised many challenges of archaeological interpretation. But when we finally came to analyse the data an overall picture seemed to emerge.

What we found was that rare, emotionally intense, communal rituals decline over the period of settlement and are replaced by more routine family-based rituals. We also saw a shift away from elaborate symbolism and imagery towards more discursive practices associated with mobile objects with standardized designs. These findings were consistent with the view that imagistic practices progressively gave way to more doctrinal ones. We also found evidence linking the rise of the doctrinal mode and levels of agricultural intensity. A less welcome discovery, from the perspective of our theoretical framework, was that these processes did not correspond to a growth in the size and density of the population. Actually, we found the reverse—the settlement became smaller and more dispersed. What we think may have happened is that as the doctrinal mode emerged, households became more independent of the communal band, and more diffuse ethnic identities encompassing larger and more dispersed populations took over from the local cult group bonded through imagistic practices. Paradoxically, as settlements thinned out and dispersed, social identities may have been greatly expanded—uniting much larger populations (Whitehouse, Mazzucato, Hodder, & Atkinson, 2014).

To test that hypothesis, we needed to go beyond Çatalhöyük and examine trends in the changing character of ritual and social morphology over a wider area and over a much longer period of time. This led to the construction of a regional database covering nearly all the archaeological sites of Anatolia and the Levant from the end of the Palaeolithic to the beginning of the Bronze Age. This labour-intensive process eventually yielded a picture that is broadly consistent with the predictions of the modes theory. In the earlier sites surveyed, ritual life bore all the hallmarks of the imagistic mode. Over time large-scale feasting declined, and instead a focus on family rituals and burials became a major focus of ritual life, a transformation that may have been linked with the emergence of much larger social groupings based on principles of descent and organized economically around the domestic mode of production (Mazzucato et al., In Prep).

A great advantage of archaeological datasets is the possibility for tracking changes over long time periods and especially some of the most consequential phases in sociocultural evolution, such as the early adoption of animal domestication and crop cultivation. A downside, however, is that the evidence from prehistory can be very limited or patchy with regard to variables of high importance. For example, to test our predictions about the changing role of imagistic practices as societies became larger and more complex, we needed to capture information on the frequency and emotionality of rituals. But given the sparsity of evidence pertaining to ritual performances in prehistory, this can be a considerable challenge. As noted above, we were able to estimate ritual frequency with regard to certain key events, such as communal feasting by dating the abundance of relevant faunal remains in midden deposits, for example. And we could infer dysphoric intensity from pictorial representations of ritual events, the presence of ceremonial knives or other embellished cutting instruments, or from signs of injury to human remains. The granularity and detail of the evidence on ritual performances improves with the advent of writing but that occurred long after the transition from foraging to farming. Increasingly, therefore, the pressure has grown to find a way of applying what is known about small-scale societies in the ethnographic record to the analysis of prehistorical social formations. This led to the development of an innovative methodological approach that that we have called 'Material Correlates Analysis' (MCA) (Gantley, Whitehouse, & Bogaard, 2018).

The basic idea behind the MCA approach is that we can leverage the very rich information available on extant cultures studied in detail by ethnographers to fill in gaps in our knowledge about prehistoric cultures. Drawing analogies between modern and ancient societies is nothing new, of course. A well-known example is the effort to use ethnographic accounts of contemporary hunting and gathering cultures to try to reconstruct the social organization of ancient foraging bands (Barnard, 2004). One of the reasons this approach has been controversial in the past, however, is that the reasons for reliance on wild food sources can be very different nowadays than in the ancient past, for example because formerly farming cultures have been driven into foraging in less hospitable environments as a consequence of disease and other consequences of colonization (Balée, 1992). Another risk is to overestimate the similarities between a single richly studied modern case study and a more ancient one, with no reliable way of distilling what is unique and what is generalizable about the contemporary example (McGranaghan, 2017). What is different about the MCA approach is that it starts by identifying a broad range of features that many modern societies of a particular type have in common and establishes which of those features are archaeologically visible in more ancient societies. It then uses a number of complimentary multivariate statistical techniques to estimate the likely presence of archaeologically inaccessible correlates of those features, thereby enabling us to fill in gaps in the prehistoric record.

Applying this general approach to our question about the role of ritual in the transition from foraging to farming, we began by establishing a wide range of features associated with the most doctrinal and imagistic cultures we could identify in the contemporary ethnographic record (Gantley, Whitehouse, & Bogaard, 2018). Our starting point was the large rituals database described above (Atkinson & Whitehouse, 2011), constructed using materials extracted from the electronic Human Relations Area Files (eHRAF). Recall that our original database contained details of hundreds of rituals selected from a sample of seventy-four cultures. Of those cultures, we now created a subset of thirty-four comprising the fifteen most imagistic (societies with the most dysphoric rituals) and the nineteen most doctrinal (societies with the most frequent collective rituals) based on analysis of 65,432 paragraphs of ethnographic description relevant to the MCA. For the archaeological dataset, we identified fifty site phases across southwest Asia (primarily Anatolia and the Levant), spanning the transition from foraging to farming from the Epipaleolithic to the Pottery Neolithic. For the thirty-four most doctrinal and most imagistic cultures in our ethnographic dataset, we identified ninety characteristics relating to ritual life, subsistence activity, and social organization that could be reliably correlated with archaeologically visible features in our archaeological dataset. Using a combination of multidimensional scaling, principal components analysis, and generalized linear modelling, it was possible to statistically estimate the likelihood of ancient societies being predominantly doctrinal or imagistic, based on degree of similarity in their material cultures with the most doctrinal or imagistic modern examples—with each archaeological site-phase being assigned a percentage probability of being doctoral or imagistic. The overall results—in terms of the percentages of sites from the sample that were classified as imagistic, doctrinal, or indeterminate—showed that the earliest (Epipaleolithic) societies, which depended primarily on foraging, exhibited more imagistic characteristics, while the most recent (Pottery Neolithic) societies, with the highest levels of agricultural intensity in our prehistoric sample, exhibited more doctrinal characteristics. The various phases of the Pre-Pottery Neolithic in between exhibited a mixture of imagistic and doctrinal features, consistent with a process of transition between the two modes of religiosity (Gantley, Whitehouse, & Bogaard, 2018). Thus, the MCA approach seeks to track broad patterns of changes in ritual life that would otherwise be hard or even impossible to discern from the archaeological evidence alone.

Conclusions

This chapter has outlined some of the general features of the modes theory and described some of the methods used to observe doctrinal and imagistic dynamics cross-culturally and throughout the human past. From early field observations and agent-based models of oscillating modes in a remote Melanesian cargo cult has blossomed a diverse body of research ranging from historical and ethnographic case studies through to statistical analyses of cross-cultural variation in ritual practices worldwide and of changing patterns of ritual and social organization over thousands of years of human prehistory.

What all this research suggests is that the sorts of collective rituals that demarcate groups and bind them together take the form of two modes of religiosity and group formation: imagistic and doctrinal. The imagistic mode appears to be the more ancient and is associated with intense but localized group bonding in small-scale societies, such as the foraging bands that dominated most of human prehistory. In the next chapter, I will attempt to tease apart the psychological processes underlying imagistic practices in more depth and will consider efforts to understand how they evolved. Later, in Chapter 4, I will turn to the rise of the doctrinal mode as a much more recent process of cultural evolution, following the invention of agriculture.

3
Imagistic Ritual, Fusion, and Self-Sacrifice

In previous chapters, I have presented evidence that the ritual stance, even in young children, motivates affiliation with groups, and that varying the frequency and emotionality of collective rituals influences the scale and intensity of the bonds formed among coparticipants. Group formation through ritual participation is arguably one of our species' most successful and yet devastating cooperative adaptations. There is much to admire about human groupishness, insofar as it gives rise to acts of altruism, loyalty, camaraderie, heroism, and love. But these qualities typically extend only to the ingroup (e.g. family, tribe, religion, ethnicity, or nation). Beyond the group, caution and suspicion reign, and when provoked by the members of rival coalitions, there can be a seemingly insatiable appetite for organized violence. Social cohesion whets the appetite for such conflict. Without cohesive groups, we would not wage wars, commit genocides, or conquer other people's lands.

One of the most potent causes of ingroup cohesion and outgroup hostility is participation in collective ritual. The modes theory, as we saw in the last chapter, proposes that different kinds of rituals contribute to group bonding in different ways, and to different degrees. Imagistic practices produce especially intense social cohesion (Whitehouse, 1995, 2000, 2004; Martin & Pachis, 2009). And one of the hallmark features of the imagistic mode is that its rituals trigger transformative experiences through the enactment of traumatic ordeals, searing themselves into the memories of participants and triggering a process of exegetical reflection that last for years, sometimes for a whole lifetime.

But why should psychological processes like memory and reflection lead to such strong forms of loyalty and self-sacrifice? In this chapter, I set out to answer that question, drawing on evidence from a wide range of psychological studies with special populations, ranging from martial arts groups to armed insurgents and from football fans to university fraternities and sororities. As I will explain, imagistic rituals increase cohesion *within groups* but, under certain circumstances, they can also intensify feelings of hostility and intolerance *between groups*. Two factors appear to play a crucial mediating role in this process. One is memory: one-off traumatic experiences, especially ones that are surprising and consequential for participants, are remembered over longer time periods (and with greater vividness) than less arousing events. Such recollections have a canonical structure, sometimes referred to as 'flashbulb memories' (Brown & Kulik, 1977; Whitehouse, 1992; Conway, 1995), specifying not only details of the event itself but what happened afterwards and who else was present. Although psychologists have long realized that memories play an important role in the formation of personal identity, the theory of imagistic practices places the role of autobiographical memory in a dramatically new light, by focusing on the effects of *sharing* such memories with others. By recalling life-changing ritual episodes, shared with other members of the group, we are establishing unique and exclusive bonds. There is little scope for adding to or subtracting from ritual groups whose membership derives from one-off experiences of this sort.

Another factor fuelling imagistic bonds within a group is *interpretive creativity*. Since the procedures entailed in rituals are a matter of stipulation and are not transparently related to overall goals (if indeed those goals are articulated at all), the meanings of the acts present something of a puzzle for participants. In the case of traumatic ritual experiences that continue to be remembered and reflected upon for many years afterwards, questions of symbolism and purpose may become a major focus of attention (Barth, 1987). The sharing of transformative, meaningful, and self-defining events can produce a powerful sense of shared group essence that group psychologists have described as 'identity fusion' (Swann et al., 2012) – a visceral feeling of oneness with other group members, linked to extreme pro-group action. The notion of an imagistic pathway to fusion and self-sacrifice has made it possible to integrate key concepts and measures from group psychology into the modes theory in a way that has stimulated a veritable industry of new empirical research with groups as diverse as revolutionary battalions (Whitehouse et al., 2014), football fans (Newson et al., 2018), Trump supporters (Kapitány et al., 2019), animal lovers (Buhrmester et al., 2018a), martial arts clubs (Kavanagh et al., 2018), victims of atrocities (Buhrmester et al., 2015), expectant mothers (Tasuji et al., 2020), and religious fundamentalists (Yustisia et al., 2020).

This heady cocktail of shared and self-shaping experience, persisting in long-term memories that prompt subsequent reflection and ritual exegesis, serves to bind together small, exclusive communities of participants in imagistic practices. Groups formed in this way display high levels of trust, cooperation, and tolerance towards fellow members. But there is also a darker side to this syndrome, which finds expression in outgroup hostility. Comparative research, both ethnographic and historical, points to widespread and longstanding links between rites of terror and chronic intergroup conflict and warfare (Sosis, Kress, & Boster, 2007). Imagistic rituals take many diverse forms, ranging from hazing practices through to initiatory ordeals such as scarification, whipping, head-biting, evulsion of the fingernails, stinging, burning, and penis bleeding (Whitehouse, 1996a). They are found in many of the world's most bellicose tribes and in modern armies (Trota & Johnson, 2004). There is evidence that they were performed at least as long ago as the Upper Palaeolithic, and it is quite possible they date back much earlier still, helping to explain not only the success of human groups competing for resources but perhaps also why the spread of modern humans into new territories was so often accompanied by violent conquest and the extermination of rival species (Whitehouse, 2004; Whitehouse et al., 2017).

Rites of Terror and Group Bonding

It has long been recognized that collective rituals are a potent source of cohesion in social groups and that the more arduous the rituals in question the more tightly they bond participants (Durkheim, 1912; Irons, 2001; Henrich, 2009; Konvalinka et al., 2011; Olivola & Shafir, 2013; Xygalatas et al., 2013). The pain and fear evinced by some collective rituals documented by anthropologists are so extreme that I have previously described them as 'rites of terror' (Whitehouse, 1996a). Procedures entailed in such rituals bear comparison with techniques of torture, and pain is often inflicted deliberately so as to maximize the traumatic impact. In addition to direct assault, such rituals commonly inflict suffering by depriving participants of rest, sleep, food, warmth, light, social contact, and other basic needs, often for extended periods (Barth, 1987; Chinnery & Beaver, 1915; Iteanu, 1990; Poole, 1982).

Although social scientists have long noted that traumatic ritual ordeals promote intense social cohesion, efforts to tease apart the psychological mechanisms involved only really took off in the 1950s; much of this early work inspired by Leon Festinger's theory of 'cognitive dissonance' (1956). For example, Aronson and Mills (1959) proposed that the endurance of painful initiations into the group is inconsistent with disliking the group, and consequently, initiates are highly motivated to believe that the group they have paid such a high price to join is worthy of their loyalty and affection. Rituals in general, of course, *incur costs* (e.g. time, labour, and psychological endurance) often with the promise of only poorly defined or indeterminate rewards, and in some cases, with no obvious payoff at all. In the case of initiations, the costs are typically extreme, for instance, involving physical or psychological tortures, with attendant risks of lifelong injuries or even death. In a now classic application of Festinger's theory, Aronson and Mills (1959) demonstrated that the more severe the requirement for entry into an artificially created group, the greater would be the participants' liking for other group members. Their explanation for this was that our feelings towards the groups we join will never be wholly positive, and the experience of *disliking* aspects of the group will be *dissonant* with the experience of having paid a price to join; this dissonance could be resolved by downplaying the costs of entry, but the greater the severity of initiations into the group, the less sustainable that strategy will become. Under these circumstances, dissonance reduction will focus instead on generating more positive evaluations of the group.

Others have suggested that participation in painful rituals serves as a costly signal of commitment to the group, thereby promoting trust and prosociality among group members (e.g. Bulbulia, 2004; Sosis, 2003). A limitation of both dissonance and costly signalling explanations of rites of terror, however, is that they assume that participation is voluntary. Although that may be true in some cases, very often it is not. Failure to submit to the ritual tortures often carries heavy penalties—ranging from social exclusion to execution (Cimino, 2011). Moreover, these theories assume that traumatic ritual ordeals are used to mark entry into a group. But this is not necessarily the case—such rituals may be performed for a wide range of stated purposes that have little or nothing to do with initiation into, or the conferment of membership of, a group (Whitehouse, 1996a; Atkinson & Whitehouse, 2011).

An addition to these previous theories is provided by the theory of imagistic bonding. This theory has the advantage of being applicable to all intensely dysphoric (e.g. painful or frightening) rituals and not only voluntary initiations. The core idea is that dysphoric rituals produce social cohesion through the sharing of exceptionally thought-provoking and life-shaping experiences, encoded in episodic memory (Whitehouse, 1992, 1995). Because these kinds of memories specify who else was present at the time, the groups they produce have rigid boundaries—members cannot be added if they are not part of the recalled episode nor can anyone who participated be excised from memory. As such, imagistic practices are associated with relatively small, face-to-face groups. In the next section I describe how, building explicitly on the research above, many of the variables mediating the relationship between shared dysphoria and group bonding have been disambiguated experimentally. This suggests that, even if we cannot rule out such explanations as cognitive dissonance and costly signalling, variables associated with the imagistic mode must also be considered as strong predictors of group cohesion, cooperation, and self-sacrifice.

Dysphoric Ritual and the Search for Meaning

In the last chapter, I described how emotionally intense splinter-group rituals in the Kivung inspired the notion of an imagistic mode of religiosity (Whitehouse, 1995), which subsequent cross-cultural and historical research suggests may be a globally recurrent feature of ritual group bonding (Whitehouse, 2000, 2004). Central to the theory of imagistic practices is the idea that dysphoric rituals are encoded as vivid and enduring memories (Whitehouse, 1992), in turn prompting considerable interpretive effort and meaning making (Barth, 1987), a process that has also been referred to as 'spontaneous exegetical reflection' (Whitehouse, 2001a; Xygalatas, 2007). In parallel ways, psychological research also pointed to the possibility that memories for traumatic experiences impact the development of personal identity (Conway, 1995; Singer & Salovey, 1993), and much empirical research has attempted to explore the mechanisms linking memory of and reflection on life-changing experiences to autobiographical narratives and the construction of the personal self (e.g. Conway et al., 2005; Cili & Stopa, 2014; Dunlop & Walker, 2013; McAdams & McLean, 2013; King & Raspin, 2004; Lilgendahl & McAdams, 2011). One of the central aims of the present chapter is to show how enduring episodic memories and the meaning and significance invested in them can contribute to processes of group alignment, cohesion, and cooperation. But the first step is to understand how emotionally intense rituals generate meaning. In this section, I review some early experimental evidence on this topic.

Our efforts to investigate the relationship between ritual, emotion, and meaning making began with the creation of artificial rituals. In one early study, for example, we had participants undergo a complex series of actions that they were told was a reconstruction of an Amazonian fertility rite (Richert, Whitehouse, & Stewart, 2005). According to our cover story, anthropologists were seeking to puzzle together the long-forgotten meanings of the acts and artefacts involved in the ancient rite and were eager to learn from the impressions and interpretations of participants in the reconstruction. The ritual involved a variety of causally opaque actions such as marching in line behind the experimenter shaking a rattle, 'washing' hands in a pile of rotting leaves, or planting sticks described as 'spears' into the earth. As part of the ritual sequence, participants were invited to place their hands in a hole in the ground while a drum played in the background. In this between-subjects design, the actions were varied such that participants in the high-arousal condition wore blindfolds when reaching into the hole. This made the experience considerably more frightening, as evidenced by self-reports of fear and apprehension gathered immediately afterwards. All participants were asked to describe their ideas about the meaning of the ritual around ten weeks later, allowing time for reflection in the intervening period. The meanings reported were scored according to exegetical volume (the number of ritual actions attributed a distinct meaning) and analogical specificity (complete source-target pairings being accorded higher scores than incomplete ones). After analyzing the data, we found that those experiencing the ritual as more frightening scored significantly higher on the meaning-making measures, supporting our hypothesis that dysphoric intensity is linked to 'spontaneous exegetical reflection' (hereafter 'SER') on ritual actions.

A limitation of the above study was that our emotion measures were based exclusively on self-report, the reliability of which was uncertain. For example, it was quite possible those in the high-arousal condition exaggerated the affective intensity of the experience or that those in the low-arousal condition underestimated it. To ensure that we had achieved a genuine polarization in arousal levels between the two conditions we sought a way of using more objective physiological measures, in addition to self-report. Eventually, we settled on a design that allowed us to measure changes in pulse and galvanic skin response (GSR). Because the GSR equipment was large and heavy and required access to power sources, we abandoned the woodland setting used in the initial studies and instead used a special facility at Queen's University Belfast, known as the Sonic Arts Research Centre. This was a musical performance space that allowed us to manipulate arousal levels by adjusting the acoustic environment in various ways, bombarding participants with sound from unexpected directions, including from under their feet, while also enabling us to use lighting effects and other props that increased the sense of drama and excitement. The ritual procedures themselves had to be carried out by participants while seated, partly because of the need to wire them up to static equipment. Despite the restrictions on movement, participants had little difficulty enacting the ritual actions according to the instructions projected onto a screen. In the low-arousal condition, they performed exactly the same procedures but under normal lighting conditions with music played at low level from a single source. The results of this second experiment confirmed by more objective measures that we were able to achieve a polarization of emotional reactions, and, like the study conducted in woodland using only self-report, the second experiment also showed that participants experiencing a stronger emotional reaction to the ritual generated more elaborate SER (see above), showing also greater depth and volume of exegetical reflection on the meaning of the ritual actions (Richert, Whitehouse, & Stewart, 2005).

One of the key questions arising from this line of research was whether rituals had to be *dysphoric* in order to maximize SER. If so, it might explain why initiations, hazing rituals, and other imagistic practices are so often painful or frightening rather than merely pleasurable or joyful. Initial efforts to explore these issues used game playing as a proxy for religious ritual. For example, in one study we explored the differential effects of euphoric and dysphoric mood on expertise and analogical reasoning as a key aspect of SER (Russell, Gobet, & Whitehouse, 2014). Previous research had shown that euphoria induces thinking on a broader canvas, whereas dysphoria induces narrower and more details-focused thinking. So, we devised experiments to explore how novices and experts performed on analogical thinking tasks relating to a ritualistic task after being primed with videos designed to trigger either euphoric or dysphoric mood. Those assigned to the euphoric condition watched a short comic performance on video, and those assigned to the dysphoric condition watched a distressing piece of video depicting the effects of nuclear war. Use of an affect grid afterwards confirmed that these videos had the intended effect on mood and thus served as an appropriate priming method. Participants were then required to perform the 'Tower of Hanoi' (TOH) task, a ritual-like procedure based on a story about a temple (reputedly in Vietnam) wherein the priests were said to move disks between pegs according to a divinely inspired algorithm. Afterwards, they were required to complete the Bear God (BG) task, which had the same rules as the TOH but very different surface features. Participants were not told that the BG tasks had the same rules, and so the question was whether their mood (induced by the videos) would affect their ability to reason analogically, connecting the hidden rules of the TOH 'ritual' to the BG 'ritual'. What we found was that, for those who were adept at performing the TOH task (our 'ritual experts'), dysphoric but not euphoric mood enhanced analogical reasoning, constituting further evidence that dysphoric rituals can increase levels of SER.

All these early findings supported the impression that unpleasant ritual ordeals have a more enduring impact on memory and subsequent exegetical reflection, suggesting that they contribute to the construction of our life histories and associated meaning making and thus might help to shape our personal identities. To the extent that these imagistic experiences are shared with others, particularly those individuals we recall being present during a ritual event, we create bonds with a group. Such groups would be expected to have tightly circumscribed boundaries because they are rooted in episodic memories for particular performances in which coparticipants feature prominently. It is impossible to add participants subsequently who are not present in one's recollections of the event, or to exclude anybody you recall having taken part. For this reason, even the earliest formulations of the modes theory proposed that, although imagistic practices produce very intense social cohesion among coparticipants, they are hard to spread to wider populations and therefore tend to be restricted to local, face-to-face groups (Whitehouse, 1995, 2000, 2004).

When the theory of imagistic rituals was initially proposed it prompted quite lively debate about why only some rituals and not others involved such high levels of sensory pageantry and emotion (McCauley, 2001; McCauley & Lawson, 2002; Whitehouse, 2004). But it rapidly became clear that many of the questions raised in these discussions hinged on issues that could only be adequately addressed through further empirical research (Barrett, 2004). This would require more relevant measures of group cohesion, as well as more sophisticated ways of conceptualizing and measuring key independent variables like ritual frequency and moderating mediators like emotion, exegetical reflection, and memory (Whitehouse, 2018a). During the 1990s, when these early debates were taking place, group psychology was still dominated by social identity theory, which emphasized alignment with group categories rather than relational networks and conceptualized social and personal identities as mutually repelling poles, such that making one more salient made the other less so (Tajfel & Turner, 1979). None of these characteristics seemed to capture the nature of group bonding through imagistic rituals where group identities seemed closely entwined with personal experience and agency. But just a decade or so later, a new construct was developed by group psychologists, dubbed 'identity fusion' (Swann et al., 2009; Swann et al., 2012). The fusion measure seemed to capture much better than social identity theory the nature and intensity of social cohesion observed in imagistic group rituals.

When Personal and Group Identities Fuse

Identity fusion—a visceral feeling of oneness with a group (Swann et al., 2009)—entails an identity configuration such that one's social identity is considered an essential aspect of one's personal self. As such, strongly fused persons report intense family-like connections to other group members, high levels of personal agency, and feelings of invulnerability in their group. In turn, strongly fused individuals exhibit an extreme propensity to make personal sacrifices for their group, for example, by expressing willingness to give blood to help victims of terrorism (Buhrmester et al., 2015) or by fighting on the frontlines in combat (Whitehouse et al., 2014).

For fused persons, any serious attack on the group is taken personally, triggering a willingness to fight and die in the group's defence (Swann et al., 2009, 2012). Although fusion may originally have been a cognitive adaptation for small-group living (Whitehouse et al., 2017), it has also been exploited and refined by religious and military traditions over the ages, in the form of a great diversity of imagistic rituals (Whitehouse & Lanman, 2014). Fusion has also been linked to extreme self-sacrifice in civil war armed groups (Whitehouse et al., 2014) and terrorist organizations engaging in suicide attacks (Whitehouse, 2018a). For those of us engaged in fusion research, it soon became clear that understanding the cognitive and evolutionary dynamics driving these forms of ingroup cooperation and outgroup hostility constituted an urgent challenge not only for scientists but also for policymakers concerned with prevention and resolution of intergroup conflict (see Chapter 6).

Fusion was initially measured using a pictorial scale (Figure 3.1) in which a small circle represented the personal self and a large circle represented the group. This was a dichotomous measure: only those choosing 'E' on the pictorial scale were 'fused', whereas those choosing options 'A–D' were not. Subsequently, a verbal scale was developed, enabling researchers to talk about degrees of fusion (e.g. 'high-' or 'low-fused' individuals) (Figure 3.2). Then, some years later a Dynamic Identity Fusion Index was developed, allowing respondents to drag the

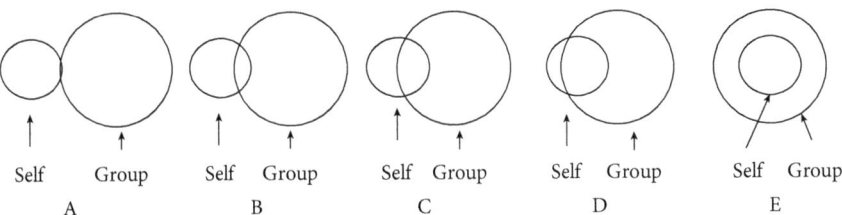

Figure 3.1 *Pictorial fusion measure*
(Source: Swann et al., 2009 based on 'Inclusion of Other in Self' (IOS) scale, e.g. Aron, Aron, & Smollan, 1992)

I am one with my country
I feel immersed in my country
I have a deep emotional bond with my country
My country is me
I'll do for my country more than any of the other group members would do.
I am strong because of my country
I make my country strong

Figure 3.2 *The verbal measure of fusion*
(Source: Gómez et al., 2011)

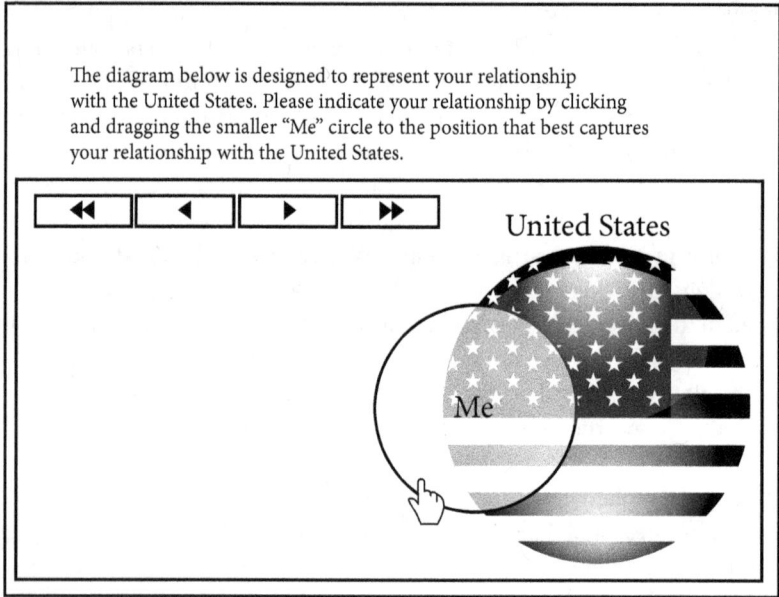

Figure 3.3 *Dynamic Identity Fusion Index*
(Source: Jiménez et al., 2015)

small circle (representing self) over the large circle (group fusion target), thus providing a continuous measure of fusion levels particularly suited to online data collection across a range of language groups (Figure 3.3).

Fusion differs from *identification* with a group category (Tajfel & Turner, 1979). In contrast to identity fusion, identification constitutes a depersonalized form of group alignment such that making group identity salient makes personal identity less accessible (and vice versa—thinking about one's personal identity—makes group identities less accessible). Although identification produces ingroup favouritism and outgroup derogation, numerous studies indicate that identity fusion is a stronger predictor of personal sacrifice for the group (Swann et al., 2009; Whitehouse, 2018a). Whereas fusion motivates extreme pro-group behaviour by tapping into personal agency (Swann et al., 2014), identification may be expected to motivate self-sacrifice only to the extent that such behaviour is endorsed by the group *and* that any self-preservation motives that conflict with group values or interests can be held at bay.

The Imagistic Pathway to Fusion

Efforts to explain the process of fusing with a group have been based upon a synthesis of research on imagistic rituals in natural settings and experimental approaches in social psychology (Whitehouse, 2018a; Reese & Whitehouse, 2021). As discussed above, imagistic rituals are thought to bind group members together by creating salient and enduring memories of shared experience. This is because imagistic experiences are not only transformative in shaping the personal self but—insofar as these experiences are shared with others—they also define the group. This would explain why personal and group identities, having both been forged by ordeals that are simultaneously life-changing for the person and defining for the group, are activated together in fused individuals. This imagistic pathway to fusion posits a causal chain from emotionally intense experiences to vivid and enduring memory to reflection on those experiences to the formation of the essential autobiographical self to feelings of shared group essence and ultimately to identity fusion and self-sacrifice.

In addition to this 'shared experiences pathway' to fusion, people may also be fused based on the perception of shared biology or 'phenotypic matching'. To the extent that personal identities are not only constructed out of transformative past experiences but also rooted in essentialized physical qualities, commonly deployed also in folk notions of kinship (e.g. based on shared blood, bones, genes, *mana*, or other essentialized qualities thought to be inherited within families), fusion is often expressed in the language of family and kinship (Swann et al., 2014; Whitehouse & Lanman, 2014). The two pathways to fusion, based on shared experience and shared biology, respectively, are depicted in Figure 3.4.

To explore both pathways to fusion in a single study group, we designed a series of experiments to disambiguate the effects on fusion of shared biology versus shared life experiences (Whitehouse et al., 2017). In the first study, we assigned 198 participants to three priming conditions in which they wrote about either a self-shaping experience, a set of traits transmitted genetically, or the changing seasons (as control). They were then asked to imagine meeting somebody who had either shared their transformative life event, had turned out to be a long-lost sibling, or was a mere stranger (control). Those in the shared experience and shared biology conditions reported higher levels of fusion with the imaginary person, although, interestingly, the effects were notably stronger for shared experience. We also designed a study with a large sample of twins to explore the

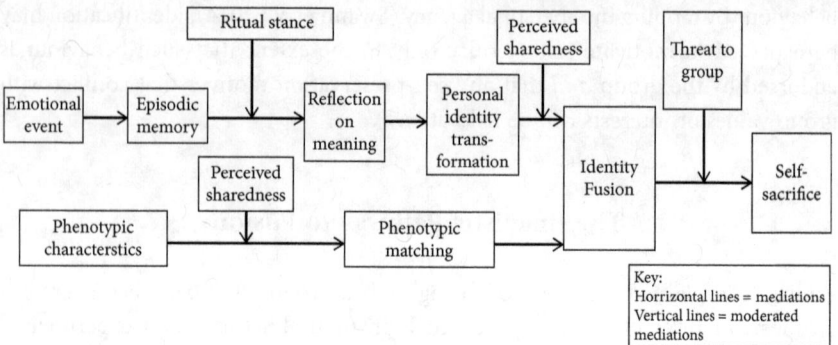

Figure 3.4 *Pathways to fusion and self-sacrifice*
(adapted from Whitehouse, 2018a)

impact of shared genes versus shared experience on levels of fusion with a sibling (Whitehouse et al., 2017). In this study, we asked 260 monozygotic and 246 dizygotic twins to describe shared transformative experiences, and we measured levels of fusion with their twin. We found that both shared biology (as measured by zygosity) and shared experience predicted fusion levels independently.

Given that the sharing of either self-defining experiences or biological traits with others can lead to fusion, it is not surprising to find that individuals commonly describe their bonds with the group using the language of kinship and familial relatedness. Moreover, both fusion and familial ties predict similar forms of commitment to the group. Indeed, a survey covering eleven countries from six continents revealed that 86.1 per cent of the 2,438 respondents expressed willingness to die for their families before any other group (Swann et al., 2014). The same survey also showed that priming feelings of shared biology among people already fused with their countries made them more willing to make extreme sacrifices for their fellow countrymen. Mediation analyses showed also that fusion impacted willingness to fight and die for country via feelings of kinship. These conclusions are supported by studies of groups actually (as opposed to hypothetically) experiencing an external threat. For example, in the wake of the 2013 Boston Marathon bombings, the willingness of locals fused with America to give blood or money to help the victims was fully mediated by feelings of psychological kinship with fellow countrymen, expressed by endorsing statements like 'members of my country are like family to me' (Buhrmester et al., 2015). And finally, studies with twins have shown that the relationship between shared genes and self-sacrificial behaviour is mediated by fusion (Vázquez et al., 2017a).

In order to unpick the causal pathway from shared autobiographical memory to fusion, it has been necessary to work closely with populations that perform emotionally intense, life-changing rituals. Although imagistic practices were once widespread in human societies, they are nowadays often confined to populations that are hard to infiltrate, such as military elites, terrorist cells, street gangs, or small-scale traditional societies using languages that few university researchers are able to speak. With the evolution of large-scale hierarchical societies, in which submission to centralized authorities and the rule of law should supersede allegiances to village and tribe, imagistic rituals have typically been outlawed or allowed to flourish only in institutions closely aligned with the ruling group. While traditions of hazing may be tolerated or even encouraged in the upper echelons of the military or in prestigious public schools and universities, the more emotionally intense rituals of ordinary folk have been quite systematically suppressed historically arguably because of the potential threat that localized cohesion presents to centralized authority. As the world's tribal societies have progressively come under the control of colonial and postcolonial state apparatus, or, in less stable countries, have actually formed the factions responsible for prosecuting civil wars, gaining access to hazing rituals for would-be researchers has become increasingly difficult and dangerous.

Nevertheless, there are some environments within easy reach of academic researchers where imagistic practices continue to persist in relatively accessible venues. Perhaps the most easily reachable of all are those hiding in open view within universities themselves, namely the hazing practices of college fraternities and sororities. In one study, we asked 146 members of American college fraternities and sororities about their experience of hazing or other initiatory ordeals (Whitehouse et al., 2017). We found that the more self-defining such ritual experiences were to the participants' personal identities, the higher their reported levels of identity fusion with their fraternity or sorority, and the more willing they were to sacrifice themselves for the sake of their group. Nevertheless, collecting data from participants in these kinds of rituals is fraught with difficulty, given that hazing is officially proscribed by university authorities and usually shrouded in secrecy. In part, this is due to the number of recorded cases in which participants have tragically died as a direct result of hazing practices. Less controversial study populations that are also often found in the vicinity of university campuses are the passionate fans of team sports. For example, our extensive research with football supporters in Brazil, the UK, Australia, and Indonesia has shown that intensely emotional shared experiences among fans of both league and national teams have all the hallmark features of the imagistic mode (including e.g. vivid episodic recall, meaningfulness, transformativeness, and feelings of shared essence) that predict high fusion scores and willingness to makes sacrifices for club or country (Newson et al., 2016; Newson et al., 2018; Newson, Buhrmester, & Whitehouse, 2021; Whitehouse et al., 2017; Buhrmester, Newson et al., 2018).

Another source of relatively accessible groups engaging in imagistic rituals are martial arts experts. For example, we used online advertisements to conduct a survey of 564 Brazilian Jiu-Jitsu (BJJ) practitioners who had undergone grading rituals to progress through the system of 'belts'. Many participants in our study had undergone extremely painful belt-whipping gauntlets as part of their promotions through the grades. We found that the emotional intensity of the grading rituals not only predicted fusion with other BJJ club members but also stated willingness to risk one's life fighting to protect the club, as well as to make various other sacrifices, such as giving up time or donating money (Whitehouse et al., 2017). Interestingly, however, it was not the dysphoric intensity of the rituals that produced these effects, as studies with other ritual communities had found, but rather the *euphoric* intensity, perhaps resulting from surmounting the whipping ordeals, that predicted elevated fusion levels. This suggests that in at least some imagistic rituals, it may not be the pain or fear that is driving subsequent memory, reflection, and meaning making but the positive feelings associated with overcoming adversity (Kavanagh et al., 2018).

Painful rituals conducted by university fraternities or sororities and martial arts groups, imposed as an entry requirement for new members, strikingly resemble the initiations of more ancient ancestral populations or small-scale indigenous groups in the rainforests of Amazonia and Melanesia or the Australian Outback. The basic logic of initiatory ordeals would probably register universal recognition in human societies, and even in those where such practices are not officially endorsed, they are commonly thought to have occurred in the past or to persist in secret or illegal organizations. As such, initiation rites may be candidates for a universal class of rituals. Nevertheless, the specific types of groups into which modern-day novices are initiated—such as undergraduate brotherhoods and sports clubs—are neither universal nor ancient. If seeking examples of human experience that lead naturally to shared group identities in broadly similar ways worldwide and throughout the human past, it makes sense to focus on those rooted in panhuman biological processes, such as birth, maturation, reproduction, and death. These shared experiences punctuating human life provide the most widely recognized rationales for rites of passage.

From the perspective of the imagistic pathway to fusion theory, however, birth and death present problematic cases insofar as neither of these generate socially salient memories. Childhood amnesia ensures that, unlike many other distressing experiences that people may share in the course of their lives, nobody remembers the ordeal of being born or circumcised in infancy. In the case of death, of course, the reason we cannot remember the experience of it is that it is, by definition, too late—all brain functions having ceased after the ordeal has concluded. On the other hand, there are some notably impactful life crisis events rooted in panhuman physiological processes that occur during phases of life when autobiographical memories can be richly encoded and subsequently recalled. One such event is a girl's first menses (menarche), which has been shown to produce enduring flashbulb memories in some cases. In one study, for example, a sample of ninety-nine women completed a 'menstrual distress questionnaire' in which they were asked how well prepared they had been in advance of the experience of menarche (Pillemer et al., 1987). This study found that the less well prepared and thus the more distressing the experience had been, the richer and more flashbulb-like were the women's subsequent recollections of the menarche. This is an instructive example of an experience common to women in all societies, worldwide and throughout the human past, potentially capable of motivating a feeling of sisterhood based on the imagistic pathway to fusion. Nevertheless, menarche is certainly not the most traumatic shared experience that women typically undergo in the course of their reproductive lives. Arguably an even stronger candidate for an imagistic experience rooted in biological universals would be that of childbirth and especially the first experience of delivering a baby. This is due to the combination of uniqueness, novelty, and high levels of emotional intensity associated with giving birth for the first time.

To explore this topic in some depth, we sampled 164 first-time mothers in America, 89 of whom were pregnant at the time of the study and 75 of whom had already given birth within the previous six months (Tasuji et al., 2020). Measures of fusion with other mothers were collected from all participants, and as predicted, those who had already been through the emotionally impactful and personally transformative process of childbirth were more fused with other mothers than those who had yet to undergo the experience. To explore whether this increase in fusion was indeed due to the perception of shared experience, as the modes theory proposes, we asked postpartum mothers to evaluate how painful their experience of childbirth had been and found that they were more fused with other mothers who had experienced similar levels of dysphoria (in line with our shared dysphoria pathway to fusion model). As discussed in some detail above, the modes theory proposes that the impact of imagistic events on group bonding works in part by transforming our personal identities in an enduring fashion, not only by searing unforgettable experiences into autobiographical memory but also by prompting patterns of subsequent reflection that shape our sense of who we are as persons and as members of groups. One of the more interesting outcomes of this study was that it showed how the relationship between emotionally intense shared experiences and identity fusion was indeed moderated in complex ways by subsequent rumination, reflection, and posttraumatic growth in first-time mothers.

Thus, a recurrent thread running through our studies linking emotionally intense events to fusion is the extent to which shared experiences are felt to be 'transformative' and self-defining. And this in turn is linked to how much people have reflected on their experiences and invested them with meaning—whether we are talking about Vietnam War veterans reflecting on their experiences of front-line combat (Whitehouse et al., 2017) or football fans reflecting on why they lost a crucial game against a rival club (Newson et al., 2016). For many, the imagistic pathway to fusion results not so much from a deliberately contrived ritual event, such as an initiation or hazing experience, or even from predictable events rooted in our biology, but from efforts to pull together as a community in the face of an unexpected ordeal or threat. An example of this is a series of studies we conducted with the victims of terrorist attacks in Northern Ireland (over many years of sectarian violence) and in Boston (following the marathon bombing in 2013) (Jong et al., 2015). In such cases we found that fusion with one's community (whether Irish Republicans, Unionists, or fellow Bostonians) was mediated by reflection on shared sufferings. Moreover, these findings were supported by experimental and not just correlational evidence.

Studies of the effects of shared suffering in very large groups have also helped us better understand how fusion resulting from imagistic experiences can influence political and religious alignments on a national or international scale. The process of fusing through shared experiences does not appear to be confined only to small, relational groups but is also capable of fuelling extended fusion among much larger ones, such as worldwide religious organizations, social movements, and pressure groups. I will turn to this topic more fully in Chapter 4, but for now, consider the following examples of extended fusion from Indonesia and America.

In Indonesia, where most people identify as Sunni Muslims, support for more extreme expressions of Islamist ideology was on the rise during the opening decades of the twenty-first century. In collaboration with researchers based in Jakarta, we designed a study with a broad cross-section of 1,320 Muslims, recruited from three sectors of the population (Kavanagh et al., 2020). The first comprised 207 members of the Prosperity and Justice Party (PKS), espousing a fundamentalist ideology with links to transnational Islamist movements such as the Muslim Brotherhood originating in Egypt. The second comprised 618 members of *Nahdlatul Ulama* (NU)—a large and inclusive religious organization reflecting more moderate Muslim teachings and practices. Our third sample comprised 495 members of the population at large in Jakarta who were not affiliated to either PKS or NU. A primary aim of our study was to explore the relationship between shared experience and extended fusion in these Indonesian samples.

To examine the effects on fusion of shared life-shaping experiences, participants were asked to write about events in their lives that were not only personally transformative but also defining for the larger-scale groups they primarily aligned with, such as 'all other Muslims in Indonesia'. We included measures of how 'transformative' those experiences had been by asking participants to rate on a scale the extent to which the events they described had impacted their identities, as well as measures of how much those experiences were felt to be shared with others. The results confirmed our prediction that both transformativeness and sharedness generate identity fusion. At the same time, however, this research encouraged us to think about the potentially complicating role of popular narratives (e.g. media coverage and ideological dissemination) in influencing the effects of major events on large-scale collective identities. According to our theoretical framework, events that are personally transformative can lead to fusion if they are evidently also shared with other group members. But many group-defining events on a national or international scale are shared vicariously, for example, through propaganda or news reports. To the extent that newsworthy events can serve as markers of group identity, they often do so in ways that are socially transmitted (our hypothesized pathway to identification) rather than personally experienced and internally processed (our hypothesized pathway to fusion). In theory, the kinds of dramatic events that end up being reported in the media could lead to both identification and extended fusion but figuring out how both come about and with what consequences is not a simple matter.

The process of reflecting on the meaning of major events that are also widely discussed and analysed in public can seem rather different from events that are confined to small relational groups, such as a military unit, whose members may talk very little about the more intense experiences they have shared together. The lines between socially learned normative beliefs and narrative conventions, on the one hand, and personally transformative memories and internal reflections on the other, can be somewhat fuzzy. For example, the 2017 inauguration ritual for President Trump was an emotionally distressing event for many US Democrats but did that make it an 'imagistic' ritual capable of generating extended fusion among those opposed to Trump's values and style of leadership? To address that question, my colleagues and I carried out a longitudinal study in a sample of 928 Americans (describing themselves, in roughly equal proportions, as Republicans, Democrats, or neither) to examine the effects of the Trump inauguration on variables hypothesized to drive identity fusion, such as emotional intensity, reflection on the event, and perceived transformativeness (Kapitány et al., 2019). In contrast with the patterns commonly observed in other studies of the effects of emotionally intense experiences on fusion, the Trump inauguration ritual did not appear to have any measurable impact on fusion among his supporters (for whom it was of course a predominantly euphoric event). But, perhaps even more remarkably, the shared dysphoria induced by the ritual among Clinton supporters did not lead to an increase in fusion (as the shared dysphoria pathway to fusion model would predict) but the opposite—a decrease in levels of fusion. For US Democrats, Trump's inauguration may have been a poor candidate for an imagistic ritual in the first place, given that it served primarily to celebrate an outgroup victory than to enact a dysphoric rite of passage for ingroup members to undergo together. But to explain specifically the *negative* effects of the event on fusion levels among Clinton supporters, it may be useful to consider factors that could have damaged feelings of alignment with the failed ingroup campaign, particularly the effects of media reporting and other forms of narrative transmission that portrayed the ingroup as 'losers' and encouraged behaviours aimed at cutting off reflected failure or 'CORFing' (Cialdini, 1976; Snyder, Lassegard, &

Ford, 1986), a form of distancing from an ingroup that may be more closely associated with identification than fusion (Haslam et al., 2009). Once again, this points to the potentially complex relationships between extended fusion and identification when experiences are shared, often vicariously through the media, in large-scale groups.

Some evidence for the imagistic pathway to fusion in large-scale groups comes from studies suggesting that reflecting on vicariously shared episodic memories can prompt changes in the essential autobiographical self over time, in turn giving rise to trait fusion with other members of the group who are presumed to have undergone similar experiences. A good example of this is a longitudinal study we carried out with donors to big cat conservation projects following the killing of a lion nicknamed 'Cecil' in 2015 by an American trophy hunter using a longbow at Hwange National Park in Matabeleland North, Zimbabwe (Buhrmester et al., 2018a). When the news of Cecil's killing went viral in the world's media outlets, tens of thousands of enraged members of the public pledged donations to support WildCRU, the Oxford-based research and conservation unit studying Cecil at the time. In collaboration with WildCRU staff, we ran surveys over six months to explore how people's reflections on the incident impacted their personal identities and their fusion not only with Cecil but with those committed to protecting lions in the wild. An important feature of this study was not only that it was able to shed light on how processes of reflection feed into feelings of shared essence, thought to underly fusion, but it revealed the extent to which feeling that one has shared personally transformative experiences with others, perhaps with people faraway or even with members of an entirely different species, can motivate increased levels of fusion and willingness to engage in prosocial action, for example, in the form of monetary donations. In short, this study demonstrated the remarkable extent to which feelings of fusion can be stretched beyond a local, relational group.

In general, fusion is also a highly durable form of group alignment. Once fused, individuals typically remain fused for life unless there are powerful reasons to doubt the feelings of shared essence on which the fusion is based. Studies with highly committed football supporters have shown that enduring memories of emotionally charged experiences of winning and losing crucial games is a better predictor of lifelong loyalty than alternative explanations, for instance, based on cognitive dissonance theory that would seek to explain ongoing commitment simply as a reflection of time previously invested in support for the club (Newson et al., 2016). Since fusion, once established, tends to last for such a long time, it is normally measured as a psychological 'trait' rather than a transitory 'state' (Swann et al., 2012; Vázquez, Gómez, and Swann, 2017). Nevertheless, it should be noted that some rituals are capable of elevating fusion among participants temporarily, for example, by reminding them of past imagistic experiences (e.g. initiations, defeats on the sports field or battle ground) or genealogical links (e.g. shared ancestry, kinship). One class of such rituals includes commemorations and memorials. Most commonly, these are designed to focus attention on shared sufferings such as the loss of loved ones during a war, terrorist attack, or natural disaster. As such they prime memories for events that were both self-shaping and group-defining, diagnostic elements of the imagistic pathway to fusion.

There are also ritual actions that fleetingly blur the boundary between personal and group identities creating 'state fusion'—that is, sensations of self and group become fused as one but only while the ritual is taking place. The most common way in which this is achieved is through social synchrony: chanting, singing, marching, swaying, or dancing in time with other group members (Reddish et al., 2013; Rennung & Göritz, 2016; Jackson et al., 2018). It is noteworthy that synchronous movement is an extremely widespread feature of collective rituals and is particularly prominent in military ceremonies ranging from the drilling and parading of modern armies to the traditional *haka* of Māori warriors and sports teams, such as New Zealand's All Blacks. This method of generating group cohesion is not strictly speaking 'imagistic', however. As noted above, its effects are confined to the moment of performance, and the illusion of oneness evaporates rapidly once the ritual is over (which may help to explain why military drilling and parading procedures are repeated over and over, even if the instrumental benefits of this repetition are unclear). Also, there is some evidence that the effects of social synchrony on prosocial action are not restricted to coparticipants but may be extended more or less indefinitely to 'others', whether or not they are sharing one's experience (Reddish et al., 2016). As such, rituals emphasizing social synchrony may help to motivate and perpetuate large-scale, routinized traditions operating in the doctrinal mode, rather than being necessarily confined to small-scale groups or imagistic cults.

Social Consequences of the Imagistic Pathway to Fusion

In studies exploring the social consequences of fusion, including those mentioned above, the propensity to engage in self-sacrifice has been measured using willingness to engage in hypothetical pro-group actions that would, if carried out, be costly to self. Among the measures used to investigate prosocial commitment of this kind, the so-called 'fight-and-die' measure capturing willingness to lay down one's life defending the group and its members, has featured prominently (Swann et al., 2010). Nevertheless, it is one thing to say that one would stop at nothing to protect an ingroup and quite another to actually put one's life on the line for the sake of others. To explore fusion's effects on *actual* acts of extreme self-sacrifice, as opposed to mere endorsement of statements expressing willingness to fight and die, we needed to identify a pool of research participants who were indeed risking their lives for each other.

In 2011, the year of the Arab Spring, we went to Libya to run a study with frontline fighters in insurgent groups that had helped overthrow and capture Muammar Gaddafi. There, we interviewed 179 members of revolutionary battalions in Misrata, Libya (Whitehouse, McQuinn et al., 2014). Roughly half the sample were frontline fighters, and the others providers of logistical support to the fighters. All reported near ceiling levels of fusion with their families, with their closest friends in the battalions, and even with the members of other battalions, but not with prorevolutionary Libyans who never joined a battalion and therefore did not fully share the intensely dysphoric experiences of participation in the 2011 uprising. In view of these high levels of fusion with multiple groups, we introduced a forced choice question: if you had to choose only one group as your primary fusion target, which would it be? And here we found a striking difference between those who faced the most traumatic ordeals of the war and those who suffered but not as intensely by working behind the scenes. Frontline fighters were nearly twice as likely (compared with providers of logistical support) to choose fellow revolutionaries over their families. This finding is further supported by studies with conventional armies, exploring the relationship between dysphoric intensity and fusion among military personnel. For example, a survey among 380 Vietnam War veterans in the USA found that intensity of dysphoric combat experience predicted fusion with fellow fighters and that this fusion also mediated willingness to support other veterans in need (Whitehouse et al., 2017).

Although the link between fusion and willingness to fight and die for the group is reasonably well established, it also seems clear that fusion alone is not sufficient to motivate violent forms of self-sacrifice. Although highly fused individuals love the group, they may not be particularly interested in outgroups, unless they pose a threat. Moreover, as we have seen, fusion is very commonly focused on peaceful rather than violent outcomes. Some studies suggest that the relationship between fusion and the fight-and-die response is mediated by outgroup threat (for a summary see Whitehouse, 2018a). When rivalries are salient, fused individuals will do more than those who are merely identified with their groups, stopping at nothing to secure their own group's interests despite the costs (Buhrmester et al., 2018b; Apps et al., 2018).

But even the 'fusion-plus-threat' explanation for violent self-sacrifice may be too simplistic. Research with football supporters in Brazil suggests that violence-condoning norms play an important role in converting high levels of fusion into acts of aggression against rival fans (Newson et al., 2018). In addition, there is some evidence that outgroup anxiety, a construct closely related to perceived outgroup threat, increases prejudice towards rival soccer fans among those who identify strongly with, but not those who are highly fused with, their football club (White et al., 2021). One possible explanation for this finding is that highly fused individuals are primarily concerned with the question of how best to advance the interests of the ingroup whether or not that involves outgroup hostility. Whenever it may seem most advantageous for the ingroup to abstain from violence, even when threatened by rival groups, highly fused individuals might self-regulate and actively prevent other group members from attacking the enemy. In such contexts, high levels of fusion with a group might motivate more Machiavellian but peaceful forms of outgroup derogation, including efforts to maintain orderliness and self-discipline within the group, rather than expressing aggression and hostility as the most effective way of advancing the ingroup's interests. Thus, it is important to realize that even if the imagistic pathway to fusion creates a willingness to do whatever it takes to protect the group and advance its interests, it does not in itself tell us much at all about how members of the group will express that commitment.

Direct evidence for this comes from studies comparing the effects of fusion on various strategies of engagement with outgroups on the part of football fans in Indonesia and Australia, respectively (Newson et al., In Prep). In Indonesia, the most highly fused football supporters we interviewed were actually less inclined to engage in violence than those who scored lower on fusion but were also members of hardcore fan clubs. By contrast, in Australia, fusion and membership of hardcore fan clubs interacted to account for reported acts of violence in the past. These observed differences could well be linked to the relatively high costs of intergroup violence among football fans in Indonesia, where the chances of a fellow supporter being killed in such clashes is much higher than in Australia. Thus, the desire to protect the ingroup may be a more compelling consideration in Indonesia when highly fused fans decide whether to encourage or prevent confrontations with outgroups. Of equal interest is that fact that fused football fans often exhibit strong prosocial tendencies towards all football supporters, including rival fans, so the relationship between love of group and hatred towards rivals is not a simple or straightforward one (Newson, Buhrmester, & Whitehouse, 2021). Above all, high levels of fusion are linked to strong forms of pro-group action but what form that action takes can be highly variable, depending on a host of contextual factors.

Fusion and Self-Sacrifice from an Evolutionary Perspective

The theory and evidence presented here suggest that willingness to make extreme sacrifices for the group stems from the perception that self and other are fused, whether that is due to shared biology or shared personally transformative experiences. Alongside these proximate explanations for extreme prosociality, it is reasonable to ask also whether the fusion mechanism has an evolved function. For fusion to evolve by natural selection the individuals most prone to fuse would need to pass on their genes. For example, taking a fatal spear to protect one's kinsmen might make sense in evolutionary terms if one stood a better chance of passing on one's genes via surviving relatives than by successfully mating oneself.

From a gene's eye point of view, the vehicle for its transmission (the individual organism) should maximize its individual fitness. Kin selection famously presents an exception: for example, self-sacrifice to save fellow group members makes sense if all members of the ingroup are closely related, as in the case in certain social insect colonies. Kin selection has been invoked to explain the empirical observation that people are more likely to endorse self-sacrifice for family than for any other group, as well as the finding that priming family ties increases the effects of fusion on self-sacrifice (Swann et al., 2014). More specifically it has been argued that shared experience, associated with the imagistic pathway to fusion, acts in much the same way as phenotypic cues—serving as a reasonably reliable proxy for genetic relatedness (Whitehouse & Lanman, 2014). This latter argument, as well as the claim that sharing core values or attitudes signals genetic relatedness (Park & Schaller, 2005; Swann et al., 2014), is premised on the assumption that having in common life-shaping experiences and/or core values served as reliable phenotypic markers in ancestral groups composed mainly of closely related individuals (Lieberman et al., 2007). In order for a propensity to sacrifice self to evolve via kin selection, members of ancestral hunter-gatherer bands would have to have been sufficiently closely related genetically. Recent research, however, has cast doubt on this assumption, suggesting that in fact both humans and chimpanzees evolved in groups of relatively distantly related individuals (Langergraber et al., 2011).

An alternative scenario, however, is based on mutualism—I'll die for you if you'll die for me if, as a consequence, we both stand less chance of dying. This could occur where the survival of group members is strongly tied to survival of the group. Such a mechanism would need to be sensitive to environmental cues, however. A group that is not at threat of being annihilated or whose members' fates are not inextricably linked to the survival of the group should not be fused, because the costs of fusion would outweigh the benefits. The logic of mutualism would require that the personal risk of dying for your fellow fighters must weigh favourably against the fitness benefits of having fellow group members looking out for you. That might have been the case, for example, if the commitment of group members to defend each other to the death meant that each individual's chances of survival and reproduction were increased. In conditions of chronic warfare, the fate of group members might be strongly tied to that of the group—such that if the group is defeated, its members will all be slain. Under these circumstances, individuals should be motivated to take extreme risks to defend the group. But such a response should typically occur only when clear individual benefits ensue; if the group is not at risk of annihilation, then its members should not be willing to lay down their lives for each other.

Evolved solutions are often multistranded. It is quite conceivable that a combination of kin selection, mutualism, and any number of additional processes fuelled the human capacity to fuse. Another mechanism could have been the conditioning of cooperation on past experience, a conclusion supported both by mathematical modelling and a wide range of empirical evidence (Whitehouse et al., 2017). Our model was based on a population comprised of a large number of groups facing two distinct kinds of challenges to survival: natural hazards (ranging from avoiding fierce animals, to maintaining fire and providing shelter) and enemy attack (e.g. from neighbouring tribes competing for the same resources). Losing battles not only harmed one's group but contributed to the success of one's enemies. By contrast, being eaten by carnivores was mainly harmful to one's group and less likely to be beneficial to other groups in the vicinity. Group flourishing meant producing offspring, while groups that got overly predated could go extinct. The individuals who made up the various groups in the model were each assigned a pair of genes, one of which made cooperative behaviour possible only after a fitness-enhancing experience and the other only after a fitness-decreasing experience. But only one of these genes could be expressed in any given individual, and all individuals in a group shared the same genetically endowed capacities in this regard. Groups were randomly assigned fitness-increasing and fitness-decreasing experiences, after which their patterns of cooperation were measured. After running many simulations in this way and allowing for the effects of mutation, recombination, and migration, we found that the gene effects on cooperation were stronger in groups that had suffered more fitness-decreasing experiences than those who had undergone more fitness-enhancing ones. Moreover, this pattern was even more pronounced when the fitness-decreasing experiences resulted from enemy attack rather than being mauled by hungry predators. The fusion mechanism, motivating self-sacrifice for the sake for the group, could have evolved in much the same way as in the simulations run on our computers.

Beyond the question of how the fusion mechanism evolved under natural selection, however, there is also the question of whether social institutions, capable of exploiting the fusion mechanism, evolved through cultural group selection. Small-scale societies are typically bound together not only by high levels of social cohesion (Whitehouse, 2004) but also by low levels of relational mobility (Yuki & Schug, 2012; Roos et al., 2014). Limited opportunities for moving away from one's natal community might be expected to produce elaborate webs of mutual obligation accompanied by careful reputation monitoring and management. Under these circumstances, fear of gossip and ostracism would help motivate prosocial behaviour and suppress hubris and selfishness. Nevertheless, when the group faces an external threat, reputational concerns may not always be sufficient to motivate high levels of prosocial risk-taking necessary to mount a collective defence. This is where fusion could have come into play. Dysphoric rituals would have served as a cultural adaptation in communities that depended on extremely high levels of social cohesion and self-sacrifice to ensure that cultural groups and their members survived and reproduced. Recent research showing that warfare intensity predicts severity of initiation rituals would support this conclusion (Sosis et al., 2007). But there may also be other circumstances in which imagistic practices have been culturally adaptive, for example in groups that engage in high-risk hunting strategies using simple technologies (Whitehouse & Hodder, 2010; Whitehouse, Mazzucatto et al., 2014). On this view, cultural institutions fostering fusion may have evolved as a way of binding together relational groups. But as social groups became larger and more complex the fusion mechanism was extended to categorical identities rather than relational networks.

Local fusion in face-to-face groups may be stronger than extended fusion with larger 'imagined communities', such as a nation or world religion whose members are too numerous to know each other personally (Swann et al., 2012). One reason for this could be that the evidence for shared experience in local communities is often more compelling than for extended groups. For example, as discussed earlier, in our research with Libyan insurgents in the 2011 uprising, we found ceiling levels of fusion with fellow revolutionaries in both local and extended groups, but on a forced choice question, almost all participants in our survey chose a relational group over an extended group category as their primary fusion target (Whitehouse, McQuinn et al., 2014). It seems plausible that this is because being able to recall the physical presence of brothers in arms or family members during particularly intense ordeals during the revolution is a stronger evidential basis for shared experience than indirect signals, such as membership of a revolutionary battalion elsewhere in the country. Moreover, in studies where we have been able to explore the development of fusion over time, based on vicariously (rather than directly) shared experiences (Buhrmester, Burnham et al., 2018), the ensuing self-sacrificial acts are far less extreme (e.g. small monetary donations) than those associated with frontline combat in Libya (e.g. jumping on a grenade to protect others).

As conditions permitted an escalation in the scale and complexity of human societies, the mechanisms for generating prosociality, cooperation, and parochial altruism would have needed to adapt and change. With the evolution of increasingly complex societies, doctrine and narrative became more standardized; beliefs more universalistic; sociocultural systems more hierarchical; and offices more professionalized. Sacred texts played an increasingly important role in the codification and legitimation of emergent orthodoxies, as religious guilds increasingly monopolized resources (Whitehouse, 2000, 2004). As societies became larger and more hierarchical, rituals were more frequently performed (Atkinson & Whitehouse, 2011), and low-frequency dysphoric rituals typical of small, cohesive social groups such as warring tribes were increasingly suppressed (Whitehouse, 1996a). Small tightly bonded groups with dysphoric rituals (e.g. hazing and initiation) posed a threat to cooperation in larger societies (creating opposing coalitions) and so were gradually 'selected out' of the cultural repertoire, at least for the population at large, and relegated to organizations loyal to rulers (e.g. militaries). In their place emerged the much more frequent rituals typical of regional and world religions, sustaining forms of group identification better suited to the kinds of collective-action problems presented by interactions among strangers, or socially more distant individuals (Whitehouse, 2004).

It is possible that all the accounts proposed above have contributed to the evolutionary history of the fusion mechanism, since these explanations are not mutually exclusive. But whatever the final account, it is also clear that shared biology and shared experience contribute to especially high levels of cohesion in kin groups, and where these features can be shared with a relational group of non-kin (local fusion) and even an entire population united by categorical ties (extended fusion), this will motivate willingness to fight and die for unrelated individuals. One of the main ways in which this kind of sharing is produced and reproduced is through the performance of imagistic rituals.

Conclusions

In this chapter, I have explored the various ways in which imagistic rituals give rise to a lasting state of identity fusion, a visceral sense of oneness with the group capable of motivating extreme forms of cooperation and self-sacrifice. Research into the imagistic pathway to fusion has revealed a complex process, starting with emotionally intense episodes that endure in memory and become a locus for subsequent reflection. When people think about the meanings of episodic life events, this changes their sense of who they are, their essential autobiographical self. This is all the more noticeable when the experiences in question take the form of emotionally intense rituals, since causal opacity amplifies the potential meaningfulness of experiences, driving the process of spontaneous exegetical reflection. When experiences of this kind are shared with others and regarded as group-defining, as well as personally transformative, this fuses together personal and group identities. I have considered a wide range of empirical evidence to support this imagistic pathway model, involving surveys and experiments with many cultural groups from around the world, engaged in activities as diverse as hazing rituals, childbirth, team sports, and armed combat. Despite important differences, all these experiences engage the processes of shared personal transformation and fusion described above. Although my main focus here has been on this imagistic pathway, I have also considered how the modes theory can be broadened to explain the ways rituals can create fusion based on phenotypic cues and psychological kinship, as well as temporary or 'state' fusion via social synchrony. Finally, I have explored possible models for the biological evolution of identity fusion, based on kin selection, mutualism, and conditioning cooperation on past experience, as well as models for the cultural evolution of imagistic institutions. Although there is still much to learn about the way rituals contribute to extreme group bonding and cooperation, an increasingly rich picture of the processes involved is now emerging based on rigorous empirical research.

4
Doctrinal Ritual, Identification, and Social Complexity

Chapter 2 introduced the theory of modes of religiosity, which proposes that collective rituals tend to cluster around two distinct attractor positions: an 'imagistic' mode in which rare but emotionally intense rituals bond together small groups of participants, and a 'doctrinal' mode in which high-frequency rituals serve to standardize a body of beliefs and practices in a large population. Chapter 3 examined in much closer detail the nature and origins of the imagistic mode, introducing the idea of a 'shared-experiences pathway' to identity fusion capable of motivating extreme self-sacrifice for the group. This chapter focuses attention on the doctrinal mode. A central idea here is that routinized rituals allow beliefs and practices to stabilize and spread, so that eventually even strangers can recognize each other as members of a common ingroup, facilitating trust and cooperation on a scale that would otherwise be impossible. In this way, doctrinal rituals herald not only the first large-scale societies but eventually also the first complex systems of governance, in which laws and societal norms can be policed via centralized bureaucracies, legal institutions, and professionalized priesthoods and militia.

Group bonding through rituals likely had important consequences for cultural group selection in the evolution of larger and more complex societies. With the advent of agriculture and the regional standardization of identity markers (e.g. rituals, customs, and belief systems), more encompassing group identities (e.g. empires, ethnic groups, and world religions) became established based on identification with much larger social categories than were imaginable in foraging worlds. In the process, our biologically evolved psychological propensity to fuse with the band in times of hardship came to be exploited in new ways. While *extended fusion* of this kind may have helped solve the complex coordination and collective action problems of large-scale societies, a darker side to this has been its capacity to motivate large-scale warfare and genocide.

One of the major challenges for archaeology is to explain how small-scale foraging groups evolved into much larger, centralized, hierarchical ones and how the expansion of the latter led to a sharp decline in the former, eventually driving the world's remaining hunter-gatherers into the least productive environments, such as the Kalahari Desert or Arctic tundra. Efforts to reconstruct these processes theoretically, for example, using phylogenetic methods (e.g. Currie et al.,

2010) or agent-based models (Salali, Whitehouse, & Hochberg, 2015), have provided valuable insights into possible mechanisms. Of even more obvious importance, however, are the patterns of evidence that can be gleaned from archaeological and historical sources (Turchin et al., 2015; Whitehouse, 2016b). Archaeologists commonly focus on the advent of crop cultivation and animal domestication as initial drivers in the rise of social complexity (Bellwood, 2005), but there is a growing recognition that changes in ritual life and community cohesion likely also played an important role in the agricultural transition (e.g. Gantley, Whitehouse, & Bogaard, 2018; Goring-Morris, 2005; Kuijt, 2000; Watkins, 2010). In this chapter, we consider evidence that an increase in the frequency of collective rituals may have contributed to the rise of larger-scale groups, eventually enabling the fixation of universalistic moral systems capable of unifying multiethnic empires. The rise of the doctrinal mode of religiosity appears to have paved the way not only for the homogenization of cultural traditions capable of spreading and stabilizing across vast territories but also a set of shared cooperative principles that allowed the spread of trading networks and allegiance to common authorities on a hitherto unimaginable scale.

The Doctrinal Pathway to Identification and Extended Fusion

When people participate in the same rituals on a daily or weekly basis, it is impossible for them to recall the details of every past performance. Instead, they represent the rituals and their meanings as *types* of behaviour—a Holy Communion or a Call to Prayer, for instance. Psychologists describe these representations as *procedural scripts* and *semantic schemas*. Scripts and schemas specify what typically happens in a given ritual and what is generally thought to be its significance. In a group whose identity markers are composed mainly of scripts and schemas, what it means to be a member of the tradition is generalized beyond people of our acquaintance, applying to everyone who performs similar acts and holds similar beliefs. Routinization of a group's beliefs and practices can therefore produce 'imagined communities' (Anderson, 1983)—large populations sharing a common tradition and capable of behaving as a coalition in interactions with nonmembers, *despite* the fact that no individual in the community could possibly know all the others, or even hope to meet all of them in the course of a lifetime.

Routinization is linked to other important effects as well. For instance, it may allow very complex networks of doctrines and narratives to be learned and stored in collective memory, making it relatively easy to spot unauthorized innovations. Rote learning, a technique of memorization long known to psychology and educationalists (Ebbinghaus, 1913), is still widely used in many elementary schools and religious organizations around the world to ensure high-fidelity transmission of approved bodies of knowledge, even though it has also been widely criticized for suppressing independent thinking (Feynman, 2005). From the viewpoint of those seeking to maintain an orthodoxy, however, the suppression of creativity may be viewed in a positive light, a way of promoting conformism to group norms, further amplifying the effects of the 'ritual stance' (Chapter 1). Part of the reason why routinization has this effect might be that having achieved procedural fluency one no longer needs to reflect on *how* to perform the ritual, in turn making one less likely to reflect on *why* one should perform it. Thus, routinization may aid the transmission of *standardized* doctrinal orthodoxies: traditions of belief and practice that are relatively *immune to innovation* and in which unintended deviation from the norm is *readily detectable* (Whitehouse, 1995, 2000, 2004).

Efforts to test these predictions empirically have included field observations, interviews, and surveys with religious adherents, as well as computational models of doctrinal transmission and identity formation. For example, in one study of evangelical Christians and members of a more mainstream Protestant church in Singapore, data from semistructured interviews was used to build semantic networks showing the extent to which religious beliefs were socially shared among adherents (Lane, 2019). Frequency of participation in the collective rituals of the tradition in both cases was linked to higher rates of shared beliefs in the group, with the more central concepts of each tradition showing the highest levels of consensus. This supports the view that ritual routinization contributes to the transmission of complex religious schemas and the stabilization of a body of teachings in doctrinal traditions.

To the extent that routinized rituals help to homogenize and spread religious beliefs, they provide a foundation for much larger-scale communities, capable of encompassing indefinitely many individuals singing from the same hymn sheet (both literally and metaphorically). Expanding the size of the ingroup in this way has implications for the scale on which people can engage in cooperative behaviour, extending both *trust* and *tolerance* even to strangers, merely because they carry the same insignia indicating shared beliefs and practices. At the same time, however, the cohesion engendered through common membership of the tradition is less intensely felt than that accomplished in small groups undergoing rare and painful rituals together. In other words, as cohesion is expanded to encompass greater populations, it is also in an important sense spread more thinly.

Perhaps part of the reason for this is that routinization produces *identification* (Tajfel & Turner, 1979), a less potent motivator of self-sacrifice than fusion (Buhrmester & Swann, 2015). Evidence for the link between routinization and identification also comes from the surveys with Singaporean Christians mentioned above. This research used measures of frequency of ritual attendance and both identification and fusion with the religion as a whole (i.e. the 'imagined community' of fellow worshippers), showing that frequency of ritual participation and identification are significantly correlated (Lane, 2019). Results indicated that the more similar the beliefs held by a group, the more strongly identified its members were. Unlike fusion, however, identification does not tap into personal identity and agency. For those who identify strongly with a group, thinking about their identities as group members makes their unique personal identities less accessible and vice versa (making one's personal identity salient, makes group roles and identities less so). In self-categorization theory, this has been described as the 'functional antagonism principle' (Turner et al., 1987), according to which identification produces a hydraulic relationship between personal and group identities, in contrast with the synergistic relationship that is diagnostic of fusion (Swann et al., 2012). The modes theory suggests that these alternate forms of group alignment, hydraulic versus synergistic, are rooted in the way human memory works.

In the doctrinal mode, group identity markers are stored and transmitted as semantic schemas and procedural scripts. Each participant in a doctrinal tradition knows that the group's unique identity markers are socially learned via imitation and testimony rather than the outcome of self-defining experiences, such as life-changing events, autobiographical memories, and personal reflections (as we have seen in the case of the imagistic pathway to fusion). This would help to explain the hydraulic relationship between personal and group identity that is a hallmark feature of identification—not only is the group an abstract semantic category rather than a face-to-face community, but what brings it into being in the first place is the sharing of conventions that come from outside of oneself and therefore do not originate in one's personal identity.

The hydraulic relationship between personal and group identities that characterizes identification would explain why, even in its strongest form, identification is a less potent driver of self-sacrifice for the group than fusion (Buhrmester & Swann, 2015). Given that self-sacrifice involves a conflict between powerful selfish interests and the demands of group loyalty, there is always a distinct possibility that the desire for self-preservation will prevail, no matter how strongly one identifies with the group. From a gene's eye point of view, it makes good evolutionary sense that the individual (as vehicle) should attempt at all costs to survive and reproduce even at the expense of all others in the group (barring scenarios based on kin selection in which closely related individuals stand a better chance of passing on one's genes). While fusion overcomes this conflict by making self and group functionally equivalent under certain circumstances, as described in the last chapter, the 'functional antagonism principle' underlying identification ensures that the conflict between self and group must be played out, and that the self will more naturally prevail. Concretely, this means that fusion should normally outperform identification when it comes to the costliest of pro-group actions. Thus, although identification is capable of unifying larger populations, the cohesion it generates is spread more thinly, with weaker behavioural outcomes.

More than thirty studies have shown that fusion is a better predictor than identification of willingness to endorse extreme self-sacrifice for the group (Buhrmester & Swann, 2015). Fusion also taps into personal agency in a way that is very different from identification. For example, using exercise to increase physiological arousal amplifies the effects of fusion, but not identification, on expressions of willingness to fight and die for the group, and likewise, threats to self cause highly fused, but not highly identified, individuals to endorse self-sacrifice more strongly (Gómez et al., 2011; Swann et al., 2009; Swann et al., 2010).

While it is tempting to view fusion and identification as distinct forms of group alignment, they can also operate in concert such that alignment with a large group category based on routinized identity markers may overlap with essentialised qualities of the personal self—whether based on shared biology or shared experience. Indeed, this is one way of conceptualizing the nature of 'extended fusion' (Swann et al., 2012). Fusion with extended group categories is commonplace in doctrinal traditions where imagined communities are attributed a common underlying essence based either on shared ancestry or histories of persecution. For example, what it means to be Jewish is often construed in terms of shared ancestry and genealogy but also a shared history of persecution, especially the rise of fascism and resulting Holocaust. This is true of many other ethnic groups too that emphasize notions of shared biological essence, as well as shared histories of suffering, for instance African Americans who describe themselves as 'brothers' and emphasize a common experience of oppression and institutionalized racism.

Given that extended fusion incorporates an element also of identification with large group categories, there may also be a heightened sensitivity to outgroup threat, not inherent in smaller fused groups. For example, although families do occasionally enter into feuding relationships, it may be more common in many societies for them either to ignore other families or to interact with them cooperatively to mutual benefit, unlike larger coalitions that may be more readily conflict-prone. On this logic, unless one's relatives are under attack in some way, most people would be inclined to take a benign view of other people's families, wishing them no harm and expecting no harm from them in turn. By contrast, identification is strongly associated with outgroup derogation (Brewer, 2001). The very process of identifying with a group, creates an avid interest in what other groups are up to, especially if they are competing for the same resources. Nevertheless, as discussed in the last chapter, when reviewing studies we have conducted with groups of football fans in Indonesia and Australia, the relationship between fusion and outgroup hostility is complex, and the presence of competition and threat are among a variety of factors that can come into play in determining the nature of pro-group action in both local and extended groups.

What does seem to be clear is that when fusion and identification both exert an influence on group alignment based on categorical rather than relational ties, the impact of both on prosocial action, including self-sacrifice, can be hard to disentangle. In the last chapter, for example, I described our efforts with Indonesian samples to investigate the possible role of major public events on cohesion with Muslims as an extended group, and explained how the vicarious sharing of events reported in the media might be capable of motivating both extended fusion and identification. Recall that part of our goal in this research was to compare group alignment and willingness to self-sacrifice between three types of Sunni Muslim groups: *Partai Keadilan Sejahtera* (PKS) (a hard line fundamentalist political party originally inspired by the Muslim Brotherhood in Egypt); *Nahdlatul Ulama* (NU) (a moderate movement following the Shafi'i school of jurisprudence); a control group of Indonesians unaffiliated to any political part or movement (Kavanagh et al., 2020). As anticipated, followers of the more extremist PKS ideology were more fused to Muslims as an extended group, compared with moderates and the general population. Indeed, thirty-six per cent of PKS supporters indicated willingness to prioritize protecting fellow Muslims as a group over their own family members, compared with only eight per cent of NU supporters and nine per cent of the general population. On the other hand, however, across all three groups, *identification* was a better predictor than fusion of stated willingness to *self-sacrifice* for other groups members. Three forms of self-sacrifice were measured: willingness to fight and die for the ingroup; parochial voting; readiness to join demonstrations to support the ingroup. It is by no means clear why, at least in this Indonesian study, identification outperformed fusion on willingness to engage in pro-group action, particularly the more extreme 'fight-and-die' measure. One possibility, however, is that strong forms of identification encouraged particularly vehement endorsement of group norms demanding self-sacrifice, and that if we had been able to adopt a behavioural measure (e.g. actual as opposed to expressed willingness to fight and die), fusion would have outperformed identification as the best predictor.

It is also possible that other psychological factors complicate the relationship between fusion and willingness to self-sacrifice in countries like Indonesia. In another recent study, for example, we found that higher scores on measures of collective narcissism and intolerance towards normative transgressions predicted higher levels of endorsement for parochial altruism among religious fundamentalists (Yustisia et al., 2020). Collective narcissism—a tendency to exaggerate positive perceptions of the ingroup—has been linked to endorsement of intergroup violence (de Zavala et al., 2009) and might help to explain unusually high rates of expressed willingness to fight and die for the group among those who also identify strongly with group ideologies and norms. Nevertheless, it should still be borne in mind that most previous studies up to now have found extended fusion to be a stronger predictor than identification of willingness to fight and die for the group (Gómez et al., 2011; Swann et al., 2009; Swann et al., 2010).

In the contemporary world, examples of extended fusion in centralized, hierarchical societies may include strong forms of alignment to political groups, unions, protected minorities, and professional guilds, as well as to religious factions and ethnicities. But throughout most of human history, prior to industrialization and the spread of more secular belief systems, most groups have subscribed to various beliefs in gods and other deities. So, although in this section we have focused on examples of extended fusion based on ethnicity, nationality, and regional alignments—group categories based primarily on shared secular beliefs and practices—the initial rise of the doctrinal mode in world history was more closely linked to supernatural belief systems and thus more obviously a mode of *religiosity* specifically. The significance of this only really becomes clear though, when we view the role of identification and extended fusion in human societies through the lens of deep history.

Sociocultural Evolution and the Doctrinal Mode of Religiosity

As discussed in Chapter 2, the first appearance of the doctrinal mode in global prehistory is strongly linked to the invention of agriculture. This link first came to light as an unexpected outcome of efforts to analyze patterns of performance frequency and emotional arousal in collective rituals from more than seventy cultures in the ethnographic record, and to relate those patterns to social features, such as group morphology and subsistence (Atkinson & Whitehouse, 2011). Increasing routinization of ritual life with the advent of farming is also consistent with the general observation that sedentism led to an increase in the diversity and volume of material culture and thus in the range of activities, both instrumental and ritualistic, associated with the production and maintenance of artefacts (Hodder, 2012). The discovery that agricultural intensity is positively correlated with the presence of routinized rituals prompts the question of whether the doctrinal mode might have been a direct outcome of the transition from foraging to farming. And the archaeological evidence would seem to support that. Both detailed case studies, for example, at the ancient site of Çatalhöyük, covering nearly two millennia during the Neolithic revolution in the Konya plain, together with the use of new statistical techniques for identifying changes in modes of religiosity across fifty sites in southwest Asia over a much longer time depth, all point to a pattern in which the imagistic mode was progressively replaced by more doctrinal practices (see Chapter 2). Here we take up the story again but focusing on a global dataset and extending further forward in history, long after the agricultural transition. In Chapter 2, we ended with the first emergence of higher frequency rituals and accordingly more standardized beliefs and practices. These innovations made it possible for much larger groups to emerge, capable of sharing identity markers that remained stable even as they spread across the landscape. But even if there were signs of increasing technical and ritual specialization as sites like Çatalhöyük, levels of social complexity remained low. There was little indication of class, stratification, rank, or hierarchy and systems of law, governance, education, public works, and so on all remained rudimentary (Hodder, 2006). How did humanity transition from flourishing but still localized settlements in the early Neolithic to much more complex and regionally distributed societies in the Bronze Age and beyond?

The work summarized in Chapter 2 relied on a combination of global ethnography gathered from contemporary societies and regional archaeology gathered from Anatolia and the Levant. A major drawback with the former approach was lack of historical depth, and with the latter, regional parochialism and restriction to only the earliest phases in the rise of agriculture. To investigate the role of the doctrinal mode in sociocultural evolution, a much larger and temporally deeper source of data was required. Partly to address this need, we created Seshat: Global History Databank (for further details on the construction process, see Chapter 7).

Seshat (named after the ancient Egyptian goddess of wisdom, knowledge, and writing) constitutes the most comprehensive body of knowledge about the human past ever assembled on a single searchable platform, enabling us to test hypotheses on a wide range of topics including the relationship between such key variables as ritual frequency and emotional intensity, group scale and cohesion, and agricultural intensity (Turchin et al., 2012; Currie et al., 2015; Turchin et al., 2015; Whitehouse, 2016b). Within the first ten years of its foundation, Seshat accumulated more than 300,000 records relating to 400 polities (independent political units). Seshat was designed to contain vast amounts of information, eventually relating to all known polities in global history. But the first priority of the Seshat team was to develop a sampling scheme covering thirty natural geographic areas (or NGAs) from around the world. We called this our *World Sample 30*.

World Sample 30 was created by first dividing the world into ten major regions—and then choosing three NGAs from each of them. Each NGA represents an area with some ecological unity, roughly 100 km by 100 km in size (although NGAs can be somewhat larger or smaller than that). To maximize variation within the sample, these three NGAs were chosen as examples of areas that developed social complexity very early (like Upper Egypt), very late (like Iceland), or somewhere in the middle (like Chuuk). The purpose of stratifying the sample in this way is to maximize variance in the data. But obviously this is all relative—so the most complex NGA in Oceania-Australia is Big Island Hawaii, which is nothing like as complex as (say) Latium. For each NGA we code data pertaining to polities (e.g. states like Egypt's classic old kingdom) or quasi-polities (e.g. subtraditions) as far back as the data will allow. This means for some NGAs there are only a few time slices, whereas Upper Egypt has around forty.

Seshat's codebook specifies more the 1500 variables of interest under major topic headings such as social complexity, religion and ritual, warfare, agriculture, and so on. These are then further subdivided into many categories. Initial efforts to measure social complexity have used fifty-one variables associated with population size, hierarchy, territory, governance, bureaucracy, infrastructure, and so on (Turchin et al., 2018). Our analyses show that these different characteristics exhibit strong relationships with each other across all our world regions. It is also clear from our analyses that social complexity evolved at widely differing time points in different parts of the world (see Figure 4.1).

Analysis of Seshat data, and especially its sophisticated measures of social complexity, allows researchers to investigate more closely the impact of sociocultural evolution on the moral fabric of society, including religious beliefs and practices. Ancient foraging societies faced many kinds of collective action problems, ranging from coordination of subsistence activities, to defending the band against raiding parties and wild animals, to resolving conflict within the group and managing bullies. Many of these problems could be quite effectively addressed using a suite of evolved psychological adaptations encouraging prosocial behaviour, reputation management, and third-party punishment (Mullins, Whitehouse, & Atkinson, 2013). Relevant adaptations available to all human populations, past and present, include shame (Fessler, 2004), empathy (Decety, 2012), kin psychology (Whitehouse & Lanman, 2014), coalitional psychology (Billig & Tajfel, 1973), among other mechanisms that help to regulate adherence to norms and the sanctioning of transgressions (Gelfand, 2018; Wright, 1994). Thus, humans naturally tend to be conditional co-operators (Fehr & Fischbacher, 2004) with a strong aversion to fairness violations (Haidt, 2012) and an appetite for 'prosocial punishment' (Fehr & Gächter, 2002). In Palaeolithic communities, these tools for prosocial living would have been readily deployed and regularly sharpened and maintained through such cultural practices as collective ritual and social synchrony (Wiltermuth & Heath, 2009), commensality and singing together (Morley, 2013), as well as potent forms of group bonding based on shared traumatic ordeals (Whitehouse, 1996, 2018). With the rise of farming and increasingly large-scale human settlements, however, the evolved moral toolkit, originally designed to enable cooperation in small groups, would have been placed under increasing stress.

Dependence on social interactions between strangers became more and more commonplace, weakening social cohesion in society at large and making it harder to detect and punish cheaters, defectors, and free-riders. The appearance of doctrinal practices would have helped with this by enabling identity markers to become standardized across expanding regions, extending social cohesion to larger groups. But the dark side to this more hierarchical form of social organization was the establishment of increasingly oppressive systems of governance, associated with the so-called archaic states (Bellah, 2011; Flannery & Marcus, 2012; Turchin, 2016). In many of these early civilizations, extreme forms of top-down coercion, including exercise of absolute power by divinely sanctioned heads of states, human sacrifice, and enslavement, were rampant (Trigger, 2003). But as societies grew to encompass hundreds of thousands and eventually millions of

DOCTRINAL RITUAL, IDENTIFICATION, AND SOCIAL COMPLEXITY   115

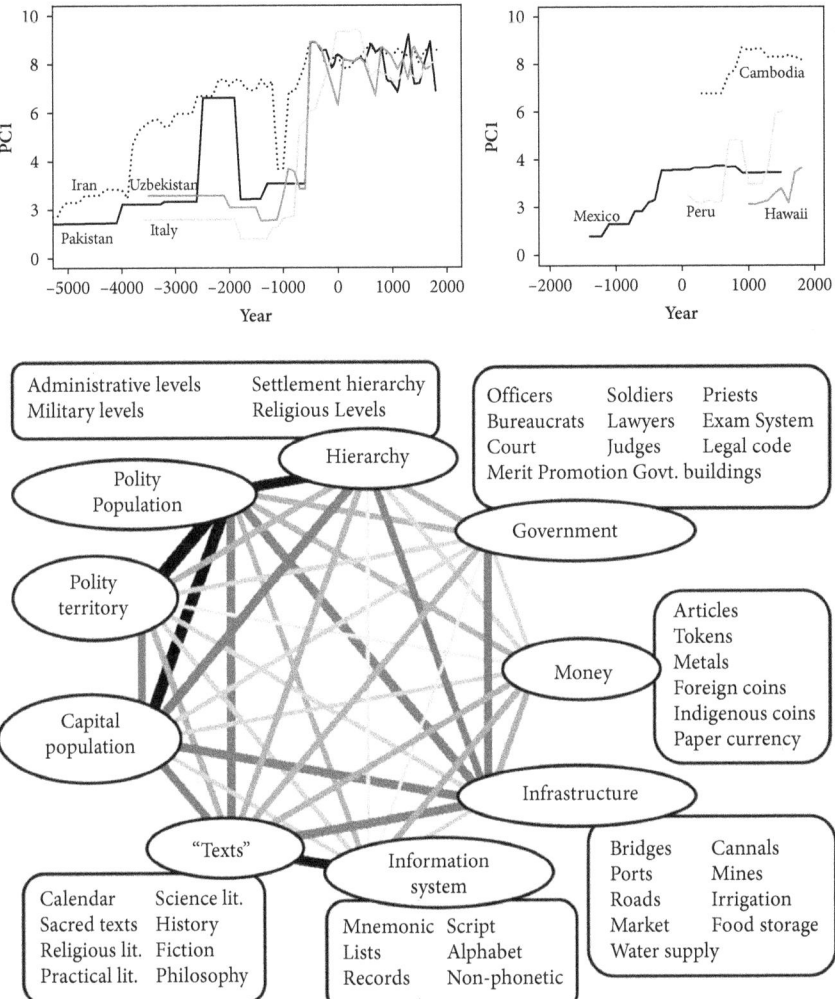

Figure 4.1 *Tracking the rise of social complexity in world history. Top panels show examples of the widely differing time points for the rise of social complexity across a selection of world regions. Bottom panel shows nine complexity characteristics (ovals) aggregating 51 variables (darker and thicker connecting lines indicate stronger correlations). All complexity characteristics are significantly correlated with one another.*
(Source: Turchin, Currie et al., 2018)

citizens, excessive inequality and political domination became a source of instability (Turchin et al., In Prep). Political domination by powerful elites was only effective up to a certain point in world history. In small, highly cohesive states, for example, the general population could be kept in check through fear of imprisonment, torture, or worse. But to the extent that factions can form and gather the collective strength to mount coups and revolutions, oppressive regimes are brittle and can break down. Rebellion may be staved off in such societies by warmongering, since this increases acceptance of despotic leadership, but the effects are hard to sustain indefinitely, and such an approach also carries the risk of invasion by more powerful adversaries. These problems are far more acute as societies become more complex and internally diverse, for example, through the absorption of multiple ethnicities and religious traditions. This marked a turning point in world history, one that took humanity back to its most ancient moral intuitions at the same time as it pushed us forward into novel forms of ideology and organized religion. This new phase in the evolution of the doctrinal mode has been widely referred to as the Axial Age.

The idea that a great moral and intellectual revolution occurred in a few regions of Eurasia during the last millennium BCE—well after the rise of complex societies—dates back at least as far as the scholarship of the French Indologist Anquetil-Duperron (1771) and the Scottish folklorist Stuart-Glennie in Scotland (1873). However, it was Karl Jaspers in mid-twentieth-century Switzerland who first popularized the term 'Axial Age' (*Achsenzeit*, in his native German) to characterize, among other developments, the rise of moralizing religions and more egalitarian principles of governance, which in turn spawned many hallmark features of modernity. Jaspers (1948, 1953) along with several later Axial Age proponents (e.g. Bellah, 2011; Eisenstadt, 1986) argue that this 'axial turn' constituted a radical departure from the coercive political systems typical of so-called archaic states headed by deified rulers, in which extreme forms of inequality, such as slavery and human sacrifice, were sanctioned. According to this theory, axial modes of thought first appeared in what is now China, India, Israel-Palestine, Iran, and Greece, finding expression in the ethical systems respectively known as Confucianism, Buddhism, Judaism, Zoroastrianism, and Greek philosophy (the five 'axial religions'). These traditions emerged over a relatively short time span, roughly 800–200 BCE. But does it really make sense to describe this period as an 'Axial Age'?

Recent analyses of Axial Age features in the Seshat databank suggests that although the idea of a single 'age' is probably misleading, some traditional notions of 'axiality', specifically the shift from coercive to more ethical forms of governance, do indeed appear to be a discernible phenomenon in global history (Whitehouse et al., 2019). At the root of this transition, however, was not so much the appearance of transcendent forms of reasoning (e.g. Bellah, 2011; Jaspers, 1953), which in any case would require further explanation in turn, but the demands of increasingly complex societies. That is, axiality appears to have arisen as a consequence of passing a certain threshold in the scale and structure of human societies, one that has been reached at different points in time in different parts of the world. Once this threshold is passed, societies must adopt more prosocial and egalitarian moral principles if they are to survive the twin spectres of external conquest and internal collapse (Turchin, 2016).

We need to be clear, however, what exactly we mean by 'axiality'. Recent efforts to identify a set of specific diagnostic features for the Axial Age have focused on twelve principles (Mullins et al., 2018): First, moralistic punishment: the principle that violations of natural morality will be punished by higher authorities, whether by means of secular or supernatural sanctions in this life or the next. Second, moralizing norms: the principle that peers and other members of a relational network are obligated to monitor and deter deviance within the community. Third, promotion of prosociality: the principle that cooperative behaviour should be actively encouraged and rewarded. Fourth, moralizing omniscient supernatural beings: the principle of an 'eye in the sky' watching over everyone, punishing sins and rewarding virtuous behaviour. Fifth, rulers are not gods: the principle that worldly leaders are merely human, just like everyone else. Sixth, equating *elites* and commoners: the principle that moral rules apply to everyone regardless of birth, breeding, and social status. Seventh, equating *rulers* and commoners: again, emphasising that moral rules apply to all. Eighth, formal legal code: the principle that rule of law is explicitly formulated. Ninth, general applicability of law: the principle that the law applies to all citizens equally. Tenth, constraint on the executive: the principle that governors' decisions can in principle be vetoed or overturned. Eleventh, professionalized bureaucracy: the principle that administration of a system of governance requires specialist skills, training, and salary. And twelfth, impeachment: the principle that excessive an arbitrary exercise of power by a ruler can lead to their removal.

Analysis of the emergence of these twelve principles across a sample of ten world regions (Japan, Cambodia, China, India, Iran, Israel-Palestine, Greece, Turkey, Egypt, and Italy), prior to the spread of modernity, shows that axiality (using the definition above) did not evolve everywhere, and in the regions where it did emerge, the patterns and rates of emergence differ (Mullins et al., 2018). For example, in Japan, Cambodia, China, and Greece, only some and not all of the twelve principles coalesced. And although the pattern across all the regions sampled was a progression from relatively few to relatively many principles being present, the path was not necessarily a linear one, with losses as well as gains along the way. Perhaps most importantly for any assessment of the Axial Age hypothesis as traditionally formulated, the greatest concentration of the twelve principles was not in the first millennium BCE, but in the two thousand years that followed. Moreover, many of the twelve principles emerged much earlier than the Jaspers model allows, and in regions that were not part of the classical model for axiality, such as Egypt and Turkey. Thus, axiality was a more complex, patchy, widely distributed, and early emerging phenomenon than the original advocates of the concept appreciated. But an even more important point to make, is that axiality involved a restoration of moral rules that had been quite systematically repressed and distorted in the archaic states that came before.

The range of behaviours judged to be morally good is actually somewhat invariable across human societies, apparently stemming from psychological predispositions emerging deep in our species' evolutionary history. The evidence for a universal human morality is compelling. For example, in a recent analysis of ethnographic writings on sixty societies worldwide, we found that seven cooperative rules (help your family, help your group, return favours, be brave, defer to superiors, divide resources fairly, and respect others' property) were considered everywhere to be morally good, and we found examples of most of them in most societies, across all cultural regions. Crucially, none of these was ever deemed morally bad (Curry, Mullins, & Whitehouse, 2019). The fact that these seven rules for cooperation are predicted by game theory and found throughout the natural world (Curry, 2016), plausibly explains why it is those solutions that are also considered morally good in all human societies.. That is, moral intuitions appear to be biologically evolved adaptations to various collective action problems. But whereas in small-scale, simple societies, innate moral predispositions may be sufficient to sustain many forms of cooperation, this is less true of larger-scale and more complex societies (Mullins, Whitehouse, & Atkinson, 2013). In the archaic states, as noted above, some of these principles were grotesquely exaggerated, such as the rule that one should defer to authority. Excessive concentration of arbitrary power in the hands of god-kings meant that the benefits for the meek were disproportionately small and the brutality of dominant individuals excessive, contrary to natural morality. Likewise, the principle of sharing these fairly was blatantly flouted by elites that hoarded wealth while large portions of the population were enslaved or impoverished. The twelve principles of axiality restored some of these natural moral rules by postulating supernatural agents who cared about social justice, family values, the rule of law, and constraining the powers of earthly rulers.

Although the exact manner in which the rules of natural morality were upheld by axial ideologies varied across world regions, the tendency towards the stepwise restoration of these values is unmistakable when viewed comparatively on a global scale over several millennia. This is arguably what we mean (or *should* mean) by 'axiality'. The question remains, however, what exactly drove this restoration of natural morality and why it took the religious and ideological forms that it did.

A plausible explanation for the rise of axiality is that societies past a certain threshold of social complexity become vulnerable to collapse, whether due to internal divisions or external attack. Some evidence for this view comes from efforts to track the rise of moralizing supernatural punishment in world history, using the Seshat database (Turchin, Whitehouse et al., 2019). In this study, as well as coding for the presence or absence of a wide range of beliefs in moralizing supernatural punishment, we also coded information pertaining to warfare and the environment. Analysis of the data showed that beliefs in moralizing gods came after the sharpest initial rises in social complexity and that both may have been driven to some extent by intergroup warfare. In particular, cavalry warfare turned out to have been a powerful factor in the appearance of moralizing religion, more so than other previously hypothesized drivers such as affluence, climate security, and reliance on pastoralism.

Using Seshat to quantify patterns such as these in world history is necessarily an incremental process, and further studies building on these findings are continuously underway. Nevertheless, it already looks as though fixation of a common moral code may well have been essential to the unification and stabilization of political systems exceeding the megasociety threshold. This could be because it established foundations for conflict management and effective cooperation in ways that regionally or ethnically diverse cultural norms and customs could not. Consider once again the case of the Kivung religious tradition discussed in Chapter 2. Recall that when the Kivung first emerged, the region was divided into numerous language groups, in turn speaking many more dialects and subscribing to locally distinctive cultural traditions encompassing at most a few thousands of individuals. Peaceful cooperation between these localized ritual communities was hard to achieve based around the procurement of brides (based on 'sister exchange') or exotic trade goods and often descended into feuding and violence. Intergroup warfare, raiding, and bride capture in the region were rampant (Whitehouse, 1995), as in other regions of New Guinea (Godelier & Strathern, 1991). Part of the reason why cooperation between these small communities was so fragile was because the provenance of moral concern was highly parochial, being based primarily on local fusion resulting from imagistic rituals and psychological kinship (see Chapter 3). But the emergence of the Kivung not only established shared identity markers, based on highly routinized rituals diagnostic of the doctrinal mode, but also a set of moral rules applicable to all followers of the movement, irrespective of language, customs, and traditional enmities.

The moral rules of the Kivung were modelled on the ten commandments of the Old Testament, learned from Roman Catholic priests and other missionaries visiting the region. Every Kivung village erected a post at its entrance on which were inscribed the Roman numerals I to X, reminding people of the ten laws that must be obeyed. Paramount among these was the commandment forbidding homicide, which in the Kivung context was taken not only as a law against murder but also warfare, raiding, and all forms of intergroup violence. These laws not only established peaceful interactions across all the formerly warring groups of the region, but they created obligations to cooperate economically, ritually, and politically despite speaking different languages and observing widely differing local customs. This allowed the Kivung to scale up cooperation to tens of thousands of followers, based on a centralized, hierarchical model for group formation borrowed from colonial administrations and Christian missions designed to unify and regulate much larger groups, running into tens or even hundreds of millions. The origins of this model in world history would seem to lie in the Axial Age.

Admittedly, the above account represents only part of the story about the rise of axiality. Nevertheless, if broadly correct, it would seem that axiality constituted a new way of restoring faith in old morals, rather than an entirely novel moral system. As such, the so-called Axial Age was not so much an age as a *stage* in the evolution of social complexity, and its distribution globally was wider and its origins historically deeper than anybody previously imagined. The initial rise of archaic states led to the distortion and repression of at least some components of natural morality and axiality provided a way of restoring those principles under the guise of a more benevolent regime of supernatural enforcement, in ways that applied equally to rich and poor, the powerful and the meek. Such a restoration was perhaps necessary for political systems to evolve beyond the megasociety threshold.

If the original function of axiality in world history was to hold together fragile, ethnically diverse coalitions, what might declining participation in organized religion mean for the future of societies today? Could secularization in Europe, for example, contribute to the unravelling of supranational forms of governance in the region? If beliefs in moralizing gods decline, what will that mean for cooperation across ethnic groups in the face of migration, warfare, or the spread of xenophobia? Or are the functions of axial religious ideologies simply being replaced by more secular ones? To answer these questions, we need increasingly to integrate findings from the cognitive, behavioural, and biological sciences with ever more sophisticated analyses of world history.

Doctrinal Religions, Credibility Enhancing or Undermining Displays, and Normative Tightness

Prior to the Neolithic revolution, imagistic practices provided a common method of generating social glue in human societies, but the doctrinal mode was unheard of. Nowadays, however, the dominance of the two modes has been more or less reversed worldwide, and the doctrinal mode reigns supreme in all but the most isolated of human societies, indeed has done so for many centuries in the Old World, and in some case for millennia. In the process, cultural evolution has wrought a diversity of changes to the dynamics of doctrinal systems in different regions and at different times. In this section, I consider how moralizing gods (Norenzayan, 2013) and credibility enhancing or undermining displays (Henrich, 2009; Turpin, Andersen, & Lanman, 2018) may have strengthened or weakened beliefs in doctrinal orthodoxies and thus their ability to facilitate trust and cooperation in changing social ecologies. I also consider how factors influencing the tightness and looseness of group norms (Gelfand, 2018) have come to impact the maintenance of orthodoxy and the standardization of ideology more generally.

In the previous section, I discussed the possibility that moralizing gods might have been necessary to sustain cooperation in large-scale societies, especially multiethnic empires where common overarching identities were lacking. But for moralizing gods to motivate prosocial action, they would have had to be believable. The idea of an 'eye in the sky' watching over everyone, punishing the wicked and rewarding the pious, may have some intuitive appeal (Boyer, 2001), but religions of that kind have always had their sceptics too, not least because such beliefs often seem to be rather convenient for power holders (Kertzer, 1988). Seeing evidence that others truly believe, however, might help to quell doubts and scepticism. It has been suggested that 'credibility enhancing displays' (CREDs) constitute culturally evolved mechanisms providing that kind of evidence (Henrich, 2009).

When a person acts in a way that would be costly and therefore inexplicable if they did not really believe what they claim, it makes their claims more believable to others. Thus, if I claim that a potentially poisonous mushroom is safe to eat, that claim appears far more believable if I proceed to eat the mushroom myself. And in the same way, it has been argued that performing costly (e.g. time-consuming) rituals make the beliefs associated with them more believable (Henrich, 2009). Such rituals, in other words, serve as CREDs, increasing the believability of doctrinal beliefs, for example, in a moralizing god. If correct, the CREDs theory would also help explain why some doctrinal traditions spread more rapidly or efficiently than others (see Figure 4.2). Conversely, traditions that fail to sustain adequate CREDs would struggle to retain their members, especially where other religions or secular ideologies are eager to recruit defectors. Worse still, religious traditions whose leaders are seen to be hypocritical, such as Catholic clergy who sought to cover up child abuse scandals in the church, may be seen as engaging in 'credibility undermining displays' (CRUDs) that contribute to even more rapid decline in belief, as has recently been observed in the Republic of Ireland, for example (Turpin, Andersen, & Lanman, 2018).

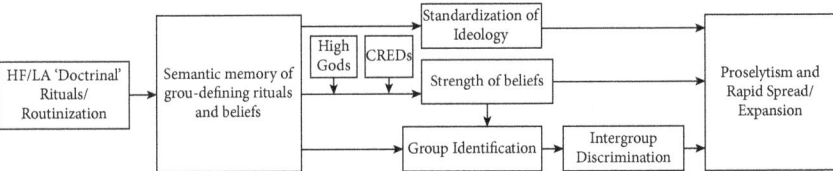

Figure 4.2 *Moralizing gods and CREDs strengthen doctrinal beliefs*
(Source: Whitehouse & Kavanagh, 2020)

As well as variables such as CREDs and CRUDs that might strengthen or weaken the links between variables within the doctrinal mode, there are also factors external to the institutional system itself that could influence its evolution. For example, although it is not yet clear how exactly the rise of agriculture led to an increase in the frequency of collective rituals and thus to the rise of the doctrinal mode, it seems possible that some third factor (i.e. neither agriculture nor routinization but related to both) somehow triggered the whole process. A plausible candidate would be increasing population densities and the spread of infectious diseases (Murray & Schaller, 2010), in turn triggering hazard precaution systems in the brain and an increased desire to engage in ritualistic behaviours (Boyer & Liénard, 2006). Another factor may have been the rise in routinized activities of all kinds as part of the emergence of a farming lifestyle and toolkit, many of which likely incorporated ritualistic elements demanding high-frequency repetition (Whitehouse & Hodder, 2010). Other factors could have come into play at once or in different degrees at different locations. Whatever the environmental (including demographic, ontogenetic, and social) variables were that originally led to the establishment of routinized rituals as agriculture emerged and spread, it is clear that some of these factors may also have influenced the nature of the doctrinal system in various ways.

For example, a growing body of empirical research suggests that when environments become harsher, for example due to natural disaster or outgroup conflict, norms are more tightly enforced (Gelfand et al., 2011). Doctrinal traditions are, of course, also normative systems, and we would expect any effects on tightness-looseness to play a significant role in their functioning (Yustisia et al., 2020). In particular, an increase in normative tightness would strengthen peer-to-peer enforcement of conformist behaviour, as well as support for the suppression by religious leaders of unauthorized deviations from the orthodox canon. This in turn would help to ensure the standardization of the tradition as a whole, necessary to ensure shared identity and cooperation (see Figure 4.3).

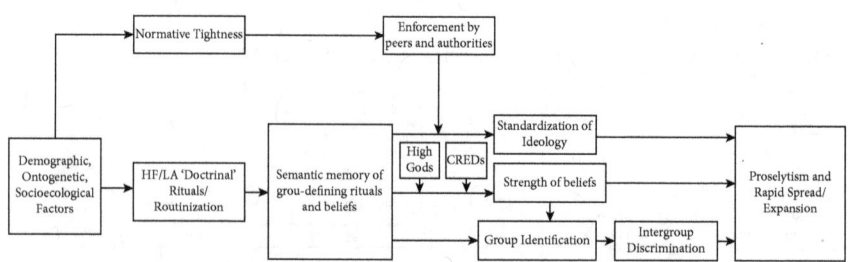

Figure 4.3 *Normative tightness promotes social enforcement increasing standardization*
(Source: Whitehouse & Kavanagh, 2020)

Relational Mobility and the Doctrinal Mode

According to the above account, the doctrinal mode contributed to the evolution of social complexity by spreading standardized identity markers and moral systems across the landscape, thus making cooperation possible in increasingly large groups. But some environments may have provided more fertile soil for the doctrinal mode than others. One factor that could plausibly have impeded the spread of doctrinal practices is *low relational mobility* (Whitehouse & Kavanagh, 2020).

Relational mobility is a measure of the extent to which people can forge new social relationships or shake off unwanted ones (Yuki & Schug, 2012; Yuki, Schug et al., 2007). Although some simple societies, such as the acephalous hunter-gatherer bands of the Kalahari Desert (Lee & DeVore, 1969), have quite flexible social groupings, enabling people to come and go freely (Woodburn, 1982), most small-scale polities exhibit very low levels of relational mobility. In some cases, this is because group membership is assigned by birth, for example, because recruitment to corporate groups (e.g. tribe, clan, or lineage) is based upon descent from a common ancestor as among the patrilineal Tallensi of West Africa (Fortes, 1945) or the matrilineal Trobriand Islanders of New Guinea (Malinowski, 1929). In other cases, it is because their imagistic rituals create lifelong bonds based on episodic memories from which coparticipants cannot be expunged and to which new persons cannot be added (Whitehouse, 2004). It has been argued that missionization is notably less efficient in societies lacking centralized hierarchies, such as West Africa, where initiation cults abound (Højbjerg, 2004), as compared with chiefdoms and traditional states where imagistic practices are less widely in evidence (Fallers, 1965). In the case of Pacific Islands societies, such differences in the rate of spread of Christianity have been attributed to the fact that converting a paramount chief in the hierarchical societies of Polynesia was a speedy way of converting an entire society, whereas missionization had to proceed one soul at a time in the smaller and more egalitarian tribes of Melanesia (Sahlins, 1963). But while that may be true, it is probably only part of the story. A major reason why imagistic groups are hard to recruit to new doctrinal religions is because their members are less open to forming new relationships or shedding established ones.

Low relational mobility may also help to explain why some regions of the world, even where social complexity emerged and spread, have appeared to be stony ground for the spread of doctrinal religions. For example, Japan has among the lowest scores on relational mobility compared with other countries around the world (Thomson et al., 2018) and also has famously low levels of doctrinal religiosity (Christianity and Islam especially having had strikingly little impact on the general population). It seems quite possible that an inability to join new groups or forge new social relationships also reduces openness to joining new

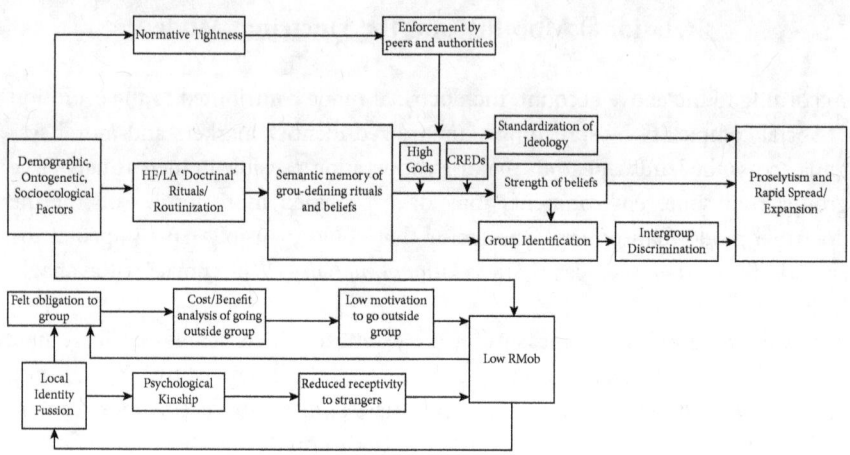

Figure 4.4 *Relational mobility and modes theory*
(Source: Whitehouse & Kavanagh, 2020)

religious organizations and adopting novel beliefs and practices. For instance, the study cited above showed that at least one of the main predictors of relational mobility is the historical subsistence strategy: dependence on cooperative rice cultivation in East Asia was linked to the need for relatively fixed social networks and bounded groups, while animal husbandry was associated with higher rates of relational mobility in Western countries. It is also possible that, despite the evident scale and complexity of Japanese society, the higher prevalence of imagistic practices there (Kavanagh, 2016; Kavanagh & Jong, 2019; Kawano, 2005; Nelson, 1996; Reader & Tanabe, 1998) is both a result of weak doctrinal regulation but also a possible reason why doctrinal systems spread less successfully there than in many other countries. That is, imagistic practices may have helped to drive down relational mobility as part of a self-amplifying feedback loop (Figure 4.4).

Conclusions

Building on the introduction to modes theory in Chapter 2, this chapter has explored in greater depth the psychology, ecology, and evolutionary history of the doctrinal mode. Psychologically, what makes doctrinal practices so revolutionary is simply an increase in performance frequency. Although it is not entirely clear why at least some collective rituals became more extensively routinized with the advent of agriculture, it is possible that the activities associated with crop cultivation and animal domestication involved more regular repetition of cooperative subsistence activities, especially within domestic units, and this provided a fabric of behavioural routines into which ritualised actions could be readily interwoven. But whatever complex of factors prompted an initial increase in ritual routinization, it laid the foundations for radically new patterns of group formation and political association. In particular, it meant that a set of identity markers (ranging from ritual actions and myths to pottery designs and clothing styles) could be standardized across increasingly large populations. I have argued that this was because deviation from the standard scripts and schemas of the ritual system could be more readily detected and punished and because routinization reduced the motivation to innovate and encouraged the entrenchment of collective habits capable of defining vast imagined communities based on likeness. A core idea here is that this mode of group alignment produces *identification*, based on the sharing of traits acquired socially from others. Since these traits are not linked to personally defining experiences or qualities, identification implies a hydraulic relationship between self and group and is thus a weaker form of social cohesion than the fusion of identities produced by imagistic practices.

With this theoretical framework in place, I turned to the question of how the doctrinal mode evolved as groups became larger and larger. This phase of social evolution was associated with the establishment of so-called archaic states, typified by the growth of deep structural inequalities and highly coercive top-down political domination by political elites. But once populations grew beyond the one million watershed, whether as a result of peaceful expansion and incorporation of neighbouring groups or through violent conquest (or both), societal resilience depended increasingly on reducing the more egregious expressions of exploitation and political domination (especially mass slavery and human sacrifice) and instead favoured the rise of ethical religions, associated with the so-called Axial Age, including moralizing gods concerned to enforce reciprocity, fairness, and other principles of cooperation in human affairs. Discernment of these patterns in world history has been greatly improved by the advent of new databanks, allowing us to quantify variables associated with social complexity, ritual routinization, and moralizing religion, and compare their patterns of emergence in a diversity of regions around the globe.

As the doctrinal mode became ever more closely associated with enforcement of universalizing moral codes, additional mechanisms came into play, strengthening commitment to dogma. A good example of this is the spread of CREDs, which encourage more effective transmission and peer enforcement of moral codes. Another set of factors helping to drive a strengthening of norms, including moral norms, in doctrinal religions took the form of psychological stressors (e.g. associated with warfare, disease, and natural disasters) which served to increase the normative tightness of doctrinal traditions. By incentivizing prosocial punishment of transgressors, these mechanisms bolstered the capacity of the doctrinal mode to foster cooperation on ever more ambitious scales, not only within state formations and regional coalitions but across increasingly far-flung imperialist colonial empires. Some parts of the world were more readily absorbed into these rapidly evolving forms of ideological, political, and commercial globalization. Low relational mobility may have slowed the rate of spread of some forms of doctrinal religion, for example in cultures where imagistic practices were still widespread, or subsistence practices helped to ossify relational networks and limit opportunities to expand one's social horizons. As such, the impact of the doctrinal mode on the evolution of complex societies was not uniformly felt around the globe but was influenced by a range of demographic, ontogenetic, and socioecological factors.

5
Ritual's Evolutionary Landscapes

Throughout this book, the extraordinary diversity of human rituals around the world and across human history has been evident. Is that variability in the form and content of human rituals due to cultural evolution or some other process? If rituals evolve then what are the units of selection? Does the evolutionary process involve random variation and selective retention as occurs in natural selection? To what extent does it depend on deliberate design and innovation? Are rituals evoked by biologically evolved mechanisms? We have already touched on some of these questions and tentatively concluded that the motivation to acquire and perform rituals is rooted in a biologically evolved predisposition to engage in overimitation (Chapter 1) but that the specific ways in which that behaviour programme is expressed have been honed by cultural evolution, perhaps especially through the innovation and spread of institutions that regulate the frequency and emotionality of collective rituals (Chapters 2, 3, and 4). In this chapter, we consider a more unified overarching framework in which to conceptualize these kinds of processes.

The tendency to study evolutionary psychology and cultural evolution in isolation is probably best explained by accidents and vicissitudes in the history of science and the way academic disciplines and fashions have formed but, from a purely theoretical perspective, these two subjects should be seen as intricately interwoven. Nevertheless, since evolutionary psychologists and cultural evolution theorists adopt divergent explanatory strategies, the natural interconnectedness of their projects is all too easily overlooked. Evolutionary psychology emphasizes the idea that culture is *evoked*, to the extent that it matches the input conditions of specialized cognitive architecture, whereas cultural evolution theory emphasizes the idea that cultural systems result from processes of *transmission* via social learning. Clearly, however, human culture is both evoked and transmitted, so the question is really about the relative contribution of both dimensions. Having acknowledged this, a key next step is to figure out a suitable framework for understanding how the two processes work together. The gap between evolutionary psychology and cultural evolution theory arguably stems from a tendency of both disciplines to emphasize problems of ultimate rather than proximate causation, focusing more on issues of function and selection than on issues of mechanism and development. What has been lacking is a more encompassing account of the various levels at which proximate explanation needs to be understood.

This chapter attempts to sketch out how a more encompassing framework for studying the evolution of rituals might look. Building on Waddington's notion of the 'epigenetic landscape', three kinds of evolutionary landscapes are disambiguated: epigenetic, cognitive-developmental, and social-historical. The discussion here focuses on ritual behaviours, but the general approach would be applicable to cultural practices more generally. The aim is to bring greater conceptual integration to a somewhat complex and messy cluster of research areas and at the same time, open up new hypotheses ripe for investigation. But first, it is helpful to explore the underling basis for the opposition of evolutionary psychology and cultural evolution theory.

Are Rituals Evoked or Transmitted?

Rituals are *evoked* to the extent that some putatively innate behavioural tendency is triggered by the presence of some standard social cue (e.g. exaggerated concern with separating and cleaning). For example, Chapter 1 set out evidence that overimitation is an innate (biologically inherited, early developing, panhuman) learning mechanism and that certain standard social cues (e.g. causally opaque actions without end-goals) trigger higher fidelity overimitation while suppressing idiosyncratic innovation. By contrast, ritual is *transmitted* to the extent that some putatively learned behavioural convention (e.g. self-crossing) is passed down through the generations as part of a particular religious tradition (in the case of self-crossing, the Roman Catholic church). Evolutionary psychologists have tended to argue that most of the ritual behaviour we observe is evoked via innate mechanisms, whereas cultural evolution theorists tend to argue that most of it is transmitted via social learning.

A concise illustration of the differences of emphasis between these two perspectives is instructively provided by a debate organized in San Diego in 2016 by the Society for Personality and Social Psychology in a symposium entitled 'Big Questions in Evolutionary Science and What They Mean for Social-Personality Psychology'. Evolutionary psychologist Leda Cosmides opened the debate by arguing that much of the content of culture is evoked rather than learned. That is, many cultural representations are the way they are because they are anticipated by evolved psychological architecture and, as such, would be motivating or memorable and therefore 'catchy' for any normal human being placed in a suitable environment. By contrast, cultural evolution theorist Joe Henrich argued that much of our cognitive architecture evolved to facilitate the acquisition of useful information that could not have been inherited genetically. That is, we have evolved to recognize and preferentially learn useful information from more experienced others. Both Cosmides and Henrich agreed that many specialized cognitive adaptations have evolved through natural selection, and both agreed that culture provides an important context for the activation of these cognitive systems. The points of disagreement between them, however, turned out to be as subtle and multifaceted as they are theoretically portentous.

For evolutionary psychologists like Cosmides, the most striking thing about cultural learning is the role of evolved psychological capacities that emerge similarly in development across all human populations, and are both highly specialized and genetically prespecified. For cultural evolution theorists like Henrich, on the other hand, evolved behaviour programmes in humans are much more open-ended and general purpose. Both acknowledge that human psychology is an outcome of biological evolution. For Cosmides, however, the emphasis is on inherited cognitive specializations—a view that is often associated with (albeit not necessarily limited to) a vision of the mind as 'modular' (Fodor, 1983; Sperber, 2001). By contrast, for Henrich the emphasis is on learning capacities (if not a more general intelligence, then at least a mind specialized for learning new skills rather than simply pulling out preformed gadgets to suit the terrain).

To the extent that having acquired fluency in the performance of a certain socially learned cultural ritual can have significant consequences for anatomy, cognition, and behaviour, Henrich argues that culture and genes can co-evolve. But whereas for Henrich this insight should have profound implications for our understanding of human psychology, Cosmides would argue that most cultural innovations are too recent to have had much effect on biological evolution via natural selection.

Lurking somewhat in the background of this particular debate is a question about whether or not culture itself evolves. Cosmides would readily acknowledge that of course rituals and other cultural representations can accumulate in a population so as to form distinctive cultural traditions and that particular domains of culture, such as technology, can become progressively more effective and efficient via processes of winnowing and selection. But she doubts whether such processes constitute a separate system of inheritance, alongside genetic inheritance, such that the two might be said to co-evolve (see also Sperber, 1996). According to Cosmides, the notion of a cultural inheritance system either requires or tends to lead to a 'mind-less' (psychologically implausible) view of cultural transmission (see also Powell & Clarke, 2012).

The debate in San Diego between Cosmides and Henrich was designed around an adversarial format, however, and veiled much common agreement. Moreover, it would surely be misleading to reduce the differences between evolutionary psychology and cultural evolution theory to the views expressed by only two academics at a single symposium. Nevertheless, a puzzling conundrum lurks beneath the surface here and deserves careful consideration. While some emphasize culture as evoked and others emphasize its transmission via social learning, all agree on many fundamental points of theory; yet they still end up concluding that what the other is studying is not what they think it is. This is reminiscent of the story of the three blind men who each feel a different part of the elephant (e.g. the tail, the trunk, and the ear) and, as a consequence, reach very different conclusions about the nature of the object before them (claiming respectively that the object is a rope, a branch, and a fan). These disagreements, however, may begin to evaporate if we augment the focus on ultimate causation and evolutionary history with a much closer consideration of proximate and ontogenetic dimensions, in a way that more fully incorporates the theories and findings of both evolutionary psychologists and cultural evolution theorists, among others.

Proximate Causation and Development in the Evolution of Ritual

The developmental pathways of biological organisms, minds, and social systems are intimately interconnected. This is not always obvious when conducting research at these different explanatory levels in light of discipline-specific questions, theories, and methods. Thus, most theories in the cognitive science of religion, for example, ignore efforts to establish the genetic and neurological foundations of religiosity. Social scientists are meanwhile notoriously skeptical of psychological and biological reductionism and seldom consider the shaping and constraining effects of cognitive and physiological processes. The resulting silo effect would not be a problem if processes unfolded at these different levels independently. But they do not. Efforts to show how they are related tend to approach the subject in a rather arbitrary and piecemeal fashion. What is needed is a more integrated conceptual scheme, one that generates systematic hypotheses and provides a more comprehensive and flexible understanding of proximate causation and development in the evolution of cultural traits, such as rituals.

A fruitful heuristic for thinking about proximate causation and development is provided by Waddington's famous notion of the 'epigenetic landscape' (1957). The basic idea is that the development of any phenotypic characteristic (whether morphological, physiological, or behavioural) is an outcome of both genetic and environmental factors in varying degrees. To represent this complex interaction, Waddington invited us to imagine a virtual landscape in which the contours vary, and to picture developing traits (e.g. organs) as marbles rolling down through that landscape, their descent corresponding to a process of maturation over time. In this elegant metaphor, genes are represented as pegs, and the effects of genes are represented as guy ropes. These guy ropes tug under the surface of the landscape so as to create furrows, canalizing development towards a steady end-state (the mature phenotype). The idea is that where the tug of genes is weaker the furrows in the landscape are shallower, and therefore environmental influences

Waddington	Epigenetic landscape
Pegs	Genes
Guy ropes	Biochemical or regulatory effects of genes.
Landscape	Sum of the effects of genes and environment in producing as table end-state.
Steep ness	Genetic robustness. Steep= genetic canalization. Shallow = plasticity
Endstate (attractor)	Mature phenotype (morphology, physiology or behaviour)

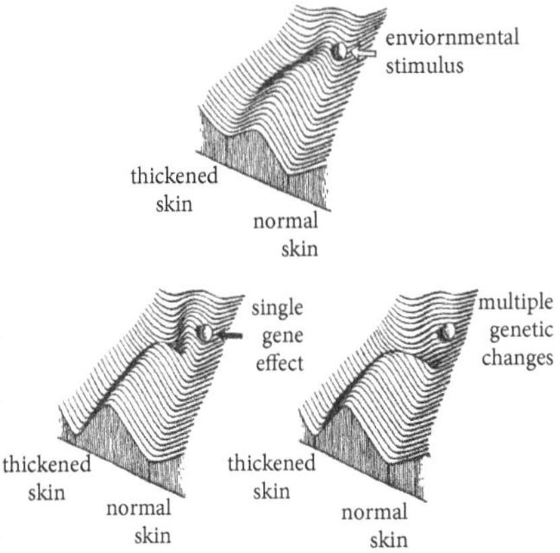

Figure 5.1 *Waddington's epigenetic landscape*
(*Source: Tavory, Jablonka, & Ginsburg, 2013*)

can push the developing phenotype onto a new path, something that could not be accomplished by the effects of genes alone.

Waddington was admittedly proposing a mixed metaphor, combining the image of a tent (the canvas of which is held taught by pegs and guy ropes) and the image of a landscape (the contours of which are formed by quite different forces, such as erosion). Although mixed metaphors are considered a faux pas in some literary circles, Waddington's works quite well because the surface of a hillside does in many ways resemble the wall of a tent. We could, however, dispense with the idea of a landscape altogether and simply think of the image of a badly pitched tent with furrowed walls and imagine developing phenotypic traits as raindrops sliding down the canvas. An added advantage of this modification is that it affords a source analogue for the environment, in the form of a gusting wind that can tauten and relax the furrows of the fabric within the constraints imposed by genetic pegs and ropes. A similar modification is proposed later in this chapter.

Others too have suggested thought-provoking revisions to the epigenetic landscape metaphor. Tavory, Jablonka, and Ginsburg (2013) have extended Waddington's metaphor as a way of understanding the development of sociocultural systems. In their new version of the metaphor, pegs represent cultural traits of various kinds—and these can canalize the development of communities in much the same way as genes can canalize the development of an organ

Jablonka	Social-developmental landscape
Pegs	Each peg is a distinctive cultural trait such as a norm, or skill, or story, or style of clothing, etc.
Guy ropes	Exert 'pull' on the landscape via their entanglements
Landscape	Sum of the effects cultural traits and agentive strategies in producing a stable end-state.
Steepness	Steep = faithful inheritance of tradition? Shallow = innovation?
End state (attractor)	A more or less stable community or tradition?

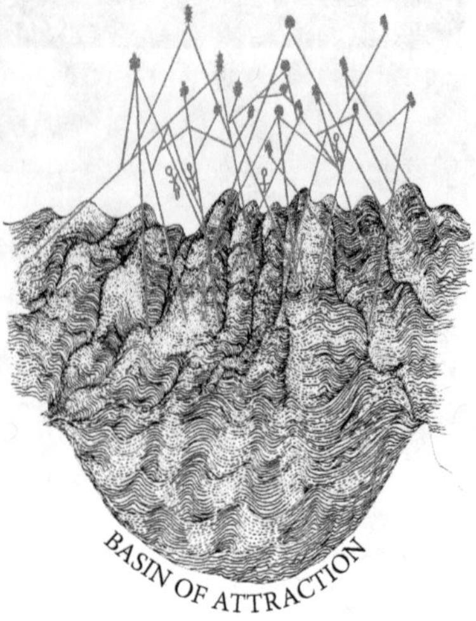

Figure 5.2 *A social-developmental landscape*
(*Source: Tavory, Jablonka, & Ginsburg, 2013*)

in the body. As in Waddington's original metaphor, the flatter parts of the landscape represent regions where the canalizing effects of pegs are less strongly exerted, allowing outside factors to push development in new directions. In the so-called social-developmental landscape these outside factors include the conscious strategies of agents in their efforts to accomplish various outcomes.

The general proposal advanced by Tavory et al. is original and thought-provoking. Nevertheless, it raises a host of unanswered questions. For example, what exactly do the pegs and guy ropes refer to in this social-developmental landscape? Do the pegs represent individual behaviours or recurrent *patterns* of behaviour at a population level? Or do they represent *cultural maps* rather than behaviours? Is the mature phenotype a cultural system or a social group (or both, or something else)?

As noted above, one of the limitations of Waddington's original analogy was that the effects of the environment are not represented pictorially, despite playing an important role in his conceptual framework. Moreover, simple one-to-one mappings of genes (pegs) and their expressions (guy ropes) do not capture well the kinds of processes described by contemporary animal geneticists. Such problems could be remedied, however, by extending Waddington's analogy such that *environmental* pegs and guy ropes *above* the landscape pull on its fabric so as to counter or exacerbate the effects of *genetic* pegs and guy ropes tugging from *below*. (These environmental dynamics need not be as Tavory et al. portray them, as we shall see.) To capture more of the complexity of the gene-phenotype relationship, instead of simple direct connections between pegs and their points of attachment to the landscape one might imagine entangled guy ropes (somewhat more along the lines of Tavory et al.'s inverted landscape but without the inversion). Moreover, although Waddington envisaged the mature phenotype as a stable resting place in the epigenetic landscape, when applying this analogy to human development, it would be more accurate to imagine the mature phenotype as a very gently descending valley floor where development proceeds slowly but doesn't come to a halt (until death), in contrast with the much faster pace of development during immaturity.

Epigenetic Landscapes

Rituals are intimately linked to physiological development in a wide range of ways, for instance by influencing diet, sexual behaviour, drug use, and many other behaviours that impact the development of the body. To take just one example, we recently conducted a study with football fans in Brazil, showing that the negative stress hormone *cortisol* was found in higher concentrations among participants fused via imagistic experiences (Newson et al., 2020). Rituals and the emotional, spiritual, and exegetical mental states to which they give rise recruit brain activity in ways that are potentially observable and measurable empirically (Newberg & Waldman, 2009). There is some evidence, for example, that imagistic experiences are physiologically related to quite well-studied neural disorders such as temporal lobe epilepsy (Persinger, 1983; Livingstone, 2005), and that feelings of transcendence induced by meditation are linked to decreased activity in the parietal lobe, a part of the brain involved in orienting the body to three-dimensional spaces (Urgesi et al., 2010). Other studies have sought to understand the biochemistry of certain aspects of ritual participation, focusing on the role of neurotransmitters like dopamine in altered states of consciousness (Previc, 2009).

Although the neurophysiology of ritual is not well understood, there have been a number of intriguing studies showing that collective rituals can have distinctive population-level effects on synchronization of brain activity. In one recent study, for example, we presented members of a Chinese ritual tradition with videos of a trusted spirit medium performing low-, medium-, or high-arousal rituals (Cho et al., 2018). Participants were assigned to either a watch-alone (individual) condition or a watch-together (group) condition. Across both conditions, participants judged higher arousal ritual to be more efficacious. Efficacy judgements in turn predicted some striking patterns in neural synchrony based on electroencephalogram (EEG) data. For example, in the group condition, participants showed increased theta-phase synchronization with others watching the same video together. Although interpretation of such findings should proceed cautiously, such research suggests that performing rituals in groups has distinctive effects on brain activation, a finding that is broadly consistent with previous studies showing that physiological arousal, as measured by heartrate, can synchronize among observers and participants who are socially or genealogically related (e.g. Konvalinka et al., 2011).

Although research into the neural correlates of ritual actions is still in its infancy, it seems reasonable to assume that the brain states that occur during and after the performance of rituals are shaped by both genes as well as culture (and culturally constructed environments). Rituals are phenotypic characteristics, just like any other, and their development can be conceptualized in Waddingtonian terms in the same way as the development of organs. By way of illustration, consider again the hazard precaution theory of ritual discussed in Chapter 2, which proposes that cultural rituals activate a cluster of brain systems evolved to respond to hazardous substances by triggering precautionary routines such as cleaning, separating, and straightening (Boyer & Liénard, 2006). The idea is that these same brain systems malfunction in patients suffering from obsessive-compulsive disorder (OCD), but where no such pathology is present, they serve a useful function biologically by causing people to handle potentially contaminating substances with special care. The hazard precaution theory proposes, however, that the same mechanism that protects us from harmful contaminants is routinely hijacked by cultural systems that mimic the relevant input, in the form of religious taboos, for example, which similarly involve concerns about coming into contact with sacred materials and substances, requiring stereotyped behavioural routines resembling those of OCD patients. This is clearly an example of ritual as an evoked trait, of the kind envisaged by Cosmides (above).

Boyer and Liénard argue that the hazard precaution system has a distinctive developmental trajectory. They cite evidence that diagnostic features of the hazard precaution system, such as concern with 'just right' object placement, cleaning, stereotypy and repetition of routines, appear around year two and peak prior to puberty. This would seem to be consistent with the hypothesis that the evolved function of the hazard precaution system is to protect against infectious or contaminating materials during vulnerable phases of development, when exploratory play and learning is most intense and therefore the risk of exposure to hazards is most acute. Boyer and Liénard also present some evidence that OCD-like thinking peaks in women during pregnancy and in men after the birth of their first child.

To conceptualize the development of the hazard precaution system in terms of the epigenetic landscape metaphor, we might envisage a topography of relatively steep valleys during adolescence, indicating somewhat stronger genetic canalization during this phase of development. Here the 'tug' of genes and their guy ropes underneath the landscape would be stronger than during most other life stages. (These effects would result from networks of genes rather than simple one-to-one mappings between genes and development.) Then there would be further valleys during reproductive phases before the landscape flattens out and a stable or 'mature' phenotype is achieved. We can extend Waddington's metaphor, however, to represent the effects of the environment on this developmental process. Exposure to cues activating the hazard precaution system might be more or less frequent or intense for different individuals depending, for instance, on how ritualistic the environment is, how much concern is expressed with issues of hygiene and boundary marking, and how great are the risks of contamination and infection. A highly ritualistic religious system, such as Judaism for instance, might serve to deepen the furrows in the landscape created by genetic canalization of the hazard precaution system and its neurological circuitry. By contrast, a more iconoclastic religious system, such as a Protestant church eschewing ritual, might soften the contours of the landscape, resulting in a different mature phenotype.

Cognitive-Developmental Landscapes

Although cognitive capacities are shaped and constrained by processes in the brain (and the genetic, cultural, and environmental influences shaping their expression and development), psychological systems are not wholly reducible to neurological ones. In order to understand the complexity of human mental life, it is necessary to formulate theories of reasoning, memory, motivation, and emotional response at a level distinct from biological events. In short, we need to postulate a cognitive-developmental landscape as well as an epigenetic one. This cognitive-developmental landscape is quite compatible with Waddington's original scheme. In this new scheme, however, pegs would represent species-specific, genetically canalized pathways in cognitive development, and guy ropes would represent evolved cognitive constraints on learning. These constraints could be very strong (e.g. the impression that rituals are magically efficacious) but with a certain amount of learning and practice, they can also be overcome to some extent (so we can appreciate that magical thinking is invalid from a scientific perspective).

	Epigenetic Landscape	Cognitive-Developmental Landscape
Pegs	Genes	Evolved cognitive capacities (does not require massive modularity)
Guy ropes	Biochemical or regulatory effects of genes	Cognitive constraints on learning
Landscape	Sum of the effects of genes and their effects plus environment on changing gravitational pull towards a stable end-state. (Environment as geology?)	Sum of the effects of cognitive constraints plus cultural scaffolding on changing gravitational pull towards a more or less stable end state.
Steepness	Steep = canalization; Shallow = plasticity	Steep = cognitive canalization; Shallow = cognitive plasticity
End stage (attractor)	Mature phenotype (morphology physiology or behaviour	Mature phenotype (stable semantic networks)

Figure 5.3 *Summary of the cognitive-developmental landscape*
(Source: Whitehouse, 2013)

The interaction of cognitive canalization and cultural learning in development results in more or less stable *semantic networks* in the minds of mature agents. Semantic networks are systems of representations, each representation being conceptualized as a node that is in turn linked to other nodes with varying frequency, credibility, and emotional salience. Not all nodes in a semantic network are equally easy to represent, believe, or remember. Some nodes or clusters of nodes are more intuitive than others, chiming more readily with maturationally natural and universal implicit beliefs (McCauley, 2011). By contrast some nodes may be more counterintuitive or form part of more elaborated clusters, making them more difficult to acquire and maintain. These features of semantic networks were discussed at some length in Chapter 2 when describing the process of building an agent-based model to simulate doctrinal-imagistic oscillations in a particular ritual tradition.

The theologically elaborated teachings of doctrinal religions are typically more counterintuitive than the 'theologically incorrect' beliefs of rank and file laity. Consider some examples from the Roman Catholic cultural system. Many Catholics in Southern Europe cross themselves upon entering a church because they have an implicit belief that God is present in holy places even though he cannot be seen or heard. This belief forms part of a network of explicit representations supported by quite simple intuitive assumptions. Mind-body dualism, for instance, has a number of intuitive properties that would appear to recur in all human populations (Cohen et al., 2011). These include the expectation that that the memories, beliefs, and desires of agents can occur outside bodies, can survive death, and can even move between bodies in the case of spirit possession or divine inspiration. Although disembodied agency is easy to represent and would therefore seem to be culturally universal, agency is intuitively tied to a location in space (Barrett & Keil, 1996) and is constrained by intuitive principles of gravity, solidity, and continuity (Meng, Nakawake, et al, 2021). Catholics do not appeal to relics several miles away but move within earshot of the relic in order to commune with it. By contrast, the Vatican teaches that God is omnipresent, a proposition that is much less intuitive and therefore difficult to implement as a guiding principle in worshipful practice. If the principle of omnipresence were really used as a guide to behaviour, self-crossing would be no more necessary in churches than in other places and it would be just as effective to address a holy relic from afar.

Similar disjunctions between intuitive lay beliefs and more counterintuitive theological systems have been observed with respect to many features of intuitive reasoning. For example, as noted in Chapter 2, our predisposition to adopt teleological explanations for the functions of material objects make it easier to represent features of the natural world as the purposeful creations of gods, ancestors, or other agents than as the products of erosion or descent with modification (Kelemen, 2004). Likewise, our intuitions about immanent justice make it easier to imagine that wicked people will get their comeuppance than to absorb the intricate and often counterintuitive propositions of moral philosophy (Binmore, 2005). To express this in Waddingtonian terms, some semantic networks are more strongly *canalized* than others in the course of development. In general, this means that intuitive nodes in semantic networks decay less rapidly than counterintuitive nodes.

Nevertheless, semantic networks can also exhibit remarkable plasticity. Rehearsal and review of a network of representations, even of a complex and counterintuitive network, can strengthen the links between nodes. Theologians overcome the limitations of intuitive reasoning, producing religious phenotypes quite different from what would be expected based on processes of cognitive canalization alone (Slone, 2004). Costly signalling (Sosis & Alcorta, 2003) and 'credibility enhancing displays' (Henrich, 2009), such as self-flagellation or large charitable donations, might also increase the plausibility of semantic networks (as discussed at some length in Chapter 4). Logic and narrative used in the teaching of religious doctrines can meanwhile help to make a body of orthodox teachings more memorable as well as more coherent and believable (Whitehouse, 2000). External mnemonics, such as sacred texts, can also help to preserve semantic networks over time (Mullins, Whitehouse, & Atkinson, 2013).

Another approach that has proven useful in the study of religion's cognitive-developmental landscape is to construct agent-based models. This allows us to vary the effects of cognitive canalization, emotional salience, repetition, conformism bias, and prestige bias. Although computational simulations cannot tell us directly about the workings of the real world, they help us understand our own theories better, enabling us to generate more precise and testable hypotheses (Whitehouse et al., 2012).

Social-Historical Landscapes

Semantic networks associated with ritual performances can be communicated as public representations, for instance, by means of procedural performances, speeches, ritual artefacts, and body decorations. Individuals sample public representations around them and update their semantic networks accordingly, with the result that meaning systems can be largely shared across entire populations. The sum of all people's semantic networks in a bounded population can be described as a 'sociocultural system'. As in Waddington's epigenetic landscape, the pegs in a sociocultural-historical landscape would represent information, but rather than pegs encoding information in genes (or in minds in the case of the cognitive-developmental landscape), pegs would now represent a set of normative beliefs and behaviours in a population, in other words, its 'social structure'. Guy ropes would now represent the implementation of these rules in practice: sometimes people follow the rule book to the letter but at other times they innovate, as their individual strategies unfold on the ground. This has been described as 'social organization' as distinct from the normative rule book of social structure (Firth, 1964). The sum of the combined effects of social structure and social organization, on the one hand, and various environmental forces acting on a population (such as invasions and natural disasters), on the other, determine its historical trajectory. Inasmuch as some sociocultural systems eventually coalesce into relatively stable forms, they may be said to achieve their mature phenotype (change becoming very gradual like the ageing process in the body). Like organisms, however, sociocultural systems have a finite lifespan (they 'rise and fall' or evolve into something else). Some never accomplish stability or die young.

The formation of some doctrinal traditions is heavily canalized by social structure, for instance, in the case of some of the stricter Protestant denominations of Christianity that maintain a rigid orthodoxy through the use of unrelenting repetition of the creed, its codification in text, and the supervisory prominence of ecclesiastical authorities. Other traditions, such as New Age cults and fashions, exhibit much greater plasticity, and the canalizing effects of social structure are weaker. Accordingly, environmental factors should have a stronger effect on the development of the tradition when normatively canalized social structure is weak, and vice-versa.

	Epigenetic Landscape	Social-Historical Landscape
Pegs	Genes	Shared semantic networks ('social structure'; institutional instruction manual)
Guy ropes	Biochemical or regulatory effects of genes	Cumulative socialbehavioural effects of the rules and models encoded in semantic networks ('social organization'; agency in action)
Landscape	Sum of the effects of genes and their effects *plus environment* on changing gravitational pull towards a stable end-state. (Environment as geology?)	Sum of the effects of social structure and organization plus environment (e.g. invasion, revolution, tsunami on changing gravitational pull towards a more or less stable end state.
Steepness	Steep = canalization; Shallow = plasticity	Steep = social structural canalization; Shallow = social structural plasticity
End stage (attractor)	Mature phenotype (morphology physiology or behaviour	Mature phenotype (more or less stable cultural system, i.e. distributed and standardized semantic network at the population level)

Figure 5.4 *Summary of the social-historical landscape*
(*Source: Whitehouse, 2013*)

Multilevel Landscapes

Epigenetic, cognitive-developmental, and social-historical landscapes shape and constrain each other. For example, genetically canalized neural systems constrain our psychological susceptibility to particular nodes in semantic networks. But practice and review of these networks can extend our capacities for reasoning and memory (outcomes in the cognitive-developmental landscape), and thus the uniformity and stability of cultural representations across human populations (outcomes in the social-historical landscape). In other words, processes unfolding in any given landscape can have major consequences for processes in all the others.

To illustrate, consider the many so-called cargo cults of Melanesia that blossomed in the wake of colonization and missionization by Western powers, mainly during the twentieth century. The term 'cargo cult' is typically used to refer to groups believing that the wealth, technology, and high standard of living in postindustrial societies have a supernatural origin and can be obtained by appealing to spirits, ancestors, or gods. A variety of epigenetic, cognitive-developmental, and social-historical processes came into play in the evolution of the cargo cult phenomenon. Moral intuitions, for example, played an important role in the cognitive-developmental landscape. Cult leaders foretold that the great imbalances of wealth between native peoples and the colonists would be levelled or

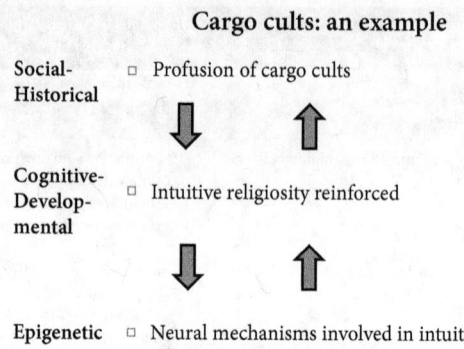

Figure 5.5 *Some causal relations between epigenetic, cognitive-developmental, and social-historical landscapes in cargo cults*
(Source: Whitehouse, 2013)

reversed and enemy tribes would be vanquished or punished. Prophets also appealed to intuitions about mind-body dualism (e.g. predicting that the spirits of the dead would be reincarnated), about the efficacy of ritual (e.g. by means of which the cargo would materialize), and about acts of creation (e.g. on the part of primordial ancestors). Little is currently known about the role of genetic processes in the development of the neural systems involved in intuitive reasoning about hazard precaution, immanent justice, mind-body dualism, and promiscuous teleology. Nevertheless, if these panhuman, early developing neural systems evolved under natural selection, then like any other innately prespecified architecture, they would have been recursively harnessed in the elaboration of historically distinctive religious traditions (see Chapter 2 for an extended discussion of this in the construction of an agent-based model). Thus, social-historical systems postulating supernatural agent concepts are able to fine-tune the maturation of intuitive reasoning in various ways, and this would naturally also impact the development of neural pathways. In such ways, these three levels of analysis are clearly interconnected (see Figure 5.5).

To explore how interactions of this kind might unfold in practice it is instructive to consider in further detail the case of the Kivung movement of New Britain, Papua New Guinea (PNG) (Whitehouse, 1995), discussed in Chapter 2. Like most Melanesian cargo cults, the Kivung was based on a set of highly intuitive propositions about human origins, the return of the ancestors, the arrival of cargo, and the righting of wrongs. But whereas all other cargo cults in New Britain had flared up and then disappeared just as rapidly, the Kivung had unusual staying power and it spread to a much larger population than any of the cults that came before. Moreover, it offered a doctrinal system and orthopraxy more elaborated than any previous cults. Some of the movement's teachings went far beyond merely intuitive ideas, postulating a complex theology comparable to missionary Christianity, with all its attendant dogmas and a

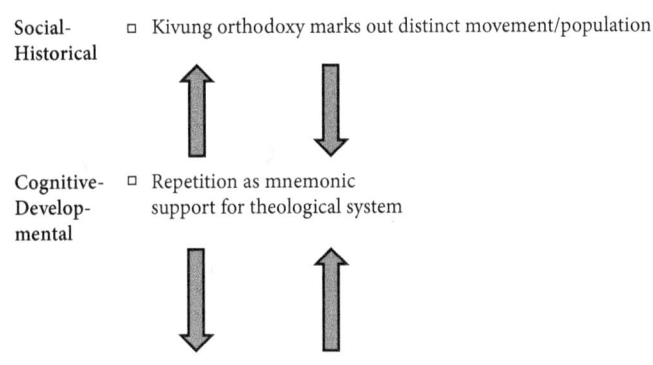

Figure 5.6 *Some causal relations between epigenetic, cognitive-developmental, and social-historical landscapes in the Kivung*
(Source: Whitehouse, 2013)

corpus of parables and stories linking them together. Kivung beliefs and practices formed an extensive religious system that became standardized in the 1960s and has remained much the same ever since. How are we to explain the success of this ritual tradition?

The Kivung was more persuasive, enduring, and widespread than other creeds in part because it exploited the cognitive-developmental landscape in a novel way. It subjected its theories and stories to frequent repetition at public gatherings. As argued in Chapter 2, this seemingly minor adjustment in the cognitive-developmental landscape allowed a single coherent body of teachings and practices to become standardized across the movement as a whole, radically changing the entire social-historical landscape (Whitehouse, 1995, 2000, 2004). It meant that much more elaborate semantic networks than those featuring in earlier cargo cults could now be sustained in memory. This would in turn have had consequences for the development of neural processes involved in semantic memory, rote learning, narrative construction, oratorical expertise, and so on but it would also facilitate the regional homogenization of the tradition and its orthodoxy at a population level (see Figure 5.6).

In the example just provided, the ramifications of a change in one landscape had feedback effects in the others. That is, a change in cognitive development (doctrinal learning through rehearsal and review) occasioned changes at both epigenetic and social-historical levels, which fed back into cognitive development by strengthening certain forms of expertise and memory from below and stabilizing normative rules from above. But one can easily imagine other patterns, for instance, where changes in the three landscapes occur in a cyclical fashion. Consider the following example.

When the Kivung was first established, its leaders declared that followers should no longer chew betel nut (a widespread and somewhat addictive practice in PNG). The explicit rationale for tabooing betel nut was that the red substance produced (and spat around on the ground) was akin to menstrual blood, considered by some of the ethnic groups joining the Kivung to be polluting and dangerous. Linking betel nut to menstrual blood suddenly made the practice of chewing seem disgusting, a transformation in the cognitive-developmental landscape of Kivung followers. An unintended consequence of this lifestyle change was the emergence of widespread dental problems, especially halitosis, which had previously been prevented by betel chewing. This change in the epigenetic landscape affected the perceived attractiveness of Kivung followers at least to outsiders, affecting processes of mate selection in the cognitive-developmental landscape. Resulting changes in patterns of marriage made the Kivung movement increasingly endogamous. This in turn sharpened the boundaries between ingroup and outgroup in the social-historical landscape. Sanctions were introduced to deter betel chewing among followers, reinforcing the normative social system but also impacting the psychological association of betel nut with sinfulness and pollution. In this way, a cyclical pattern of reinforcement for this novel aspect of life in the Kivung became established.

Of course, there are many other patterns of this kind that could be hypothesized using the landscape metaphor. The examples given here are merely to show how this can open up a new perspective on processes of religious evolution, and sociocultural evolution more generally.

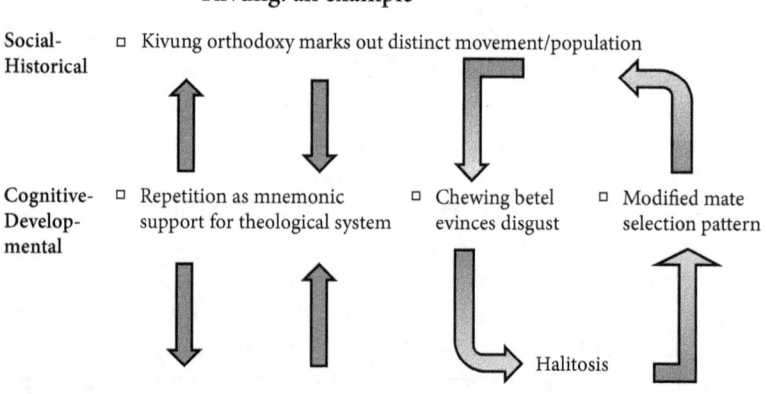

Figure 5.7 *Further causal relations between epigenetic, cognitive-developmental, and social-historical landscapes in the Kivung*
(Source: Whitehouse, 2013)

Conclusions

The landscapes metaphor brings conceptual integration to a very complex set of relationships between proximate causation and development in the evolution of rituals and ritual systems. Magical thinking, mind-body dualism, creationism, and a host of other patterns of reasoning commonly associated with religious ritual systems derive at least partly from evolved neural processes that are also influenced in development by social and cultural environments. This is hardly controversial, and yet the ways in which these levels interact are not very thoroughly understood, and the situation is easily oversimplified.

The dominant paradigm in evolutionary psychology, which sees culture as primarily evoked rather than transmitted, has found rich expression in the cognitive science of religion (White, 2021). For many contributors to that field, the main challenge of explaining religion is to identify a set of universal cognitive predispositions and susceptibilities to believe certain things rather than others (e.g. Boyer, 2001; Barrett, 2004; Slone, 2004). While this has undoubtedly produced much important research, it tends to overlook the fact that all religious representations are embedded in cultural systems with highly variable content and structure. These systems sometimes foreground intuitive ideas but can also exclude or obscure them with widely varying consequences for history, individual experience, and physiological processes—all of which often have important feedback effects. At the same time, however, it is not enough to gloss over all this complexity by conceptualizing it as a generic process of cultural transmission facilitated by a simple set of open-ended learning programmes, which is perhaps closer to the strategy commonly adopted in the field of cultural evolution theory. What is required is a framework that integrates but also extends both approaches.

As well as capturing and integrating more of the complexity inherent in processes of sociocultural evolution, the multilevel landscape framework opens up new hypotheses. If we look more closely at ritual systems through the lens of the epigenetic landscape metaphor, we begin to ask not only about processes in the brain but in the organism as a whole. The role of betel nut in dental hygiene is a fairly random example, but consider how many religions taboo recreational drugs, most commonly alcohol. How has this affected or been affected by cognitive development for individuals growing up in culturally heterogeneous cities, where alcohol is freely available and widely used, and how has this impacted or been influenced by processes of sociocultural reproduction and change? Questions crossing the boundaries of biology, individual psychology, and social systems are seldom asked or only posed in a way that is narrowly focused on the seemingly idiosyncratic interests of particular researchers, rather than being systematically derived from a single overarching conceptual framework. Although this chapter only sketches the contours of how such a framework might be developed, the aim is to stimulate further theorizing and empirical research that would refine and improve the approach, so that it can be rendered more precisely, and its implications fleshed out more comprehensively. Some of the challenges this presents for science, and potential strategies for overcoming them, are discussed in the final chapter. But first, let us consider what might be gained from applying these ideas to practical problems in society at large, the topic of the next chapter.

6
Challenges for Society

The theories and findings described in this book have ramifying implications for all of us as citizens, and for those responsible for formulating and implementing public policy. The modes theory sets out to explain how rituals produce different types and intensities of social glue, and this in turn constrains what kinds of cooperation are possible and on what scale coordinated effort can occur. So, the question then inevitably arises: could we (and relatedly, *should* we) redesign or modify our rituals or try to manage their effects in an effort to make us more ethical co-operators?

Many collective action problems depend on social glue and cooperation. On a global scale, for example, extreme poverty is a scourge on humanity that could be solved quite rapidly with sufficient commitment worldwide to creating and implementing the mechanisms necessary to redistribute wealth, and wealth-producing opportunities, more equitably (Singer, 1999). Likewise, the most disastrous effects of global heating might be averted if action were taken more swiftly by all of us, in a more coordinated fashion (Sheppard, 2012). Much the same could be said about other global challenges, many of which are interrelated, such as forced migration, resource depletion, preventable disease, warfare, modern slavery, terrorism, global food security, and human rights violations. The fundamental insight that social glue can be used to tackle all these problems around the world may sound overoptimistic or even naïve. No doubt, however, our palaeolithic ancestors would have been just as sceptical if assured that one day humans would live in societies comprising millions of people, obeying laws made by governments representing all of them, enforced by a professionalized police force and funded through a system of wealth contributions to a cumulative central pool. Supposing it had somehow been possible to communicate such a vision coherently and intelligibly thousands of years ago, before the advent of agriculture, it would surely have sounded like the stuff of dreams. And yet precisely such a transformation—from small-scale groups with very limited means of keeping the peace between them into large-scale centralized political organization—did indeed occur at multiple locations around the world, before spreading and eventually overtaking most of the habitable world. And in some regions, the speed of this transition was quite breath taking.

In the Pomio-Baining region of Papua New Guinea where I carried out fieldwork in the late 1980s (see Chapter 2), the transition from small-scale, face-to-face communities to large-scale, centralized, hierarchical societies encompassing multiple ethnic groups took only a few years to accomplish. This was because

Pomio-Baining people were in possession of a blueprint for building a large-scale doctrinal movement provided by talented indigenous leaders well versed in the ways of missionary Christianity and colonial administration. Similar processes took much longer (thousands of years) in regions like the Mediterranean, North Africa, and East Asia (see Chapter 4) and that is because the evolution of social complexity had to proceed from scratch. Neither our Neolithic ancestors at the dawn of agriculture, nor even the most inspired visionaries of the great bronze age civilizations, had the benefit of seeing what sorts of innovations and compromises would be needed to enable multi-ethnic empires to flourish and spread. In the present era, we similarly lack a detailed blueprint for collective action on a global scale, but we can build such a thing from the ground up if we are able to combine the relevant sciences in an effective way. This is where the multilevel landscapes approach, set out in the last chapter, has potentially significant practical ramifications.

Human worlds are never shaped exclusively at the level of biology, mind, or institutional history alone. They are continuously shaped by *all three* and by the *relationships* between all three. Scientists have appreciated this fact, and its policy implications, more readily in some domains than in others (Jablonka, 2016). For example, it has been recognized for some time that urban poverty is a trap, into which individuals can easily become ensnared by adopting strategies to which any of us would naturally be prone in similar circumstances. These strategies include future discounting (e.g. resulting in risky resource procurement strategies and teenage pregnancies) and criminal coalitional behaviour (e.g. in the form of street gangs, drug cartels, terrorist organizations, and hooligan groups), giving rise to undesirable outcomes that are hard to reverse, such as incarceration, substance dependencies, and high defection costs if seeking to extricate oneself from criminal networks. These strategies are not only a product of processes at the cognitive-developmental level, however. They are also shaped by social-historical and epigenetic landscapes, that can ensnare individuals within self-reproducing systems or 'vicious cycles.' For example, one feature of the social-historical landscape associated with urban poverty in the contemporary world is reliance on cheap, mass-produced, high-energy foods which, given an evolved human fondness for sweet and fatty foodstuffs (a universal predisposition in the cognitive-developmental landscape), encourages overconsumption, which in turn produces consequences at the epigenetic level, such as early sexual maturation (McBride, Paikoff, & Holmbeck, 2003). This then links back to behaviour via cognitive-developmental processes in the form of early sexual debut, teenage pregnancies, and increased existential insecurity which, unsurprisingly, feeds back into the propagation of social-historical environments, including parasitic forms of capitalism (e.g. multinational supermarket chains and fast food outlets exacerbating demand for unhealthy foods in deprived neighbourhoods) that make extrication from the poverty trap still harder to accomplish.

But while some aspects of the multilevel landscape framework have been deciphered in a few fairly random domains, such as the study of urban poverty traps, it is seldom realized that the same logic applies to all other aspects of human life, and thus of public policy, including the most pressing collective action problems currently facing our species as a whole. Consider, for example, the problem of how best to respond to a global pandemic. In formulating and publicly justifying measures to manage the threat of viral infection, governments naturally seize upon evidence from scientists working on dynamics in the epigenetic landscape, such as the search for vaccines capable of establishing population immunity. But less immediately obvious to politicians, who after all must respond under pressure to fast-changing conditions, is the scientific evidence pertaining to cognitive-developmental and social-historical landscapes and their interactions. One way to illustrate how greater attention to multilevel interactions could improve public policy is to consider how the UK government responded to, and perhaps inadvertently contributed to, high rates of infection during the early phases of the Covid-19 pandemic of 2020–2021.

Multilevel Landscapes and Public Policy

UK residents who lived through the lockdowns of that period will probably recall innumerable government statements announcing the latest rules on social distancing, school attendance, travel restrictions, closure of nonessential businesses, and other measures intended to reduce spiralling infection rates. Although many of these announcements curtailed people's freedoms in ways normally more familiar in the curfews of totalitarian regimes, there appeared to be widespread public support for them. Politicians were keenly aware of this. Indeed, sensitivity to public opinion, stoked by ratings-driven news reporting, helped contribute to a seemingly incessant stream of novel measures and three-part slogans during the initial phases of the pandemic crisis. Nevertheless, the more the government announced lockdown measures in response to public demand, the more alienated and distrustful the general populace seemed to become, bemoaning lack of clarity and consistency in the formulation of the latest rules and regulations. If the government had been better informed on the relevant scientific research relating to social-historical and cognitive-developmental landscapes, as it had been on the projections of epidemiological models (and if policy makers had understood better the *relationships* between all three levels) they might have presented lockdown announcements and implementations somewhat differently.

For example, measures to combat the pandemic threat in the UK were often accompanied by vocal demands in the media for rituals with opaque but compellingly prescriptive instructions rather than instrumental measures that could be adapted flexibly to novel situations. Whenever the desire for a new orthopraxy (explicit do's and don'ts, leaving minimal room for interpretation or unintended deviation) was not felt to be adequately met, this caused disgruntlement in the general population, undermining trust in the government and commitment to well-intentioned measures. In other words, at the same time as new restrictions were being presented as instrumentally necessary for the good of the nation, there was also apparently a strong public (and media) preference for firmer normative rules. Instead of trying to exhort people to exercise common sense in preventing viral infection, the government may have been better advised to meet public demand for clear normative conventions that could be applied irrespective of changing conditions and situations encountered on the ground. By and large, people (and reporters) appeared to want rules not tools. By why? Part of the answer to this question is an early developing species-specific disposition to adopt the ritual stance when causally opaque behaviours are prescribed using appropriate social cues, as described at length in Chapter 1.

A particularly germane source of insight into the cognitive-developmental landscape influencing public reactions to the handling of lockdowns may be found in the literature on so-called normative protest observed among toddlers. Studies have shown that when children as young as two to three years old are shown a novel action described as 'daxing' (a made-up verb) subsequent performances of that same action that depart from the originally modelled version elicit vocal objections ('normative protest'), imploring the experimenter to do it 'properly' (Rakoczy, Warneken, & Tomasello, 2008). Note that this insistence on daxing 'correctly' is cued simply by the attribution of a conventional term to the action in question, despite the fact that daxing is an entirely novel feature of the child's cultural environment and is devoid of any obvious instrumental value or usefulness. Building on this point early on in the book, I presented in some detail a growing body of scientific evidence suggesting that children everywhere display an early developing propensity to imitate causally opaque behaviour, all the more so if that behaviour is unrelated to any kind of end goal. The more the causal link between action and outcome is irretrievably severed, the more precisely children will follow the rules of the ritual and the less likely they will be to invent their own versions or deviate from the normative script.

Government lockdown announcements did not take account of this important facet of human nature because it was not presented to policymakers as part of a framework that connected up the relevant bodies of knowledge in ways that could maximally inform decision-making. Consequently, politicians overemphasized end goals and the need to exercise common sense and sound judgement in achieving them. The Prime Minister himself frequently exhorted the public to acknowledge the necessity of lockdown measures by appealing to instrumental reasoning rather than to ritual obligation and the affiliative motivations undergirding it. By contrast, media reporting focused heavily on the way reactions to these announcements were filtered through the ritual stance, emphasizing the desire to implement conventions without reference to instrumental rationales. High-profile examples reported in the media included overzealous applications of newly announced rules by the police, such as fining people for pausing to sit alone on park benches, or driving slightly more than a vaguely recommended distance in order to exercise at an isolated location. Policing decisions of that kind were not driven by a concern to prevent a member of the public from infecting others so much as by a desire to implement an arbitrary procedural script: a ritual. And rather than ask what instrumental considerations should guide our implementation of social distancing measures, many members of the public clamoured to know what precise distance one should or should not drive, in order to be acting within the rules.

Nevertheless, there are also times when people want tools not rules, and indeed it is quite possible that the UK public were ambivalent about the desire for a ritualistic framework in managing the pandemic. Many also complained that lack of instrumental transparency in government guidelines was more troubling than a lack of specificity and consistency about the new orthopraxy. Establishing what the public wanted would have required better psychometric measures and data than were available at the time. But there are also compelling theoretical grounds for thinking that any tendency to adopt either a ritual or instrumental stance on government pandemic measures was likely to have been shaped and constrained by both epigenetic and social-historical factors. We should therefore look to all levels in our multilevel landscape model to achieve a fuller understanding of people's attitudes and behaviours.

Consider the following example, which recalls the logic of urban poverty traps. In the UK's epidemiological landscape, many dramatic events were taking place during the epidemic, the most salient of which were sharply rising infection rates, which, while impacting population immunity in ways that were highly contested at the time, were even more immediately triggering a cascade of precautionary reactions at the level of the cognitive-developmental landscape. Rising infection rates and Covid testing increased the probability that any individual would either be positively diagnosed with the virus or have a personal, relational tie to someone who was. This in turn would have undoubtedly amplified the mortality salience of the pandemic threat (Pyszczynski et al., 2020) as no longer something that just dominates the media and is observed from a distance, but something that is increasingly experienced directly in people's personal lives. This in turn would be predicted to trigger hazard precaution routines (Boyer & Liénard, 2006)—stereotyped behaviours, such as hand washing, associated not only with contagion avoidance and (in pathological manifestations) obsessive-compulsive behaviour but also, of particular relevance here, widely observed in cultural rituals from all around the world (Dulaney & Fiske, 1994). This, coupled with socially and historically ingrained scripts and schemas concerning what to expect in a national crisis made the top-down imposition of rituals from central government more normative and thus desirable, despite the material costs and curtailments of personal freedoms. Against such a backdrop, it is easy to understand the British demand for rules rather than tools, and why failure to provide these in the desired manner resulted in disaffection and wavering support for the Prime Minister and his cabinet.

Viewing these issues through the lens of the multilevel landscape approach, thus encourages us to consider what kinds of social cues, embedded in government responses to the pandemic threat, particularly encouraged ritual rather than instrumental stances to be adopted by the media and the general public, or the other way around. This motivates a much wider range of questions than those briefly reviewed above; all of which, however, warrant thorough empirical investigation. Many of these questions are directly prompted by the modes theory, as set out in this book. For example, mask-wearing was already a ritualized group identity marker prior to the 2020 pandemic, being notably more widespread among the East Asian diaspora, so to what extent did ingroup-outgroup thinking affect the take-up of masks in the general population (a question primarily about ritual routinization, identification, and intergroup relations as discussed in Chapter 4)? How might these ingroup and intergroup dynamics in turn have impacted the epigenetic landscape in terms of rates of infection, wider public health consequences, and population immunity (along the lines of the model discussed in Chapter 5)? How do directly experienced versus reported events at the epigenetic level filter back upwards into the cognitive-developmental landscape, and what cognitive mechanisms are activated in the process (including but not limited to those discussed in Chapter 1)? To what extent do shared experiences of illness and self-isolation or the deleterious effects of lockdowns, such as loss of income or access to support networks, foster imagistic processes, analogous to those associated with the pain of childbirth or the ordeals of frontline combat (Chapter 3)? How does the routinization of novel normative conventions, associated with social or physical distancing, impact patterns of identification, tightness-looseness, or other aspects of everyday social psychology (Chapter 4)? And how do all these processes in turn impact demand for more lockdowns and associated rules and rituals from governments that may be concerned more with remaining in power than exercising it in the long-term national interest—a situation perhaps best understood at the level of the social-historical landscape (the present consideration)?

One of the main factors impeding a multilevel approach to collective action problems is that the historical depth and pace of scientific research is uneven across levels. The sciences relevant to understanding epigenetic landscapes are substantially more precise and theoretically advanced than those focusing on the levels above, in part because the biological sciences have longer histories but mainly because their subject matter is inherently less complex and (as argued in the next chapter) better grounded in evolved intuitions. Conversely, while social-historical landscapes may be documented in fine-grained detail, engagement with scientific methods is often scant, and what passes as 'theory' is not scientific at all (and may even be presented as anti-science or 'anti-scientistic'). Although these issues are largely set aside for the next chapter, they are relevant here because they limit what can reasonably be said about the relevance of modes theory for public policy at this stage in the development of scientific knowledge. Pointing to questions about the relationships between processes within and between our multilevel landscapes is all very well, but it is still too soon to answer them with any confidence, let alone to do so comprehensively. Instead, the rest of this chapter is devoted to flagging up some of the key ways in which existing research based on the modes theory could reasonably be applied to public policy issues in the here and now. This involves focusing mainly on the current state of the art when it comes to understanding the psychological drivers of cooperation in the cognitive-developmental landscape.

A key point to keep in mind here is that cooperation at a global level and cooperation within or between families constitute extremes of a continuum. In between are many other scales of cooperation that can only be activated by applying social glue. The cooperative challenges facing humanity at this mid-range level include the prevention or containment of localized forms of intergroup conflict, such as clashes between rival football fans, ethnic groups, and sectarian coalitions, all of which have been a focus of research by those engaged in the study of imagistic dynamics, discussed in the next section. Other examples of problems to which the modes theory has been applied focus on doctrinal dynamics at a national level, such as the rise of populism in America and the causes and effects of Brexit in the UK, considered later in this chapter. The modes theory is likewise generating novel proposals for the creation of diagnostic tools for conflict prediction, ways of mobilizing imagistic pathways to fusion in order to reduce the numbers of people in prison, methods of harnessing doctrinal rituals to coordinate action on the climate crisis, and the fostering of barrier-crossing leadership to combat the deleterious effects of polarization and online echo chambers. All of these proposals—set out in more detail in this chapter—are driven by research based on the theories and methods described step by step throughout the book.

The next section focuses in on problems and solutions related to the management of *imagistic* practices. Later, in the final section, I will turn to problems and solutions related to the management of *doctrinal* practices. A major insight emerging from this research is that we now stand on the cusp of a new Axial Age—one in which the overriding challenge is to channel social glue at all levels, from family networks to global governance, and to develop a universal moral compass, endorsing panhuman principles of peaceful cooperation for the betterment of all.

Imagistic Pathways to Intergroup Violence

Throughout this book, we have seen that imagistic rituals generate an extremely powerful type of social glue, known as identity fusion. Highly fused individuals express willingness to do whatever it takes to protect the group, even to engage in acts of extreme self-sacrifice. This insight has also helped to shape closely related theories of violent extremism, such as the 'devoted actor model' (Atran, 2016), which emphasizes the motivating power of sacred values (Tetlock, 2003; Tetlock et al., 2000; Atran & Axelrod, 2008) in ways that are readily assimilated into fusion frameworks (e.g. Atran et al., 2014; Atran & Goméz, 2018).

As discussed in some detail in Chapter 3, a limitation of much early fusion research was that it relied heavily on purely hypothetical scenarios to assess willingness to engage in pro-group behaviours, such as the so-called fight-and-die measure (Swann et al., 2010). One of the drawbacks of this measure is that fighting and dying are not the same thing. Clearly, to die for one's group is a far bigger self-sacrifice than merely to fight for one's group when the risk of dying is small (Hansen, 2018). This problem can only be overcome to a limited extent by the use of trolley problems as a quasi-behavioural outcome measure (Swann et al., 2009), but even then, the scenarios are hypothetical and do not necessarily tell us how people would respond in real-world situations when presented with an opportunity to save the group at the expense of one's own life (Whitehouse, 2018a). In order to study such extreme scenarios in an ethical fashion, it became obvious that we needed to conduct surveys and experiments in field settings where people really were putting their lives at risk for one another.

An example of this is the research we conducted in Libya during 2011, the year of the popular uprising during which hordes of ordinary citizens rejected Muammar Gaddafi's *jamahiriyya* (state of the masses) and took up arms to repel government forces on the streets, thousands of them losing their lives in the process (Whitehouse et al., 2014; see also Chapter 3, above). But there are also circumstances in which the same psychological processes unfold in natural settings with less extreme consequences, for example, leading to only sporadic or localized killings, nonfatal injuries, or damage to property, rather than to full-scale civil war (e.g. Buhrmester et al., 2014). At the root of these patterns of behaviour, imagistic practices commonly lurk.

A good example of this emerged from recent research into the effects of initiation rituals on intergroup violence in rural Cameroon (Buhrmester, Zeitlyn, & Whitehouse, 2020). The African Union has estimated that some 43 per cent of Africa's landmass is utilized by pastoralists, but as pressures on land use have intensified due to mining, commercial agriculture, and the climate crisis, conflict between farmers and herders has intensified. In Nigeria alone during just the first six months of 2018, it has been estimated that some 1300 deaths resulted from such clashes and some 300,000 people were forced to flee their homes (Nnoko-Mewanu, 2018). Farmers in West Africa commonly allege that herders are damaging their crops or making unsubstantiated territorial claims, while herders claim that the lands increasingly coming under cultivation are their traditional grazing routes. Most of the violence is sporadic and localized, but there is also obvious potential for these patterns of intergroup conflict to escalate into organized terrorism or ethnic cleansing (Moritz, 2010). Understanding the psychological factors that turn interpersonal conflict into larger scale intergroup violence is clearly important in this context. One possible explanation for conflict escalation is the presence of high levels of identity fusion in communities, resulting from imagistic ritual traditions. Given the evidence of a link between fusion and willingness to fight and die to protect the group when it comes under attack (Chapter 3), it seems reasonable to ask whether the presence of imagistic initiation rituals in West Africa might explain increased prevalence of farmer-herder violence.

To test that hypothesis, we ran a survey in rural Cameroon among a sample of Mambila farmers (Buhrmester, Zeitlyn, & Whitehouse, 2020). Mambila men traditionally organize an annual ritual, usually translated as 'the Masquerade' (suàgà bɔ sep), during which masked figures run amok through villages, causing mischief and scattering objects in their path. Women and children are expected to run for cover during these visits. And each year, a new cohort of boys is initiated into the cult by means of a terrifying enforced confrontation with the masked figure in an enclosed space. Within moments of this encounter, the boys typically flee screaming, while initiated men attempt to block their escape, increasing their sense of panic. Many features of this ritual bear comparison with the initiation rites of the Mali Baining of New Britain that originally inspired the notion of an imagistic mode (Whitehouse, 1995), or the many other 'rites of terror' in which children, as part of their initiation into adulthood, are chased by masked figures while fearing for their lives (Whitehouse, 1996).

In our survey of 398 Mambila men, roughly half the sample had undergone the suàgà imagistic rite of passage, while the other half had not. We measured fusion with various groups, most importantly the Mambila people, and asked a series of questions about willingness to engage in violence to defend fellow group members. In line with our predictions, we found that initiation into the masquerade, as well as fusion with the Mambila, predicted willingness to engage in violent self-sacrifice. Given that the experience of being initiated occurred on average thirty years before our survey was conducted, our findings among the Mambila are consistent with the theory that imagistic rituals have a lifelong impact on group bonding and willingness to defend the group. But of even more immediate practical importance, this study may help to explain why Mambila farmers leap to each other's aid so swiftly when conflict with herders occurs, and thus why violence can often escalate so rapidly.

Comparable findings come from studies of violence among rival football fans who have previously been bonded through imagistic rituals. Contrary to the popular perception that football-related violence is perpetrated mainly by individuals who are socially maladjusted (Lawther, 1972; Zani & Kirchler, 1991; Wakefield & Wann, 2006), our studies of 'superfan' groups in Brazil (*torcidas organizadas*) suggest that a more potent root cause of conflict between rival fans may be fusion, especially when combined with histories of past violence (Newson et al., 2018). Like the highly fused Mambila initiates in Cameroon, members of *torcidas organizadas* in Brazil are often involved in violent clashes with rival supporters, in ways that can lead to rapid escalation and loss of life (Murad, 2013; Raspaud & Da Cunha Bastos, 2013). And, also just like the Mambila initiates, members of superfan groups in Brazil are highly fused with each other and with their clubs. Of the 465 participants in one of our studies, 44.1 per cent described themselves as members of *torcidas organizadas*, exhibiting higher fusion levels than ordinary fans and a history of more violent altercations with rival fans. These superfans also considered themselves more likely to be involved in violent clashes in the future. By contrast our measures of social maladjustment failed to predict either fusion or intergroup violence. Previous research among football fans has repeatedly shown that the pathway to fusion lies in *shared dysphoric experiences*, most notably experiences of losing football matches. Although vicarious defeats on a sports field are not the same thing as undergoing the ordeals of initiation among the Mambila, both are imagistic in the sense that they involve forms of suffering that are remembered over the lifespan, that may be profoundly self-shaping, and that are crucially also shared with other members of the group. Moreover, both the masquerade in Cameroon and the sufferings of football fans are highly ritualistic in nature, involving a variety of irremediably causally opaque elements, from the wearing of traditional Mambila masks to the donning of team regalia, and from the performance of dances in West African villages to the synchronized chanting of fans in a football stadium. These imagistic experiences not only give rise to fusion but also help to explain why members of the group leap to each other's aid when under attack, and thus why intergroup skirmishes can escalate so rapidly.

Armed with these research findings, what can be done to reduce or rechannel the behavioural outcomes of imagistic group bonding? One obvious way in which the theory and evidence discussed in this book could be used to prevent intergroup conflict would be to provide a set of diagnostic tools for detecting individuals or populations at risk of turning to violent extremism as a way of defending the group. Civil wars, terrorist atrocities, revolutions, riots, and popular uprisings all too often catch the world by surprise. Admittedly, once violence has become a standard method of advancing group causes in a given region, sectarian clashes and terrorist atrocities are more expectable. But even where extremist ideology has taken root and suicide attacks are commonplace, it can be hard to pinpoint which individuals are most likely to engage in nonviolent forms of resistance and which will engage in acts of murderous self-sacrifice. What is needed is a 'Volatility Index' (VI)—a set of robust psychological predictors of violence that, if detected early, could lead to preventative action both at a population level and in the apprehension of individuals at risk. In what follows, I describe how such a measure might look, and how it may be applied to achieve consensual rather than repressive outcomes.

A central idea here is that when VI values rise above a certain threshold, it should be possible to develop and apply a variety of interventions to calm things down. Such measures are commonly associated with the notion of 'deradicalization', but this arguably mislabels the problem as being fundamentally about ideology. Our research suggests that the root of the problem is *how we bond with groups*, and therefore the real challenge is to find a way of *defusing* violent extremists (Whitehouse, 2016c). Defusion should not be understood as a process of 'deprogramming' or mind control, still less should it be construed as part of a punitive framework aimed at deterring unwanted behaviours by means of coercion or the threat of coercion. It is a cause for concern, for example, that under the Terrorism Act 2000, it became illegal in the UK to make statements expressing support for prohibited groups, and those convicted of such offences could face lengthy prison sentences (Whitehouse, 2018b). If violent extremism is fomented by powerful forms of shared experience rather than by ideology, curtailing freedom of speech may be the wrong place to start in efforts to stem the problem and could even backfire by making groups that already feel threatened, become even more volatile. Rather, a more effective approach to tackling terrorism might begin by establishing a collaborative process involving both extremists *and* more moderate members of their communities, families, and other relational networks. Indeed, an important implication of the approach proposed here is that efforts to reduce the human costs of population-level volatility would actually fail if applied repressively and can only work successfully if pursued in a fashion that is consistent with respect for human rights. So, how might the VI diagnostic tool work in practice? And, following on from this, how can defusion programmes be put into effect?

At a population level, the basic logic underlying the VI approach is that fusion leads to volatility via a series of mediating moderators, such as perceived outgroup threat, violence-condoning norms, and the absence of peaceful alternatives. So, the first step is to measure these constructs in a suitably diverse array of countries around the world, initially prioritizing any subgroups that have endured collective ordeals, for example, as a result of histories of persecution or repression. Previous research has shown that the pictorial measure (described in Chapter 3 and displayed in Figure 3.1) is well-suited to comparative fusion studies spanning multiple languages and cultural groups (Whitehouse, 2018a). Only a small proportion of the most highly fused populations, however, are liable to turn to violence as a means of defending the group or advancing its interests. So, as well as measuring fusion levels, it is also necessary to take into account additional factors such as magnitude of threat, carefully disambiguating relevant dimensions—including perceived immediacy, credibility, severity, and consequentiality of the threat. In addition, as discussed in Chapter 3, research with football fans suggests even a combination of high levels of fusion and perceived outgroup threat is no guarantee of volatility—indeed, if the group's best interests are served by fending off threats in a nonviolent fashion, fusion can motivate peaceful forms of resistance, potentially including costly expressions of passivism (e.g. conscientious objectors). It would therefore be important to consider also other factors, such as the strength of violence-condoning norms or the belief that peaceful recourse has proven to be useless or unachievable. Although the number of such factors is probably quite small, further research is urgently needed to whittle down the list of measures capable of capturing most of the variation across volatile populations worldwide. One such measure might be entitativity.

Entitativity is the tendency to treat all members of an outgroup as the same or functionally equivalent (Kahn, Klar, & Roccas, 2017). Viewing members of a group as a single entity is highly relevant to intergroup conflict because it means, for example, that if an outgroup is considered responsible for a crime, then all its members are equally culpable and therefore punishable. This logic is often expressed by those responsible for terrorist atrocities, for instance arguing that even though victims may include unarmed civilians, they are all infidels in the eyes of God or all equally to blame for the sins of their forefathers and thus tarred with the same brush. In response to the imagistic-pathway-to-fusion theory (Whitehouse, 2018a), it has been argued that entitativity could explain why fusion increases willingness to fight and die (Choi et al., 2018). It could, of course, be the other way around: entitativity increases the effects of fusion on willingness to fight and die. Moreover, it is possible that entitativity and violence-condoning norms could work together in driving violent intergroup conflict. These are all issues that should be prioritized in future research. As the empirical evidence grows, the VI could be suitably refined and calibrated to provide an increasingly precise predictive tool that could enable governments, NGOs, international bodies, and grassroots communities to help head off violence before it occurs or escalates.

As well as operating at a population level, another version of the VI could be developed to identify *individuals* at risk of engaging in violent extremism. While it may be tempting to focus all our attention on overt expressions of ideological extremism, this could be a poor predictor of violent *behaviour*. Even if extreme beliefs were a necessary condition for extreme behaviour, there are far too many people who harmlessly subscribe to extreme beliefs for this to be used as a way of predicting who will actually commit a terrorist atrocity in the future. To address this needle-in-a-haystack problem, we need a method of singling out a small minority of potential terrorists from much larger populations of avowed extremists before they engage in illegal actions, and thus before any punitive interventions from law enforcement agencies would come into play. The focus would instead be on turning those individuals away from the pathway to violence by engaging the support of their relational networks (as discussed shortly). The VI could provide a framework within which interventions could be developed, based on a data-driven approach that is continually updated in light of new evidence.

Measuring fusion and threat in populations with extremist beliefs is possible in some countries like Indonesia, where support for the goals of jihadist and hardline fundamentalist groups is widespread (e.g. Yustisia et al., 2020; Kavanagh et al., 2020). But in countries with Muslim minorities, for example, in Europe and the USA, accessing those holding similar views is much more difficult. One way of studying such groups is to track their behaviour online. Julia Ebner, one of the world's leading experts in online undercover research on extremist groups (Ebner, 2017, 2020), has been developing ways of detecting the predictors of violence, including imagistic experiences and indicators of fusion, in the chatrooms and other online platforms frequented by extremists. Ebner's project in our lab group at the University of Oxford seeks to develop a set of diagnostic tools for identifying highly fused extremists who are most likely to engage in acts of violent extremism, as opposed to merely echoing the views of a much larger number of people who subscribe to extremist beliefs and attitudes.

Once it has been satisfactorily established that the VI can be used to accurately detect and measure the risk that individuals or entire populations will turn to violence, the next challenge is to act swiftly to prevent violence from actually erupting. This will require a toolkit for defusing those most likely to engage in acts of violent self-sacrifice. In contrast with the approach adopted by deradicalization programmes, such as the UK's Prevent Strategy, I propose that the starting point for defusion techniques should not be the person's extreme beliefs or ideological commitments. These may be regarded as secondary characteristics that are probably best set aside during the initial stages of defusion. The first priority should be to unpick the pathway to fusion—the meaningful, life-changing experiences through which personal identity is forged, and the convictions of sharedness that fuse the individual to a group. Insofar as there is an adequate sense of trust and easy rapport with the interviewer, our experience is that most people will eagerly talk to researchers about their most transformative life experiences. Promoting trust of this kind is most likely to succeed if defusion efforts engage the support of the communities in which volatility levels are high or rising.

At the core of the fusion process is the belief that personally transformative experiences and their meanings are shared with other group members. It follows that anything capable of undermining this belief also undermines fusion. On that basis, the most effective pathway to defusion is to facilitate reasonable doubt about the sharedness of personally transformative experiences. Defusion interventions would need to be conducted in a way that is motivating and authentic for participants and carried out in settings that resemble and engage existing patterns of social interaction as fully as possible. If the goal is for fused individuals to discover that other members of their group have not really shared exactly the same experiences or have interpreted them very differently, the most natural way to facilitate that discovery is to encourage conversations focused on memories of, and reflections on, past experiences.

This will not always be as easy as it sounds. In many groups that have been fused via the imagistic pathway, conversations about shared dysphoric experiences may rarely occur in the natural course of things. In the case of military groups, this is often linked to macho norms. Thus, although highly fused soldiers who have seen active service together may hold regular reunions and other gatherings during peacetime, they seldom talk about their experiences of battle. Indeed, it would be socially inappropriate to do so in most social gatherings. In the case of the initiation cults of Melanesia and West Africa described above, the activities and artefacts involved in the rituals are subject to stringent taboos and shrouded in secrecy. Given that the social function of imagistic practices is typically to fuse groups that depend on each other in the face of extreme external threat, norms forbidding open discussion about imagistic experiences would have helped prevent defusion. Such norms have, however, been changing in professional armies and it is now standard practice in the US military, for example, to engage in extensive debriefing after a military engagement involving injury or loss of life.

The conceptual framework I have advanced in this book would predict that groups engaging in prolonged discussion in the aftermath of imagistic experiences—if this discussion revealed a lack of sharedness (e.g. focusing on mutually inconsistent or simply different aspects of the event)—would experience lower levels of fusion than those who observe a collective silence. Thus, one way to defuse would-be violent extremists might be to mirror the modern debriefing techniques of the military by establishing discussion groups for extremists that are managed by a respected, but more moderate, facilitator. Obviously, such interventions would need to observe very strict rules to avoid a situation in which the interactions merely reinforce ideological commitments rather than disrupting the conviction of shared experience. But given that ideological transmission is linked to identification rather than fusion, a weaker form of group alignment (see Chapter 4), this is a risk worth taking and might be ameliorated by ensuring that facilitators are sufficiently well-trained. Moreover, whereas such interventions should begin simply by opening up awareness of unshared aspects of experience *within* the group, they might also progressively focus attention on shared aspects of experience *across* groups, potentially also encompassing outgroups. Such an approach may be more likely to soften hard-line attitudes and reduce willingness to engage in violence compared with efforts that begin and end with ideology.

Defusion at the level of the population could realistically be achieved in much the same fashion. As a result of basic data collection for the VI, a multicountry comparative dataset could be generated, detailing the most salient shared experiences giving rise to fusion in each population and specifying measurable threat levels at any given point in time. Whenever a VI warning threshold is exceeded, this might trigger intervention programmes designed to increase levels of public discussion on the diversity of past experiences, bringing to attention the heterogeneous nature of people's personal memories and interpretative frameworks. This could be achieved through the involvement of moderate groups, leaders, and journalists across the political spectrum in the countries concerned and orchestrated by local people in concert with international NGOs, building on the theoretical framework provided in this book. Defusion programmes operating in this way would focus their efforts on the free expression of personal experiences rather than on politically sensitive issues such as extreme belief or outgroup threat. In other words, such interventions would be directed at the least contentious, but also the most psychologically salient, level—the root motivations to engage in violent self-sacrifice.

The above proposals are admittedly broad-brush since many of the details of interventions will need to be fleshed out once the VI has been developed, and the interventions themselves would also need to be adapted to local circumstances in countries where data are collected. Before rolling out such programmes, there would also be thorny ethical issues to address, requiring a maximally consultative and consensual process. But unless we establish a suitable evidence-based theoretical framework to start with, genuinely effective preventative interventions may never be possible. In order to illustrate how the transition from theory to evidence and from evidence to intervention can work in practice, consider the following ways in which we are now applying what we have learned about the imagistic mode to tackle the problem of ex-offender recidivism in the UK.

As discussed in several chapters of this book, football fandom is a source of intense social cohesion all around the world. Indeed, crowd spectator sports are as close as many people nowadays ever get to the experience of imagistic rituals and fusion with a group that is larger than one's family. As discussed above, imagistic practices and the groups they produce are mostly outlawed or at least on the fringes of law-abiding society in most modern states, operating largely underground or on the margins of society, for example, in the form of motorcycle gangs, guerrilla forces, paramilitaries, and criminal cartels. But in the world of football fandom, imagistic bonding has tended to persist, and this may be because it is comparatively easy to regulate and police, at least in most countries, most of the time. When rival teams encounter each other in a sports ground, it can feel very much like tribal warfare, but losing a match is not really the same thing as losing a battle, and participants rarely die. Moreover, the experiences of winning and losing for supporters are entirely vicarious—they do not themselves risk injury on the pitch or endure the psychological pressures of taking a crucial penalty kick in front of a large audience. For all these reasons, football fandom is only mildly imagistic compared with the initiation rites of the Mambila or the forms of shared suffering endured by warring militia in the Middle East. As a result, football fans constitute a *relatively* 'safe' population in which to study the imagistic pathway to fusion. But this also makes fandom a potentially potent source of social glue that can be used to produce peaceful prosocial outcomes. The challenge is to harness fusion in football to tackle collective action problems in positive, consensual ways. This is the goal of the Twinning Project.

The Twinning Project was created in 2018 by David Dein, former vice-president of the Football Association and of Arsenal Football Club in the UK. The vision is to twin every prison in the UK with a local professional football club to provide inmates with an opportunity to get involved in the sport, improve their health and fitness, align themselves with positive values, and acquire transferrable skills that will be recognized by future prospective employers. The overarching goal is to strengthen the resolve of ex-offenders to 'go straight' and make a positive contribution to society. In 2019, Dein invited one of my research teams, led by postdoctoral researcher Martha Newson, to investigate the effectiveness of the Twinning Project. This led to the design of a longitudinal study to explore how the imagistic pathway to fusion with football and with the values of the Twinning Project can help reduce rates of recidivism among ex-prisoners (Newson & Whitehouse, 2020). Recent research with parolees suggests that prison populations may have unusually low rates of fusion with family compared with the population at large, and with society at large (Whitehouse & Fitzgerald, 2020). When prisoners do fuse, it is often with criminally inclined 'fusion families'—kin-like units forged through the shared dysphoria of prison life. An undesirable side-effect of these strong bonds with other offenders is that, although they may provide the only forms of social support available in prison and perhaps also post release, they can reinforce patterns of reoffending and increase the chances of ending up back behind bars. What makes the Twinning Project special is that it provides a novel fusion target, strongly linked to law-abiding values, including healthy living, avoidance of drugs, punctuality, loyalty to group, and other qualities that improve the ex-offender's prospects of success outside of prison.

The causes of recidivism cannot be addressed exclusively by targeting the psychology and behaviour of ex-offenders, however. 'Going straight' after leaving prison also requires a supportive receiving community. One of the areas in which a lack of support is most keenly felt is the job market. Employers are wary of the risk of hiring workers with criminal records, especially in jobs requiring some degree of responsibility and trust. The Twinning Project can help in this respect by providing participants in the programme with certification of their successful performance in a number of areas of relevance to employers. But there is also the potential to harness the cohesion of football fandom to increase the willingness of the community to help those coming out of prison. The homepage of the Twinning Project website quotes Jesse Jackson's epithet: 'Don't look down on someone, unless you are helping them up.' This ethos is spreading, following the launch of the Twinning Project to an audience of tens of thousands of supporters at Wembley Stadium in 2018.

The idea that shared experience can help to improve the willingness of the receiving community to help ex-prisoners establish new lives on the 'outside' has also been demonstrated experimentally. In a recent study, we presented prospective employers with an opportunity to review job applications from ex-offenders in light of information about experiences of bereavement, a common life-shaping event (Buhrmester & Whitehouse, In Prep). Our goal was to find out whether the sharing of such life experiences would influence fusion with ex-offenders and concomitant willingness to offer second chances. Initial analysis of the data suggests that focusing attention on the shared experience of being bereaved significantly increases fusion, not only making prospective employers more likely to offer job opportunities but also contributing to a broader range of community reintegration efforts and even to donating money to support reintegration programmes. Thus, simply encouraging people to think about how their own life-shaping experiences are shared by others, and particularly those with whom they may not previously have considered themselves to have anything in common, can help to foster cohesion and cooperation across groups, perhaps also reducing suspicion, prejudice, and other factors impeding peaceful coexistence and cooperation. In short, since the imagistic pathway to fusion is based on meaningful shared experiences, it could be harnessed not only to strengthen the resolve of ex-offenders to stay out of prison but also to motivate the receiving community to help them reintegrate and find jobs.

Doctrinal Pathways to Populism, Polarization, and Global Action

In contrast with the very intense social cohesion and extreme forms of self-sacrifice that imagistic practices produce, the doctrinal mode gives rise to ingroup favouritism and outgroup derogation associated with a form of group alignment that social psychologists refer to as *identification*. Even though, as we have seen, identification does not tap into personal agency, as in the case of fusion, it is nevertheless a highly effective way of motivating quite strong forms of cooperation with anonymous others who display the same identity markers, within so-called imagined communities too large for their members to know each other personally. Large-scale cooperation motivated by identification can take violent forms, from lynching and mob justice to participation in state violence and warfare. Identification is 'weaker' than fusion (even extended fusion) in the sense that its capacity to motivate self-sacrifice is lower. Nevertheless, identification provides a very effective way of motivating behaviours that are not offputtingly costly to self. An example is willingness to make small gifts to charity anonymously in order to contribute to a prosocial outcome. Another instance is voting behaviour, which carries low cost to the voter and can be motivated not only by self-interest (e.g. to support policies that lower the tax burden) but by a desire to advance the interests of one's imagined community based on ingroup categorical ties and outgroup derogation (e.g. in support of anti-immigration policies). These are examples of pro-group action that do not require fusion, merely a sense of belonging and an associated desire to act (and to be seen to act) as a good and loyal citizen.

Some of these patterns of identification can be linked to perceptions of vicariously shared suffering, promoting 'extended fusion' (as discussed at length in Chapter 4). For example, many of those voting to leave the European Union in the UK's 2016 Brexit referendum were motivated not only by the promise of personal gain, although that was surely a factor, but also by a desire to see Britain prevail in competition with various outgroups (including not only the various countries of Europe but also immigrants from poorer countries around the world seeking a better life in the UK). An interesting feature of these large-scale patterns of pro-group voting is that they can be motivated not only by identification with an ingroup but also forms of extended fusion with outgroups. For example, the latter seems to have been a powerful explanatory factor in the voting behaviour of Remainers in the Brexit referendum.

Just prior the 2016 referendum, we measured fusion with the UK and Europe in a sample of 212 voters in the UK, comprising both supporters of the campaign for Britain to leave the European Union ('Leavers') and of the campaign to remain within it (Curry, Buhrmester, & Whitehouse, 2019). Contrary to popular stereotypes, we found that Leavers were not more fused or identified with Britain than Remainers. On the contrary, fusion and identification with Britain was similarly high for supporters of both camps. Given the association between identification and outgroup derogation, why then did Remainers who were already extendedly fused with Britain lack a hostile view towards Europe, preferring to stay within the EU? Our answer was that Remainers were more highly bonded with Europe than were Leavers, and this bonding was based as much on extended fusion as it was on identification.

Although the Brexit situation may reflect long-term divergences in patterns of extended fusion across the UK electorate, the outcome of the referendum also served as a potent shared experience, creating new forms of group alignment. For many Remainers, for example, the referendum result came as a profound shock, prompting a realization that the UK was more divided and the Leave campaign stronger than many had previously appreciated. To the extent that Remainers now realized that they were in the minority, if only marginally, they rapidly became an embattled group, one that was not only based on identification with a new category ('Remainers') but also created perceptions of vicariously shared dysphoric experience (losing the referendum) that was strong enough to produce extended fusion. This was confirmed by a recent longitudinal survey investigating the effects of remembering and reflecting on the Brexit referendum of 2016 across two time points: May 2017 (i.e. nearly a year after the result of the referendum became known) and March 2018 (i.e. about ten months after the first questionnaire was completed). Our aim in this study was to explore how the emotional intensity of Remainers' reactions to the referendum result, and their reflections on those memories over time, affected their levels of fusion versus identification with other Remain supporters (Muzzulini et al., Under Review). Initial data analysis confirmed that the more intense and visceral people's memories were of the encoding event (upon first hearing the result of the referendum), and the more they had reflected on that event subsequently, the more fused they were with other Remainers. Also as predicted, the shared memories that explained higher levels of fusion did not contribute to higher levels of identification, providing support for our hypothesis that the reason fusion taps into personal agency is because it involves the sharing of personally salient memories with others (see Chapter 3). At the same time, these findings were also consistent with the theory that identification is based on sharing values, beliefs, and practices acquired socially from other members of the group and therefore is not affected by people's self-defining memories and transformative life experiences (see Chapter 4).

For many, the Brexit referendum may have resembled an imagistic ritual, in the sense that it entailed a certain amount of pomp and ceremony involving campaign buses and other causally opaque elements, while also evincing strong emotions, both positive and negative, among the general public. Although the main dividing lines between Remainers and Leavers were surely based on identification with large-scale group categories (based on routinized norms and identity markers acquired socially), as is typical of the doctrinal mode, these group attachments were also augmented in many cases by extended fusion based on shared experience. In particular, the outcome of the referendum was undoubtedly a shared *dysphoric* experience for those opposed to Brexit. Of course, it was not intended to have that effect, nor was it conducted in order to mark a change of status or achieve some other outcome that could be regarded as beneficial to Remainers as a group, and so it was not an imagistic ritual in the more usual sense. Nevertheless, in terms of the modes theory, patterns of large-scale group bonding that occur in response to national events can have both doctrinal and imagistic elements. While they may involve the creation and transmission of identity markers that demarcate large group categories associated with doctrinal orthodoxies of various kinds (including secular ideologies and political credos), they can also mobilize feelings of shared experience around episodic memories, fusing people to extended group categories in a fashion that is more typical of the imagistic mode.

One of the most remarkable strengths of the doctrinal mode is thought to be its capacity to spread a corpus of teachings and ritual practices to a large population rapidly and efficiently so as to establish very large-scale traditions. Even if the forms of pro-group commitment this evinces are rooted only in identification—or in its strongest form, extended fusion—that can still be sufficient to motivate forms of cooperation that can bring about consequential changes on a grand scale. This is illustrated by the way large-scale doctrinal religions successfully induce billions of people around the world to attend regular forms of collective worship or to donate money. Often these acts are, taken in isolation, relatively small sacrifices—just a few hours a week or tapping a manageable proportion of one's income. But over time they amount to much more significant investments. An incalculably large amount of potentially productive labour time is expended on worship in churches, synagogues, mosques, and temples around the world, and vast sums of money are cumulatively amassed by the world's religious traditions every year. These represent formidable cooperative achievements, and they have the potential to be applied to a much wider range of collective action problems.

Consider, for example, the untapped potential of the world's doctrinal religions to motivate action on the climate crisis. There are already some striking examples of initiatives aimed at doing exactly that (Whitehouse, 2020), such as the EcoSikh movement that set out to plant a million new trees worldwide to celebrate the five hundred and fiftieth anniversary of Guru Nanak's birth or the creation of 'Vegan-adan' as a meat-free alternative to Ramadan. The potential for such projects to be taken up in other religious traditions is obvious. All the world religions and their offshoots provide scriptural support for stewardship for the planet, and all have the cohesive strength and organizational machinery necessary to emulate the tree-planting Sikh initiative. The idea of celebrating major religious anniversaries by performing acts that can help to slow down global heating is both simple and achievable, at least in theory. Moreover, the idea of using religious teachings to influence dietary practices, even tabooing particular foods, is long-established, so there is no reason why novel restrictions on consumption of foods that are causing the most widespread damage to the environment could not be endorsed through the efforts of doctrinal religions, as the Vegan-adan initiative demonstrates.

Harnessing religion to tackle environment problems need not rely only on scriptural endorsement but should also tap into intuitive morality. As discussed in Chapter 4, during the initial rise of doctrinal religions in world history, some moral domains were prioritized over others, often in line with quite oppressive forms of top-down coercion. The so-called axial age and the rise of the ethical religions, from which modern doctrinal traditions are descended, restored a more balanced moral economy in which fairness and reciprocity were prized alongside more hawkish values, such as deference to authority and courage in battle. It was argued in Chapter 4 that as political systems grew in size beyond the 'mega-society' threshold (around a million individuals), naked political domination epitomized by human sacrifice and the deification of rulers was no longer sustainable. But the ways in which the Axial religions created more balanced and consensual moral systems differed from one tradition to the next. This forged new and highly successful religious traditions but ones that were capable of expanding largely in competition with others. This helped to harden doctrinal disagreements, motivating holy wars and crusades, the destructive consequences of which still resonate down through the centuries and continue to shape patterns of intergroup conflict in the world today. A key question is whether we could imagine, and even help to bring about, more globally consensual forms of religiosity and moral thinking, starting perhaps with shared concern for environmental issues.

To explore the potential to strengthen our shared moral repertoire as applied to environmental issues, we conducted an analysis of the academic literature on cooperative conservation, accessed through an online archive known as Web of Science (Curry et al., 2019). More specifically we were looking for references to conservation efforts that included mention of any of the seven forms of cooperation that our previous research had shown to be judged morally good in a sample of sixty cultures selected from the ethnographic record so as to maximize diversity (Curry, Mullins, & Whitehouse, 2019). As noted in Chapter 4, this earlier study had produced strong evidence for seven universal moral rules: help your group, support your family, return favours, be brave, defer to superiors, divide resources fairly, and respect other people's property. In theory, all seven domains might be deployed to support environmental goals and conservation efforts. For instance, I have mentioned how loyalty to a religious group could be used to motivate activities such as tree planting. But it is just as easy to imagine arguments that emphasise other moral domains: care for kin, such as the need to protect the futures of our children and grandchildren; heroism, expressed, for instance, as a call to arms in the war against global heating; deference and awe, in the form of respect towards the findings of science or the beauty of the natural world; fairness, emphasizing the need to share the earth with millions of other species; and respect for property, insofar as many species have been around for longer than *homo sapiens* and, on those grounds, may be said to have a plausible claim to prior possession. Obviously, these are just examples, and the possibilities for moral arguments invoking each of the seven domains are legion.

Nevertheless, our literature search, which produced 910 citations relating to cooperative conservation, showed that the vast majority of arguments on the topic of conservation (85 per cent of all citations found) related to just *one* of the seven moral domains: reciprocity. It is not clear why reciprocity holds special appeal as an argument in the conservation literature, but what this does reveal is a missed opportunity for environmentalists to exploit a wider range of potentially compelling and universal moral arguments. This may be true not only of efforts to conserve biodiversity or address the planetary climate crisis, but also a much wider range of large-scale collective action problems.

To exploit previously untapped potential for coordinated action on key global problems, it will be vital to establish ways of rendering our universal moral intuitions in a common language, one that transcends the boundaries of established group alignments. This will likely require new forms of leadership. Most traditional leaders rise to prominence because they are credible advocates for the interests of the groups they represent, by helping to motivate and enforce prosocial behaviour within the group and through statesmanlike efforts to position the group competitively in its dealings with rivals and outgroups. While this kind of intragroup leadership will undoubtedly always inspire support and admiration, there is a growing need on the world stage for barrier-crossing leaders capable of recognizing and valuing the goals of outgroups in ways that also help to advance the needs of their ingroups more effectively than barrier-bound leadership alone could accomplish.

A concrete example of barrier-crossing leadership is provided by the career of Nelson Mandela, who was famously imprisoned on counts of sabotage and conspiracy under the apartheid regime in South Africa. Despite the fact that Mandela witnessed brutal ill-treatment of his ingroup and endured decades of incarceration, following his release, he campaigned tirelessly for interracial reconciliation, eventually unifying a new South Africa as its first black president and subsequently becoming a world leading statesman combating poverty and Aids. More recent, if less famous, examples of barrier crossers include Lord John Alderdice, who, as leader of the Alliance Party, helped establish the peace process in Northern Ireland after decades of sectarian conflict by persuading unionist leaders to enter into dialogues with Sinn Fein, a party they had previously refused to engage with due to its close ties with nationalist paramilitaries. Another example would be Mustafa Cerić, who served as the Grand Mufti of Bosnia and Herzegovina and was the recipient of numerous awards for promoting interfaith understanding and peaceful coexistence. Although such leaders are much less common than intragroup leaders, examples may be found, if only at grassroots level, in many of the world's most embattled groups.

The question what makes a barrier-crossing leader, and especially what motivates them often in the face of opposition not only from outgroups but from within their own ranks, is crucial to address if we are to establish ways of fostering this sort of leadership. One possibility is that barrier crossers are exceptionally good at taking the perspectives of others and thus seeing more than one side to every situation. Another is that they recognize the significance of shared experiences on both sides of intergroup conflicts and, for that reason, are more fused with outgroups than other members of their ingroup would typically be. To explore whether either or both of these factors could help to explain what motivates barrier-crossing leadership, we designed a study with sixty leaders drawn from three groups that had experienced long-term discrimination in different ways: African Americans in New Orleans, travellers in Omagh, and Muslims in London

(Buhrmester, Cowan, & Whitehouse, Under Review). Roughly half our sample of leaders were barrier crossers who worked extensively with their group's traditional enemies or oppressors, while the other half were more typical barrier-bound leaders, committed to advancing the interests of their ingroups with little concern for any other group. We invited both kinds of leaders to fill out a lengthy questionnaire in which we probed their perceived skills at perspective taking, their most meaningful life-changing experiences, and their fusion levels with both ingroup and outgroup. Our results showed that there were no significant differences between barrier crossers and intragroup leaders on self-reported perspective-taking abilities—if anything, intragroup leaders considered themselves better at this. It is possible that barrier crossers had a more acute awareness of the difficulties of seeing the other person's point of view and were more modest in self-appraisal as a consequence. But even so, there was no evidence that perspective-taking abilities differed markedly between the two types of leaders. Where a more striking pattern of difference emerged was on the shared experience and fusion questions. Compared with intragroup leaders, the barrier crossers reported higher levels of shared dysphoric experience and higher levels of fusion with members of outgroups. This suggests that at least one of the drivers of barrier-crossing leadership is an awareness that burdens and sufferings are often shared by groups on both sides of a divide, and this can help to motivate the search for solutions to intergroup conflicts in ways that benefit all parties.

Barrier-crossing leadership may well be the key to establishing moral norms that are not only rooted in our universal evolved preferences but formulated in a doctrinally standardized way that can be shared by all, irrespective of religion, creed, ideology, or ethnicity. It also seems plausible that leaders who convincingly signal that they share in the sufferings of humankind as a whole, rather than just some sector of it, will serve as ideal harbingers of universal morality, an approach that has an illustrious pedigree in the history of messianic and prophetic religions and their descendants. If a globalizing morality could indeed be formulated and spread effectively, it will need to be embedded into the fabric of people's lives as part of our routinized ritual practices, because that is how the doctrinal mode achieves uniformity and stability in any system of beliefs and values. Until now, culture has been globalized mainly through processes of commercialization by multinational conglomerates or through various entertainment industries, for example, in the form of music and movies. When new ideologies spread, they are commonly embedded in an organization, such as a religion or political party, claiming a monopoly on truth and situating itself, more or less explicitly, in competition with other such organizations. Consequently, such groups are trapped in a zero-sum game, acquiring a greater share of the market only at the expense of rivals. The key question facing humankind in the twenty-first century is whether we can transcend these forms of parochialism in at least some key domains of life—not in a way that dilutes local traditions and national identities but in a way that fosters commitment to cooperation on a global canvas to ensure peace and sustainable forms of prosperity for all of us.

Conclusions

In this chapter, and throughout the book, I have argued that collective rituals produce social cohesion, in turn motivating cooperation of various kinds. I have also presented a range of evidence that the performance frequency and emotional intensity of rituals influence the scale on which cooperation is possible and the degree to which people will be willing to make sacrifices for the sake of the group. Studies designed to test the modes theory have shown that imagistic rituals produce a very powerful form of social cohesion known as identity fusion, capable of motivating extreme forms of pro-group action. Nevertheless, there is clearly a dark side to this form of group bonding, for when the group is felt to be under threat, fusion creates a powerful urge to defend the group no matter what the cost. This can result in acts of terrorism, as well as heroism, the difference between the two often being largely a matter of which group you belong to. To avoid the more destructive outcomes of fusion, the framework advanced in this book suggests that we need to defuse those bent on violence or, where practicable, rechannel fusion into more peaceful forms of cooperation. The latter may be most readily achievable in mildly imagistic ritual domains, such as football fandom. The passionate commitment and loyalty of football fans could be harnessed to help ex-offenders align with law-abiding relational groups or networks and at the same time could help to generate the trust and goodwill of prospective employers to help them reintegrate after leaving prison. Such programmes could be replicated in many countries with sizeable prison populations and cohesive fan bases associated with spectator sports (football is just one example).

There is also reason to hope that doctrinal practices will increasingly be harnessed in ways that can help us to address larger scale cooperation problems, such as climate change. One example considered here has been the potential role of the world religions and their offshoots to mobilize identification and extended fusion in support of practical contributions to stewardship of the planet, including tree planting and dietary change. More ambitiously still, we may look forward to the emergence and spread of a new kind of global morality, building on universal cooperative instincts while also enriching them with a set of culturally specific norms and doctrines that have the potential to be accepted on a global scale. In this way, we might create a meaningful and durable sense of world citizenship, augmenting more localized or regionally distinctive traditions.

The idea that all humans might join together as a single community, based on shared experience, moral values, and collective goals, may sound naïve or unrealistic. But the modes theory, based on decades of scientific research, suggests that such a global community is psychologically possible. Up until now, identification has dominated the rise of nation states, while extended fusion has been its servant in two world wars and numerous regional conflicts. Unfortunately, identification not only produces ingroup favouritism but also fuels outgroup derogation. Fusion is different, however. Fused individuals do not seem to need an outgroup in order to feel bonded to their ingroup. Likewise, extended fusion does not necessarily require a rival or enemy group. As long as the emphasis is on personally meaningful shared experiences, rather than on socially learned identity markers and outgroup threats, people can unite without needing also to oppose those who choose not to join. This makes the prospect of fusion with humanity at large, a very real possibility.

The term 'Anthropocene' (Waters et al., 2016) conveys the idea that the world is now entering a new geological epoch—a depressingly apocalyptic phase in the life of a planet despoiled by the insatiable selfishness of one species. But humanity is also capable of sculpting a very different future for the world. To realize this potential, it will be necessary to harness the shared experiences of humanity today and tie them to universal intuitions in novel ways. As we have seen, there is strong evidence that humans everywhere judge at least seven cooperative rules to be morally good: help your group, support your family, return favours, be brave, defer to superiors, divide resources fairly, and respect other people's property. I have argued that these principles could be applied to environmental issues, but these same universal intuitions could also help motivate action to combat other global problems, including extreme poverty, intergroup hatreds and conflicts, and human rights abuses. Elaborating a moral framework for tackling collective action problems in a form that is palatable to all the peoples of the world may not be the hardest part, however. Spreading and embedding this framework so that it transcends and blends with all others presents an even greater challenge. It will likely require new forms of barrier-crossing leadership and new kinds of global rituals. But if we can encourage and facilitate this process, future historians may view this, our present epoch, as one the greatest Axial Ages in world history—an age ushered in not by the most destructive species our planet has seen but by the most cooperative.

7
Challenges for Science

I have argued that a fuller understanding of the nature of ritual, and of its causes and consequences, must address all four of Tinbergen's questions concerning function, mechanism, history, and development. The first question is in many ways the most elusive because it requires us to reconstruct the selection pressures at work in ancient ancestral environments, as well as the sequence in which novel adaptations came into being. These are daunting requirements. Direct evidence from the archaeological record is often too sparse to permit detailed reconstruction of the evolutionary history of ritual behaviours on that basis alone and so indirect methods also have an important role to play, such as mathematical simulations based on tentative assumptions and inferences using ethnography, experimental psychology, and cross-species comparisons.

Moreover, much remains unknown about how the ritual stance fits into human psychology as a whole. Is it related to the evolution of language, for example, as a by-product of the need for children to acquire a vast lexicon? After all, the vocabulary of every human language, like a society's unique repertoire of rituals, is established by convention rather than because the words or actions relate to features of the environment in a causally intuitive way (odd cases, such as onomatopoeia, excepted). Or are the roots of the ritual stance to be found instead in the overimitation of potentially useful but only half understood instrumental behaviours, as in the case of resolvably opaque technologies, such artefacts with hidden mechanisms, and irremediably opaque magical variants, such as voodoo dolls? These scenarios and others may have some *prima facie* plausibility, but more research is needed before much can be said with confidence.

Likewise, we know relatively little about the range of social cues that activate the ritual stance. Perhaps the expectation of learning something technically useful is cued by signals of experience, competence, and confidence, whereas expectations of learning rituals and conventions are cued by signals of group consensus or the popularity of the model. Are we more likely to want to join in a ritual if it is modelled by somebody of high social status in our peer group or if it is simply popular among our peers? Are ritual traditions conserved more faithfully than instrumental techniques? Do techniques spread across cultural group boundaries more readily than rituals conferring identity? Do the rituals of higher status groups spread across cultural boundaries faster than those of lower status groups?

The idea that ritual and instrumental stances have discrete functions, grounded in distinct evolved mechanisms, has many ramifications that have yet to be fully explored. While ritual and instrumental stances may seem like relatively small and subtle capacities or predispositions, I have argued that they facilitated a quantum leap in the proliferation and spread of new cultural forms. This is because, working together, these two stances on the imitation of modelled behaviour enabled humans (uniquely among other primates) to conserve, as well as innovate, in cultural systems—to store the hard-won discoveries of forebears and generate those novel discoveries in the first place (Legare & Nielsen, 2020). This 'ratchet effect' made the evolution of increasingly elaborate sociocultural institutions and technologies inevitable. As culture itself evolved, it changed the niches occupied by our forebears and thereby established increasingly rich and diverse epigenetic landscapes that can only be properly understood through their articulation with cognitive-developmental and social-historical ones as well (see Chapter 5).

So, where does this leave the scientific study of ritual? I would argue that it places us at a very portentous, albeit challenging, stage in the scientific study of culture—one in which the potential rewards of transdisciplinary collaboration are richer than they have ever been before. If we are to realize that potential, however, we need to overcome a series of major hurdles to the advancement of collaborative social science. In this chapter, I attempt to describe some of the most significant impediments and discuss how these might be addressed. I begin by arguing that the very enterprise of social science is inherently *unnatural*, given our uniquely human evolved psychology, and this may explain why the study of the social has proven harder to get off the ground, in comparison with many other life sciences. Then I consider how the resulting lack of consensus on basic matters of epistemology and method has contributed to the creation of theoretical and methodological divisions in the social sciences in the alternate guises of the 'two cultures problem' and the 'silo effect'. Nevertheless, I go on to explore how a fuller understanding of the nature and origins of all these problems can help us to surmount them.

Key to the hoped-for renaissance in the science of the social is a more *problem-centred* approach to transdisciplinary collaboration. Achieving knowledge synthesis across the humanities and sciences, and the many silos they contain, is not simply a matter of persuading academics from disparate disciplines to talk to each other. Since interdisciplinarity has long been explicitly encouraged by funding bodies and university management, meetings of academics from different disciplines are commonplace. But the results can be quite disappointing, with people from different academic traditions simply 'talking past' each other. Where such encounters turn into real collaborations, discussion is typically focused on a problem that everyone agrees must be solved. Such an approach requires participants to conceptualize the problem in a mutually intelligible fashion, so that they can then pool their knowledge to help solve it. This process often requires a sound understanding of how different kinds of knowledge can be deployed to tackle a problem from a variety of angles or how methods can be combined and adapted to generate novel datasets. I argued in Chapter 3, for example, that explaining the evolution of extreme forms of cooperation required mathematical models, the assumptions of which must be evidence-based (e.g. informed by ethnographic field observation), in order to generate plausible predictions that can be tested using psychological experiments and surveys (Whitehouse et al., 2017). This kind of knowledge synthesis only works, however, if everyone involved is committed to defining a common problem and adapting their tools and expertise to solve it, or at least bring the team closer to solving it via cumulative theory building and testing. Based on this reasoning, I argue in this chapter for an ambitious new vision for the future of social science that, if we understand and avoid the pitfalls, is capable of cumulative theory-building comparable to that of the most advanced neighbouring sciences.

The revival of anthropology's scientific ambitions, while retaining its commitment to qualitative ethnography in maximally diverse local settings, has a particularly important role to play in this new vision. Even the most ambitious sciences of the social up until now have been hidebound by dependence on unrepresentative samples of humanity, mainly selected from student populations at predominantly Western universities. And, just as troublingly, many of the core questions that have been asked about human nature are rooted more in ethnocentric stereotypes than in the weight of evidence from indigenous or ancient cultures studied by diminishingly small numbers of humanities scholars. I argue that anthropology has a special role to play in rectifying this imbalance and helping to bring about the necessary synthesis of knowledge across science and humanities disciplines engaged in psychological, historical, social, and behavioural research programmes, joining them together into a new and indivisible whole via problem-centred collaborations.

The Unnaturalness of Social Theory

The history of social theory is in many ways a history of intellectual warfare, in which the casualties have been heavy and territorial gains only limited and fleeting. We see this pattern most strikingly, perhaps, in the history of sociocultural anthropology (hereafter simply 'anthropology'). Looking back on it, many of anthropology's internal battles, like those of warring tribes and states, have not led to consensual advancements. Even at the most broad-brush level, changes in the intellectual centre of gravity—for example, from the sciences to the humanities and back again—may seem more like the ebb and flow of tides rather than a cumulative process of directed change. Why is that?

Anthropology originally fashioned itself as an ambitious new science, capable of posing and possibly even answering big questions about human nature and the evolution of sociocultural systems (e.g. Malinowski, 1944). But anthropologists lost confidence in this ambitious enterprise and became increasingly convinced that they belonged in the world of the humanities, perhaps as a branch of history (Evans-Pritchard, 1962), or philosophy (Spiro, 1996 Jackson, 2013; cf. Gellner, 1992). I have argued in this book, however, for a return to the original commitment to science. To accomplish this reversal decisively and rigorously will require new ways of gathering and analysing comparative data on the world's cultures so as to build upon the past findings of ethnography, and also delve into the underlying causes of human behaviour using the methods of experimental psychology and related fields, such as behavioural economics, neuroscience, and agent-based modelling. To achieve this vision, however, deep collaboration will be necessary not only between anthropologists and cognitive scientists but also historians and archaeologists, many of whom also align with the humanities and may be wary of, or even hostile to, the methods and goals of science. Nevertheless, this cannot be a process of simply reversing the earlier retreat from science or abandoning the achievements of humanities-based anthropology. Ideally, anthropology would help lead the effort to bring the human sciences and humanities disciplines into closer dialogue as part of an overarching collaborative enterprise. In an effort to understand why this has so far proven difficult to achieve, I argue in this chapter that social theory has been held back by strongly held but seemingly conflicting intuitions about the fundamental nature of 'the social'. This is arguably due in large part to the fact that our cultural institutions have evolved faster than our psychological capacities for conceptualizing them. A potted history of anthropology may help to illustrate this point.

Anthropology began by asking big questions about the origins and causes of human nature, society, culture, and history. The intellectual founders of the field, in the nineteenth and early twentieth centuries, were enchanted by the idea that societies evolve and they made some important contributions to understanding the processes involved. An example of this is the rise of Marxist anthropology (Bloch, 1975), which offered a seemingly compelling evolutionary theory of technological and economic determinism. According to Marx's theory (1977 [1859]), forces of production determined the kinds of production relations that prevailed in a given social formation, while the forces and relations of production together determined the form and function of the legal, political, ideological, and religious institutions (the 'superstructure'), in line with ruling-class interests. This all sounds conceptually coherent and perhaps even plausible, but for the theory to be testable, it was clearly necessary to draw sharp distinctions between causes (e.g. production relations) and effects (e.g. legal institutions). This meant, for example, providing a way of conceptualizing relations of production that was sufficiently distinct from legal rights of ownership for it to make sense to describe the former as 'determining' the latter. Efforts to accomplish this by couching production relations in terms of the *power* to use and exploit productive forces while describing legal arrangements in terms of *rights* (McMurtry, 1978) were vulnerable to the charge of tautology and made the theory difficult and perhaps impossible to test scientifically.

The limitations of early explanatory ambitions in anthropology, together with growing anxiety about the association between those ambitions and imperial colonial projects, brought grand theoretical aspirations almost to the brink of extinction. This intellectual retreat began with a shift away from *why*-type questions towards *how*-type questions. Instead of asking about causes and origins (why are societies and cultures the way they are?), anthropologists increasingly restricted themselves to problems of function and structure (How do sociocultural systems fit together?). The French anthropologist, Claude Lévi-Strauss, among other influential anthropologists of the twentieth century, never entirely reconciled himself to this demotion of the explanatory enterprise. As his British colleague Meyer Fortes once wistfully observed, the 'lure of the *pourquois*' remained irresistible for Lévi-Strauss—albeit tantalizingly out of reach (1980: 198). By the close of the twentieth century, however, even generalizing efforts in the study of structure and function appeared to some anthropologists hopelessly unproductive. Many had by then abandoned science altogether in favour of exclusively humanist agendas, concerned with interpretation, phenomenology, literary theory, postmodern critique, and constructed realities (Marcus & Fischer, 1986; Norris, 1979; Tyler, 1986; Viveiros de Castro, 2012; Holbraad & Pedersen, 2017).

Almost unobserved, however, some of anthropology's neighbours had been making some startling discoveries. After a long period in the theoretical wilderness, largely in the grip of behaviourism, psychology underwent a dramatic revolution, sparked mainly by the invention of computers. The middle of the twentieth century heralded the appearance of radically new models of information processing which, taken together with advances in evolutionary biology and the neurosciences, opened up a new window on human psychology and its evolutionary history. In particular, over several decades, a substantial corpus of experimental evidence was rapidly built up, pointing to the presence of at least four 'core knowledge' systems for representing objects, actions, number, and space (Spelke & Kinzler, 2007). The term 'core' was used to indicate a growing consensus—based especially on developmental evidence cross-culturally and comparative studies of primate behaviour—that these systems were evolved features of human psychology. Indeed, over the same few decades, evolutionary psychology generated a rich evidence base for extensive modular specializations in the human cognitive repertoire, suggesting that many psychological predispositions and susceptibilities are genetically inherited rather than being the constructs of any particular cultural environment or history (Buss, 2005). Such features are typically thought to emerge in a similar fashion in all normal human beings without the need for deliberate instruction or training (barring pathology—itself often a valuable source of insight into natural cognition) (e.g. Farah & Wallace, 1992; Hillis & Caramazza, 1991).

These aspects of our evolved psychology arguably shape and constrain sociocultural systems even if reciprocally, at least some of those features may also be 'tuned' by cultural environments (McCauley, 2011). Accordingly, evolved features of human minds would seem to be necessary for a fuller understanding of economic behaviour, political strategizing, and systems of kinship, marriage, and descent (to take some of anthropology's traditional heartland subject areas), as well as more fashionable areas of research among contemporary ethnographers, such as the study of performance, art, and display, or of materiality, discourse, and embodiment.

Nevertheless, although anthropologists have long recognized the need to integrate their findings with those of neighbouring human sciences (Gellner, 1985), interest in this kind of integration dwindled in the closing decades of the twentieth century. According Pascal Boyer (2011), anthropologists instead became increasingly preoccupied with the production of 'salient connections', while the value of erudite scholarship and the systematic testing of scientific theories declined. Symptoms of these trends, Boyer argued, included low levels of agreement on what constituted authoritative work, or what methods of assessing the relative worth of competing contributions should be applied. In place of textbooks setting out widely agreed-upon theories, methods, and findings of the discipline, students were increasingly required to recount histories of ever changing and contested perspectives. Intellectual factions would coalesce around fashion-leaders and then disperse. And the argument of authority (despite the contested nature of that authority) came to eclipse evidential support as the primary means of persuasion. Boyer's bleak diagnosis, though not uniquely applicable to anthropology, is concerning. Anthropology began with scientific ambitions, and it proceeded to build up an impressive corpus of scholarship on comparative ethnography (e.g. in the highly specialized study of systems of kinship, marriage, and descent). Meanwhile, however, science and rigorous scholarship have come to be relatively devalued.

Part of the explanation for this disappointing trajectory may be that reasoning about sociocultural phenomena does not come naturally. That is, humans as a species lack dedicated intuitive machinery for reasoning about highly elaborated social morphology. As our societies have grown in size and complexity, we have witnessed the emergence of a vast plethora of specialized offices and corporate groups based on a broad range of sorting principles: kinship, descent, rank, caste, ethnicity, nationality, and so on. Categories of office, coalition, and class are no more than idealized models of how the social world is organized, rather than precise descriptions of how it operates on the ground (Firth, 1964; Leach, 1954), but they provide robust schemas for individual behaviour, establishing cultural patterns over time that serve to perpetuate those schemas. Nevertheless, many of the highly elaborated schemas required to live in a sprawling, stratified society are a relatively modern and potentially dispensable accretion to human thinking, too recent in our evolutionary history to have led, via natural selection, to specialized cognitive skills for reasoning about social complexity. The same cannot be said for patterns of thinking in many other ontological domains.

As part of our evolutionary endowment, we possess dedicated intuitive machinery for reasoning about physical properties (e.g. solidity and gravity) (McCloskey, 1983; Povinelli, 2000), biological properties (e.g. essentialized differences between natural kinds) (Carey, 1985; Leslie, 1994; Bloom, 2000), and psychological properties (e.g. a capacity to empathize with suffering) (Preston & de Waal, 2001). Our intuitive physics, intuitive biology, and intuitive psychology may have to be substantially revised in light of the discoveries of *scientific* physics/biology/psychology, but our intuitions often *also* deliver useful reference points and pedagogic tools. For instance, although our intuitions about the discreteness and stability of natural kinds are inconsistent with the diachronic character of evolutionary processes, the taxonomies they produce do provide a convenient on-the-hoof framework within which to conceptualize the plants and animals we encounter.

Problems arise, however, when some of our intuitively grounded ontological commitments also serve as markers of identity. In order to function in that way, such commitments must cause us to differ discernibly from other people so as to become a locus of conflict. If you and I share the intuitively grounded explicit belief that all features of the natural environment are the outcome of intentional design, then we can live in peace with that commonly held presumption. If, however, somebody challenges our beliefs with an alternative account (e.g. that the features in question were caused by some non-agentic process), we have a basis for conflict, especially where competition for resources, either symbolic or material (or both), depends on who comes down on which side of the debate. In this particular case, some evolutionary biologists and their supporters have been drawn into protracted disputes with young-earth creationists and proponents of intelligent design. In scientific circles, however, these kinds of battles tend to be somewhat peripheral to the day-to-day business of formulating hypotheses and gathering data to test them. Any competent biologist, even one who sympathizes with certain notions of intelligent design, would (despite this peculiarity) be doing the same kind of science as anybody else in that field. Likewise, if an astrophysicist has theistic commitments these would not necessarily affect in any way the quality of her scientific research on the origins of the universe. Imagine, by contrast, a domain of scholarly enquiry that based its theories on multiple and conflicting intuitions about the basic nature of the phenomena under study. It would struggle to get off the ground because of interminable turf wars among competing coalitions with widely differing foundational assumptions about the nature and purpose of scholarly enquiry. Unfortunately, we do not have to imagine it. That is exactly the problem, or at least I would argue that it has been the problem historically, with the social sciences in general and with anthropology in particular.

Since we lack dedicated cognitive machinery for reasoning about social complexity, we are prone to *borrowing* intuitions proper to *alien* ontological domains. Consequently, social scientists at turns reify institutions, biologize social categories, anthropomorphize offices, and mentalize corporate groups. This does not mean that our borrowed intuitions are applied inappropriately. It might, of course, if those intuitions badly distort what could have been profitably learned through the application of scientific methods. But even if they help rather than hinder understanding, the fact that our intuitions about the social are borrowed and potentially competing can make disagreements much harder to resolve. Consider the following examples in scholarly sociologizing.

Instances of *teleological* reasoning about the social are rampant in functionalist traditions in the social sciences. The theory of social functions, as elaborated by several generations of British anthropologists since Malinowski (1922), maintains that every social institution serves to bolster some other institution (or cluster of institutions) so as to contribute to the maintenance of stable social systems (e.g. Evans-Pritchard, 1940; Radcliffe-Brown, 1952; Firth, 1951). Thus, the ritualized abuse of a monarch in some African kingdom might have the social function of giving public expression to structural tensions running through society (e.g. between commoners in opposition to an exploitative aristocracy and monarchy, or between loyal commoners and the king in opposition to plotting royal heirs, and so on) while publicly affirming in the concluding rites that unification of the kingdom is both necessary and desirable in spite of this (Gluckman, 1962b). At the core of this mode of social theorizing is the idea that rituals are like tools, with specific functions, and offices (e.g. the kingship) and social categories (e.g. commoner clients) are like artefacts that are made and remade through the application of those tools. Marxist scholars have often adopted similar strategies of reasoning, except that the functions of political, legal, and religious institutions are typically said to serve the interests, not of society as a whole, but of a particular sector of society, namely the ruling class (Bloch, 1983). To reiterate, there is nothing inherently wrong with these functionalist arguments, but they can come into conflict with other strategies of sociological reasoning based on alternative intuitions.

For example, just as we are tempted to borrow from teleological artefact cognition when reasoning about complex sociocultural phenomena, we are no less inclined to draw on our *intuitive psychology* in response to much the same phenomena of interest. For instance, the so-called 'culture and personality school' in American anthropology, inspired by the ideas of Franz Boas and Sigmund Freud, was premised on the idea that variable child-rearing practices lead to the predominance of certain personality types at a population level, allowing us to generalize about tribes and nations rather as we might about the character of a particular individual (classic examples of this approach include Mead, 1928; Benedict, 1935; Wallace, 1970). In France, also, the tendency to anthropomorphize social groups and categories has been a recurrent theme, featuring prominently for instance in the ideas of *L'Année Sociologique*, whose members wrote enthusiastically about such things as 'collective memory' (Halbwachs, 1950) and 'collective conscience' (Durkheim, 1933[1893]). Some of these ideas have enjoyed a renaissance in recent years to the extent that by the time I graduated from Cambridge in the early 1990s, it was practically impossible to find a major conference in any of the arts, humanities, or social science disciplines that did not in some way emphasize the theme of memory, and, in particular, its putatively collective or social character as understood by social theorists. While there is nothing inherently wrong with either functionalist or psychological perspectives on the domain of the social, because they are rooted in contrasting intuitions, they seem all too readily to involve radically distinct and opposed world views, thereby assigning their followers to 'camps', between which the serious student may feel compelled to choose.

In the same way as we might readily deploy teleological or anthropomorphic reasoning in sociological theorizing, so we may also be inclined to treat certain types of persons as natural kinds based on analogical extension of intuitive knowledge about the biological world. The temptation to biologize the social world grows stronger as societies become larger and more heterogeneous and the division of labour more elaborate. It is no accident that Emile Durkheim coined the term 'organic solidarity' to characterize this type of social morphology (1933[1893]). Biologizing the social can lead us also to essentialize institutions, especially where particular offices or membership of social groups and categories are transmittable from parent to offspring. Where that is not the case (e.g. where there is great occupational mobility, where people join and leave clubs and associations at will, and where religious affiliations are chosen rather than ascribed), we may be less likely to essentialize the social. Nevertheless, where people's roles and identities are determined by birth and shared with ancestors, the speciation of social categories may well become much harder to resist.

Despite or perhaps because of the tendency for the average person to biologize social categories (e.g. in racial stereotyping), this way of reasoning is highly problematic for liberal academics, and with good reason. The efforts, particularly in the nineteenth century, to carve up humanity into distinct races based on phenotypic characteristics seems to most contemporary social scientists at least as distasteful as it is biologically indefensible (Peers, 2007). That is not to say that intuitive biology has ceased to play a role in social theorizing, however. A particularly widespread, if largely unexamined anthropological practice is (and probably has always been) to talk about cultural traditions as at least implicitly analogous to biological species, especially when threatened with extinction. There are striking continuities, for instance, between the ways in which some anthropologists reason about the rights of small-scale societies to preserve their traditional beliefs and practices, and the ways in which conservationists campaign for the protection of endangered species (cf. the 'Declaration on Anthropology and Human Rights' adopted by the American Anthropological Association). Even though anthropologists have become increasingly sensitive to the contested nature of cultural traditions and their embedding in wider regional and global processes of economic expansion and political struggle, there remains a widespread intuition that *all* traditions should be respected and preserved, that there is no moral high ground beyond the local cultural universe from which we can justly impose reform. From that relativistic perspective, cultural and linguistic diversity comes to be valued by more or less explicit comparison with the taxonomic richness and diversity of the natural world.

The trouble with grounding our ideas about the sociocultural realm in intuitive thinking borrowed from other domains is not merely that we may discover these to be inadequate tools for the job. To some extent that may be inevitable, since social and cultural institutions are not really physical artefacts, organisms with essences, or minds with collective personalities or memories. If that were the only problem, however, it would be relatively easy to surmount (in comparison with the more intractable problem to which we presently turn). After all, mature sciences are accustomed to explaining that our intuitions—for instance, about the cosmos or the natural world or the mind—are only going to take us so far, and then we have to abandon them. It is not that those intuitions then disappear. It may still seem to us that the sun moves across the sky (rather than the Earth around the sun) or that some kind of intentional agent is responsible for selecting the characteristics of biological species (rather than effects of random mutation and ecology on the fitness of organisms). Nevertheless, with sufficient education and intelligence, we can realize and remember, when reasoning explicitly, that things are not as they seem. Where it gets more complicated, however, is when people's *identities* become wrapped up in a particular intuitive construal of the world. This is how Galileo found himself under house arrest as a punishment for his heretical claims about the structure of the solar system. Even today some intuitive forms of Biblical literalism are belligerently espoused by Christian fundamentalists. The problem gets more intractable still when the same phenomena attract mutually exclusive and competing intuitive claims, on which professional reputations are pinned.

Every time a new school of thought has emerged in anthropology, anchored in borrowed intuitions, it has eventually provoked a backlash of objections from those inspired by alternative intuitions. Often the arguments are less about the issues at stake and more about whose intuitions should prevail. Ultimately, however, all are losers. Functionalism, for instance, is now considered a dirty word in anthropology, whereas it once had been a more or less paradigmatic method of ethnographic enquiry (Holmwood, 2005). Why? On the surface, objectors pointed to lacunae in the functionalist world view. Although we could trace the functions of real tools and artefacts to the intentions of ancestors (and sometime historical individuals), nobody could explain how institutions came to have the useful properties that functionalists ascribed to them. There were other sources of embarrassment too: anthropologists found that societies were seldom, if ever, trapped in a state of functionally integrated equilibrium; looking a little closer we always found a writhing morass of contestation and struggle rather than consensus and harmony; looking a little longer invariably revealed upheaval and transformation rather than societal stability and integration. Although often cited as the reason for functionalism's downfall, however, such considerations are not as serious as critics have been wont to claim. There is no reason why tendencies toward functional integration should be impossible to demonstrate in principle, and arguably these have been repeatedly demonstrated in practice.

Before we can begin to contemplate solutions to this conundrum, however, we have to attend to an even more serious problem. Disillusioned by all attempts to discover a sociological method grounded in stable intuitions, social theorists in the second half of the twentieth century began to look for ideas with increasing desperation almost *anywhere*. The structure of natural language seemed to be a promising starting point, not least because of its systemic character. Claude Lévi-Strauss's structuralist paradigm (1966) was inspired in no small part by the linguist Ferdinand de Saussure's (1959) observation that not only are most of the sounds of a words discernible only on the basis of arbitrary phonological differences ('bat' being distinguishable from 'mat' by utilizing natural differences between plosive and nasal sounds) but so too are many of the conceptual structures to which those sounds refer (e.g. 'river' being distinct from a 'stream' in English because the former is larger and wider, while *'fleuve'* is distinct from *'riviere'* in French because the former flows into the sea) (Leach, 1989). Both the phonological and semantic properties of words seemed to be determined by arbitrary *systems* of differences, an insight that Lévi-Strauss and his followers enthusiastically transferred and extended in the analysis of a wide variety of cultural forms: myths, rituals, kinship, descent, marriage, culinary traditions, and so on. This way of thinking emphasized the relativity of cultural systems, both in terms of directly observable properties (behaviours and artefacts) and interiorized but distributed inner states (meanings and values). Nevertheless, it also arguably over-egged the importance of binary logic in both language and culture (Boyer, 1993). After all, much of the conceptual content entailed by the concept 'river' is held in common with the concept *'fleuve'*, and not all variability across languages/cultures may be said to result from arbitrary differences between signs (e.g. the sounds of speech or the concepts they signify).

Lévi-Strauss's structuralism, however important its insights may have been, was soon abandoned and replaced by more fashionable strategies, based on still other competing intuitions. For example, Clifford Geertz's brand of 'interpretivism' sought to detach sociocultural phenomena from mental activity entirely, arguing that culture occupies an ontological domain of its own, and can only be described and interpreted in terms belonging to that domain (for a critical discussion, see Strauss & Quinn, 1997). These developments, as well as the rise of many varieties of poststructuralist and postmodernist critique, all have something in common: they take sociocultural phenomena to be fundamentally text-like, allowing interpretive flights of fantasy extending far beyond the dull world in which everyday culture is produced and transmitted. Authors rapidly became enchanted by the suggestiveness of their own language through the creation of jargon and stylistic innovations, decorating the limited interpretations of informants with vastly more fanciful and appealing interpretations of their own (for an erudite critique of this trend, see Gellner, 1992). In this runaway inflation of ideas, almost anything goes, as long as it is new and different. Soon the idea of culture as text is not enough, it must be continuously reconceived (Coombe, 2008), for instance, as something to be experienced (Hastrup & Hervik, 1994), embodied (Pedwell, 2010), or, as one influential anthropologist has suggested, 'enwinded' (Ingold, 2007).

A potentially more consensual alternative is to seek an encompassing scientific framework on which to construct our questions and pursue answers. Such a framework exists in the form of evolutionary theory. Since at least the time of Darwin, evolutionary theory has proven to be an exceptionally robust method of explaining the anatomy, appearance, behaviour, psychology, history, and development of our species. Despite some false starts and blind alleys, efforts to explain recurrence and diversity of sociocultural traits within this framework, both in humans and other animals, is generating cumulative and, therefore, increasingly sophisticated bodies of theory based on the formulation of precise and testable hypotheses (Sosis & Alcorta, 2003; Henrich & Henrich, 2007; Boyd & Richerson, 2005; Henrich, 2016; Richerson et al., 2016). Admittedly, evolutionary explanations of sociocultural phenomena sneak in old arguments and their intuitive assumptions through the back door. The notion, for instance, that a certain kind of institution might help to reproduce the society in which it occurs (in evolutionary formulations a perfectly respectable hypothesis) surely just reinstates the functionalist teleology that anthropology long ago abandoned. Recall, however, that the main problem with functionalism was that it failed to specify the mechanism by which socially useful traits came into being. The intuitive solution alone might lead quite erroneously to notions of intentional design rather than to Darwinian evolution (Wilson, 2002). It is precisely these missteps that rigorous evolutionary science can help us to avoid. I have argued in this book that we need to fractionate sociocultural phenomena into component features that are explainable in terms of discrete suites of causes rather than relying merely on intuitive forms of reification and anthropomorphism. By adopting this strategy, we may improve the prospects of cumulative theory building, such that seemingly interminable turf wars between those holding competing intuitions might instead give way to new forms of transdisciplinary alliance and collaboration, building on and, where appropriate, replacing our borrowed intuitions with a genuine *science of the social*.

The Two Cultures Problem and the Silo Effect

I have argued that progress in the social sciences has been held back by wars waged under the flags of competing intuitions, but it has surely also been impeded by the assignment of the sciences and humanities to institutionalized and seemingly unbridgeable camps within academia—a phenomenon popularly known as the 'two cultures problem'. At the core of this problem is the tendency for humanities scholars and scientists to be poorly informed about the nature of the work being undertaken on the other side of the divide, and to adopt a hostile attitude towards each other's basic assumptions, methods, and goals, even (or perhaps especially) when these are not well understood. As such, the two academic tribes live and work more or less in isolation from one another, and occasional encounters range from suspicious to openly hostile. C. P. Snow, who first coined the term 'two cultures' to describe the problem (1959), attributed some of the blame for it to early specialization in the British schooling system. But the two cultures problem is globally distributed in the academy rather than confined to any one country, and its roots are deeper than simply the lack of early exposure to a broad range of academic subjects during development.

The division of the academy into two culturally distinct camps may be explained at least in part within the framework of dual stance theory, as elaborated in Chapter 1. Recall that this theory postulates, first, an *instrumental stance*, focused on acquiring causally transparent (or at least potentially causally transparent) behaviours as a way of understanding and manipulating the physical world ever more effectively. Most of what passes as science, and everything we class as technology, is produced largely in the spirit of the instrumental stance—of wishing to know how things work in order to control and harness them. By contrast, the *ritual stance* focuses on acquiring behaviours that are *not only* causally opaque, but in a way that is assumed to be *irremediable*. Irremediable causal opacity is a defining feature of all forms of normative convention, but this is also true of magic and art. Earlier in this book, I devoted considerable space to discussing why conventional and magical actions may be seen as expressions of the ritual stance. But I have avoided, until now, any mention of the psychological origins of *art* (e.g. painting, sculpture, and music), which a moment's reflection reveals to be a very closely related phenomenon.

Art, like ritualized behaviour, is always at least partially opaque, and irremediably so. Each conceptual move, each stroke of the brush, each change of tone or cadence, is irreducible to a set of physical-causal motivations. And so, just like ritual, art attracts exegesis—efforts to interpret the meaning, significance, or allegorical intent of the narrative, composition, or melody. Some art may be quasi-instrumental, just like a magical ritual, except that the end goal is less often to heal than to disturb, or at least to provoke an aesthetic reaction or appraisal. At any rate, however, art (like magic and convention) engages the ritual stance, while science more prominently triggers an instrumental stance. This is clearly a matter of degree, as in all domains of human activity, but the difference of emphasis is written deep into the code of what makes art, art and science, science. And this may go a long way to explaining why the two cultures have come to live under a form of academic apartheid.

The idea that the arts and humanities cleave more strongly than science to the ritual stance is impressionistic and would at least need to be rendered more precisely to be investigated empirically. Armed with suitable measures, it would be similarly possible to establish whether some sciences are more ritualistic than others, and likewise if that is also the case when comparing across humanities disciplines. But whichever disciplines end up scoring high or low on such a measure, we would expect scholars aligning with the more ritualistic ones to be more highly attuned to issues of belonging, fashion, and tribal loyalty, to cherish and display proudly the norms and conventions that define them, and to act as coalitions when competing for resources in central university administrations. We would also predict that rank and authority would feature highly, if subtly, in such groups, perhaps emphasizing more heavily the importance of lengthy inductions into the group via protracted periods of doctoral training and postdoctoral apprenticeship. As such, mentoring might be valued more dearly than collaboration. By contrast, we might predict that in disciplines where the instrumental stance is more salient, competition for resources would be more individualistic, that what you can do would matter more than who you are, and that demonstrable competence or skill would explicitly trump seniority or rank when placed head-to-head. These are all potentially testable predictions, but for now it is at least worth noting that dual stance theory (Jagiello, Heyes, & Whitehouse, Under Review) could help to explain the persistence of the two cultures problem. As argued at numerous junctures elsewhere in this book, gaining a fuller understanding of the cognitive-developmental roots of human behaviour, and how these relate not only to epigenetic landscapes below and social-historical arrangements above, is arguably the first step towards consensual change in society (beginning, in this case, with our universities).

Whether or not the arts and humanities are more ritualistic than the sciences, the *social and behavioural* sciences which are often awkwardly located somewhere in the middle, undoubtedly suffer from an acute 'silo effect'. This is to be seen, for example, in the tendency for disciplines to create unnecessary jargon or arcane skill sets unshared by other fields, even neighbouring ones. In the world of business and information technology, silos are management systems that cannot operate in conjunction with others and so become isolated. In the academy, silos make communication across disciplinary boundaries difficult by creating seemingly incommensurate constructs, methods, and terminology associated with discrete fields of research. Based on a survey conducted in 2015, sampling 236 founding members of the Cultural Evolution Society, we identified 422 distinct challenges facing the new field, but the most commonly cited of these 'grand challenges' was *knowledge synthesis* (Brewer et al., 2017)—that is, the ability to overcome the silo problem so as to integrate knowledge from disparate disciplines (Ensor, 1988).

If there is to be a successful science of the social, it will need to embed the expertise of humanities scholars at its very core. All too often, experimental psychologists derive their hypotheses from common-sense (often ethnocentric) assumptions about human nature rather than from close engagement with ethnography, history, and archaeology. I would argue that the most important contributions of social science must always depend upon qualitative engagement with human worlds through the practice of ethnography, historiography, and archaeological reconstruction, as well as the insights of related empirical humanities scholarship on such topics as world history, music, art, literature, and architecture. Deep interpretative engagement with these human worlds, for example, via participant observation, dialogue, and inspection of manuscripts, artworks and artefacts of all kinds, should provide the bedrock on which knowledge about the social can be adequately supported. The humanities alone, however, cannot build cumulatively on these foundations without the help of scientific theory and method. This requires skill sets that go beyond the work of observation, description, and interpretation. Needed also are strategies for rigorous comparison, measurement, and hypothesis testing. Scientists are long accustomed to tackling such problems in fields such as physics, biology, and even psychology, but there is much catching up to do in the sciences of the social. This will not be achieved, however, simply by debating the philosophical merits of relativism or constructivism as creeds, worldviews, or systems of thought. Real progress, I would argue, depends on adopting a more pragmatic approach, via *problem-centred* engagement with data.

Problem-centred approaches to research are remarkably rare in the humanities and even in many social sciences. They are also not well incentivized, exacerbating the silo problem. Commonly, careers are advanced by contributing to a local field of scholarship, since this is how invitations to conferences, publishing opportunities, and academic jobs are secured. As a result, many of those who have valuable expertise to bring to a problem-centred interdisciplinary project, for example, on ethnographic or historical variation, may have had little or no experience of working collaboratively and be understandably wary of investing time and effort in such an enterprise. Funding bodies have a role to play by incentivizing science-based projects requiring meaningful contributions from scholars with expertise in ethnography, language, art, religion, archaeology, or history who are willing to learn how to contribute to problem-centred collaborative research while also teaching and sharing their knowledge as widely as possible. But university departments and faculties can also contribute to fostering interdisciplinary research, for example, through more joint appointments, cross-departmental degree programmes, coordinated sabbatical opportunities, and international exchange programmes.

Problem-centred research needs to be pursued using diachronic, as well as synchronic, datasets in the social sciences. Recall that Tinbergen's four whys emphasize phylogeny and ultimate causation as well as development and proximate mechanisms. While field projects designed collaboratively by psychologists, sociologists, and anthropologists may be the best way to address the latter two whys, history and selective pressures in sociocultural evolution are often best studied in collaboration with historians, archaeologists, and evolutionary modellers. In order for this to succeed, the data generated by these disciplines needs to be analysed quantitatively as well as qualitatively. Here again, this can present formidable resourcing challenges.

A good example is the Seshat: Global History Databank project (see Chapter 4). Seshat was first established as part of a project I directed with support from the UK's Economic and Social Research Council (ESRC), aimed at combining approaches to the study of ritual from cognitive science, anthropology, evolutionary biology, archaeology, and history. My fellow co-founders of Seshat, Peter Turchin (overall director of the databank) and Pieter François (the first postdoctoral researcher employed to help us set it up), were responsible for delivering the historical component of the ESRC project. Our aim was to establish a way of quantifying patterns of recurrence and diversity in world history in various domains of religion, ritual, politics, economics, and technology (Whitehouse, 2016b). This meant repackaging information about the human past in a way that would be analysable statistically.

When we started to construct Seshat, it was obvious that the greatest impediment to quantifying and tracking the appearance and distribution of traits in world history was the fact that these traits were not organized into packages that could be directly measured or compared. For example, the same trait was often assigned a unique label in different regions of the world or in different time periods within the same region. In order to tackle this problem, we created a codebook in which hundreds of traits of interest could be defined in such a way that their presence or absence (or some numerical measure of their magnitude) could be coded for, and thus compared directly across space and time. This required extensive collaboration between evolutionary theorists, computer scientists, mathematical modellers, and statisticians, on the one hand, and historians, classicists, and archaeologists on the other—disciplines with different research cultures and little or no experience of working together. Moreover, it required the involvement of academics at all stages of career—from established scholars and scientists to postdoctoral researchers, research assistants, and students—all of whom were needed not only to source and check data but to help us establish the basic design of the database. Since no individual could master all the toolkits necessary to accomplish this, extensive collaboration emerged as the only way forward. But that meant more scholars and scientists needed to share at least the basics of a common language and theoretical framework.

Seshat thus requires a vast amount of specialist knowledge, not only of history and prehistory, but also of various branches of computer science necessary to curate and organize its data. In addition, it relies on relevant fields of statistics to analyse the data, and theoretical frameworks from fields as diverse as evolutionary biology, anthropology, and agent-based modelling to hone the hypotheses to be tested and to design the variables in the codebook. Even more dauntingly, this very diverse knowledge needs to be coordinated in quite specific ways to address agreed-upon research questions. This kind of extensive and deep collaboration is not easy, or cheap. Seshat has already cost many millions of pounds and a vast amount of volunteer labour-power to set up, and only after nearly a decade of collaborative effort did the first waves of data analysis begin to appear in published articles (e.g. Turchin et al., 2018; Mullins et al., 2018). More research based on Seshat data is continually appearing, and there is potential to continue generating further studies in this way for many decades to come. Nevertheless, core funding is necessary to maintain databases of this kind and for statistical analysis of world history to become sustainable in the long run, it will be necessary to establish new resourcing models, for example, by embedding the approach institutionally as part of basic education or university degree programmes in the social sciences.

Although the challenges described above are daunting, I have argued throughout this book that we can best make rapid progress by grounding the study of humanity (including human social, political, and economic lives and histories) in the evolutionary sciences. This would help not only to break down the conceptual and terminological boundaries between the various sciences of the social but also to connect them to all the other related sciences, including neuroscience, genetics, epidemiology, primatology, and (of course) evolutionary biology. Although there have been understandable reasons why these disciplines have evolved into more or less distinct silos, the intellectual costs of this are inordinately high. We can no longer afford to pursue social science and humanities research in ways that are detached from each other or from the rest of science. While there will still be greater overlap between some disciplines than others, creating an impression of 'neighbouring' fields, the evolutionary perspective allows us to see them as all related and commensurate. Moreover, it becomes clear that from the perspective of one discipline the relevance of another is not fixed, but is a result of the kind of problem being investigated. This section has set out to show how such an integrated framework for the human sciences might look (at least from one set of perspectives), while the next section is primarily about the practical impediments to deep cross-cultural comparison and collaboration that must be overcome to put such an ambitious vision into practice.

Diversifying Cross-Cultural Comparison and Collaboration

One increasingly obvious reason why transdisciplinary research into the causes and consequences of human culture is hard to achieve is that it needs to take account of global variation and not oversample convenient but unrepresentative populations, such as university undergraduates. This means running studies (including surveys and experiments) in the field as well as the lab. Historically, however, participants in psychological studies are overwhelmingly WEIRD—that is, they are sampled from cultures that are predominantly Western, Educated, Industrialized, Rich, and Democratic (Henrich et al., 2010). This not only produces a very biased impression of human nature in general, but also skews our research in the direction of particular kinds of cultural groups. For example, it biases us to think of rituals as the preserve only or primarily of doctrinal religions, particularly the 'Abrahamic' ones (Willard et al., 2020). Overcoming the WEIRD problem is not simply a matter of sampling populations outside Europe and North America; it is about developing research questions that are shaped and informed by knowledge of the world's extant and historical cultures and conducted in field settings that are relatively hard for social scientists, typically based in urban research universities, to access. This is a formidable challenge because when psychological studies are conducted in the field with the collaboration of local experts, it takes a very long time for shared understandings among researchers to become adequately established and longer still to conduct the necessary qualitative research in local communities before ecologically valid experiments, surveys, and quantitative analysis can be systematically undertaken.

Participant observation allows ethnographers to describe cultural systems holistically, and that is perhaps anthropology's greatest strength (Parkin, 2007). Nevertheless, observation and description are not the same as explanation. To understand the causes of the phenomena observed in the field requires carefully controlled experiments and systematic comparison across space and time. Field sites have a vital role to play at this level as well. But when experiment and comparison are the goal, fieldwork starts to look very different. Research teams get larger, field sites need to start communicating with each other, and the whole enterprise of data gathering and analysis needs to be scaled up and, to some extent, centrally coordinated.

Much of the research described in the core chapters of this book was conducted in non-Western cultures including non-literate or semiliterate populations in places like rural Vanuatu and Cameroon or among relatively deprived groups in urban settings, such as the *favelas* of Brazil or the street traders of Indonesia. In choosing field locations for the study of ritual modes, my colleagues and I have sought to maximize cultural variability in our samples, something that can be important for a wide variety of reasons. For example, one of the theoretical debates discussed earlier in this book focuses on the extent to which ritual behaviours are evoked or transmitted (see Chapter 5). Investigating this question requires empirical studies that allow us to adjudicate between these two possibilities. It is all too easy to fall prey to the widespread, if implicit, misconception that just because behaviour is universal it must be innate and therefore evoked, whereas if it is variable, it must be learned and therefore culturally transmitted. But this can be overly simplistic and misleading.

Moral norms may differ cross-culturally not primarily because of histories of cultural transmission, but because different environments present varied cooperation problems that require different moral rules to solve (Curry, Mullins, & Whitehouse, 2019). And the same applies to rituals. For example, in Chapter 1 we considered a series of studies showing that when children believed that a regularly enacted group behaviour was a normative convention rather than an instrumental action, they performed better on a task involving delayed gratification (Rybanska et al., 2016). This could have been due to culturally transmitted ideas, for example, because the children had learned that participation in rituals (conventional behaviours) requires a respectful attitude, tamping down impulsivity and consequently making them better able to wait for a reward. But it could just as easily have been a result of panhuman, evoked psychological propensities or susceptibilities. After all, as a consequence of the need to pay attention to all aspects of behaviour in an irremediably opaque procedural string, action parsing for ritual actions might reasonably be expected to require a higher cognitive load than for instrumental actions, and thus participating in novel rituals might be expected to 'train up' executive control systems, improving the ability to defer gratification. One way to investigate these hypotheses was to compare the results achieved using a sample of European children and participants of the same age in a village in Vanuatu, where deference to tradition is much more strongly emphasized via cultural transmission. What we found were similar effects of ritual participation on both participant pools, suggesting that the effects on future discounting are not primarily a result of cultural learning (see Chapter 1).

Nevertheless, carrying out valid cross-cultural comparative studies based on experiments in the field can be extremely difficult and entails a high risk of failure. For example, consider the following study conducted in another part of Vanuatu, on the island of Tanna. This was a community that had consciously decided to remain aloof from Western influences, choosing to wear traditional clothing (penis sheaths or grass skirts) and relying mainly on subsistence crops in preference to shop-bought goods. Our aim was to run a version of the child study described above, focusing on the effects of ritual framings on the ability to delay gratification, but in this case with an adult sample. In our experiment, all participants were invited to participate in a small collective ritual in which a stone was passed in a circle of four individuals, comprising the experimenter, two research assistants, and the participant. Half the participants were assigned to a ritual condition (in which the stone-passing task was described convincingly as a forgotten local tradition and referenced to a genuine but little-known local myth), and half the participants were assigned to an instrumental condition (in which the task was explained equally plausibly as a form of exercise to improve posture and strengthen the back). After this performance, participants were paid in salt (rather than money, for reasons explained below). They were offered the opportunity to receive one cup of salt immediately or one-and-a-half cups three days later. We predicted that participants in the ritual condition would be more likely to delay gratification. As beguilingly simple as this research design may sound, implementation raised innumerable problems, many of which we have found to be quite common in field settings, illustrating the challenges of running experiments in non-WEIRD populations.

It was imperative for the success of this field experiment that participants did not have an opportunity to learn about the experiences of others who performed the same task. To try to achieve privacy, we conducted the study in a sheltered outdoor space as far away from domestic dwellings as possible and we asked villagers not to approach unless it was to participate in the research. We also asked participants not to talk about their experiences with others in the village until the work was complete. In practice, these rules were impossible to enforce. People did observe curiously from a distance, prior to participating, and it is also highly likely that they discussed their experiences afterwards. Whereas in a lab setting privacy can usually be assured, this is seldom the case in the field, and, consequently, there is always a high risk that the purpose of experimental manipulations will be easily detected, and their effects therefore compromised.

Another feature of this field experiment that proved problematic was the mode of payment. The government body regulating research activities in this region of Vanuatu discouraged the use of currency as payment for participation in research on the grounds that monetarizing such transactions can create expectations that could hamper future research. Salt was considered a more appropriate form of remuneration because it is valued as a flavour enhancer but not easily procured locally, at least in the region we were working. Nevertheless, when running the study, it soon became clear that the use of salt as a measure of ability to defer gratification impacted the behaviour of female participants very differently from that of males. Whereas men were more likely to wait to obtain a bigger reward after a three-day delay in the ritual condition, women were more likely to take the offer of salt immediately, irrespective of the condition to which they were assigned. The reason for this was that they were eager to use the salt at once in preparing food, in a way that was less of a pressing concern for the men. As a result of these sorts of problems, the results of this study were never published.

Team-based fieldwork is costly, logistically complicated, and prone to a wide range of setbacks, as in the example just presented. One way of reducing these risks and increasing efficiency is to combine forces with other research teams that have overlapping goals. For example, my data collection efforts in Vanuatu have been successfully coordinated with other research groups, including Quentin Atkinson's lab group at the University of Auckland and Cristine Legare's lab group at the University of Texas. If all teams require the same basic demographic data from the communities in which research is to be conducted, this can be gathered more efficiently and cheaply by joining forces and sharing datasets. Moreover, even on those occasions when field experiments fail, vital experience may be acquired that can lead to improved research design on subsequent studies. For example, the unpublished study on Tanna provided essential training that subsequently resulted in successful data collection on a much more ambitious collaborative experiment in the months that followed.

Because of the high costs involved, running field-based experiments using staff and students from another country may only be advisable in regions where local scientific expertise is unavailable. During our research in Vanuatu, for example, the country did not have a university-based department of experimental psychology capable of running the kinds of field studies described above. There were, however, many well-educated students in the country's capital who were willing to collect survey data not only in the city but also in the many island communities from which the student population was drawn. Consequently, another way in which we have been able to obtain data from non-WEIRD countries has been to provide training to teams of students as interviewers and to work with them collaboratively to design survey instruments. Such an approach is more efficient and cost-effective than sending overseas scientists into the field, and it has the advantage of leveraging local expertise, including fluency in local languages, familiarity with relevant cultural norms, and ability to incentivize research participation in communities unfamiliar with survey methods. Admittedly, this approach to collecting data is not costless—it does still require sending scientists overseas to provide training and usually also depends on being able to find local collaborators capable of coordinating the work of student volunteers and managing budgets.

Working with local communities in these ways, whether directly or through locally trained researchers (or both), can be a very rewarding process of consensus building. This often means ensuring that the process of conducting research is beneficial to participants, and never merely extractive. Such research cannot progress by advancing the careers of foreign researchers without fully remunerating local informants' time and effort and maximizing opportunities for knowledge exchange, training, and the formation of longer-term collaborative networks. It is equally important to establish mutually enriching relationships with the communities in which research is conducted. It is not necessarily sufficient, or even possible, simply to remunerate key informants, gatekeepers, and other research participants by means of wages or other forms of payment. In some situations, the kind of labour involved in research participation is not appropriately commoditized, carrying with it instead a host of reciprocal moral obligations. And quite commonly what research participants and local collaborators seek most is access to external resources (e.g. healthcare or political representation), protection from intrusive commercial interests (e.g. foreign logging and mining companies), or the ability to acquire public goods (e.g. electricity supply or water tanks). Sometimes, the most valuable contributions of long-term ethnographic work result from the role of the anthropologist as advocate in dealings with authorities external to the community, as a result of deep and extensive local consultation with a wide range of stakeholders, including those whose voices are seldom heard in public life (James, 2007). Bridging between local communities, in which research is conducted, and more powerful stakeholders, such as governments and commercial interests, or organizations whose acquisitive goals are not ostensibly material, such as missionaries or ideologues, might be seen as quite basic goals in the type of long-term cross-cultural research envisaged here. Arguably the most valuable products of field research are the least commonly explored, such as the potential to develop consensual solutions to locally recognized collective action problems, via a collaborative approach to applied social science. This potential is best realized by making the research not only descriptive and interpretive but also scientific, and therefore capable of contributing to policy impacts that are evidence-based and potentially generalizable, as long as they are rolled out through deep consultation and consensus-building from the outset.

In some non-WEIRD regions of the world, there are also local scientists who can take the lead on the design and implementation of study designs and can provide highly trained research staff and doctoral students capable of carrying out the data collection. For example, in Indonesia we have developed longstanding collaborations with permanent faculty at Persada University in Jakarta, through which several waves of empirical research have been conducted, including large surveys based on interviews with research participants from a variety of cultural and religious groups, including populations that would have been impossible to access as foreign researchers. This approach does still require regular face-to-face meetings to discuss research design, provide training, and plan data collection, but much of the implementation can be undertaken by collaborators based in the country under the mentorship of tenured university faculty. This has resulted in publications that are spearheaded by our Indonesian colleagues (e.g. Yustisia et al., 2020), as well as ones led by members of our own research team at the University of Oxford (e.g. Kavanagh et al., Under Review). Thus, the incentives driving collaboration in such cases obviously include advancement of collective knowledge and individual academic career development, and not just monetary remuneration or resource redistribution.

While one or the other (or both) of the above models can be used to collect data in most countries around the world, there are some regions in which it is neither possible to conduct field-based studies directly nor to gather data indirectly in collaboration with local universities. Examples include regions in which state failure or chronic violence mean that foreign researchers cannot gain access and that local universities (if they are still functioning) are unable to provide suitable collaborators. This has been the case in several countries in the Middle East where we have sought to collect data, including Syria, Iraq, Afghanistan, and Libya. In the case of Libya, we were originally able to conduct research in the country directly during the Arab Spring of 2011, with the extensive assistance of local revolutionary leaders and their battalions (Whitehouse et al., 2014). Nevertheless, after the insurgency, access to groups that were able to provide reasonably secure environments for foreigners to collect data proved increasingly difficult. We therefore switched to a strategy of collecting data through organizations that already had local researchers embedded in Libya. This had the disadvantage that we were unable either to interview informants in the field ourselves or to provide training for research assistants directly or *in situ*, but it did at least mean that data collection could be accomplished from a distance, with supervision provided indirectly from our universities in the UK and the USA, allowing us to carry out regular checks on data quality remotely (Buhrmester et al., Under Review).

Yet another way of accessing non-WEIRD populations is to collaborate with ethnographers who have long-term field experience and extensive regional knowledge and networks. This is often the least expensive way of doing comparative studies while benefitting from a high level of local expertise. But it is also relatively hard to find willing collaborators in anthropology departments, largely due to the 'two cultures' problem described above. A rare example of an anthropologist who conducts field-based experiments with behavioural economists and group psychologists is David Zeitlyn at the University of Oxford (Thomae, Zeitlyn, & Van Vugt, 2013; Buhrmester, Zeitlyn, & Whitehouse, 2020). Zeitlyn has been carrying out fieldwork in Mambila communities in rural Cameroon for several decades, and due to his extensive ethnographic knowledge and local connections, he was able to mobilize teams of research assistants to run surveys in the region designed in collaboration with fellow researchers at Oxford's School of Anthropology and Museum Ethnography (some of the results of this work were discussed in the last chapter; see also Buhrmester, Zeitlyn, & Whitehouse, 2020). One of the many benefits of this kind of collaboration is that ethnographers typically visit their field sites annually as a matter of course, and so comparative projects can become integrated into such visits without incurring significant extra costs. It could revolutionize efforts to combat the WEIRD problem if more anthropologists were willing to participate in problem-centred collaborations of the kind illustrated by the research described in this book. Such collaborations constitute one of the most significant ways in which the two cultures can be reconciled and academic silos effectively bridged.

An important feature of all the approaches to collaborative data collection described above, is that they differ markedly from the role of government anthropologists of yesteryear, who were appointed by colonial administrations with the explicit goal of gathering useful intelligence on subject populations to facilitate various kinds of imperialist projects, including the goals of extractive industries and of missionization, sometimes with only a veneer of concern for the welfare of indigenous populations. A strong and very understandable desire to distance the work of ethnography from such insidious forms of collusion has loomed large in the way anthropology reshaped its identity as a discipline in the second half of the twentieth century. But there is also a worthy alternative to anthropologists aligning themselves with the oppressed and exploited and that is to work with *all* levels of society to create fairer and more inclusive institutions from which everyone can benefit. Doing so consensually with maximum transparency, and in a way that is informed by scientific research, may lead to much better outcomes for all than approaches that are based merely on taking sides and which therefore lack credibility in the eyes of all key stakeholders. Appreciating the importance of inclusion is central to the idea of 'barrier-crossing leadership' discussed at some length in Chapter 6 and is just as applicable to the practice of social science as it is the work of parliamentarians, activists, or religious authorities.

One of the reasons why anthropology can play a potentially central role in bringing science to bear on the pursuit of social justice is that its practitioners often have very strong local networks, potentially bridging local communities with policy makers. Anthropologists are also uniquely placed to help researchers to tackle the problems of WEIRD sampling, silos, and the two cultures at the same time. Moreover, anthropology is the broadest of all the human sciences. It can naturally incorporate the concerns of the humanities with the local and particular but, at the same time, its historical emphasis on cross-cultural comparison via long-term field research makes it also uniquely placed to address questions of global recurrence and variation in human thinking, behaviour, and social organization, vital to the production of generalizing social theory. Despite the growth of anti-scientific trends in the discipline, at the core of anthropology remains an enduring commitment to the production of careful and rigorous ethnography. It is noteworthy also that some of the most important developments in social anthropology have been spearheaded by scholars with a keen interest in evolutionary theories (e.g. Bateson, 1972; Douglas, 1966; Goody, 1977; Gell, 1988; Lévi-Strauss, 1966; Lewis, 1988; James, 2003) or cognitive scientists with an anthropological background (e.g. Sperber, 1996; Boyer, 2001; Atran, 2002). Anthropology has made (and continues to make) valuable contributions that will, if we are wise, be put to increasingly effective use in the scientific study of our species' social and cultural achievements.

Conclusions

The challenges we face in building a more thoroughgoing science of the social are undoubtedly daunting, but the solutions are also potentially emancipating. Over the past century or more, anthropologists have posed many big questions about the nature and origins of culture, including the role played by rituals in establishing cohesive traditions of various kinds. The modes theory, among other efforts to contribute answers to these big questions, has prompted efforts to formulate precise and testable hypotheses, and to investigate them empirically, using methods borrowed from whatever sources happen to be most relevant and readily available. But that process has still left many questions unanswered or only partially answered. To advance further we need to address the two cultures problem. This problem no doubt has multiple causes, some of which are historically contingent and institutionalized. But one of the most difficult obstacles to overcome appears to be *psychological* in origin, stemming from a lack of evolved intuitive machinery for reasoning about the social, at least at the level of group categories as opposed to relational, interpersonal networks and dyadic ties. As a consequence, it is tempting to borrow intuitions from ontological domains that are entirely irrelevant to understanding the social, with the result that basic assumptions are constantly being critiqued or 'deconstructed' and basic scientific theory-building cannot easily get off the ground.

Evolutionary thinking provides a solution to this predicament, at least in theory. In practice, however, progress will also depend on overcoming the silo problem in academia. If we are to learn general lessons from world history, for example, historians specializing in a great diversity of regions and periods will have to develop commensurate constructs and terms of reference and they will need to work effectively with analysts of big data, including statisticians and mathematical modellers. Experimental psychologists and other social scientists will need to find ways of working in a greater diversity of non-WEIRD field settings, either directly or in collaboration with local universities. Anthropologists have a special contribution to make to comparative cross-cultural projects, but this will require a fundamental change of epistemological outlook and a renewed commitment to problem-centred interdisciplinary collaboration.

Even assuming that all academic researchers who are currently engaged in the study of human thinking, behaviour, and its products become increasingly open to the idea of developing a grand intellectual vision of the human sciences integrated under the umbrella of a shared evolutionary framework, there would still remain many formidable practical hurdles to realizing that vision. Some of these hurdles are the result of long histories of disciplinary isolation (the silo problem, discussed above) which make retooling costly at many levels and hard to incentivize. Sampling the diversity of contemporary cultural systems around the world is also challenging, as is the problem of how to organize the data from human history and prehistory in ways that facilitate comparison and sequencing. Overcoming these hurdles will not be easy, or cheap. As prosaic as it may seem to dwell on these collective action problems and potential practical solutions, it is an essential exercise if we are collectively to make progress towards a new and better future for the science of the social.

Epilogue

The ritual animal longs to belong. From infancy, we copy those around us in order to be like others, to be one with the tribe. Other primates will copy behaviour that leads to transparent benefits, such as access to food. But only humans promiscuously copy actions that have no obvious instrumental purpose. Moreover, we do so all the more fastidiously when there is no hope of attributing a transparent causal structure to the observed behaviour. As argued at length in Chapter 1, this propensity to imitate actions that are *irremediably* opaque lies at the root of all human rituals. The main motivation to copy such behaviour is the desire to affiliate, and we imitate with higher fidelity when ostracism threats are cued, apparently as a re-inclusion behaviour. Thus, what motivates children to acquire the rituals of their surrounding communities is the hope of learning how to conform and gain acceptance rather than how to acquire some technically useful skill.

Ritual and instrumental learning can be hard to disambiguate. In terms of their observable features, there may be nothing to distinguish them since both may involve the copying of behaviour that has a non-obvious causal structure. The difference lies only in the actor's attitude or 'stance'. Whereas the instrumental learner assumes that there is a potentially knowable causal structure lurking behind the modelled actions, the ritual performer assumes there is not, and that correct performance is therefore a matter of carrying out the actions in the stipulated or 'proper' fashion. Correspondingly, ritual and instrumental stances may be sensitive to very different social cues: the latter attending more to signals of competence and experience; the former being more attuned to signals of peer group acceptance and popularity.

The human yearning to be part of a group yields many benefits, facilitating loyalty, trust, generosity, and a wide range of cooperative outcomes. Often the benefits of ritual participation extend only to members of the ingroup. But ingroup bonding through rituals can also sometimes help to solve *intergroup* collective action problems, in the absence of overarching leadership. For example, in a classic ethnographic account of life in a Nigerian Ibo village in the early twentieth century, Margaret Green (1947) documented the various ways in which the British colonial policy of indirect rule ran into difficulties. This policy, first developed as a way of harnessing the indigenous hierarchies of South Asia, involved appointing traditional leaders or figures of authority as official agents of the colonial administration. This was not only cheaper and more efficient than training local officials from scratch but also provided a way of tapping into existing power relations and their traditional mechanisms of legitimation. But while this may have been an effective administrative method in India, it was hard to find local leaders in some West African cultural groups. In the case of the Ibo of Agbaja region, Nigeria, collective-actions problems were often solved not under the direction of a figure of authority, but through the mechanism of 'dual division', whereby two distinct 'halves' of the village competed to carry out collective tasks, such as cleaning of the village, more speedily or effectively than their rivals. Thus, while the rituals of Ibo moieties created strong cohesion and loyalty with the group, they also motivated participation in projects that assured benefits *beyond* the group. This was something the colonial authorities struggled to understand and which, in any case, was probably not congenial from the perspective of their goals, which had to do with extraction and control rather than fostering peace, human rights, equality, prosperity, and quality of life in local communities.

While intergroup competition does not necessarily descend into conflict, producing a tragedy of the commons, there is undoubtedly a darker side to the ways in which rituals create group cohesion, fuelling outgroup hostility. In Chapters 2 and 3, I described in some detail how the more emotionally intense rituals of small relational groups can produce a form of group cohesion so strong that it motivates members of the group to fight and die for one another when the group comes under attack. Dubbed the 'imagistic mode of religiosity', this form of group bonding has been strongly associated with small-scale groups that require strong incentives to stick together in the face of danger, such as military groups. Group psychologist, Bill Swann, developed a way of conceptualizing and measuring this very strong form of social cohesion, which he referred to as 'identity fusion' because it involves the fusion of personal and group identities (Swann et al., 2012). In this book, I have reviewed a wide range of studies suggesting that fusion results from feelings of shared essence, in turn an outcome of at least two general pathways: a shared experiences pathway, whereby life-changing experiences are also felt to define the group, and a shared biology pathway, whereby cues of genetic relatedness create strong feelings of psychological kinship.

It has long been recognized that emotionally intense rituals are linked to strong forms of pro-group action, but the mechanisms responsible for this are still hotly debated. Are painful or gruelling rituals forms of costly signalling? Are they a way of forcing new group members to pay heavy upfront costs? Are they ways of exploiting cognitive dissonance effects so that people feel a stronger liking for their groups than they otherwise would? These and other explanations for costly rituals have been advanced in the past and could all contain important truths, in which case the relevant question is how these various elements in the jigsaw puzzle fit together. The imagistic pathway to fusion is one of the explanations for strong pro-group action currently available. Unlike many other frameworks, the modes theory posits a time delay between ritual ordeals and their subsequent effects on prosocial behaviour. This is because personally transformative experiences can take months or even years to process via repeated acts of remembering and reflecting on events and their meaning. This potentially long-drawn-out process is thought to shape not only the essential personal self but also one's group identity, causing the two to fuse. But longitudinal studies of how this psychological process of self-making unfolds are still relatively sparse, and so we do not know for sure how long these processes can take. It is also not entirely clear how the emotional valence of experiences impacts the ritual's downstream psychological and behavioural outcomes. Some studies suggest that dysphoric rituals are more impactful than euphoric ones, but the distinction is not always easy to maintain, in part because overcoming a painful or frightening ordeal can produce strongly positive emotions. What does seem to be increasingly clear, however, is that the conviction of having shared personally transformative experiences with others leads inexorably to identity fusion, and this, in turn, motivates very strong forms of pro-group action.

I have argued that imagistic group bonding would have been beneficial to group survival throughout human prehistory, allowing bellicose tribes and their members to survive and reproduce at the expense of militarily weaker ones. But in the modern world, this way of fusing with a group has also produced much more destructive behaviours, ranging from suicide terrorism to gangland violence, that have deleterious effects not only for the group's enemies but also for its own members. Part of the problem is that imagistic group formation now occurs in a world populated with much bigger groups armed with more powerful weaponry. Whereas ancient foragers raided their immediate neighbours, capturing brides and plundering other resources, intergroup conflict was not on a scale comparable to that of modern genocides or imperialistic invasions. The lethality of today's arsenals, even those mobilized by non-state armed groups, is far greater, and the scale and destructiveness of conflicts correspondingly far more devastating.

At the same time, however, rituals have also helped to drive the rise of social complexity, enabling peaceful cooperation to be extended to ever larger groups. Human societies have been able to grow dramatically in size partly because their systems of governance have become more centralized and hierarchical. But even before inequalities of power and wealth emerged, the scale on which populations were able to share the same identity markers expanded in an unprecedented way. This involved a sea change in the way cultural beliefs and practices spread and stabilized. In particular, ritual routinization seems to have provided a way of integrating the group's identity markers into day-to-day life, making deviations from the standard script easier to detect and suppress. Dubbed the 'doctrinal mode of religiosity', this form of group bonding facilitated the standardization of rituals, narratives, and dogmas in much larger populations, carried by relatively small numbers of revered teachers (e.g. prophets, gurus, and priests). In Chapters 2 and 4, I reviewed a range of evidence from archaeology suggesting that the doctrinal mode began to form with the advent of farming, heralding the rise of the first large-scale societies (Whitehouse & Hodder, 2010; Gantley, Whitehouse, & Bogaard, 2018). As priesthoods became professionalized and technologies for storing information grew, the tendency towards homogenization and standardization of creeds grew stronger. Centralization and hierarchy facilitated tighter policing of emergent orthopraxy and orthodoxy. Inscribing practices, ranging from story boards that help stabilize narratives to full-blown literacy, allowed doctrines to be more fully elaborated, eventually leading to the creation of holy books and other sacred texts that laid the foundations for philosophical traditions, legal systems, and political constitutions.

Although the appearance of more doctrinal rituals appears to have contributed to a rise in the scale of human cooperation, archaic states dominated by divinized leaders and powerful elites would not appear until much later (Sterelny, 2019). These early states were oppressive places to live unless you were part of the ruling class. Extreme forms of inequality were rampant, expressed in horrific practices like human sacrifice and cruelly exploitative institutions, such as mass slavery. But just like modern dictatorships, these ancient forms of satrapy proved increasingly unstable. As ancient empires grew larger through conquest and the expansion of trade, they also became internally more diverse ethnically and religiously, such that cohesion became harder to achieve and the polity increasingly vulnerable both to external invasions and internal rebellions (Turchin, 2007). This may have been the main precipitating condition for the rise of the Axial Age and the spread of more egalitarian ethics, emphasizing principles of fairness and reciprocity (see Chapter 4). Societies that adopted these new ethical religions and evolved beyond the 'mega-threshold' of around one million individuals, also tended to adopt moralizing religions that promised a system of supernatural punishment for non-cooperators and rewards for the loyal, just, and trustworthy.

This extraordinary growth in the scale of human societies and the spread of common beliefs and practices around the world have produced challenges as well as opportunities. The ritual animal evolved in relational groups where everybody knew everybody else. Nowadays, however, humans live in groups that are far too large for their members to be personally acquainted. The small-group psychology of our ancestral past is therefore being pushed to its limits, and in some ways, beyond them, often with unfortunate results. In Chapters 5 and 7, we considered some of the scientific challenges this has presented us with and how we might overcome them. In Chapter 6, we considered a few of the most pressing political challenges faced by the ritual animal in an increasingly globalized environment where cooperation sometimes needs to occur at the level of a global community rather than only that of the polity and its subgroups.

The scientific challenges we have considered are broadly of two kinds: conceptual and practical. The ritual animal evolved to reason about worlds in which social relationships were mostly interpersonal and the challenges they presented best addressed through intuitive psychology and localized forms of group bonding. Techniques facilitating mastery of the natural world required an intuitive grasp of basic physics and biology, and a mind adept at causal reasoning. What it did not require was an ability to think about highly specialized systems of governance, legal codes, international relations, or principles of economics. In short, the human brain did not evolve to make sense of or manipulate complex social formations. When reasoning sociologically, the limits of our intuitions are quickly reached, and beyond that we tend to borrow ideas from other ontological domains—readily biologizing ethnic groups or reifying institutions. An elaborated solution to this problem is presented in Chapter 5, based on an extension of the idea of 'epigenetic landscapes' to encompass cognitive-developmental and social-historical ones. Whether or not this conceptual scheme proves fruitful, some kind of evolutionary framework is required—one that transcends the currently unappealing choice between the modular mind of evolutionary psychology or the domain-general mind of cultural evolution theory, while still combining the best of both.

In Chapter 6, I described a set of political challenges that the ritual animal must solve if the world is to avoid the most destructive effects of modern warfare, global heating, pandemics, and other problems that grow increasingly pressing. The solutions proposed here involve harnessing the potential of both imagistic and doctrinal modes of group bonding to achieve more peaceful and humanitarian forms for cooperation. Although the imagistic mode has fuelled some of the most violent expressions of intergroup hatred over the millennia, the bonds at the core of it are familial. Identity fusion is most commonly experienced among close kinsmen, where it serves to motivate lifelong caretaking and the pooling of resources. In other words, the same feelings that bind together a 'band of brothers' on the battlefield are also commonly found between genetically related brothers and sisters. So, while there are undoubtedly fused groups bent on acts of terrorism and violence, for whom lasting rehabilitation may require defusion, there are also groups in society for whom more fusion may actually be a positive thing. For example, I have argued that ex-offenders emerging from prison, who may have never enjoyed the benefits of fusion with family or with any group, could be helped along the way to a more productive, law-abiding way of life by fusing with sports clubs and the healthy lifestyles they can promote. Likewise, the fusion experienced by fans of the same sports clubs could be harnessed to provide practical help and support for those re-entering society and seeking employment.

Many of the *scientific* challenges with which the ritual animal is confronted are also of a very practical kind. In Chapter 7, I reviewed some of the problems that must be overcome in academia, and suggested a variety of pragmatic solutions. Arguably the most daunting of all is the so-called silo problem—the fact that academic disciplines have tended to develop their own theories, methods, goals, jargons, interpretive frames, and proprietorial datasets. This can make communication between them extremely difficult, especially if they also adhere to fundamentally incompatible epistemologies, as may be the case when comparing the world views of some humanities scholars with those of scientific reductionists. These problems are exacerbated by the tendency of the ritual animal to form groups and coalitions, whether in the guise of academic departments and faculties or research teams, fields, and entire disciplines.

I have argued that the best way to overcome these challenges is to develop programmes of problem-centred research. When people agree what the problem is that needs to be solved, the barriers to communication and collaboration dissolve more easily. For example, those interested in studying the role of ritual in the evolution of social complexity want to understand what motivates participation in rituals and how rituals affect our feelings and attitudes towards the group. These are questions that inevitably require the involvement of psychologists. This is the case both from a developmental angle (to explain how and why children absorb the rituals of the communities they are born into) and from a proximate perspective (to understand the immediate triggers for ritual behaviour, whether at the level of subjective experience or patterns of blood flow or neuronal activation in the brain). But it is also the case when it comes to understanding how rituals produce social glue and motivate cooperation—this too is a question about human psychology, and especially group psychology. At the same time, we cannot restrict ourselves to psychological questions that can only be answered through surveys and experiments because the evolution of social complexity unfolds across the world's cultures and over many millennia of human history. This requires the involvement of ethnographers, historians, and archaeologists (and others who deal with the challenges of describing and interpreting human behaviour in natural settings). As I have argued throughout this book, we need to look at the role of ritual in a range of environments, not only as historical or regional case studies but also in ways that can be quantified on a global scale. This raises many more specific challenges associated with multi-sited fieldwork and database construction and analysis.

Although this book has attempted to lay out the evidence for a particular theoretical framework—the 'modes theory', which seeks to explain how imagistic and doctrinal rituals have shaped the evolution of social complexity—a more fundamental goal has been to show how theories of this kind can be progressively tested through problem-centred collaboration. Thus, investigating the modes theory has involved long-term collaborations with developmental psychologists (conducting experiments in both lab and field), social psychologists (running surveys and experiments with a broad range of special populations around the world, from religious groups to football fans), and neuroscientists (looking at the effects of ritual participation on the brain). It has also taken us into past worlds in collaboration with archaeologists (from in-depth qualitative studies at particular sites to analysing data statistically across hundreds of sites) and historians (involving the creation of Seshat, an ambitious new database of world history covering hundreds of polities over thousands of years). The book provides examples of all these problem-centred collaborations, acknowledging limitations and pitfalls, as well as discoveries and breakthroughs. What matters is not only where this now leaves us, which is inevitably just a fleeting moment in the history of science, but also where it may lead in the future and how we might best facilitate further progress.

Finally, one of the most ambitious proposals advanced in this book is that the modes theory could be further developed to help devise solutions to global collective action problems. The archaic states produced a moral imbalance that needed to be corrected by the ethical transformations commonly associated with the Axial Age, in order for societies to continue to grow. But we are now reaching a new threshold requiring urgent action on a world stage. Humans everywhere have the same basic moral instincts, but they are manifested in regionally diverse ways, giving expression to different priorities and combinations of moral concerns. Still, the fact that there is a universal moral compass (Curry, Mullins, & Whitehouse, 2019) is a cause for hope. It is not hard to imagine a globally emergent doctrinal system specifying an ethical framework on which all could agree, grounded in universal moral intuitions but oriented very specifically to the most urgent global challenges facing us in the twenty-first century. It was a vision of this kind that led to the Universal Declaration of Human Rights in 1948, in the wake of the horrors of World War II, but the thirty-point document agreed by the United Nations was not grounded explicitly in our evolved moral instincts, nor was it (or could it have been) attentive to all the global challenges we now face. Above all, it emphasized only the rights of individuals and groups but not their responsibilities to humanity at large. We now need to create something fresh: a universal declaration of human *obligations*, perhaps.

The obligations we have to each other and to our planet at this juncture in world history, spring from our more ancient evolved psychological commitments to family and local community. These obligations are fundamentally about loyalty, caring, reciprocity, courage, respect, fairness, and ownership. To the extent that people everywhere agree that these things are good, the challenge is to apply those values to all the major collective action problems facing our world and make it our duty to see that they inform the decisions of our leaders. This will also mean demanding a new kind of leadership—one that looks beyond the boundaries of the ingroup, seeking opportunities to secure benefits for all groups. Every one of us is capable of fusing to humanity at large, and indeed to the diversity of the natural world on the planet we all share. As I have shown, a growing body of data from surveys and experiments indicates that the pathway to identity fusion begins with the recognition of shared essence. The potential for such a recognition becomes stronger all the time, as the planet becomes increasingly connected through the internet, and many of the same experiences that have shaped our essential autobiographical selves, from the trials of adolescence to the ordeals of global pandemics, are also to some extent shared by others all around the world. As we strive to combat racism and fuel instead the recognition that we are all members of one species, we may also strive to extend that intuition of shared biological essence to all other outgrowths on the tree of life with which we share a common ancestry. Joining in new rituals that emphasize these sorts of shared experiences and shared bodies will be vital because, in the end, our fates are entwined, and the ritual animal is, well, just another animal.

References

Aberle, David F. (1960). The Influence of Linguistics on Early Culture and Personality Theory. In Gertrude E. Dole & Robert L. Carneiro (Eds.), *Essays in the Science of Culture: In Honor of Leslie A. White*, pp. 1–29. New York: Crowell.

Allen, M. R. (1967). *Male Cults and Secret Initiations in Melanesia*. Melbourne: Melbourne University Press.

Anderson, B. (1983). *Imagined Communities: Reflections on the Origin and Spread of Nationalism*. London: Verso.

Anderson, J. R. (1983). *The Architecture of Cognition*. Cambridge, MA: Harvard University Press.

Anquetil-Duperron, Abraham-Hyacinthe. (1771). *Zend-Avesta: Ouvrage de Zoroastre; Contenant les idées théologiques, physiques et morales de ce législateur*. 2 vols. Paris: Tilliard.

Apps, Matthew A.J, McKay, Ryan, Azevedo, Ruben, Whitehouse, Harvey, & Tsakiris, Manos (2018). Not on My Team: Medial Prefrontal Cortex Contributions to Ingroup Fusion and Fairness. *Brain and Behaviour*, 8(8): e01030.

Aron, A., Aron, E., & Smollan, D. (1992). Inclusion of Other in the Self Scale and the structure of interpersonal closeness. *Journal of Personality and Social Psychology*, 63, 596–612.

Aronson, E. & Mills, J. (1959). The Effect of Severity of Initiation on Liking for a Group. *Journal of Abnormal and Social Psychology*, 59(2): 177–81.

Asad, T. (1988). Towards a Genealogy of the Concept of Ritual. In W. James & D. H. Johnson (Eds.), *Vernacular Christianity: Essays in the Social Anthropology of Religion Presented to Godfrey Lienhardt*, pp. 73–87. New York: Lilian Barber Press.

Atkinson, Quentin D. & Whitehouse, Harvey (2011). The Cultural Morphospace of Ritual Form: Examining Modes of Religiosity Cross-culturally. *Evolution and Human Behaviour*, 32(1): 50–62.

Atran, Scott (2002). *In Gods We Trust*. New York: Oxford University Press.

Atran, Scott (2016). The Devoted Actor: Unconditional Commitment and Intractable Conflict across Cultures. *Current Anthropology*, 57. https://www.journals.uchicago.edu/doi/full/10.1086/685495.

Atran, Scott & Axelrod, Robert (2008). In Theory: Reframing Sacred Values. *Negotiation Journal*, 24(3): 221–46.

Atran, S. & Gómez, Á. (2018). What Motivates Devoted Actors to Extreme Sacrifice, Identity Fusion, or Sacred Values? *Behavioral and Brain Sciences*, 41: E193. https://doi.org/10.1017/S0140525X18001565.

Atran, Scott, Sheikh, Hammad, & Gómez, Ángel (2014). For Cause and Comrade: Devoted Actors and Willingness to Fight. *Cliodynamics*, 5: 41–57.

Baal, J. van (1981). *Man's Quest for Partnership: The Anthropological Foundations of Ethics and Religion*. Assen: van Gorcum.

Baaren, Th.P. van (1983). A Short Meditation upon the Theme of Ritual. In J. G. Platvoet (Ed.), *Analysis and Interpretation of Rites: Essays to D.J. Hoens*, pp. 189–90. The Hague: Boekencentrum.

Balée, William L. (1992). People of the Fallow: A Historical Ecology of Foraging in Lowland South America. In Kent H. Redford & Christine J. Padoch (Eds.), *Conservation of Neotropical Forests*, pp. 35–57. New York: Columbia University Press.

Barnard, A. (Ed.) (2004). *Hunter-Gatherers in History, Archaeology and Anthropology*. Oxford: Berg.

Barrett, J. L. & Keil, F. C. (1996). Conceptualizing a Nonnatural Entity: Anthropomorphism in God Concepts. *Cognitive Psychology*, 31: 219–47.

Barrett, J. L. (2004). *Why Would Anyone Believe in God?* Walnut Creek, CA: AltaMira Press.

Barrett, J. L. (2012). *Born Believers: The Science of Children's Religious Belief*. New York: Free Press.

Barth, F. (1975). *Ritual and Knowledge Among the Baktaman of New Guinea*. New Haven, CT: Yale University Press.

Barth, F. (1987). *Cosmologies in the Making: A Generative Approach to Cultural Variation in Inner New Guinea*. Cambridge: Cambridge University Press.

Bateson, Gregory (1972). *Steps to an Ecology of Mind: Collected Essays in Anthropology, Psychiatry, Evolution, and Epistemology*. Chicago: University of Chicago Press.

Bateson, P. & Laland, K. N. (2013). Tinbergen's Four Questions: An Appreciation and An Update. *Trends Ecology & Evolution*, 28: 712–18.

Bayly, S. (2004). Conceptualizing from Within: Divergent Religious Modes from Asian Modernist Perspectives. In H. Whitehouse & J. Laidlaw (Eds.), *Ritual and Memory: Towards a Comparative Anthropology of Religion*, pp. 111–134. Walnut Creek, CA: AltaMira Press.

Beck, R. (2004). 'Four Men, Two Sticks, and a Whip: Image and Doctrine in a Mithraic Ritual. In H. Whitehouse & L. H. Martin (Eds.), *Theorizing Religions Past: Archaeology, History, and Cognition*, pp. 87–104. Walnut Creek, CA: AltaMira Press.

Bell, Catherine (1992). *Ritual Theory, Ritual Practice*. New York: Oxford University Press.

Bell, Catherine (1997). *Ritual: Perspectives and Dimensions*. New York: Oxford University Press.

Bellah, Robert N. (2011). *Religion in Human Evolution: From the Paleolithic to the Axial Age*. Cambridge, MA: Harvard University Press.

Bellwood, P. (2005). *First Farmers: The Origins of Agricultural Societies*. Oxford: Blackwell Publishing.

Benedict, Ruth (1935). *Patterns of Culture*. London: Routledge and Kegan Paul.

Bering, J. M. (2006). The Folk Psychology of Souls. *Behavioural and Brain Sciences*, 29: 453–62. http://dx.doi.org/10.1017/S0140525X06009101.

Berner, U. (2004). Modes of Religiosity and Types of Conversion in Medieval Europe and Modern Africa. In H. Whitehouse & L. H. Martin (Eds.), *Theorizing Religions Past: Archaeology, History, and Cognition*, pp. 157–172. Walnut Creek, CA: AltaMira Press.

Bersabe, Rosa & Arias, Rosario Martınez (2000). Superstition in Gambling. *Psychology in Spain*, 4: 28–34.

Berwick, David A. (2007). *Beating the Bounds in Georgian Norwich*. Norfolk: Larks Press.

Billig, M. & Tajfel, H. (1973). Social categorization and similarity in intergroup behaviour. *European Journal of Social Psychology*, 3(1): 27–52.

Binmore, K. G. (2005). *Natural Justice*. New York: Oxford University Press.

Bleak, Jared L. & Frederick, Christina M. (1998). Superstitious Behaviour in Sport: Levels of Effectiveness and Determinants of Use in Three Collegiate Sports. *Journal of Sport Behaviour*, 21: 1–15.

Bloch, Maurice (1974). Symbols, Song, Dance and Features of Articulation Is religion an extreme form of traditional authority? *European Journal of Sociology*, 15(1): 54–81.

Bloch, Maurice (Ed.) (1975). *Marxist Analysis and Social Anthropology* (ASA Studies 3). London: Malaby Press.
Bloch, Maurice (1983). *Marxism and Anthropology: The History of a Relationship*. Oxford: Oxford University Press.
Bloch, M. (1992). *Prey into Hunter*. Cambridge: University Press.
Bloch M. & Parry, J. (Eds.) (1982). *Death and the Regeneration of Life*. Cambridge: Cambridge University Press.
Bloom, Paul (2000). *How Children Learn the Meanings of Words*. Cambridge, MA: MIT Press.
Bloom, Paul (2004). *Descartes' Baby: How the Science of Child Development Explains What Makes Us Human*. New York: Basic Books.
Bocock, R. (1974). *Ritual in Industrial Society: A Sociological Analysis of Ritualism in Modern England*. London: George Allen & Unwin.
Bodenhorn, B. (1990). I'm Not the Great Hunter, My Wife Is. *Etudes Inuit Studies*, 14: 55–74.
Boesch, Christophe & Boesch-Achermann, Hedwige (2000). *The Chimpanzees of the Taï Forest: Behavioural Ecology and Evolution*. Oxford: Oxford University Press.
Bourdieu, Pierre (1977). *Outline of a Theory of Practice*. Cambridge: Cambridge University Press.
Boyd, R. & Richerson, P. J. (1985). *Culture and the Evolutionary Process*. Chicago: University of Chicago Press.
Boyd, R. & Richerson, P. J. (2005). *Not by Genes Alone: How Culture Transformed Human Evolution*. Chicago: University of Chicago Press.
Boyer, Pascal (1993). Cognitive aspects of religious symbolism. In Pascal Boyer (Ed.), *Cognitive Aspects of Religious Symbolism*, pp. 4–47. Cambridge: Cambridge University Press.
Boyer, P. (1994). *The Naturalness of Religious Ideas: A Cognitive Theory of Religion*. Berkeley: University of California Press.
Boyer, P. (2001). *Religion Explained: The Human Instincts That Fashion Gods, Spirits and Ancestors*. New York: Basic Books.
Boyer, P. (2011). From Studious Irrelevancy to Consilient Knowledge: Modes of Scholarship and Cultural Anthropology, In E. Slingerland & M. Collard (Eds.), *Creating Consilience*, pp. 113–129. New York: Oxford University Press.
Boyer, P. (2019). Informal Religious Activity Outside Hegemonic Religions: Wild Traditions and Their Relevance to Evolutionary Models. *Religion, Brain, and Behavior* Vol.10(4), pp. 459–472. https://doi.org/10.1080/2153599X.2019.1678518.
Boyer, P. & Liénard, P. (2006). Why Ritualized Behaviour? Precaution Systems and Action Parsing in Developmental, Pathological and Cultural Rituals. *Behavioural and Brain Sciences*, 29(6): 595–612. https://doi.org/10.1017/S0140525X06009332.
Brewer, M. B. (2001). Ingroup Identification and Intergroup Conflict: When Does Ingroup Love Become Outgroup Hate? In R. D. Ashmore, L. Jussim, & D. Wilder (Eds.), *Rutgers Series on Self and Social Identity; Vol. 3. Social Identity, Intergroup Conflict, and Conflict Reduction*, pp. 17–41. Oxford: Oxford University Press.
Brewer, J. Peregrine, P., Gelfand, M., Jackson, J., MacDonald, I., Richerson, P. Turchin, P. et al. (2017). Grand Challenges for the Study of Cultural Evolution. *Nature Ecology & Evolution. Nature Ecology & Evolution*, Vol.10(4), pp. 459–472. https://doi.org/10.1038/s41559-017-0070.
Brown, P. (1972). *The Chimbu*. Cambridge, MA: Schenkman.
Brown, Roger & Kulik, James (1977). Flashbulb Memories. *Cognition*, 5(1): 73–99. https://doi.org/10.1016/0010-0277(77)90018-X.

Buchsbaum, D., Gopnik, A., Griffiths, T. L., & Shafto, P. (2011). Children's Imitation of Causal Action Sequences Is Influenced by Statistical and Pedagogical Evidence. *Cognition*, 120(3): 331–40. https://doi.org/10.1016/j.cognition.2010.12.001.

Buhrmester, Michael, Burnham, Dawn, Johnson, Dominic, Curry, Oliver S., Macdonald, David, & Whitehouse, Harvey (2018a). How Moments Become Movements: Shared Outrage, Group Cohesion, and the Lion That Went Viral. *Frontiers in Ecology and Evolution*, 6. https://doi.org/10.3389/fevo.2018.00054.

Buhrmester, M. B, Cowan, M., & Whitehouse, H. (Under Review). What Motivates Barrier-Crossing Leadership?

Buhrmester, M. D., Fraser, W. T., Lanman, J. A., Whitehouse, H., & Swann, W. B., Jr. (2015). When Terror Hits Home: Identity Fused Americans Who Saw Boston Bombing Victims as 'Family' Provided Aid. *Self and Identity*, 14(3): 253–70. https://doi.org/10.1080/15298868.2014.992465.

Buhrmester, Michael D., Newson, Martha, Vázquez, Alexandra, Hattori, Wallisen Tadashi, & Whitehouse, Harvey (2018b). Winning at Any Cost: Identity Fusion, Group Essence, and Maximizing Ingroup Advantage. *Self and Identity*, 17(5): 500–16. https://doi.org/10.1080/15298868.2018.1452788.

Buhrmester, M. D. & Swann, W. B., Jr. (2015). Identity fusion. *Emerging Trends in the Social and Behavioral Sciences: An Interdisciplinary, Searchable, and Linkable Resource*. 1–15. https://doi.org/10.1002/9781118900772.etrds0172.

Buhrmester, M.D., Swann, W.B., Everington, A., Hafid, L., & Whitehouse, H. (Under Review). Brothers No More: Shifting group alignments in the failed state of Libya.

Buhrmester, M. D., Zeitlyn, D., & Whitehouse, H. (2020). Ritual, Fusion, and Conflict: The Roots of Agro-Pastoral Violence in Rural Cameroon. *Group Processes and Intergroup Relations*. https://doi.org/10.1177/1368430220959705.

Bulbulia, J. (2004). Religious costs as adaptations that signal altruistic intent. *Evolution and Cognition*, 10, 19–42.

Bulbulia, J., Geertz, A. W., Atkinson, Q. D., Cohen, E. A., Evans, N., François, P., et al. (2013). The Cultural Evolution of Religion. In P. J. Richerson & M. H. Christiansen (Eds.), *Cultural Evolution: Society, Technology, Language, and Religion (Strungmann Forum Reports)*, pp. 381–404. Cambridge, MA: MIT Press.

Bull, M. & Mitchell, Jon P. (Eds.) (2015). *Ritual, Performance and the Senses*. London: Bloomsbury Academic.

Burger, Jerry M. & Lynn, Amy L. (2005). Superstitious Behaviour Among American and Japanese Professional Baseball Players. *Basic and Applied Social Psychology*, 27: 71–6.

Brunton, R. (1980). Misconstrued Order in Melanesian Religion. *Man*, 15(1), New Series: 112–28. https://doi.org/10.2307/2802005.

Buss, D. M. (Ed.) (2005). *The Handbook of Evolutionary Psychology*. Hoboken, NJ: Wiley.

Buttelmann, D., Carpenter, M., Call, J., & Tomasello, M. (2007). Enculturated Chimpanzees Imitate Rationally. *Developmental Science*, 10(4), PMID: 17552931.

Callan M. J., Ellard, J. H., & Nicol, J. E. (2006). The Belief in a Just World and Immanent Justice Reasoning in Adults. *Personality and Social Psychology Bulletin*, 32(12): 1646–58.

Callan, Mitchell J., Sutton, Robbie M., Harvey, Annelie J., & Dawtry, Rael J. (2014). Immanent Justice Reasoning: Theory, Research, and Current Directions. In James M. Olson & Mark P. Zanna (Eds.), *Advances in Experimental Social Psychology*, Volume 49, pp. 105–161. London: Academic Press. https://doi.org/10.1016/B978-0-12-800052-6.00002-0.

Carey, Susan. (1985). *Conceptual Change in Childhood*. Cambridge, MA: MIT Press.

Carley, K. M. & Kaufer, D. S. (1993). Semantic connectivity: An approach for analyzing symbols in semantic networks. *Communication Theory* 3: 183–213.

Case, Trevor I., Fitness, Julie, Cairns, David R., & Stevenson, Richard J. (2004). Coping with Uncertainty: Superstitious Strategies and Secondary Control. *Journal of Applied Social Psychology, 34*: 848–71.

Chasteen, John Charles (2004). *National Rhythms, African Roots: The Deep History of Latin American Popular Dance.* Albuquerque: University of New Mexico Press.

Chinnery, E.W. P. & Beaver, W. N. (1915). Notes on the Initiation Ceremonies of the Koko, Papua. *Journal of the Royal Anthropological Institute, 45*: 69–78.

Chinnery E. W. P. & Haddon, A. C. (1917). Five New Religious Cults in British New Guinea. *Hibbert Journal, 15*: 448–63.

Cho, Philip S., Nicolas Escoffier, Yinan Mao, April Ching, Christopher Green, Jonathan Jong, and Harvey Whitehouse (2018). Groups and Emotional Arousal Mediate Neural Synchrony and Perceived Ritual Efficacy. *Frontiers in Psychology, 9*: 1664–1078. https://doi.org/10.3389/fpsyg.2018.02071.

Choi, Virginia K., Joshua C. Jackson & Michele J. Gelfand (2018). The role of entitativity in perpetuating cycles of violence. *Behavioral and Brain Sciences, 41*: 16–17. doi:10.1017/S0140525X18002042, e196.

Cialdini, R. B. (1976). Basking in Reflected Glory: Three (football) Field Studies. *Journal of Personality and Social Psychology, 34*(3): 366–75.

Cili, S. & Stopa, L. (2014). The Retrieval of Self-defining Memories Is Associated with the Activation of Specific Working Selves. *Memory, 23*(2): 233–53. https://doi.org/10.1080/09658211.2014.882955.

Cimino, A. (2011). The Evolution of Hazing: Motivational Mechanisms and the Abuse of Newcomers. *Journal of Cognition and Culture, 11*: 241–67.

Clark, A. L. (2004). Testing the Two Modes Theory: Christian Practice in the Later Middle Ages. In H. Whitehouse & L. H. Martin (Eds.), *Theorizing Religions Past: Archaeology, History, and Cognition*, pp. 125–142. Walnut Creek, CA: AltaMira Press.

Clegg, J. M. & Legare, C. H. (2016). A Cross-Cultural Comparison of Children's Imitative Flexibility. *Developmental Psychology, 52*(9): 1435–44. https://doi.org/10.1037/dev0000131.

Coombe, Rosemary (2008). Encountering the Postmodern: New Directions in Cultural Anthropology. *Canadian Review of Sociology, 282*: 188–205.

Collinson, P. (1997). From Iconoclasm to Iconophobia: The Cultural Impact of the Second English Reformation. In P. Marshall (Ed.), *The Impact of the English Reformation 1500–1640*, pp. 278–307. London: Arnold.

Cohen, E. E. A. (2007). *The Mind Possessed: The Cognition of Spirit Possession in an Afro Brazilian Religious Tradition.* New York: Oxford University Press.

Cohen, E. A., Burdett, E., Knight, N., & Barrett, J. (2011). Cross-Cultural Similarities and Differences in Person-Body Reasoning: Experimental Evidence from the UK and Brazilian Amazon. *Cognitive Science, 35*(7): 1282–1304.

Cohen, Gillian (1989). *Memory in the Real World.* Hove: Laurence Erlbaum Associates.

Connerton, Paul (1989). *How Societies Remember.* Cambridge: Cambridge University Press.

Conway, M. A. (1995). *Flashbulb Memories: Essays in Cognitive Psychology.* Hillsdale, NJ: Lawrence Erlbaum Associates, Inc.

Conway, M. A., Wang, Q., Hanyu, K., & Haque, S. (2005). A Cross-Cultural Investigation of Autobiographical Memory: On the Universality and Cultural Variation of the Reminiscence Bump. *Journal of Cross-Cultural Psychology, 36*: 739–49. https://doi.org/10.1177/0022022105280512.

Corriveau, K. H., DiYanni, C. J., Clegg, J. M., Min, G., Chin, J., & Nasrini, J. (2017). Cultural Differences in the Imitation and Transmission of Inefficient Actions. *Journal of Experimental Child Psychology*, *161*: 1–18.

Currie, T. E., Greenhill, S. J., Gray, R. D., Hasegawa, T., & Mace, R. (2010). Rise and Fall of Political Complexity in Island South-East Asia and the Pacific. *Nature*, *467*: 801–4. Pmid:20944739.

Currie, Thomas E., Bogaard, Amy, Cesaretti, Rudolf, Edwards, Neil R., François, Pieter, Holden, Phillip B., et al. (2015). Agricultural Productivity in Past Societies: Toward an Empirically Informed Model for Testing Cultural Evolutionary Hypotheses. *Cliodynamics: The Journal of Quantitative History and Cultural Evolution*, *6*(1): 24–56.

Curry, O. S. (2016). Morality as Cooperation: A Problem-Centred Approach. In T. K. Shackelford & R. D. Hansen (Eds.), *The Evolution of Morality*, pp. 27–51. Cham, Switzerland: Springer International Publishing.

Curry, Oliver S., Buhrmester, Michael, & Whitehouse, Harvey (2019). *Brexiteers Are Not More British, Just Less European*. OSF project. June 21, Osf.io/crv6a.

Curry, Oliver S., Hare, Darragh, Hepburn, Cameron, Johnson, Dominic D. P., Buhrmester, Michael, Whitehouse, Harvey, et al. (2019). Cooperative Conservation: Seven Ways to Save the World. *Conservation Science and Practice*. https://doi.org/10.1111/csp2.123.

Curry, Oliver S., Mullins, Daniel A., & Whitehouse, Harvey (2019). Is It Good to Cooperate? Testing the Theory of Morality-as-Cooperation in 60 Societies. *Current Anthropology*, *60*(1). https://doi.org/10.1086/701478.

Clegg, J. M. & Legare, C. H. (2016). A Cross-Cultural Comparison of Children's Imitative Flexibility. *Developmental Psychology*, *52*(9): 1435–44.

Decety, J. (2012). *Empathy: From Bench to Bedside*. Cambridge, MA: MIT Press.

Dennett, D. (1987). *The Intentional Stance*. Cambridge, MA: MIT Press.

de Zavala, A. G., Cichocka, A., Eidelson, R., & Jayawickreme, N. (2009). Collective narcissism and its social consequences. *Journal of Personality and Social Psychology*, *97*(6), 1074–1096. https://doi.org/10.1037/a0016904

Diener, E., Lusk, R., DeFour, D., & Flax, R. (1980). Deindividuation: Effects of Group Size, Density, Number of Observers, and Group Member Similarity on Self-Consciousness and Disinhibited Behaviour. *Journal of Personality and Social Psychology*, *39*: 449–59. https://doi.org/10.1037/0022-3514.39.3.449.

Douglas, Mary (1966). *Purity and Danger: An Analysis of Concepts of Pollution and Taboo*. London: Routledge.

Dulaney, S. & Fiske. A. P. (1994). Cultural Rituals and Obsessive-Compulsive Disorder: Is There a Common Psychological Mechanism? *Ethos*, *22*(3): 243–83.

Dumont, Louis (1980). *Homo Hierarchicus: The Caste System and Its Implications*. Chicago: University of Chicago Press.

Dunlop, W. L. & Walker, L. J. (2013). The Life Story: Its Development and Relation to Narration and Personal Identity. *International Journal of Behavioural Development*, *37*: 235–47. https://doi.org/10.1177/0165025413479475.

Durkheim, É (1933[1893]). *On the Division of Labor in Society*. Trans. George Simpson. London: The MacMillan Company.

Durkheim, É. (1912). *Les Formes élémentaires de la vie religieuse/The Elementary Forms of Religious Life*. Paris: Alcan.

Ebbinghaus, H. (1913). *Memory: A Contribution to Experimental Psychology*. New York: Teachers College, Columbia University.

Ebner, Julia (2017). *The Rage: The Vicious Circle of Islamist and Far-Right Extremism*. New York: Bloomsbury.

Ebner, Julia (2020). *Going Dark: The Secret Social Lives of Extremists*. New York: Bloomsbury.
Eisenstadt, Shmuel N. (1996). *Japanese Civilization: A Comparative View*. Chicago: The University of Chicago Press.
Ember, C. R., & Ember, M. (1998). Cross-cultural research. In H. R. Bernard (Ed.), *Handbook of Methods in Cultural Anthropology*. (pp. 647–687). Walnut Creek, CA: AltaMira.
Ensor, Phil (1988). The Functional Silo Syndrome. *AME Target, Summer*: 16.
Erickson, P. (2017). *A History of Anthropological Theory*. Toronto: University of Toronto Press.
Evans-Pritchard, Edward Evan (1937). *Witchcraft, Oracles and Magic Among the Azande*. Oxford: Clarendon Press.
Evans-Pritchard, E. E. (1940). *The Nuer*. Oxford: Oxford University Press.
Evans-Pritchard, E. E. (1962). *Anthropology and History: Essays in Social Anthropology*. London: Faber and Faber.
Fallers, Lloyd A. (1965). *Bantu Bureaucracy: A Century of Political Evolution Among the Basoga of Uganda*. Chicago: University of Chicago Press.
Farah, M. J. & Wallace, M. A. (1992). Semantically-Bounded Anomia: Implications for the Neural Implementation of Naming. *Neuropsychologia, 30*: 609–21.
Fehr, E. & Fischbacher, U. (2004). Third-party punishment and social norms. *Evolution and Human Behavior, 25*(2): 63–87.
Fehr, E., Gächter, S. (2002). Altruistic punishment in humans. *Nature, 415*: 137–140. https://doi.org/10.1038/415137a.
Felson, Richard B. & Gmelch, George (1979). Uncertainty and the Use of Magic. *Current Anthropology, 20*: 587–9.
Fernandez, J. W. (1971). Persuasions and Performances: Of the Beast in Every Body... and the Metaphors of Everyman. In C. Geertz (Ed.), *Myth, Symbol, and Culture*, pp. 39–60. New York: Norton.
Festinger, L. (1957). *A Theory of Cognitive Dissonance*. Stanford, CA: Stanford University Press.
Fessler, Daniel M. T. (2004). Shame in Two Cultures: Implications for Evolutionary Approaches. *Journal of Cognition and Culture, 4*(2): 207–62.
Feynman, R. P. (2005). *The Pleasure of Finding Things Out: The Best Short Works of Richard P. Feynman*. New York: Basic Books.
Fincher, C. L. & Thornhill, R. (2012). Parasite-Stress Promotes In-group Assortative Sociality: The Cases of Strong Family Ties and Heightened Religiosity. *Behavioral and Brain Science, 35*(2): 61–79.
Firth, Raymond (1951). *Elements of Social Organization*. London: Routledge.
Firth, Raymond (1964). *Essays on Social Organization and Values*. London: University of London Athlone Press.
Fiske, A. P. & Haslam, N. (1997). Is Obsessive-Compulsive Disorder a Pathology of the Human Disposition to Perform Socially Meaningful Rituals? Evidence of Similar Content. *Journal of Nervous & Mental Disease, 185*: 211–22.
Flannery, Kent & Marcus, Joyce (Eds.) (2012). *The Creation of Inequality. How Our Prehistoric Ancestors Set the Stage for Monarchy, Slavery and Empire*. Cambridge, Massachusetts: Harvard University Press.
Flynn, E. & Smith, K. (2012). Investigating the Mechanisms of Cultural Acquisition: How Pervasive Is Overimitation in Adults? *Social Psychology, 43*(4): 185–95. https://doi.org/10.1027/1864–9335/a000119.
Fodor, J. A. (1983). *The Modularity of Mind*. Cambridge, MA: MIT Press.
Fortes, Meyer (1945). *The Dynamics of Clanship Among the Tallensi: Being the First Part of an Analysis of the Social Structure of a Trans-Volta Tribe*. Oxford: Oxford University Press.

Fortes, Meyer (1980). Anthropology and the Psychological Disciplines. In Ernest Gellner (Ed.), *Soviet and Western Anthropology*, pp. 195–216. London: Duckworth.

Frazer, James (1922). *The Golden Bough: A Study in Magic and Religion*. New York: Macmillan.

Gantley, Michael, Bogaard, Amy, & Whitehouse, Harvey (2018). Material Correlates Analysis (MCA): An Innovative way of Examining Questions in Archaeology Using Ethnographic Data. *Advances in Archaeological Practice*, 6(4): 328–41. https://doi.org/1.1017/11p.2018.9.

Gardiner, A. K. (2014). Beyond Irrelevant Actions: Understanding the Role of Intentionality in Children's Imitation of Relevant Actions. *Journal of Experimental Child Psychology*, 119: 54–72. https://doi.org/10.1016/j.jecp.2013.10.008.

Geertz, C. (1966). Religion as a Cultural System. In M. Banton (Ed.), *Anthropological Approaches to the Study of Religion*, pp. 1–46. London: Tavistock Publications.

Gelfand, M.J. (2018). *Rule Makers, Rule Breakers:* How Tight and Loose Cultures Wire Our World. New York: Scribner.

Gelfand, M.J., Raver, J., Nishii, L., Leslie, L., Lun, J., Lim, B. C., et al. (2011). Differences Between Tight and Loose Societies: A 33-Nation Study. *Science*, 33: 1100–4.

Gell, Alfred (1988). Technology and Magic. *Anthropology Today*, 4(2): 6–9.

Gellén, Kata & Buttelmann, David (2018). Rational Imitation Declines Within the Second Year of Life: Changes in the Function of Imitation. *Journal of Experimental Child Psychology*. https://doi.org/10.1016/j.jecp.2019.04.019.

Gellner, David (1988). Priesthood and Possession: Newar Religion in the Light of Some Weberian Concepts. *Pacific Viewpoint*, 29(2): 119–43.

Gellner, David (1992). *Monk, Householder, and Tantric Priest: Newar Buddhism and Its Hierarchy of Ritual*. Cambridge: Cambridge University Press.

Gellner, David, Currey, Oliver C., Cook, Joanna, Alfano, Mark, & Venkatesen, Soumhya (2020). Debate: Morality Is Fundamentally an Evolved Solution to Problems of Social Cooperation. *Journal of the Royal Anthropological Institute (N.S.)*, 26: 415–27.

Gellner, Ernest (1969). A Pendulum Swing Theory of Islam. In R. Robertson (Ed.), *Sociology of Religion: Selected Readings*, pp. 127–138. Harmondsworth: Penguin.

Gellner, Ernest (1992). *Postmodernism, Reason, and Religion*. London: Routledge.

Gellner, Ernest (1985). *Relativism and the Social Sciences*. Cambridge: Cambridge University Press.

Gergely, G., Bekkering, H., & Király, I. (2002). Rational Imitation in Preverbal Infants. *Nature*, 415: 755.

Gergely, G. & Csibra, G. (2005). The Social Construction of the Cultural Mind: Imitative Learning as a Mechanism of Human Pedagogy. *Interaction Studies*, 6: 463–81.

Gergely, G. & Csibra, G. (2006). Sylvia's Recipe: The Role of Imitation and Pedagogy in the Transmission of Cultural Knowledge. In N. J. Enfield & S. C. Levenson (Eds.), *Roots of Human Sociality: Culture, Cognition, and Human Interaction*, pp. 229–55. Oxford: Berg Publishers.

Gluckman, Max (Ed.) (1962a). *Essays on the Ritual of Social Relations*. Manchester: Manchester University Press.

Gluckman, M. (1962b). *Order and Rebellion in Tribal Africa*. London: Cohen and West.

Gmelch, George (1971). Baseball Magic. *Society*, 8: 39–41.

Gmelch, George (1992). Superstition and Ritual in American Baseball. *Elysian Fields Quarterly*, 11: 25–36.

Godelier, M. & Strathern, M. (1991). *Big Men and Great Men: Personifications of Power in Melanesia*. Cambridge: Cambridge University Press.
Goffman, Erving (1967). *Interaction Ritual: Essays in Face to Face Behavior*. New York: Anchor Books.
Goldschmidt, W. R. (1966). *Comparative Functionalism: An Essay in Anthropological Theory*. Berkeley & Los Angeles: University of California Press.
Gómez, Á, Brooks, M.L., Buhrmester, M. D., Vázquez, A., Jetten, J. & Swann, W. B., Jr. (2011). On the nature of identity fusion: Insights into the construct and a new measure. *Journal of Personality and Social Psychology. 100(5):* 918–933. https://doi.org/10.1037/a0022642
Goody, Jack (1977). *The Domestication of the Savage Mind*. Cambridge: Cambridge University Press.
Gopnik, A. (2000). *The Scientist in the Crib: What Early Learning Tells Us About the Mind*. London: HarperCollins Publishers.
Goring-Morris, A. N. (2005). Life Death and the Emergence of Differential Status in the Near Eastern Neolithic: Evidence from Kfar Hahoresh, Lower Galilee, Israel. In: J. Clarke (Ed.), *Archaeological Perspectives on the Transition and Transformation of Culture in the Eastern Mediterranean*, pp. 89–105. Oxford: Oxbow Books.
Gragg, D. L. (2004). Old and New in Roman Religion: A Cognitive Account. In H. Whitehouse & L. H. Martin (Eds.), *Theorizing Religions Past: Archaeology, History, and Cognition*, pp. 69–86. Walnut Creek, CA: AltaMira Press.
Green, Margaret M. (1947). *Igbo Village Affairs: Chiefly with Reference to the Village of Umbueke Agbaja*. London: Routledge.
Gunter, Gebauer & Wulf, Christoph (1996). *Mimesis: Culture, Art, Society*. Berkeley: University of California Press.
Haidt, J. (2012). The righteous mind: Why good people are divided by politics and religion. New York: Pantheon.
Halbwachs, Maurice (1950). *La Mémoire Collective*. Paris: Presses Universitaires de France.
Hansen, I. G. (2018). The Analytic Utility of Distinguishing Fighting from Dying. *Behavioural and Brain Sciences, 41(e192):* 24–5. https://doi.org/10.1017/S0140525X18000249.
Harrington, J. R. & Gelfand, M. J. (2014). Tightness–Looseness Across the 50 United States. *Proceedings of the National Academy of Sciences USA, 111:* 7990.
Harris, P. L. (2012). *Trusting What You're Told: How Children Learn from Others*. Cambridge, MA: Harvard University Press.
Harrison, Simon J. (1991). *Stealing People's Names: History and Politics in a Sepik River Cosmology*. Cambridge Studies in Social and Cultural Anthropology. Cambridge: Cambridge University Press.
Hastrup, Kirsten & Hervik, Peter (1994). *Social Experience and Anthropological Knowledge*. London: Routledge.
Henrich, J. (2009). The Evolution of Costly Displays, Cooperation and Religion: Credibility Enhancing Displays and Their Implications for Cultural Evolution. *Evolution and Human Behaviour, 30(4):* 244–60. https://doi.org/10.1016/j.evolhumbehav.2009.03.005.
Henrich, J. (2016). *The Secret of Our Success: How Culture Is Driving Human Evolution, Domesticating Our Species, and Making Us Smarter*. Princeton, NJ: Princeton University Press.
Henrich, J., Heine, S. J., & Norenzayan, A. (2010). The Weirdest People in the World. *Behavioural and Brain Sciences, 33(2–3):* 61–83.

Henrich, N. & Henrich, J. (2007). *Why Humans Cooperate: A Cultural and Evolutionary Explanation.* Oxford: Oxford University Press.

Herold, J., McKay, R., & Whitehouse, H. (2013). Catholic Guilt? Recall of Confession Promotes Prosocial Behaviour. *Religion, Brain, and Behaviour,* 3(3): 201–9.

Herrenschmidt, O. (1982). Sacrifice: Symbolic or Effective? In M. Isard & Pierre Smith (Eds.), *Between Belief and Transgression: Structuralist Essays in Religion, History, and Myth,* pp. 24–42. Chicago: University of Chicago Press.

Herrmann, Patricia A., Legare, Cristine H., Harris, Paul L., & Whitehouse, Harvey (2013). Stick to the Script: The Effect of Witnessing Multiple Actors on Children's Imitation. *Cognition,* 129: 536–43.

Hertz, Robert (1960). *Death and the Right Hand.* Trans. R. Needham & C. Needham. New York: The Free Press.

Hillis, A. E. & Caramazza, A. (1991). Category-Specific Naming and Comprehension Impairment: A Double Dissociation. *Brain,* 114: 2081–94.

Hinde, R. A. (2005). Modes Theory: Some Theoretical Considerations. In H. Whitehouse, & R. N. McCauley (Eds.), *Mind and Religion: Psychological and Cognitive Foundations of Religiosity,* pp. 31–56. Walnut Creek, CA: AltaMira Press.

Hitchens, Christopher (2007). *God Is Not Great: How Religion Poisons Everything.* London: Atlantic Books.

Hobson, N. M., Gino, F., Norton, M. I., & Inzlicht, M. (2017). When Novel Rituals Lead to Intergroup Bias: Evidence from Economic Games and Neurophysiology. *Psychological Science,* 28(6): 733–50.

Hoehl, S., Zettersten, M., Schleihauf, H., Grätz, S., & Pauen, S. (2014). The Role of Social Interaction and Pedagogical Cues for Eliciting and Reducing Overimitation in Preschoolers. *Journal of Experimental Child Psychology,* 122: 122–33. https://doi.org/10.1016/j.jecp.2013.12.012.

Hodder, Ian (2006). *The Leopard's Tale: Revealing the Mysteries of Çatalhöyük.* New York: Thames & Hudson.

Hodder, Ian (2012). *Entangled: An Archaeology of the Relationships Between Humans and Things.* New Jersey: Wiley-Blackwell.

Højbjerg, C. K. (2004). Universalistic Orientations of an Imagistic Mode of Religiosity. In H. Whitehouse & J. Laidlaw (Eds.), *Ritual and Memory: Towards a Comparative Anthropology of Religion,* pp. 173–186. Walnut Creek, CA: AltaMira Press.

Holbraad, M. & Pedersen, M. (2017). *The Ontological Turn: An Anthropological Exposition (New Departures in Anthropology).* Cambridge: Cambridge University Press. https://doi.org/10.1017/9781316218907.

Holmwood, J. (2005). Functionalism and its critics. In A. Harrington (Ed.) *Modern Social Theory: An Introduction.* Oxford: Oxford University Press. Pp 87-109.

Homans, George C. (1941). Anxiety and Ritual: The Theories of Malinowski and Radcliffe-Brown. *American Anthropologist,* 43(2):164–72.

Hood, Bruce M. (2009). *Supersense: Why We Believe in the Unbelievable.* New York: HarperOne.

Horner, V. & Whiten, A. (2005). Causal Knowledge and Imitation/Emulation Switching in Chimpanzees (*Pan troglodytes*) and Children (*Homo sapiens*). *Animal Cognition,* 8: 164–81.

Horton, Robin (1993). *Patterns of Thought in Africa and the West: Essays on Magic, Religion and Science.* Cambridge: Cambridge University Press.

Houseman, Michael & Carlo Severi (1998). *Naven or the Other Self. A Relational Approach to Ritual Action.* Leiden: Brill.

Hove, M. J. & Risen, J. L. (2009). It's All in the Timing: Interpersonal Synchrony Increases Affiliation. *Social Cognition, 27*(6): 949–60.

Howe, L. (2004). Late Medieval Christianity, Balinese Hinduism, and the Doctrinal Mode of Religiosity. In H. Whitehouse & J. Laidlaw (Eds.), *Ritual and Memory: Towards a Comparative Anthropology of Religion*, pp. 135–154. Walnut Creek, CA: AltaMira Press.

Hugh-Jones, S. (1994). Shamans, Prophets, and Priests. In N. Thomas & C. Humphrey (Eds.), *Shamanism, History, and the State*, pp. 32–75. Ann Arbor: University of Michigan Press.

Humphrey, C. & Laidlaw, J. (1994). *The Archetypal Actions of Ritual: A Theory of Ritual Illustrated by the Jain Rite of Worship*. Oxford: Clarendon Press.

Hviding, E. (1996). *Guardians of Morovo Lagoon: Practice, Place, and Politics in Maritime Melanesia*. Honolulu: University of Hawaii Press.

Ingold, T. (2007). Earth, Sky, Wind, and Weather. *The Journal of the Royal Anthropological Institute, 13*: S19–S38.

Irons, W. (2001). Religion as a Hard-to-Fake Sign of Commitment. In R. Nesse (Ed.), *Evolution and the Capacity for Commitment*, pp. 292–309. New York: Russell Sage Foundation.

Iteanu, A. (1990). The Concept of the Person and the Ritual System: An Orokaiva View. *Man (N.S.), 25*: 35–53.

Jablonka, E. (2016). Cultural Epigenetics. *The Sociological Review.* 64(1_suppl): 42–60. doi:10.1111/2059-7932.12012.

Jackson, M. (2013). *Lifeworlds: Essays in Existential Anthropology*. Chicago: University of Chicago Press.

Jackson, J. C., Jong, J., Bilkey, D., Whitehouse, H., Zollmann, S., McNaughton, C., et al. (2018). Synchrony and Physiological Arousal Increase Cohesion and Cooperation in Large Naturalistic Groups. *Nature: Scientific Reports, 127*. https://doi.org/10.1038/s41598-017-18023-4.

Jagiello, Robert, Heyes, Cecilia, & Whitehouse, Harvey, (Under Review) Tradition and Invention: The Dual Stance Theory of Cultural Evolution.

James, Wendy (2003). *The Ceremonial Animal: A New Portrait of Anthropology*. Oxford: Oxford University Press.

James, Wendy (2007). *War and Survival in Sudan's Frontierlands: Voices from the Blue Nile*. Oxford: Oxford University Press.

Jaspers, Karl. (1948). "The Axial Age of Human History." Commentary 6: 430.

Jaspers, Karl. (1953). The Origin and Goal of History. Translated by Michael Bullock. New Haven: Yale University Press.

Jiménez, J. Gómez, Á., Buhrmester, M. D., Vázquez, A., Whitehouse, H., & Swann, W.B., Jr. (2015). The Dynamic Identity Fusion Index (DIFI): A New Continuous Measure of Identity Fusion for Web-based Questionnaires. *Social Science Computer Review*. Volume 34 Issue 2, April 2016 pp. 215–228. https://doi.org/10.1177/0894439314566178.

Johnson, Dominic (2015). *God is Watching You: How the Fear of God Makes Us Human*. Oxford: Oxford University Press.

Johnson, K. (2004). Primary Emergence of the Doctrinal Mode of Religiosity in Prehistoric Southwestern Iran. In H. Whitehouse & L. H. Martin (Eds.), *Theorizing Religions Past: Archaeology, History, and Cognition*, pp. 45–68. Walnut Creek, CA: AltaMira Press.

Jong, Jonathan, Whitehouse, Harvey, Kavanagh, Christopher, & Lane, Justin (2015). Shared Negative Experiences Lead to Identity Fusion via Personal Reflection. *PLOS One*. https://doi.org/10.1371/journal.pone.0145611.

Juillerat, B. (1980). Order or Disorder in Melanesian Religion. *Man (NS), 15*: 732–4.

Kapferer, B. (1991). *A Celebration of Demons: Exorcism and the Aesthetics of Healing in Sri Lanka*. Washington, DC: Smithsonian Institution Press.

Kahn D. T., Klar Y., & Roccas S. (2017). For the Sake of the Eternal Group: Perceiving the Group as Trans-generational and Endurance of In-group Suffering. *Personality and Social Psychology Bulletin*, 43(2): 272–83.

Kapitány, R., Kavanagh, C. M., Buhrmester, M., Newson, M., & Whitehouse, H. (2019). Ritual, Identity Fusion, and the Inauguration of President Trump: A Pseudo-experiment of Ritual Modes Theory. *Self and Identity*, 22 February: 293–323. https://doi.org/10.1080/15298868.2019.1578686.

Kapitány, R., Kavanagh, C. M., Whitehouse, H., & Nielsen, M. (2018). Examining Memory for Ritualized Gesture in Complex Causal Sequences. *Cognition*, 181: 46–57. https://doi.org//10.1016/j.cognition.2018.08.005.

Kapitány, R. & Nielsen, M. (2015). Adopting the Ritual Stance: The Role of Opacity and Context in Ritual and Everyday Actions. *Cognition*, 145: 13–29 https://doi.org/10.1016/j.cognition.2015.08.002.

Kapitány, R. & Nielsen, M. (2016). The Ritual Stance and the Precaution System: The Role of Goal-Demotion and Opacity in Ritual and Everyday Actions. *Religion, Brain, and Behaviour*, 7(1): 27–42.

Karmiloff-Smith, A. (1992). *Beyond Modularity: A Developmental Perspective on Cognitive Science*. Cambridge, MA: MIT Press.

Kavanagh, C. M. (2016). Religion Without Belief. *Aeon Magazine*. https://aeon.co/essays/can-religion-be-based-on-ritual-practice-without-belief.

Kavanagh, C. M. & Jong, J. (2019). Is Japan Religious? *Journal for the Study of Religion, Nature and Culture*, 14(1): 152–80. https://doi.org/10.1558/jsrnc.39187.

Kavanagh, C. M., Jong, J., McKay, R., & Whitehouse, H. (2018). Positive Experiences of High Arousal Martial Arts Rituals Are Linked to Identity Fusion and Costly Progroup Actions. *European Journal of Social Psychology*, Volume 49, Issue 3, pp. 461–481. https://doi.org//10.1002/ejsp.2514.

Kavanagh, Christopher M., Kapitány, Rohan, Putra, Idhamsyah Eka, & Whitehouse, Harvey (2020). Exploring the Pathways Between Transformative Group Experiences and Identity Fusion. *Frontiers in Psychology*, 11: 1172. https://doi.org/10.3389/fpsyg.2020.01172.

Kawano, S. (2005). *Ritual Practice in Modern Japan: Ordering Place, People, and Action*. Honolulu: University of Hawaii Press.

Kelemen, D. (1999). Why Are Rocks Pointy? Children's Preference for Teleological Explanations of the Natural World. *Developmental Psychology*, 35: 1440–52. http://dx.doi.org/10.1037/0012-1649.35.6.1440.

Kelemen, D. (2004). Are Children 'Intuitive Theists'? Reasoning About Purpose and Design in Nature. *Psychological Science*, 15(5): 295–301. https://doi.org/10.1111/j.0956-7976.2004.00672.x.

Kelemen, D. & DiYanni, C. (2005). Intuitions About Origins: Purpose and Intelligent Design in Children's Reasoning About Nature. *Journal of Cognition and Development*, 6: 3–31.

Kertzer, D. (1988). *Ritual, Politics, and Power*. New Haven, CT: Yale University Press.

Ketola, K. (2005). *An Indian Guru and His Western Disciples: Representation and Communication of Charisma in the Hare Krishna Movement*. PhD Dissertation, University of Helsinki, Finland.

Kristoffer, N. & Sørensen, J. (2011). Spontaneous Processing of Functional and Non-functional Action Sequences. *Religion, Brain, and Behaviour*, 1(1): 18–30.

Khaldūn, Ibn (1958 [1377]). *The Muqaddimah: An Introduction to History*. Trans. Franz Rosenthal, from Arabic in 3 Vols. New York: Princeton University Press.

King, L. A. & Raspin, C. (2004). Lost and Found Possible Selves, Subjective Well-being, and Ego Development in Divorced Women. *Journal of Personality*, 72: 603–32. https://doi.org/10.1111/j.0022-3506.2004.00274.x.

Konvalinka, I., Xygalatas, D., Bulbulia, J., Schjødt, U., Jegindø, E.-M.E., Wallot, S., Van Orden, G. & Roepstorff, A. (2011). Synchronized arousal between performers and related spectators in a fire-walking ritual. *Proceedings of the National Academy of Sciences of the United States of America*, bind 108, nr. 20, s. 8514-8519. https://doi.org/10.1073/pnas.1016955108

Kreinath, J., Snoek, J., & Stausberg, M. (2007). *Theorizing Rituals: Annotated Bibliography of Ritual Theory, 1966-2005*. Leiden: Brill.

Kuijt I. (2000). Keeping the Peace: Ritual, Skull Caching and Community Integration in the Levantine Neolithic. In I. Kuijt (Ed.), *Life in Neolithic Farming Communities: Social Organization, Identity, and Differentiation*, pp. 37-163. New York: Kluwer Academic/Plenum Publishers.

La Fontaine, J. S. (1985). *Initiation: Ritual Drama and Secret Knowledge Across the World*. Harmondsworth: Penguin Books.

Laidlaw, J. (2004). "Embedded Modes of Religiosity in Indic Renouncer Religions" In H. Whitehouse & J. Laidlaw (Eds.), *Ritual and Memory: Towards a Comparative Anthropology of Religion*, pp. 89-110. Walnut Creek, CA: AltaMira Press.

Lane, J. E. (2019). The Evolution of Doctrinal Religions: Using Semantic Network Analysis and Computational Models to Examine the Evolutionary Dynamics of Large Religions [PhD thesis], University of Oxford.

Langergraber, K., Schubert, Grit, Rowney, Carolyn, Wrangham, Richard, Zommers, Zinta & Vigilant, Linda (2011). Genetic Differentiation and the Evolution of Cooperation in Chimpanzees and Humans. *Proceedings of the Royal Society*, 278: 2546–52.

Lawther, J. D. (1972). *Sport Psychology*. Hoboken: NJ: Prentice-Hall.

Leach, Edmund (1954). *Political Systems of Highland Burma: A Study of Kachin Social Structure*. London: University of London Athone Press.

Leach, Edmund (1989). *Claude Lévi-Strauss*. Chicago: University of Chicago Press.

Leacock, E. (1978). Women's Status in Egalitarian Society: Implications for Social Evolution. *Current Anthropology*, 19: 247–74.

Lee, Richard & DeVore, Irven (1969). *Man the Hunter*. Chicago: Aldine Publishing Co.

Legare C. H. & Nielsen M. (2015). Imitation and Innovation: the dual engines of cultural learning. 16. Feature article in *Trends in Cogn. Sci.* 19, 688–699. doi:10.1016/j.tics.2015.08.005.

Legare C. H. (2019). The development of cumulative cultural learning. *Ann. Rev. Dev. Psychol.* 1, 119–147. doi:10.1146/annurev-devpsych-121318-084848.

Legare, C. H. & Nielsen, M. (2020). Ritual Explained: Interdisciplinary Answers to Tinbergen's Four Questions. *Philosophical Transactions of the Royal Society B, 375*: 20190419. http://dx.doi.org/10.1098/rstb.2019.0419.

Legare, Cristine H. & Souza, André L. (2012). Evaluating Ritual Efficacy: Evidence from the Supernatural. *Cognition*, 124(1): 1–15.

Legare, Cristine H., Wen, Nicole J., Herrmann, Patricia A., & Whitehouse, Harvey (2015). Imitative Flexibility and the Development of Cultural Learning. *Cognition*, 142: 351–61. https://doi.org/10.1016/j.cognition.2015.05.020.

Leslie, Alan M. (1994). Pretending and Believing: Issues in the Theory of ToMM. *Cognition*, 50: 211–38.

Lévi-Strauss, Claude (1966). *The Savage Mind*. Chicago: University of Chicago Press.

Lewis, Gilbert (1988). *Day of Shining Red: An Essay on Understanding Ritual*. Cambridge: Cambridge University Press.

Lieberman, D., Tooby, J., & Cosmides, L. (2007). The Architecture of Human Kin Detection. *Nature, 445*: 727–31.

Lilgendahl, J. P. & McAdams, D. P. (2011). Constructing Stories of Self-Growth: How Individual Differences in Patterns of Autobiographical Reasoning Relate to Well-being in Midlife. *Journal of Personality, 79*: 391–428. https://doi.org/10.1111/j.1467-6494.2010.00688.x.

Lincoln, Bruce (1987). Ritual, Rebellion, Resistance: Once More the Swazi Ncwala. *Man (N.S.), 22*(1): 132–56.

Livingstone, Kenneth R. (2005). Religious Practice, Brain, and Belief. *Journal of Cognition and Culture, 5*(1–2): 75–117.

Loncke, Sandrine (2008). *Mémoire et Transmission Musicale dans une Société Nomade. L'exemple des Peuls Wodaabe du Niger*, Paris: Cahiers d'ethnomusicologie.

Lyons, D. E., Damrosch, D. H., Lin, J. K., Macris, D. M., & Keil, F. C. (2011). The Scope and Limits of Overimitation in the Transmission of Artefact Culture. *Philosophical Transactions of the Royal Society of London. Series B, Biological Sciences, 366*(1567): 1158–67. https://doi.org/10.1098/rstb.2010.0335.

Lyons, D. E., Young, A. G., & Keil, F. C. (2007). The Hidden Structure of Overimitation. *Proceedings of the National Academy of Sciences of the United States of America, 104*(50): 19751–6. https://doi.org/10.1073/pnas.0704452104.

Malinowski, Bronislaw (1922). *Argonauts of the Western Pacific, an Account of Native Enterprise and Adventure in the Archipelagoes of Melanesian New Guinea*. New York: E.P. Dutton and Co.

Malinowski, Bronislaw (1929). *The Sexual Life of Savages in North-Western Melanesia: An Ethnographic Account of Courtship, Marriage and Family Life Among the Natives of the Trobriand Islands, British New Guinea*. London: George Routledge and Sons.

Malinowski, Bronislaw (1935). *Coral Gardens and Their Magic: A Study of the Methods of Tilling the Soil and of Agricultural Rites in the Trobriand Islands*. London: Allen and Unwin.

Malinowski, Bronislaw (1944). *A Scientific Theory of Culture, and Other Essays*. Chapel Hill: University of North Carolina Press.

Malinowski, Bronislaw (1945). *Magic, Science and Religion and Other Essays*. Garden City, New York: Doubleday.

Marcus, George E. & Fischer, Michael M. J. (1986). *Anthropology as Cultural Critique: An Experimental Moment in the Human Sciences*. Chicago: University of Chicago Press.

Martin, L. H. & Pachis, P. (2009). *Imagistic Traditions in the Graeco-Roman World: A Cognitive Modeling of History of Religious Research*. Athens: Ekdoseis Vanias.

Marx, Karl (1977 [1859]). *A Contribution to the Critique of Political Economy*. Moscow: Progress Publishers.

Mauldin, Barbara (2004). *Carnaval!* Seattle: University of Washington Press.

Mauss, M. (1979). Relations Between Psychology and Sociology. London: Routledge and Kegan Paul.

Mazzucato, Camilla, Bogaard, Amy, Nugent, Selin, Atkinson, Quentin, François, Pieter, & Whitehouse, Harvey (In Prep). The Role of Ritual in the Neolithization of the Near East: A Multivariate Statistical Approach to the Levantine and Central Anatolian Archaeological Evidence.

McAdams, D. P. & McLean, K. C. (2013). Narrative Identity. *Current Directions in Psychological Science, 22*: 233–8. https://doi.org/10.1177/0963721413475622.

McArthur, M. (1971). Men and Spirits in the Kunimaipa Valley. In L. R. Hiatt & C. J. Jayawardena (Eds.), *Anthropology in Oceania*. Sydney: Angus & Robertson.

McBride, C. K., Paikoff, R. L., & Holmbeck, G. N. (2003). Individual and Familial Influences on the Onset of Sexual Intercourse Among Urban African American Adolescents. *Journal of Consulting and Clinical Psychology*, 71(1): 159–67.
McCauley, C. & Moskalenko, S. (2008). Mechanisms of Political Radicalization: Pathways Toward Terrorism. *Terrorism and Political Violence*, 20: 415
McCauley, R. N. (2001). Ritual, Memory, and Emotion: Comparing Two Cognitive Hypotheses. In J. Andresen (Ed.), *Religion in Mind: Cognitive Perspectives on Religious Belief, Ritual, and Experience*, pp. 115–140. Cambridge: Cambridge University Press.
McCauley, Robert N. (2011). *Why Religion Is Natural and Science Is Not*. New York: Oxford University Press.
McCauley, Robert N. & Thomas Lawson, E. (2002). *Bringing Ritual to Mind: Psychological Foundations of Cultural Forms*. New York: Cambridge University Press.
McCauley, Robert N. & Harvey Whitehouse (Eds.) (2005). *The Psychological and Cognitive Foundations of Religiosity*, Special Issue of *Journal of Cognition and Culture*, 5(1–2).
McCloskey, M. (1983). Intuitive Physics. *Scientific American*, 248(4): 122–30.
McGranaghan, M. (2017). Ethnographic Analogy in Archaeology: Methodological Insights from Southern Africa. *Oxford Research Encyclopedia of African History*. https://oxfordre.com/africanhistory/view/10.1093/acrefore/9780190277734.001.0001/acrefore-9780190277734-e-213.
McGuigan, N., Gladstone, D., & Cook, L. (2012). Is the Cultural Transmission of Irrelevant Tool Actions in Adult Humans (Homo sapiens) Best Explained as the Result of an Evolved Conformist Bias? *PLOS One*, 7(12): e50863. https://doi.org/10.1371/journal.pone.0050863.
McGuigan, N., Makinson, J., & Whiten, A. (2011). From Over–imitation to Super–copying: Adults Imitate Causally Irrelevant Aspects of Tool Use with Higher Fidelity than Young Children. *British Journal of Psychology*, 102(1): 1–18. https://doi.org/10.1348/000712610X493115.
McKay, R. & Whitehouse, H. (2015). Religion and Morality. *Psychological Bulletin*, 141(2): 447. http://dx.doi.org/10.1037/a0038455.
McMurtry, John (1978). *The Structure of Marx's World-View*. Princeton, NJ: Princeton University Press.
Mead, Margaret. (1928). *Coming of Age in Samoa: A Psychological Study of Primitive Youth for Western Civilisation*. New York: Morrow.
Meng, X., Nakawake, Y., Hashiya, K., Burdett, E., Jong, J., & Whitehouse, H. (2021). Preverbal infants expect agents exhibiting counterintuitive capacities to gain access to contested resources. *Sci Rep* 11, 10884 https://doi.org/10.1038/s41598-021-89821-0
Mesoudi A, Whiten A, Laland KN. (2006). Towards a unified science of cultural evolution. *Behavioral and Brain Sciences*, 29(4): 329-47; discussion 347-83. https://doi.org/10.1017/S0140525X06009083. PMID: 17094820.
Michaels, Axel (2016). *Homo Ritualis: Hindu Ritual and Its Significance to Ritual Theory*. Oxford: Oxford University Press.
Miles, L. K., Nind, L. K., & Macrae, C. N. (2009). The Rhythm of Rapport: Interpersonal Synchrony and Social Perception. *Journal of Experimental Social Psychology*, 45(3): 585–9.
Mithen, S. (2004). From Ohalo to Çatalhöyük: The Development of Religiosity During the Early Prehistory of Western Asia, 20,000–7000 BC. In H. Whitehouse & L. H. Martin (Eds.), *Theorizing Religions Past: Historical and Anthropological Perspectives*, pp. 17–44. Walnut Creek, CA: AltaMira Press.
Mitkidis, Panagiotis, Leonard, Pierre, Nielbo, Kristoffer L., & Sørensen, Jesper (2014). Does Goal Demotion Enhance Cooperation? *Journal of Cognition and Culture*, 14: 26372. https://doi.org/10.1163/15685373-12342124.

Moritz, M. (2010). Understanding Herder-Farmer Conflicts in West Africa: Outline of a Processual Approach. *Human Organization*, 69(2): 138–148.

Morley, I. (2013). *The Prehistory of Music: Human evolution, archaeology, and the origins of musicality.* Oxford: Oxford University Press.

Mullins, Daniel A., Daniel Hoyer, Christina Collins, Thomas Currie, Kevin Feeney, Pieter François, Patrick E Savage, Harvey Whitehouse, and Peter Turchin. (2018). A Systematic Assessment of the Axial Age Thesis using global comparative historical evidence. *American Sociological Review*. doi:10.1177/0003122418772567.

Mullins, D., Whitehouse, H., & Atkinson, Q. (2013). The Role of Writing and Recordkeeping in the Cultural Evolution of Human Cooperation. *Journal of Economic Behaviour and Organization*, 90(Supplement, June): S141–51.

Murad, M. (2013). Práticas de violência e mortes de torcedores no futebol brasileiro. *Revista USP*, (99), 139–52.

Murdock, G. P. (1967). *Ethnographic Atlas: A Summary.* Pittsburgh: The University of Pittsburgh Press.

Murray, D., & Schaller, M. (2010). Historical prevalence of infectious diseases within 230 geopolitical regions: a tool for investigating origins of culture. *Journal of Cross-Cultural Psychology*, 41(1), 99–108. https://doi.org/10.1177%2F0146167210394451.

Muzzulini, Barbara, Rohan Kapitány, Valerie van Mulukom & Harvey Whitehouse, (In Prep). Shared Flashbulb Memories lead to Identity Fusion: Recalling the Defeat in the Brexit Referendum Produces Strong Psychological Bonds among Remainers.

Nadel, S. F. (1954). *Nupe Religion.* London: Oxford University Press.

Nagell, K., Olguin, R. S., & Tomasello, M. (1993). Processes of Social Learning in the Tool Use of Chimpanzees (*Pan troglodytes*) and Human Children (*Homo sapiens*). *Journal of Comparative Psychology*, 107: 174–86. https://doi.org/10.1037/0735-7036.107.2.174.

Nelson, J. K. (1996). *A Year in the Life of a Shinto Shrine.* Seattle: University of Washington Press.

Newberg, A. B. & Waldman, M. R. (2009). *How God Changes Your Brain: Breakthrough Findings from a Leading Neuroscientist.* New York: Ballantine Books.

Newson, Martha, Bortolini, Tiago Soaries, da Silva, Ricardo, Buhrmester, Michael, & Whitehouse, Harvey (2018). Brazil's Football Warriors: Social Bonding and Intergroup Violence. *Evolution and Human Behaviour*. 39(6): 675–683. https://doi.org/10.1016/j.evolhumbehav.2018.06.010.

Newson, Martha, Buhrmester, Michael, Wibisono, Susilo, Black, Clancy, Gonsalokrale, Karen, Knijnik, Jorge, et al. (Submitted). Why Do Strong Forms of Social Cohesion Produce Both Peaceful and Violent Intergroup Behaviours Among Football Fans and Radical Muslims?

Newson, Martha, Michael Buhrmester, Fiona White, Karen Gonsalkorale, Clancy Black, Jorge Knijnik, Susilo Wibisono, Vici Sofianna Putera, Harvey Whitehouse (In Prep). Ingroup Causes of Intergroup Violence among Hardcore Football Fans and Islamist Fundamentalists.

Newson Martha, Buhrmester, Michael D., & Whitehouse, Harvey (2016). Explaining Lifelong Loyalty: The Role of Identity Fusion and Self-Shaping Group Events. *PLOS One*, 11(8): e0160427. https://doi.org/10.1371/journal.pone.0160427.

Newson, M., Shriamizu, V., Buhrmester, M., Hattori, W., Jong, J., Yamomoto, E. M., et al. (2020). Devoted Fans Produce More Cortisol When Watching Live Soccer Matches. *Stress and Health*, 36(2): 220–7. https://doi.org/10.1002/smi.2924.

Newson, M. & Whitehouse, H. (2020). The Twinning Project: How football, the beautiful game, can be used to reduce reoffending. *Prison Service Journal*. 248: 28–31.

Newson, M., Buhrmester, M., & Whitehouse, H. (2021). United in defeat: Shared suffering and group bonding among football fans. *Managing Sport and Leisure*. DOI: 10.1080/23750472.2020.1866650.
Nielbo, Kristoffer L. & Sørensen, Jesper (2011). Spontaneous Processing of Functional and Non-functional Action Sequences. *Religion, Brain & Behaviour*, 1(1): 18–30. https://doi.org/10.1080/2153599X.2010.550722.
Nielbo, K. & Sørensen, J. (2015). Attentional Resource Allocation and Cultural Modulation in a Computational Model of Ritualised Behaviour. *Religion, Brain & Behaviour*, 6(4): 318–35.
Nielsen, M. & Tomasello, K. (2010). Overimitation in Kalahari Bushman Children and the Origins of Human Cultural Cognition. *Psychological Science*, 21(5): 729–36.
Nielsen, M., Mushin, I., Tomasello, K., & Whiten, A. (2014). Where Culture Takes Hold: 'Overimitation' and Its Flexible Deployment in Western, Aboriginal, and Bushmen Children. *Child Development*, 85(6): 2169–84. https://doi.org/10.1111/cdev.12265.
Nnoko-Mewanu, J. (2018). Farmer-Herder Conflicts on the Rise in Africa. *Human Rights Watch. Inter Press Service (IPS) News Agency*. https://www.hrw.org/news/2018/08/06/farmer-herder-conflicts-rise-africa.
Norbeck, Edward (1963). African Rituals of Conflict. *American Anthropologist*, 65: 1254–79.
Norenzayan, Ara (2013). *Big Gods: How Religion Transformed Cooperation and Conflict.* Princeton, NJ: University Press.
Norris, Christopher (1979). *Deconstruction: Theory and Practice.* New York: Routledge.
Olivola, C. Y. & Shafir, E. (2013). The Martyrdom Effect: When Pain and Effort Increase Prosocial Contributions. *Journal of Behavioural Decision Making*, 26: 91–105. https://doi.org/10.1002/bdm.767.
Pagel, M., Atkinson, Q. & Meade, A. (2007). Frequency of word-use predicts rates of lexical evolution throughout Indo-European history. *Nature*, 449: 717–720. https://doi.org/10.1038/nature06176.
Park, J. H. & Schaller, M. (2005). Does Attitude Similarity Serve as a Heuristic Cue for Kinship? Evidence of an Implicit Cognitive Association. *Evolution and Human Behaviour*, 26: 158–70.
Park, J. H., Schaller, M., & Van Vugt, M. (2008). Psychology of Human Kin Recognition: Heuristic Cues, Erroneous Inferences, and Their Implications. *Review of General Psychology*, 12(3): 215–35.
Parkin, D. (1991). Ritual as Spatial Direction and Bodily Division. In D. de Coppet (Ed.), *Understanding Rituals*, pp. 11–25. London: Routledge.
Parkin, D. (2007). Introduction: Emergence and Convergence. In David Parkin & Stanley Ulijaszek (Eds.), pp. 1–20. *Holistic Anthropology: Emergence and Convergence.* New York and Oxford: Berghahn Books.
Payne, Richard K. (2004). Ritual Syntax and Cognitive Theory. *Pacific World: Journal of the Institute of Buddhist Studies*, 6(3): 195–227.
Pedwell, Carolyn (2010). *Feminism, Culture and Embodied Practice: The Rhetorics of Comparison.* London: Routledge.
Peel, J. D. Y. (2004). Divergent Modes of Religiosity in West Africa. In H. Whitehouse & J. A. Laidlaw (Eds.), *Ritual and Memory: Towards a Comparative Anthropology of Religion* 11–30. Walnut Creek, CA: AltaMira Press.
Peel, J. D.Y. (2004). Modes of Religiosity and Dichotomous Theories of Religion. In H. Whitehouse & J. A. Laidlaw (Eds.), *Ritual and Memory: Toward a Comparative Anthropology of Religion*, pp. 11–30. Walnut Creek, CA: AltaMira Press.

Peers, Laura. (2007). On the Social, the Biological and the Political: Revisiting Beatrice Blackwood's Research and Teaching. In David Parkin & Stanley Ulijaszek (Eds.), *Holistic Anthropology: Emergence and Convergence*, pp. 127–147. Oxford: Berghahn Books.

Persinger, M.A. (1983). Religious and Mystical Experiences as Artifacts of Temporal Lobe Function: A General Hypothesis. *Perceptual Motor Skills*, 57: 1255–1262. http://dx.doi.org/10.2466/pms.1983.57.3f.1255

Pew Research Center (2007). Pew Research Global Attitudes Project. http://www.pewglobal.org/2007/10/04/chapter-3-viewsof-religion-and-morality/.

Piaget, J. (1928). La Causalité Chez L'Enfant. *British Journal of Psychology*, 18: 276–301.

Pillemer, David, Koff, Elissa, Rhinehart, Elizabeth, & Rierdan, Jill (1987). Flash Bulb Memories of Menarche and Adult Menstrual Distress. *Journal of Adolescence*, 10: 187–9. https://doi.org/10.1016/S0140-1971(87)80087–8.

Pew Research Center. (2007). Pew Research Global Attitudes Project. http://www.pewglobal.org/2007/10/04/chapter-3-viewsof-religion-and-morality/.

Platvoet, J. G. (1995). Ritual in Plural and Pluralist Societies: Instruments for Analysis. In Jan G. Platvoet & Karel van der Toorn (Eds.), *Pluralism & Identity: Studies in Ritual Behaviour*, pp. 25–51. Leiden: Brill.

Poole, F. J. P. (1982). The Ritual Forging of Identity: Aspects of Person and Self in Bimin-Kuskusmin Male Initiation. In G. H. Herdt (Ed.), *Rituals of Manhood: Male Initiation in Papua New Guinea*, pp. 99–154. Berkeley: University of California Press.

Povinelli, Daniel (2000). *Folk Physics for Apes*. Oxford: Oxford University Press.

Powell, Russell & Clarke, Steve (2012). Religion as an Evolutionary Byproduct: A Critique of the Standard Model. *British Journal for the Philosophy of Science*, 63: 457–86.

Preston, Stephanie D. & de Waal, Frans B. M. (2001). Empathy: Its Ultimate and Proximate Bases. *Behavioural and Brain Sciences*, 251: 1–20.

Previc, Fred H. (2009). *The Dopaminergic Mind in Human Evolution and History*. Cambridge: Cambridge University Press.

Pyszczynski, T., Lockett, M., Greenberg, J., & Solomon, S. (2020). Terror Management Theory and the COVID-19 Pandemic. *Journal of Humanistic Psychology*, 61(2). https://doi.org/10.1177/0022167820959488.

Pyysiäinen, I. (2004). Corrupt Doctrine and Doctrinal Revival: On the Nature and Limits of the Modes Theory. In Harvey Whitehouse & Luther H. Martin (Eds.), *Theorizing Religions Past: Historical and Archaeological Perspectives on Modes of Religiosity*, pp. 173–196. Walnut Creek, CA: AltaMira Press.

Pyysiäinen, I. & Hauser, M. (2010). The Origins of Religion: Evolved Adaptation or Byproduct? *Trends in Cognitive Sciences*, 14: 104–9. http://dx.doi.org/10.1016/j.tics.2009.12.007.

Radcliffe-Brown, A. R. (1952). *Structure and Function in Primitive Society*. London: Cohen and West.

Rakoczy, Hannes, Warneken, Felix, & Tomasello, Michael (2008). The Sources of Normativity: Young Children's Awareness of the Normative Structure of Games. *Developmental Psychology*, 44(3): 875–81. https://doi.org/10.1037/0012-1649.

Rakoczy, H. & Schmidt, M. F. (2013). The Early Ontogeny of Social Norms. *Child Development Perspectives*, 7(1): 17–21.

Raspaud, M. & Da Cunha Bastos, F. (2013). Torcedores de futebol: Violence and Public Policies in Brazil Before the 2014 FIFA World Cup. *Sport in Society*, 16: 192–204.

Reader, I. & Tanabe, G. J. (1998). *Practically Religious: Worldly Benefits and the Common Religion of Japan*. Honolulu: University of Hawaii Press.

Reddish, P., Fischer, R., & Bulbulia, J. (2013). Let's Dance Together: Synchrony, Shared Intentionality and Cooperation. *PLOS One, 8*(8): e71182. https://doi.org/10.1371/journal.pone.0071182.

Reddish, P., Tong, E. M. W., Jong, J., Lanman, J. A., & Whitehouse, H. (2016). Collective Synchrony Increases Prosociality Towards Non-performers and Out-group Members. *British Journal of Social Psychology, 55*(4): 722–38. https://doi.org/10.1111/bjso.12165.

Redfield, Robert (1955). *The Little Community: Viewpoints for the Study of a Human Whole.* Chicago: University of Chicago Press.

Reese, E. & Whitehouse, H. (2021). The Development of Identity Fusion. *Perspectives on Psychological Science.* doi:10.1177/1745691620968761.

Rennung, M. & Göritz, A. S. (2016). Prosocial Consequences of Interpersonal Synchrony: A Meta-analysis. *Zeitschrift für Psychologie, 224*(3): 168–89. http://dx.doi.org/10.1027/2151-2604/a000252.

Richerson, P., Baldini, R., Bell, A. V., Demps, K., Frost, K., Hillis, V., et al. (2016). Cultural Group Selection Plays an Essential Role in Explaining Human Cooperation: A Sketch of the Evidence. *Behavioral and Brain Sciences, 39*: e30. https://doi.org/10.1017/S0140525X1400106X. Epub 2014 Oct 28. PMID: 25347943.

Richert, R. A., Whitehouse, H., & Stewart, E. A. (2005). Memory and Analogical Thinking in High-Arousal Rituals. In H. Whitehouse & R. McCauley (Eds.), *Mind and Religion: Psychological and Cognitive Foundations of Religiosity,* pp. 127–45. Walnut Creek, CA: AltaMira Press.

Ridley, Matt (1993). *The Red Queen: Sex and the Evolution of Human Nature.* New York: The Viking Press.

Roos, P., Gelfand, M. J., & Nau, D. (2014). High Strength of Ties and Low Mobility Enable the Evolution of Third Party Punishment. *Proceedings of the Royal Society B, 281*: 20132661. https://doi.org/10.1098/rspb.2013.2661.

Ross, L., Greene, D., & House, P. (1977). The 'False Consensus Effect': An Egocentric Bias in Social Perception and Attribution Processes. *Journal of Experimental Social Psychology, 13*(3): 279–301.

Rozin, P. (1999). Food Is Fundamental, Fun, Frightening, and Far-Reaching. *Social Research, 66*(1), 9–30. http://www.jstor.org/stable/40971298/.

Rudski, Jeffrey M. & Edwards, Ashleigh (2007). Malinowski Goes to College: Factors Influencing Students' Use of Ritual and Superstition. *Journal of General Psychology, 134*: 389–403.

Russell, Yvan I., Gobet, Fernand, & Whitehouse, Harvey (2014). Mood, Expertise, Analogy, and Ritual: An Experiment Using the Five-Disc Tower of Hanoi. *Religion, Brain, and Behaviour, 6*(1): 67–87. https://doi.org/10.1080/2153599X.2014.921861.

Rybanska, Veronika, McKay, Ryan, Jong, Jonathan, & Whitehouse, Harvey (2018). Rituals Improve Children's Ability To Delay Gratification. *Child Development, 89*(2): 349–59. https://doi.org/10.1111/cdev.12762.

Sahlins, M. D. (1963). Poor Man, Rich Man, Big-man, Chief: Political Types in Melanesia and Polynesia. *Comparative Studies in Society and History, 5*(3): 285–303.

Sahlins, Marshall (1974). *Stone Age Economics.* London: Routledge.

Salali, G. D., Whitehouse, H., & Hochberg, M. E. (2015). A Life-Cycle Model of Human Social Groups Produces a U-Shaped Distribution in Group Size. *PLOS One, 10*(9): e0138496. https://doi.org/10.1371/journal.pone.0138496.

Saussure, Ferdinand de (1959). *Course in General Linguistics.* New York: Philosophical Library.

Schechner, R. (1977). *Essays on Performance Theory, 1970–1977*. New York: Drama Book Specialists.

Schjoedt, U., Sørensen, J., Nielbo, K., Xygalatas, D., Mitkidis, P., & Bulbulia, J. (2013). Cognitive Resource Depletion in Religious Interactions. *Religion, Brain & Behaviour*, 3(1): 39–55.

Schmitt, S. A., McClelland, M. M., Tominey, S. L., & Acock, A. C. (2015). Strengthening School Readiness for Head Start Children: Evaluation of a Self-Regulation Intervention. *Early Childhood Research Quarterly*, 30: 20–31. https://doi.org/10.1016/j.ecresq.2014.08.001.

Schunk, Dale H. (2008). *Learning Theories: An Educational Perspective*. Hoboken, NJ: Prentice Hall.

Seligman, Adam B., Weller, Robert P., Puett, Michael J., & Simon, Bennett (2008). *Ritual and Its Consequences: An Essay on the Limits of Sincerity*. Oxford: Oxford University Press.

Shankland, D. (2004). Modes of Religiosity and the Legacy of Ernest Gellner. In H. Whitehouse & J. A. Laidlaw (Eds.), *Ritual and Memory: Toward a Comparative Anthropology of Religion*, pp. 31–48. Walnut Creek, CA: AltaMira Press.

Sheppard, Stephen R. J. (2012). *Visualizing Climate Change: A Guide to Visual Communication of Climate Change and Developing Local Solutions*. London: Routledge.

Shore, Brand (1996). The Absurd Side of Power in Samoa. In Richard Feinberg & Karen Ann Watson-Gegeo (Eds.), *Leadership and Change in the Western Pacific. LSE Monographs on Social Anthropology*, pp. 142–186. Oxford: Berg.

Singer, Peter (1999). The Singer Solution to World Poverty. *The New York Times Magazine*, September 5: 60–3.

Singer, J. A. & Salovey, P. (1993). *The Remembered Self: Emotion and Memory in Personality*. New York: Free Press.

Slone, J. (2004). *Theological Incorrectness: Why Religious People Believe Things They Shouldn't*. New York: Oxford University Press.

Smith, Jonathan Z. (1987). *To Take Place: Toward Theory in Ritual*. Chicago: University of Chicago Press.

Smith, Robertson W. (1889). *Lectures on the Religion of the Semites: First Series*. London: Adam and Charles Black.

Snyder, C. R., Lassegard, M., & Ford, C. E. (1986). Distancing after Group Success and Failure: Basking in Reflected Glory and Cutting Off Reflected Failure. *Journal of Personality and Social Psychology*, 51(2): 382–8.

Sosis, R. (2003). Why Aren't We All Hutterites? Costly Signaling Theory and Religious Behaviour. *Human Nature*, 14: 91–127.

Sosis, R. & Alcorta, C. (2003). Signaling, Solidarity, and the Sacred: The Evolution of Religious Behaviour. *Evolutionary Anthropology*, 12: 264–74.

Sosis, Richard & Bressler, Eric R. (2003). Cooperation and Commune Longevity: A Test of the Costly Signaling Theory of Religion. *Cross-Cultural Research*, 37(2): 211–39.

Sosis, R., Kress, H. C., & Boster, J. S. (2007). Scars for War: Evaluating Alternative Signaling Explanations for Cross-cultural Variance in Ritual Costs. *Evolution and Human Behaviour*, 28(4): 234–47.

Sperber, Dan (1996). *Explaining Culture: A Naturalistic Approach*. Oxford: Blackwell.

Sperber, D. (2001). Mental Modularity and Cultural Diversity. In H. Whitehouse (Ed.), *The Debated Mind: Evolutionary Psychology Versus Ethnography*, pp. 23–56. Oxford: Berg.

Spelke E.S. & Kinzler, K.D. (2007). Core knowledge. *Dev Sci*. 10 (1):89-96. https://doi: 10.1111/j.1467-7687.2007.00569.x. PMID: 17181705.

Spiro, Melford E. (1996). Postmodernist Anthropology, Subjectivity, and Science. A Modernist Critique. *Comparative Studies in Society and History*, 38(1): 759–80.

Staal, F. (1989). *Rules Without Meaning: Ritual, Mantras and the Human Sciences*. New York: Peter Lang.
Stark, R., & Bainbridge, W. (1979). Of Churches, Sects, and Cults: Preliminary Concepts for a Theory of Religious Movements. *Journal for the Scientific Study of Religion,18*(2), 117–131. https://doi:10.2307/1385935
Stark, Rodney, & Glock, Charles Y. (1971). Dimensions of Religious Commitments. In Roland Robertson (Ed.), *Sociology of Religion: Selected Readings*, pp. 253–61. Harmondsworth: Penguin Books.
Sterelny, Kim (2019). Religion: Costs, Signals, and the Neolithic Transition. *Religion, Brain & Behavior*, 3: 303–20. https://doi.org/10.1080/2153599X.2019.1678513.
Stewart, Pamela & Strathern, Andrew (2014). *Ritual: Key Concepts in Religion*. London: Bloomsbury.
Strauss, Claudia & Quinn, Naomi (1997). *A Cognitive Theory of Cultural Meaning*. Cambridge: Cambridge University Press.
Strathern, Alan (2019). *Unearthly Powers: Religious and Political Change in World History*. Cambridge: Cambridge University Press.
Stuart-Glennie, J. (1873). *In the Morningland: Or, the Law of the Origin and Transformation of Christianity – Vol. 1: The New Philosophy of History*. London: Longmans, Green, and Company.
Subbotsky, E. (2004). Magical Thinking in Judgments of Causation: Can Anomalous Phenomena Affect Ontological Causal Beliefs in Children and Adults? *British Journal of Developmental Psychology*, 22: 123–52.
Swann, W. B., Jr., Buhrmester, M., Gómez, Á., Jetten, J., Bastian, B., Vázquez, A., et al. (2014). What Makes a Group Worth Dying for? Identity Fusion Fosters Perception of Familial Ties, Promoting Self-Sacrifice. *Journal of Personality and Social Psychology*, 106(6): 912–26.
Swann, W.B., Jr., Gómez, A., Dovidio, J. Hart, S., & Jetten, J. (2010). Dying and Killing for One's Group: Identity Fusion Moderates Responses to Intergroup Versions of the Trolley Problem. *Psychological Science*, 21(8): 1176–83.
Swann, W. B., Jr., Gómez, A., Seyle, C., & Morales, F. (2009). Identity Fusion: The Interplay of Personal and Social Identities in Extreme Group Behaviour. *Journal of Personality and Social Psychology*, 96: 995–1011.
Swann, W. B., Jensen, Jolanda, Gómez, Ángel, Whitehouse, Harvey, & Bastian, Brock (2012). When Group Membership Gets Personal: A Theory of Identity Fusion. *Psychological Review*, 119(3): 441–56.
Swanson, G. E. (1960). *The Birth of the Gods: The Origin of Primitive Beliefs*. Ann Arbor: University of Michigan Press.
Tajfel, H. & Turner, J. C. (1979). An Integrative Theory of Intergroup Conflict. In W. G. Austin & S. Worchel (Eds.), *The Social Psychology of Intergroup Relations*, pp. 33–47. Monterey, CA: Brooks-Cole.
Tambiah, S. J. (1979). A Performative Approach to Ritual. *Proceedings of the British Academy*, 65: 113–69.
Taniguchi, Y. & Sanefuji, W. (2017). The Boundaries of Overimitation in Preschool Children: Effects of Target and Tool Use on Imitation of Irrelevant Actions. *Journal of Experimental Child Psychology*, 159: 83–95.
Tasuji, T., Reese, E., Van Mulukom, V., & Whitehouse, H. (2020). Band of Mothers: Childbirth as a Female Bonding Experience. *PLOS One*. 15(10): e0240175. https://doi.org10.1371/journal.pone.0240175.
Tavory, Iddo, Jablonka, Eva, & Ginsburg, Simona (2013). The Reproduction of the Social: A Developmental System Approach. In: Linnda R. Caporael, James Griesemer, &

William Wimsatt (Eds.), *Developing Scaffolds in Evolution, Culture and Cognition: Vienna Series in Theoretical Biology*, pp. 307–325. Cambridge, MA: MIT Press.

Tennie, C., Call, J., & Tomasello, M. (2009). Ratcheting Up the Ratchet: On the Evolution of Cumulative Culture. *Philosophical Transactions of the Royal Society of London. Series B, Biological Sciences*, 364(1528): 2405–15. https://doi.org/10.1098/rstb.2009.0052.

Tetlock, P. (2003). Thinking the Unthinkable: Sacred Values and Taboo Cognitions. *Trends in Cognitive Science*, 7: 320–4.

Tetlock, P. E., Kristel, O. V., & Elson, B. (2000). The Psychology of the Unthinkable: Taboo Trade-offs, Forbidden Base Rates, and Heretical Counterfactuals. *Journal of Personality and Social Psychology*, 78: 853–70.

Thomae, M., Zeitlyn, D., & Van Vugt, M. (2013). Intergroup Contact and Rice Allocation via a Modified Dictator Game in Rural Cameroon. *Field Methods*, 25(1): 74–90.

Thomson, R., Yuki, M., Talhelm, T., Schug, J., Kito, M., Ayanian, A. H., et al. (2018). Relational Mobility Predicts Social Behaviors in 39 Countries and Is Tied to Historical Farming and Threat. *Proceedings of the National Academy of Sciences*, 115(29): 7521–6. https://doi.org/10.1073/pnas.1713191115.

Tinbergen, N. (1951). *The Study of Instinct*. Oxford: Clarendon.

Tinbergen, N. (1963). On Aims and Methods of Ethology. *Zeitschrift für Tierpsychologie*, 20: 410–33. http://dx.doi.org/10.1111/j.1439-0310.1963.tb01161.x.

Tomasello, M., Kruger, A. C., & Ratner, H. H. (1993). Cultural Learning. *Behavioral and Brain Sciences*, 16: 495–511.

Tominey, S. L. & McClelland, M. M. (2011). Red Light, Purple Light: Findings from a Randomized Trial Using Circle Time Games to Improve Behavioral Self-Regulation in Preschool. *Early Education and Development*, 22: 489–519. https://doi.org/10.1080/10409289.2011.574258.

Trigger, Bruce G. (2003). *Understanding Early Civilizations*. Cambridge: Cambridge University Press.

Trota, B. & Johnson, J. (2004). A Brief History of Hazing. In J. Johnson & M. Holman (Eds.), *Making the Team: Inside the World of Sport Initiations and Hazing*, pp. x–xvi. Toronto, Canada: Canadian Scholars' Press Inc.

Turchin, Peter (2007). *War and Peace and War: The Rise and Fall of Empires*. New York: Plume.

Turchin, Peter (2016). *Ultrasociety: How 10,000 Years of War Made Humans the Greatest Cooperators on Earth*. Chaplin, CT: Beresta Books.

Turchin, Peter, Brennan, Rob, Currie, Thomas E., Feeney, Kevin C., François, Pieter, Hoyer, Daniel, et al. (2015). Seshat: The Global History Databank. *Cliodynamics: The Journal of Quantitative History and Cultural Evolution*, 6(1): 77–107.

Turchin, Peter, Currie, Thomas E., Whitehouse, Harvey, François, Pieter, Feeney, Kevin, Mullins, Daniel, et al. (2018). Quantitative Historical Analysis Uncovers a Single Dimension of Complexity that Structures Global Variation in Human Social Organization. *Proceedings of the National Academy of Sciences of the United States of America (PNAS)*, 115(2): E144–51.

Turchin, P. Dupeyron, A., Currie, T. E, Whitehouse, H., François, P., Feeney, K. C., Hoyer, D., et al. (In Prep). The Rise and Fall of Human Sacrifice in the Evolution of Social Complexity.

Turchin, P., Whitehouse, H., François, P., Hoyer, D., Nugent, S., Larson, J., et al. (2019). Explaining the Rise of Moralizing Religions: A test of Competing Hypotheses Using the Seshat Databank. https://doi.org/10.31235/osf.io/2v59j.

Turchin, Peter, Whitehouse, Harvey, François, Pieter, Slingerland, Edward, & Collard, Mark (2012). A Historical Database of Sociocultural Evolution. *Cliodynamics: The Journal of Quantitative History and Cultural Evolution*, 3(2): 271–93.

Turpin, H., Andersen, M., & Lanman, J. (2018). CREDs, CRUDs and Catholic Scandals: Experimentally Investigating the Effects of Religious Paragon Behaviour on Co-religionist Belief. *Religion, Brain and Behavior*, 9(6): 1–13.

Turner, J. C., Hogg, M. A., Oakes, P. J., Reicher, S. D., & Wetherell, M. S. (1987). *Rediscovering the Social Group: A Self-Categorization Theory*. Oxford: Blackwell.

Turner, V. W. (1967). *The Forest of Symbols: Aspects of Ndembu Rituals*. Oxford: Clarendon Press.

Turner, Victor (1969). *The Ritual Process: Structure and Anti-Structure*. Chicago: Aldine Publishing.

Turner, Victor (1974). *Dramas, Fields, and Metaphors: Symbolic Action in Human Society*. Ithaca, NY: Cornell University Press.

Tuzin, Donald (1980). *The Voice of the Tambaran: Truth and Illusion in Ilahita Arapesh Religion*. Berkeley: University of California Press.

Tyler, Stephen. (1986). 'Post-modern Ethnography: From Document of the Occult to Occult Document. In James Clifford & George E. Marcus (Eds.), *Writing Culture: The Poetics and Politics of Ethnography*, pp. 112–140. Berkeley: University of California Press

Urgesi C, Aglioti SM, Skrap M, Fabbro F. (2010). The Spiritual Brain: Selective cortical lesions modulate human self-transcendence. Neuron. *65(3)*:309-19. doi: 10.1016/j.neuron.2010.01.026. PMID: 20159445.

Van Gennep, A. (1960 [1909]). *The Rites of Passage*. Chicago: University Press.

Vázquez, A., Gómez, Á., Ordoñana, J. R., Swann, W. B., & Whitehouse, H. (2017). Sharing Genes Fosters Identity Fusion and Altruism. *Self and Identity*, 16(6): 684–702. https://doi.org/10.1080/15298868.2017.1296887.

Vázquez, Alexandra, Gómez, Ángel & Swann, William B. (2017b). Do Historic Threats to the Group Diminish Identity Fusion and Its Correlates? *Self and Identity*, 16(4): 480–503. https://doi.org/10.1080/15298868.2016.1272485.

Vial, T. (2004). Modes of Religiosity and Changes in Popular Religious Practices at the Time of the Reformation. In H. Whitehouse & L. H. Martin (Eds.), *Theorizing Religions Past: Historical and Archaeological Perspectives*, pp. 143–156. Walnut Creek, CA: AltaMira Press.

Viveiros de Castro, E. (2012). *Cosmological Perspectivism in Amazonia and Elsewhere. HAU: Masterclass Series*, 1: 45–168.

Vredenburgh, C., Kushnir, T., & Casasola, M. (2015). Pedagogical Cues Encourage Toddlers' Transmission of Recently Demonstrated Functions to Unfamiliar Adults. *Developmental Science*, 18(4): 645–54. https://doi.org/10.1111/desc.12233.

Waddington, C. H. (1957). *The Strategy of the Genes*. London: Allen & Unwin.

Wakefield, K. L. & Wann, D. L. (2006). An Examination of Dysfunctional Sport Fans: Method of Classification and Relationships with Problem Behaviours. *Journal of Leisure Research, 38*: 168.

Wallace, Anthony F. C. (1970). *Culture and Personality*, 2nd ed. New York: Random.

Ward-Jackson, Philip (2011). *Public Sculpture of Historic Westminster: Volume 1 (Public Sculpture of Britain LUP)*. Liverpool: Liverpool University Press.

Waters, C. N., Zalasiewicz, J., Summerhayes, C., Barnosky, A. D., Poirier, C., Gałuszka, A., et al. (2016). The Anthropocene Is Functionally and Stratigraphically Distinct from the Holocene. *Science*, 351(6269). https://doi.org/10.1126/science.aad2622.

Watkins, T. (2010). New Light on Neolithic Revolution in Southwest Asia. *Antiquity*, *84*(325): 621–34.

Watson-Jones, Rachel, Legare, Cristine H., Whitehouse, Harvey, & Clegg, Jennifer (2014). Task-Specific Effects of Ostracism on Imitation of Social Convention in Early Childhood. *Evolution and Human Behaviour*, *35*(3): 204–10.

Watson-Jones, Rachel E., Whitehouse, Harvey, & Legare, Cristine H. (2015). In-group Ostracism Increases High Fidelity Imitation in Early Childhood. *Psychological Science*, *27*(1). https://doi.org/10.1177/0956797615607205.

Watts, J., Sheehan, O., Atkinson, Q. D., Bulbulia, J., & Gray, R. D. (2016). Ritual Human Sacrifice Promoted and Sustained the Evolution of Stratified Societies. *Nature*, *532*: 228–31.

Weber, Max (1947). *The Theory of Social and Economic Organization*. New York: The Free Press and the Falcon's Bring Press.

Weber, Max (1958 [1916]). *The Religion of India: The Sociology of Hinduism and Buddhism*. Glencoe: Free Press.

Werbner, R. P. (Ed.) (1977). *Regional Cults*. London: Academic Press.

Wilson, Monica (1957). *Rituals of Kinship Among the Nyakusa*. London: Oxford University Press.

White, Claire (2021). *An Introduction to the Cognitive Science of Religion: Connecting Evolution, Brain, Cognition, and Culture*. London: Routledge.

White, Fiona A., Newson, Martha, Verrelli, Stefano, & Whitehouse, Harvey (2021). Pathways to Prejudice and Outgroup Hostility: Group Alignment and Intergroup Conflict Among Football Fans. *Journal of Applied Social Psychology*. *00*: 1-7. https://doi.org/10.1111/jasp.12773

Whitehouse, H. (1992). Memorable Religions: Transmission, Codification, and Change in Divergent Melanesian Contexts. *Man (N.S.)*, *27*(3): 777–97. Reprinted in P. Pachis & D. Wiebe (Eds.) (2014), *In the Sights of History and the Cognitive Sciences*, pp. 479–510. Sheffield: Equinox Publishing.

Whitehouse, H. (1995). *Inside the Cult: Religious Innovation and Transmission in Papua New Guinea*. Oxford: Oxford University Press.

Whitehouse, H. (1996a). Rites of Terror: Emotion, Metaphor, and Memory in Melanesian Initiation Cults. *Journal of the Royal Anthropological Institute (N.S.)*, *2*(4): 703–15. Reprinted in John Corrigan (Ed.) (2004), *Religion and Emotion: Approaches and Interpretations*. Oxford: Oxford University Press.

Whitehouse, H. (1996b). Jungles and Computers: Neuronal Group Selection and the Epidemiology of Representations. *Journal of the Royal Anthropological Institute (N.S.)*, *1*: 99–116

Whitehouse, H. (2000). *Arguments and Icons: Divergent Modes of Religiosity*. Oxford: Oxford University Press.

Whitehouse, H. (2001a). Transmissive Frequency, Ritual, and Exegesis. *Journal of Cognition and Culture*, *1*(2): 167–82.

Whitehouse, H. (Ed.) (2001b). *The Debated Mind: Evolutionary Psychology Versus Ethnography*. Oxford: Berg.

Whitehouse, H. (2002). Religious Reflexivity and Transmissive Frequency. *Social Anthropology*, *10*(1): 91–103.

Whitehouse, H. (2003). Why Do We Need Cognitive Theories of Religion? In T. Light & B. C. Wilson (Eds.), *Religion as a Human Capacity: A Festschrift in Honor of E. Thomas Lawson*, pp. 65–88. Leiden: Brill.

Whitehouse, H. (2004). *Modes of Religiosity: A Cognitive Theory of Religious Transmission*. Walnut Creek, CA: AltaMira Press.

Whitehouse, H. (2008). Cognitive Evolution and Religion; Cognition and Religious Evolution. In J. Bulbulia, R. Sosis, E. Harris, R. Genet, C. Genet & K.Wyman (eds.) *The Evolution of Religion: Studies, theories, and critiques*, Santa Margarita, CA: Collins Foundation Press.

Whitehouse, H. (2011). The Coexistence Problem in Psychology, Anthropology, and Evolutionary Theory. *Human Development, 54*: 191–9.

Whitehouse, Harvey (2012a). Ritual, Cognition, and Evolution. In R. Sun (Ed.), *Grounding the Social Sciences in the Cognitive Sciences*, pp. 265–284. Cambridge, MA: MIT Press.

Whitehouse, Harvey (2012b). Human Rites: Rituals Bind Us, in Modern Societies and Prehistoric Tribes Alike. But Can Our Loyalties Stretch to All of Humankind? *Aeon*. http://www.aeonmagazine.com/being-human/harvey-whitehouse-ritual/.

Whitehouse, H. (2013a). Three Wishes for the World (with Comment). *Cliodynamics, 4*(2): 281–323.

Whitehouse, H. (2013b). Immortality, Creation, and Regulation: Updating Durkheim's Theory of the Sacred. In Dimitris Xygalatas & Lee W. McCorkle (Eds.), *Mental Culture: Classical Social Theory and the Cognitive Science of Religion*, pp. 66–79. Durham, NC: Acumen.

Whitehouse, H. (2013c). Rethinking Proximate Causation and Development in Religious Evolution. In P. J. Richerson & M. H. Christiansen (Eds.), *Cultural Evolution: Society, Technology, Language, and Religion (Strungmann Forum Reports)*, pp. 350–364. Cambridge, MA: MIT Press.

Whitehouse, H. (2016a). Developing the Field Site Concept for the Study of Cultural Evolution (with Comment). *Cliodynamics, 7*(2): 228–87.

Whitehouse, H. (2016b). Ritual and Social Evolution: Understanding Social Complexity Through Data. In B. Bozic, et al. (Eds.), *Computational History and Data-Driven Humanities*, pp. 1–12. Springer, Cham. https://doi.org/10.1007/978-3-319-46224-01.

Whitehouse, H. (2016c). What Motivates Extreme Self-Sacrifice? *Pacific Standard, 9*(2): 26–31.

Whitehouse, H. (2018a). Dying for the Group: Towards a General Theory of Extreme Self-Sacrifice. *Behavioural and Brain Sciences, 41*(e192): 1–62. https://doi.org/10.1017/S0140525X18000249.

Whitehouse, H. (2018b). The Dark Side to Loving a Group. In K. Almqvist & A. Linklater (Eds.), *Nations, States, and Empires: Perspectives from the Engelsberg Seminar 2017*, pp. 213–219. Stockholm: Axel and Margaret Ax:son Johnson Foundation.

Whitehouse, H. & Fitzgerald, R. (2020). Fusion and Reform: The Potential for Identity Fusion to Reduce Recidivism and Improve Reintegration. *Anthropology in Action.* 27 (1): 1–13. https://doi:10.3167/aia.2020.270101

Whitehouse, H., François, P., Savage, P. E., Currie, T. E., Feeney, K. C., Cioni, E., et al. (2020). A New Era in the Study of Global History Is Born but It Needs to Be Nurtured. *Journal of Cognitive Historiography, 5*(1–2): 142–58. https://doi.org/10.1558/jch.39422.

Whitehouse, Harvey & François, Pieter (2017). Ritual, Emotion, and Power. In Merridee L. Bailey & Katie Barclay (Eds.), *Emotion, Ritual and Power in Europe, 1200–1920*, pp. 285–303. London: Palgrave Macmillan.

Whitehouse, Harvey, François, Pieter, Cioni, Enrico, Levine, Jill, Hoyer, Daniel, Reddish, Jenny, et al. (2019). Conclusion: Was There Ever an Axial Age? In Daniel Hoyer & Jenny Reddish (Eds.), *The Seshat History of the Axial Age*, pp. 395–408. Chaplin, CT: Beresta Books.

Whitehouse, H. & Hodder, I. (2010). Modes of Religiosity at Çatalhöyük. In I. Hodder. (Ed.), *Religion in the Emergence of Civilization: Çatalhöyük as a Case Study*, pp. 122–145. Cambridge: Cambridge University Press.

Whitehouse, Harvey, Jong, Jonathan, Buhrmester, Michael D., Gómez, Ángel, Bastian, Brock, Kavanagh, Christopher M., et al. (2017). The Evolution of Extreme Cooperation via Intense Shared Experiences. *Nature: Scientific Reports*, 7(44292). https://doi.org/10.1038/srep44292.

Whitehouse, Harvey, Kahn, Ken, Hochberg, Michael E., & Bryson, Joanna J. (2012). The Role for Simulations in Theory Construction for the Social Sciences: Case Studies Concerning Divergent Modes of Religiosity. *Religion, Brain, and Behaviour*, 2(3): 182–201.

Whitehouse, Harvey & Kavanagh, Christopher M. (2021). What Is the Role of Ritual in Binding Communities Together? In Justin Barrett (Ed.), *OUP Handbook on the Cognitive Science of Religion*, pp. . Oxford: Oxford University Press.

Whitehouse, H. & Laidlaw, J. (2004). *Ritual and Memory: Towards a Comparative Anthropology of Religion*. Walnut Creek, CA: AltaMira Press.

Whitehouse, Harvey & and Laidlaw, James (Eds.) (2007). *Religion, Anthropology and Cognitive Science*, Durham: Carolina Academic Press.

Whitehouse, H. & Lanman, J. A. (2014). The Ties That Bind Us: Ritual, Fusion and Identification. *Current Anthropology*, 55(6): 674–95. https://doi.org/10.1086/678698.

Whitehouse, Harvey & McCauley, Robert N. (Eds.) (2005). *Mind and Religion: Psychological and Cognitive Foundations of Religiosity*, Walnut Creek, CA: AltaMira Press.

Whitehouse, Harvey & McQuinn, Brian (2012). Ritual and Violence: Divergent Modes of Religiosity and Armed Struggle. In M. Juergensmeyer, M. Kitts, & M. Jerryson (Eds.), *Oxford Handbook of Religion and Violence*, pp. 597–619. Oxford: Oxford University Press.

Whitehouse, H., McQuinn, B., Buhrmester, M., & Swann, W. B. (2014). Brothers in Arms: Warriors Bond Like Family. *Proceedings of the National Academy of Sciences*, 111(50): 17783–5. Early Edition. www.pnas.org/cgi/doi/10.1073/pnas.1416284111.

Whitehouse, H. & Martin, L. H. (Eds.) (2004). *Implications of Cognitive Science for the Study of Religion*, Special Issue of *Method and Theory in the Study of Religion*, 16(3): ISSN 0943-3058 (print), 1570–0682 (online).

Whitehouse, H. & Martin, L. H. (Eds.) (2005). History, Memory, and Cognition, Special Issue of *Historical Reflections/Réflexions Historiques*, 31(2): 307–18.

Whitehouse, H., Mazzucato, C., Hodder, I., & Atkinson, Q. D. (2014). Modes of Religiosity and the Evolution of Social Complexity at Çatalhöyük. In Ian Hodder (Ed.), *Vital Matters: Religion in the Organization and Transformation of a Neolithic Society*, pp. 134–156. Cambridge: Cambridge University Press.

Whiten, A. (2017). A Comparative and Evolutionary Analysis of the Cultural Cognition of Humans and Other Apes. *Spanish Journal of Psychology*, 19: E98.

Whiten, A., Allan, G., Devlin, S., Kseib, N., Raw, N., & McGuigan, N. (2016). Social Learning in the Real-World: 'Over-Imitation' Occurs in Both Children and Adults Unaware of Participation in an Experiment and Independently of Social Interaction. *PLOS One*, 11(7): e0159920. https://doi.org/10.1371/journal.pone.0159920.

Whiten, Andrew, McGuigan, Nicola, Marshall-Pescini, Sarah, & Hopper, Lydia M. (2009). Emulation, Imitation, Over-imitation and the Scope of Culture for Child and Chimpanzee. *Philosophical Transactions of the Royal Society B: Biological Sciences*, 364: 2417–28.

Whitson, J. A. & Galinsky, A. D. (2008). Lacking Control Increases Illusory Pattern Perception. *Science*, 322(5898): 115–17.

Willard, Aiyana, Baimel, Adam, Turpin, Hugh, Jong, Jonathan, & Whitehouse, Harvey (2020). Rewarding the Good and Punishing the Bad: The Role of Karma and Afterlife Beliefs in Shaping Moral Norms. *Evolution and Human Behaviour*, 41(5): 385–96.

Williams, F. E. (1928). *Orokaiva Magic*. London: Humphrey Milford.
Wilson, D. S. (2002). *Darwin's Cathedral: Evolution, Religion, and the Nature of Society*. Chicago: University of Chicago Press.
Wilson, D. S. (2020). *This View of Life: Completing the Darwinian Revolution*. New York: Knopf Doubleday.
Wiltermuth, S. S. & Heath, C. (2009). Synchrony and Cooperation. *Psychological Science 20*: 1–5. https://doi.org/10.1111/j.1467-9280.2008.02253.x.
Womack, Mari (1992). Why Athletes Need Ritual: A Study of Magic Among Professional Athletes. Shirl J. Hoffman (Ed.), *Sport and Religion*, pp. 191–202. Champaign, IL: Human Kinetics.
Woodburn, James (1982). Egalitarian Societies. *Man, NS, 17*(3): 431–51.
Worsley, Peter (1957). *The Trumpet Shall Sound: A Study of Cargo Cults in Melanesia*. London: MacGibbon & Kee.
Wright, Perry B. & Erdal, Kristi J. (2008). Sport Superstition as a Function of Skill Level and Task Difficulty. *Journal of Sport Behaviour*, 31: 187–99.
Wright, Robert (1994). *The Moral Animal: Evolutionary Psychology and Everyday Life*. London: Abacus.
Wulf, Christoph (2013). *Anthropology: A Continental Perspective*. Chicago: University of Chicago Press.
Xygalatas, D. (2007). *Firewalking in Northern Greece: A Cognitive Approach to High-Arousal Rituals*. PhD Dissertation, Queen's University Belfast, UK.
Xygalatas, Dimitris (2012). *The Burning Saints: Cognition and Culture in the Fire-walking Rituals of the Anastenaria*. London: Routledge.
Xygalatas, D., Mitkidis, P., Fischer, R., Reddish, P. Skewes, J., Geertz, A. W., Roepstorff, A., & Bulbulia, J. (2013). Extreme Rituals Promote Prosociality. *Psychological Science, 24*(8): 1602–5.
Young, Michael W. (1972). *Fighting With Food: Leadership, Values and Social Control in a Massim Society*. Cambridge: Cambridge University Press.
Yuki, M. & Schug, J. (2012). Relational Mobility: A Socioecological Approach to Personal Relationships. In O. Gillath, G. E. Adams, & A. D. Kunkel (Eds.), *New Directions in Close Relationships: Integrating Across Disciplines and Theoretical Approaches*, pp. 137–51. Washington, DC: American Psychological Association.
Yuki, M., Schug, J., Horikawa, H., Takemura, K., Sato, K., Yokota, K., & Kamaya, K. (2007). *Development of a Scale to Measure Perceptions of Relational Mobility in Society* Center for Experimental Research in Social Sciences, Hokkaido University [Working Paper].
Yustisia, W., Putra, I. E., Kavanagh, C., Whitehouse, H., & Rufaedah, A. (2020). The Role of Religious Fundamentalism and Tightness-Looseness in Promoting Collective Narcissism and Extreme Group Behavior. *Psychology of Religion and Spirituality, 12*(2): 231–40. http://dx.doi.org/10.1037/rel0000269.
Zani, B. & Kirchler, E. (1991). When Violence Overshadows the Spirit of Sporting Competition: Italian Football Fans and Their Clubs. *Journal of Community and Applied Social Psychology*, 1: 5–21.

Author Index

For the benefit of digital users, indexed terms that span two pages (e.g., 52–53) may, on occasion, appear on only one of those pages.

Aberle, D. F. 53–4
Alcorta, C. 46–7, 137, 181–2
Andersen, M. 120–1
Anderson, B. 107
Anquetil-Duperron, A. 116
Apps, M. A. J. 100
Arias, R. M. 38–9
Aron, E. & A. 89
Aronson, E. 46–7, 84
Asad, T. 5
Atkinson, Q. 49–50, 54–5, 74–5, 78–80, 85, 104–5, 112–14, 118, 137
Atran, S. 152, 193
Axelrod, R. 152

Bainbridge, W. 62–3
Balée, W. L. 79
Barnard, A. 79
Barrett, J. L. 36–7, 54–5, 88, 136–7, 143
Barth, F. 41–2, 44–5, 57, 83–6
Bateson, P. 2
Bateson, G. 193
Bayly, S. 72
Beaver, W. N. 84
Beck, R. 71–2
Bell, C. 4–7, 15
Bellah, R. N. 114–17
Bellwood, P. 106–7
Benedict, R. 53, 177–8
Bering, J. M. 60
Berner, U. 72
Bersabe, R. 38–9
Berwick, D. A. 9–10
Billig, M. 114
Binmore, K. G. 137
Bleak, J. L. 38–9
Bloch, M. 4–5, 10, 12–13, 15, 40–1, 173–4, 177
Bloom, P. 60–2, 176
Bocock, R. 4–5
Bodenhorn, B. 9
Bogaard, A. 78–80, 106–7, 198–9
Boster, J. S. 38–9, 76, 83–4
Bourdieu, P. 4–5

Boyd, R. 50, 181–2
Boyer, P. 4–5, 30–1, 33–4, 44–6, 48–9, 61–2, 121–2, 134, 143, 149–50, 175, 180, 193
Bressler, E. R. 46–7
Brewer, J. 183–4
Brewer, M. B. 110
Brown, R. 82–3
Brown, P. 48
Brunton, R. 44–5
Buhrmester, M. 22, 54–5, 83, 89, 92–3, 98, 100–1, 104, 108–10, 152–3, 161–2, 166–7, 192–3
Bulbulia, J. 55–6
Burger, J. M. 38–9
Burnham, D. 104
Buss, D. M. 174–5
Buttlemann, D. 27–8

Call, J. 24
Callan, M. J. 61–2
Caramazza, A. 174
Carey, S. 176
Carley, K. M. 60
Case, T. I. 38–9
Chasteen, J. C. 48
Chinnery, E. W. P. 84
Cho, P. S. 133–4
Choi, V. K. 156
Cialdini, R. B. 97–8
Cili, S. 85–6
Cimino, A. 85
Clark, A. L. 69–70
Clarke, J. 129
Clegg, J. M. 27
Cohen, E. A. 60, 136–7
Connerton, P. 4–5
Conway, M. A. 82–3, 85–6
Coombe, R. 180–1
Corriveau, K. H. 27
Cosmides, L. 129–30, 134
Cowan, M. 166–7
Currie, T. 106–7, 113, 115
Curry, O. S. 5–6, 22, 118, 162, 165, 188, 202

Da Cunha Bastos, F. 154
de Waal, F. B. M. 176
de Zavala, A. G. 111
Decety, J. 114
Dennett, D. 27–8
DeVore, I. 8–9, 123
DiYanni, C. J. 61–2
Douglas, M. 5, 10, 15, 193
Dulaney, S. 4–5, 149–50
Dunlop, W. L. 85–6
Durkheim, É. 10, 84, 177–8

Ebbinghaus, H. 19, 107–8
Ebner, J. 157
Edwards, A. 38–9
Eisenstadt, S. N. 116
Ellard, J. H. 61–2
Ember, C. R. & Ember, M. 74
Ensor, P. 183–4
Erdal, K. J. 38–9
Evans-Pritchard, E. E. 36–7, 172–3, 177

Fallers, L. A. 123
Farah, M. J. 174–5
Fehr, E. 114
Felson, R. B. 38–9
Fernandez, J. W. 4–5
Fessler, D. M. T. 114
Feynman, R. 107–8
Fincher, C. L. 5
Firth, R. 138, 175–7
Fischbacher, U. 114
Fiske, A. P. 4–5, 149–50
Fitzgerald, R. 21–2
Flannery, K. 114–16
Fodor, J. A. 129
Ford, C. E. 97–8
Fortes, M. 123
François, P. 185
Frederick, C. M. 38–9

Gächter, S. 114
Galinsky, A. D. 38–9
Gantley, M. 78–80, 106–7, 198–9
Gardiner, A. K. 27
Geertz, C. 47, 180–1
Gelfand, M. J. 45, 114, 120–2
Gell, A. 193
Gellén, K. 28
Gellner, D. 5–6, 44, 53–4, 58, 172–3, 175, 180–1
Ginsburg, S. 131–2
Gluckman, M. 4–5, 8–9, 43, 177
Gmelch, G. 38–9
Gobet, F. 87–8

Godelier, M. 119
Goffman, E. 4–5
Goldschmidt, W. R. 49–50
Gómez, Á. 98–9, 110–11, 152
Goody, J. 193
Gopnik, A. 28
Goring-Morris, A. N. 106–7
Göritz, A. S. 99
Gragg, D. L. 54–5
Green, M. 196–7
Greene, D. 47
Gunter, G. 29

Haidt, J. 114
Halbwachs, M. 177–8
Hansen, I. G. 152
Harrison, S. J. 9–10
Haslam, N. 97–8
Hastrup, K. 180–1
Heath, C. 6–7, 48, 114
Henrich, J. 24, 50, 84, 120–1, 129–30, 137, 181–2
Hermann, P. A. 28, 32
Hertz, R. 10–12
Hervik, P. 180–1
Heyes, C. 26–7, 182
Hillis, V. 174–5
Hinde, R. A. 54–5
Hobson, N. M. 46–7
Hochberg, M. E. 106–7
Hodder, I. 19, 24, 54–5, 76–9, 103–4, 112–13, 122, 197–8
Højbjerg, C. K. 72–3, 123
Holbraad, M. 174
Holmbeck, G. N. 146
Holmwood, J. 179–80
Homans, G. C. 38–9
Hood, B. M. 36–7, 60
Horner, V. 27
Horton, R. 37–8
House, P. 47
Houseman, M. 4–5
Hove, M. J. 4–5
Howe, L. 72–3
Humphrey, C. 40–1
Hviding, E. 9–10

Ingold, T. 180–1
Irons, W. 84
Iteanu, A. 84

Jablonka, E. 131–2
Jackson, J. C. 99
Jackson, M. 172–3

Jagiello, R. 26–7, 182
James, W. 190–1, 193
Jaspers, K. 116–17
Jiménez, J. 90
Johnson, D. 61
Johnson, K. 54–5
Johnson, J. 83–4
Jong, J. 31, 54–5, 95–6, 123–4
Juillerat, B. 44–5

Kahn, D. T. 156
Kapferer, B. 4–5
Kapitány, R. 4–6, 26–8, 30–2, 54–5, 83
Kaufer, D. S. 60
Kavanagh, C. M. 5–6, 54–5, 83, 93–4, 96, 110–11, 121–4, 157, 191
Kawano, S. 123–4
Keil, F. C. 27, 136–7
Kelemen, D. 60–2, 137
Kertzer, D. 4–9, 43, 47, 121
Ketola, K. 54–5
Khaldūn, I. 46–7
King, L. A. 85–6
Kinzler, K. D. 174–5
Kirchler, E. 154
Klar, Y. 156
Konvalinka, I. 84, 133–4
Kreinath, J. 4–5
Kress, H. C. 38–9, 76, 83–4
Kristoffer, N. 30–1
Kuijt, I. 106–7
Kulik, J. 82–3

La Fontaine, J. S. 4–5
Laidlaw, J. 40–1, 54–5, 72
Laland, K. N. 2, 50
Lane, J. E. 54–5, 107–9
Langergraber, K. 102
Lanman, J. A. 6–7, 19, 51, 89, 91, 102, 114, 120–1
Lassegard, M. 97–8
Lawson, E. T. 4–5, 58, 88
Lawther, J. D. 154
Leach, E. 4–5, 40–1, 175–6, 180
Leacock, E. 7
Lee, R. 9, 123
Legare, C. H. 3, 26–9, 34, 39, 170–1, 190
Leslie, A. M. 176
Lévi-Strauss, C. 174, 180, 193
Lewis, G. 193
Lieberman, D. 102
Liénard, P. 4–5, 30–1, 48–9, 61–2, 122, 134, 149–50
Lilgendahl, J. P. 85–6
Lincoln, B. 43

Livingstone, K. R. 133
Lynn, A. L. 38–9
Lyons, D. E. 27

Makinson, J. 27
Malinowski, B. 7–8, 15, 49–50, 123, 172–3
Marcus, J. 114–16
Marcus, G. E. 174
Martin, L. H. 18, 54–5, 57, 82
Marx, K. 173–4
Mauldin, B. 8–9
Mauss, M. 10
Mazzucato, C. 78
McAdams, D. P. 85–6
McArthur, M. 44–5
McBride, C. K. 146
McCauley, R. N. 4–5, 36–7, 54–5, 58, 88, 136, 174–5
McClelland, M. M. 31
McCloskey, M. 176
McGranaghan, M. 79
McGuigan, N. 27
McKay, R. 31, 47–8
McLean, K. C. 85–6
McMurtry, J. 173–4
McQuinn, B. 55, 99, 104–5
Mead, M. 177–8
Meade, A. 50
Meng, X. 136–7
Mesoudi, A. 50
Mills, J. 46–7, 84
Mithen, S. 54–5
Mitkidis, P. 30–1
Moritz, M. 152–3
Morley, I. 114
Mullins, D. 5–6, 22, 49, 114, 117–18, 137, 165, 185, 188, 202
Murad, M. 154
Murdock, G. P. 74
Murray, D. 122
Muzzulini, B. 162–3

Nadel, S. F. 4–5
Nagell, K. 27
Nakawake, Y. 136–7
Nelson, J. K. 123–4
Newberg, A. B. 133
Newson, M. 21–2, 54–5, 83, 93, 95–6, 98–101, 133
Nicol, J. E. 61–2
Nielbo, K. L. 30–2
Nielsen, M. 3–5, 26–8, 30–1, 170–1
Nnoko-Mewanu, J. 152–3
Norbeck, E. 43
Norenzayan, A. 120–1

Olguin R. S. 27
Olivola, C. Y. 84

Pachis, P. 18, 54–5, 57, 82
Pagel, M. 50
Paikoff, R. L. 146
Park, J. H. 102
Parkin, D. 4–5, 187
Parry, J. 12–13, 15
Payne, R. K. 4–5
Pedersen, M. 174
Pedwell, C. 180–1
Peel, J. D. Y. 53–4, 72
Peers, L. 178–9
Persinger, M. A. 133
Piaget, J. 28
Pillemer, D. 94–5
Platvoet, J. G. 4–5
Poole, F. J. P. 84
Povinelli, D. 176
Powell, R. 129
Preston, S. D. 176
Previc, F. H. 133
Pyysiäinen, I. 54–5, 58
Pyszczynski, T. 149–50

Quinn, N. 180–1

Radcliffe-Brown, A. R. 15, 177
Rakoczy, H. 148
Raspaud, M. 154
Raspin, C. 85–6
Reader, I. 123–4
Reddish, P. 99
Redfield, R. 43
Rennung, M. 99
Richerson, P. 50, 181–2
Richert, R. A. 86–7
Ridley, M. 48
Risen, J. L. 4–5
Roccas, S. 156
Roos, P. 103–4
Ross, L. 47
Rozin, P. 48–9
Rudski, J. M. 38–9
Russell, Y. I. 87–8
Rybanska, V. 31, 188

Sahlins, M. 7, 123
Salali, G. D. 106–7
Salovey, P. 85–6
Sanefuji, W. 27
Saussure, F. 180
Schaller, M. 102, 122

Schechner, R. 4–5
Schjoedt, U. 31–2
Schmitt, S. A. 31
Schug, J. 103–4, 123
Schunk, D. H. 19
Seligman, A. B. 40–1
Severi, C. 4–5
Shafir, E. 84
Shankland, D. 43, 72
Sheppard, S. R. J. 145
Shore, B. 8–9
Singer, P. 145
Singer, J. A. 85–6
Slone, J. 67, 137, 143
Smith, J. Z. 4–5
Smith, K. 27
Smith, R. W. 46–7
Smollan, D. 89
Snoek, J. 4–5
Snow, C. P. 182
Snyder, C. R. 97–8
Sørensen, J. 30–2
Sosis, R. 38–9, 46–7, 76, 83–5, 103–4, 137, 181–2
Souza, A. L. 39
Spelke, E. S. 174–5
Sperber, D. 74, 129, 193
Spiro, M. E. 172–3
Staal, F. 4–5, 40–1
Stark, R. 62–3
Stewart, P. 4–5, 86–7
Stopa, L. 85–6
Strathern, A. 4–5, 44, 119
Stausberg, M. 4–5
Strauss, C. 180–1
Stuart-Glennie, J. 116
Subbotsky, E. 36–7
Swann, W. B. 18, 83, 88–92, 98–9, 102, 104, 108–11, 152, 193

Tajfel, H. 19–20, 88, 90–1, 108–9, 114
Tambiah, S. J. 4–5
Tanabe, G. J. 123–4
Taniguchi, Y. 27
Tasuji, T. 83, 95
Tavory, I. 131–3
Tennie, C. 24
Tetlock, P. E. 152
Thomae, M. 192–3
Thomson, R. 123–4
Thornhill, R. 5
Tinbergen, N. 2–3, 185
Tomasello, M. 24, 27, 148
Tominey, S. L. 31

Trigger, B. G. 114–16
Trota, B. 83–4
Turchin, P. 106–7, 113–19, 185–6, 199
Turner, V. W. 4–5, 15, 53–4
Turner, J. C. 19–20, 88, 90–1, 108–9
Turpin, H. 120–1
Tuzin, D. 41–2
Tyler, S. 174

Urgesi, C. 133

Van Baal, J. 4–5
Van Baaren, T. P. 4–5
Van Gennep, A. 4, 131
Van Vugt, M. 192–3
Vázquez, A. 18, 92, 98–9
Vial, T. 70–1
Viveiros de Castro, E. 174

Waddington, C. H. 128, 131–3, 135, 137
Wakefield, K. L. 154
Waldman, M. R. 133
Walker, L. J. 85–6
Wallace, M. A. 174–5
Wallace, A. F. C. 177–8
Wann, D. L. 154
Ward-Jackson, P. 8

Warneken, F. 148
Waters, C. N. 169
Watkins, T. 106–7
Watson-Jones, R. E. 26–8, 33–4
Weber, M. 44
White, F. A. 100–1
White, C. 143
Whiten, A. 27, 38, 50
Whitson, J. A. 38–9
Willard, A. 187
Wilson, D. S. 2, 4–5, 181–2
Wiltermuth, S. S. 6–7, 48, 114
Womack, M. 38–9
Woodburn, J. 123
Worsley, P. 9
Wright, P. B. 38–9
Wright, R. 114
Wulf, C. 4–5

Xygalatas, D. 43, 54–5, 84–6

Young, M. W. 7–8, 27
Yuki, M. 103–4, 123
Yustisia, W. 83, 111, 122, 157

Zani, B. 154
Zeitlyn, D. 152–3, 192–3

Subject Index

For the benefit of digital users, indexed terms that span two pages (e.g., 52–53) may, on occasion, appear on only one of those pages.

Agriculture (*see also* Neolithic) 7, 17–18, 55, 76, 81, 106, 112–13, 122, 124–5, 145–6, 152–3
Agent-Based Models 64–8, 137–8
Anastenaria 57–8
Anatolia 78
Anthropology 7–8, 10, 15, 22, 40–1, 68–74, 172–82, 185–7, 192–3
Archaeology 2–4, 54–5, 68–74, 106–7, 113, 184–5, 198–9
Axial Age 114–20, 125, 151, 199
Azande 36–7

Baktaman 57
Barrier-Crossing Leadership 151, 166–9
Brain Scanning 1–2, 133–4
Bravery 8–9
Brexit 22, 151, 162–3
Bronze Age 78, 145–6

Candomblé 39–40
Çatalhöyük 76–8, 112–13
Catholics 42–3, 71
Causal opacity 2–3, 7, 16–17, 24–5, 27–46, 49, 57, 86, 128, 147–8, 154, 162–3, 182
Cecil The Lion 98
Child Development (*see also* Developmental Psychology) 1–3, 6–7, 24–5, 27–35, 49, 51–2, 61, 85–6, 94–5, 135, 143–4, 148, 153, 170, 188, 196, 201
Christianity (*see also* Missionaries, Catholics, Protestants) 7–8, 58–9, 68–71, 73, 108–9, 119–20, 123–4, 138, 140–1, 145–6, 179
Climate Change 22, 145, 151–3, 164–5, 168, 200
Cognitive-Developmental Landscape (*see also* Multilevel Landscapes, Waddington, C. H.), 135–42, 148–51
Cognitive Optimum Effect 46
Cohesion (*see* Fusion, Identification)
Cooperation (*see also* Fusion, Identification, Morality):
 And collective ritual 46–8
 Conditioned on Past Experience 44, 51, 102–3, 105

 And Goal-demotion 30–1
 And Imagistic Mode 83–6, 89, 105
 And Public Policy 145, 151, 161–9, 200–1
 Scale of 44–6, 104–6, 114, 119–26, 151, 198–9
 And Social Synchrony 48
 Varieties of 6–10, 118, 188
Costly signalling 85, 137, 197–8
Covid-19 21, 147, 149–50
CREDs and CRUDs 121–6
Cultural Evolution 19, 24, 46–51, 112–20, 127–44, 185, 199–200

Defusion 155–9, 200
Developmental Psychology (*see also* Child Development) 28, 201–2
Doctrinal Mode (*see also* Modes of Religiosity) 17–18, 19–21, 55, 60, 68–73, 77–81, 99, 106–26, 161–8, 198–200
Dysphoria 74–6, 85, 87–8, 95, 97–8, 160

Epigenetic Landscape (*see also* Multilevel Landscapes, Waddington, C. H.), 20–1, 74–6, 128, 130–5, 139–42, 146–7, 149–51, 170–1, 183, 199–200
Euphoria 5–6, 41, 75–6, 87–8, 93–4, 97–8, 197–8
Evolutionary Psychology 2, 127–30, 143, 174–5, 199–200
Experiments 3–4, 27–34, 38–9, 54–5, 85–92, 148, 152, 161, 170–5, 184, 187–95, 201–3

Familial Ties 7, 19, 89, 91–2, 100, 110, 200
Fairness 9, 114, 125, 164–5, 193
Farmer-Herder Conflict 152–3
Football 21–2, 83, 93, 95–6, 98–101, 133, 154–6, 159–61, 168
Fusion (*see also* Barrier-Crossing Leadership, Brexit, Cooperation, Imagistic Mode, Volatility Index):
 Evolution of 19, 101–5
 Extended fusion 19–20, 22, 161–5
 And Imagistic Practices 83, 88–101, 105
 As Psychological Construct 18

SUBJECT INDEX   239

And Violence 21–2, 100–1
And Peaceful Pro-Group Action 21–2, 100–1, 159–61, 168–9, 196–203

Galvanic Skin Response 86–7
Group Bonding (*see* Group Psychology, Fusion, Identification)
Group Psychology 1–2, 83, 88, 199, 201

Haka (*see also* Māori) 99
Hazard Precaution System 48–9, 62, 122, 134–5
Hierarchy 8–9, 42–4, 57–8, 69, 112–15, 198–9
History 68–74
Human Relations Area Files 74, 79–80
Human Sacrifice 114–16, 125–6, 199

Ibo 196–7
Identification 19–20, 22, 34, 69, 90–1, 96–8, 106–26, 150, 158, 161–4, 168–9
Identity Fusion (*see* Fusion)
Imagistic Mode, (*see also* Modes of Religiosity), 17–19, 21–2, 46, 55–8, 64–74, 76, 105, 112–13, 119–21, 123–6, 133, 150–61, 163, 166, 168, 197–8, 200–2
Immanentism Versus Transcendentalism 44–6
Immanent Justice 61–3, 66, 137, 139–40
Initiation 13–15, 44, 51, 56–7, 68–9, 74–6, 84–8, 94–6, 98–9, 103–5, 123, 152–4, 158–60
Intergroup Conflict 21–2, 83–4, 89, 151–6, 164–7, 198

Kivung 58–69
Kunimaipa 44–5
Kwakiutl 53

Libyan Revolution 100, 104, 152, 192
Loyalty 6–7, 10, 17–18, 27–8, 46–7, 82–4, 98–9, 109, 160, 165, 168, 183, 196–7

Magical Rituals 25, 36–40
Māori (*see also* Haka) 99
Mambila 153–4, 159–60, 192–3
Material Correlates Analysis (MCA) 78–80
Memory 3–6, 53, 56, 77, 82–3, 85–6, 88, 91–5, 105, 107–9, 121–2, 124, 135, 139, 141, 177–8
Mind-Body Dualism 60–3, 66, 136–7, 139–40, 143
Missionaries 58–9, 119–20, 140–1, 145–6, 190–1
Mithraism 71–2
Modelling 28–35, 54–5, 64–8, 79–80, 102–3, 119–20, 148, 170–3, 185–6, 194, 196
Modes of Religiosity (*see also* Doctrinal Mode, Imagistic Mode) 17–20, 53–81, 112–13

Morality, (*see also* Cooperation) 117–20, 164–5, 167–8
Multilevel Landscapes (*see also* Cognitive-Developmental Landscape, Epigenetic Landscape, Social-Historical Landscape) 139–42, 145–51

Neolithic (*see also* Agriculture) 7, 19–20, 79–80, 112–13, 145–6
Normative Tightness (*see* Tightness-Looseness)

Offenders 21–2, 151, 155, 159–61, 168, 200
Orokaiva 39
Ostracism 16, 33–4, 103–4, 196
Overimitation 16, 24–52, 128, 170

Palaeolithic 55, 78, 83–4, 114, 145
Phenotypic matching 91–2, 102, 105
Polarization 161–8
Prisoners (*see* offenders)
Public Policy (*see also* Climate Change, Covid-19, Farmer-Herder Conflict, Populism, Twinning Project, Volatility Index) 4, 21, 145–51, 190–1, 193, 196–7
Pomio Kivung (*see* Kivung)
Populism 161–8
Promiscuous Teleology 61–3, 66, 139–40
Property 9–10, 118, 165
Protestants 43, 68–71, 108, 135, 138

Quimbanda 39–40

Reciprocity 7–8, 19, 51, 125, 164–5, 199, 202–3
Relational Mobility (RMob) 103–4, 123–6
Rites of Passage 1, 4–5, 7, 13, 94, 97–8, 153
Rites of Terror 18, 83–5, 153
Ritual (*see also* Rites of Passage, Rites of Terror, Ritual Form Hypothesis, Ritual Stance versus Instrumental Stance, Symbolist School):
  Definitions of 4–5
  And Delayed Gratification 31–2, 188
  And Exegesis 40–6, 54, 69, 72–3, 83–4, 182–3
  Frequency of 17–19, 45–6, 53–81, 88, 104–9, 112–13, 122, 124–5, 127, 136, 168
Ritual Form Hypothesis 5
Ritual Stance Versus Instrumental Stance, 16–17, 25–40, 49, 149–50, 170–1, 182–3, 196
Routinization 4–5, 19, 45–6, 58, 107–9, 112–13, 121–2, 124–5, 150, 198–9

Self-Sacrifice 2–3, 15–16, 19–20, 51, 82–105
Seshat 20, 113–21, 201–2

SUBJECT INDEX

Shared Experience 18, 54, 91–9, 102, 104–5, 110, 150, 155, 157–69
Simbu 20–1
Silo Effect 48, 130, 171, 182–95, 200–1
Social-Historical Landscape (*see also* Multilevel Landscapes, Waddington, C. H.) 21, 138–42, 146–7, 150
Social Theory 22–3, 172–82, 193
Spontaneous Exegetical Reflection (SER) 85–8, 105
Surveys 10, 20–1, 78, 92–4, 98, 100, 104–5, 108–9, 152–3, 162–3, 171–2, 183–4, 187, 190–3, 201–3
Swazi 43
Symbolist School 10–16
Synchrony 4–7, 32, 48–9, 76, 99, 105, 114, 133–4

Tallensi 123

Tedium Effect 58, 65, 67–8
Tightness-Looseness 45, 120–6, 150
Tinbergen's Four Whys 2–3, 170
Transformative Experiences 82, 91–101, 157–8, 197–8
Trobrianders 38–9, 123
Trump Inauguration 97–8
Twinning Project 160–1
Two Cultures Problem 171, 182–7, 192–4
Twins 91–2

Volatility Index (VI) 21–2, 154–8

WEIRD Problem 187–94

Yafar 44–5

Zulu 43

The manufacturer's authorised representative in the EU for product safety is Oxford University Press España S.A. of el Parque Empresarial San Fernando de Henares, Avenida de Castilla, 2 – 28830 Madrid (www.oup.es/en or product.safety@oup.com). OUP España S.A. also acts as importer into Spain of products made by the manufacturer.